D0936427

Masters of War

Masters of War

Military Dissent and Politics in the Vietnam Era

ROBERT BUZZANCO

University of Houston

CAMBRIDGE
UNIVERSITY PRESS

Barry University Library
Miami, Fla. 33161

Published by the Press Syndicate of the University of Cambridge
The Pitt Building, Trumpington Street, Cambridge CB2 1RP
40 West 20th Street, New York, NY 10011-4211, USA
10 Stamford Road, Oakleigh, Melbourne 3166, Australia

© Cambridge University Press 1996

First published 1996

Printed in the United States of America

Library of Congress Cataloging-in-Publication Data
Buzzanco, Robert.
Masters of war : military dissent and politics in the Vietnam era
/ Robert Buzzanco.
p.   cm.
Includes bibliographical references and index.
ISBN 0-521-48046-9
1. Vietnamese Conflict, 1961–1975 – Protest movements – United
States. 2. United States – Armed Forces – Political activity.
3. United States – Politics and government – 1963–1969. 4. United
States – Politics and government – 1969–1974. I. Title.
DS559.62.U6B89   1996
959.704'3373 – dc20   95-16226
                                                   CIP

A catalog record for this book is available from the British Library.

ISBN 0-521-48046-9 Hardback

DS
559.62
.U6
B89
1996

In Memory of

Nick Buzzanco
(1918–1994)

Mary Tornabene Buzzanco
(1923–1979)

and

Jeane Wilson Kelso
(1924–1994)

I am convinced that if we are to get on the right side of the world revolution, we as a nation must undergo a radical revolution of values. When machines and computers, profit and property rights are considered more important than people, the giant triplets of racism, materialism, and militarism are incapable of being conquered.

Martin Luther King, Jr.
4 April 1967

Contents

Acknowledgments

I would like to thank those institutions whose financial contributions helped me write this book. The John F. Kennedy and Lyndon B. Johnson Presidential Libraries, and the Ohio State History Department, generously supported my research. Most notably, the Marine Corps Historical Foundation awarded me its dissertation fellowship in 1991, which not only paid the bills but also gave me access to the wonderful collections and staff at Building 58 at the Washington Navy Yard.

Jack Shulimson, the Marines' senior historian on Vietnam, helped me in ways too numerous to mention by leading me to important documents or inviting me to discussions of Vietnam during lunch at the "O" Club. Similarly, David Humphrey introduced me to the relevant files on Vietnam at the LBJ Library and diligently processed the innumerable declassification requests I filed over the years. I would also like to thank the staffs at the Washington National Records Center (especially Rich Boylan and Charles Shaughnessy), the National Archives (particularly Wilbert Mahoney), the Eisenhower Library, the Kennedy Library, the Seeley Mudd Manuscript Library, the Hoover Institution, the Military History Institute, the Center of Military History, and the Greenbelt Public Library (especially Lucy Duff).

I would also like to thank the editors of *Diplomatic History*, *Political Science Quarterly*, and *Vietnam Generation* for granting permission to reproduce parts of this book that previously appeared in those journals.

I want to express my most sincere gratitude to everyone who read and commented upon my work, including Walter LaFeber, George

McT. Kahin, John Prados, Bob McMahon, Melvin Small, Sandra Taylor, Harry Basehart, James Wirtz, and Kurt Schultz. Special thanks go to those scholars who took time out from their busy schedules to read the entire manuscript, including my good friend, personal copyeditor, and Vietnam Vet Woody Woodruff, Peter Hahn, Warren Van Tine, Marilyn Young, Richard Immerman, Gabriel Kolko, and Noam Chomsky. Gary Hess and David Anderson, the readers for Cambridge, will always have a special place in my heart. Their careful appraisal of my original manuscript and their excellent criticisms prompted me to undertake an agonizing reappraisal of my work and, as a result, produce a more nuanced and, I believe, more useful book.

On a more personal level I would like to thank my colleagues at Prince George's Community College, my coconspirators in Greenbelt, and Jan Hallenbeck, who taught me how to write at Ohio Wesleyan. While in graduate school at Ohio State, I was fortunate to have Marvin Zahniser and Warren Van Tine as my M.A. advisors, and even luckier to work with Michael J. Hogan on my doctorate. Mike Hogan kept me on schedule and always tolerated my views on Vietnam; maybe some day he'll even agree with me on Kennedy's responsibility for the war.

Keith Olson, a man of unique integrity at the University of Maryland, introduced me to this topic a decade ago when he told me about David Shoup, a former Marine commandant who became an outspoken opponent of the war and American imperialism generally. Without Keith's advice, and continued friendship, I would probably be completing a study of organized labor and foreign policy during the cold war.

Diane Shelton, my acupuncturist-cum-guru, not only helped restore my health, but also showed me how to think in new, different ways. Her wisdom is only matched by her skill with the needles.

I can never adequately describe how much I appreciate Bill Walker. I met Bill during my senior year at Ohio Wesleyan; I asked him if I could take an independent study with him on the Vietnam War, but warned him that "I don't know anything about it." He apparently did not believe me at the time, but a few weeks later, after I completely misrepresented several readings he had assigned, he glared at me and said, "You were right, you don't know anything about Vietnam." I trust his opinion has shifted somewhat since then. In the years since that initial encounter, Bill has been my dear friend, fellow researcher, and frequent guest, even though he does watch pro golf on television. He has constantly challenged my work, always raising my ire but also forcing me to reconsider dogma. As he said to me in the dedication to his opium book, *hasta la victoria siempre.*

My sister, Marilyn Roberts, has always been a great friend as well, and I'll always appreciate her love and support. My wife, Jane Kelso, and our son, Kelsey Niccolo Sandino Buzzanco, are as responsible for this book as I. Jane supported me, emotionally and financially, through a decade of graduate school without once pressuring me to finish my dissertation faster or to get a real job. Her work in taking on the NRA as the national grass-roots coordinator for Handgun Control, Inc., will also serve as a constant reminder, as Marx put it, that we not only have to study the world but try to change it. Our son Kelsey grew up with this book, and they both brought me pain and joy, though more of the latter. He's a great and unique kid who may turn out like either Abbie Hoffman or Ollie North, and I think there's a consensus on which is preferable.

Finally, I'd like to say a few words about the three people to whom this book is dedicated, my parents Mary and Nick Buzzanco and Jane's mom Jeane Kelso. Mom died before I even graduated from college but had already instilled in me an appreciation for learning. Jeane Kelso and my dad died within weeks of each other in early 1994, literally days before I learned that Cambridge would publish this book. Jeane loved history and took great pride in having a historian join the Kelso family. My dad, as a Class A Laborer for the Niles, Ohio, Water Department and a long-time union president, instilled in me working-class values and a Sicilian's distrust of all forms of authority. He always resented the Archie Bunker caricature of his generation and spoke out against class oppression, racism, militarism, and injustice. My joy at finishing this book is tempered by the absence of such loved ones, but, as Lou Reed said, there's a bit of magic in everything, and then some loss to even things out.

Abbreviations

ARVN	Army of the Republic of Vietnam
BLT	Battalion Landing Team
CG	Civil Guard
CI	Counterinsurgency
CIA	Central Intelligence Agency
CINCPAC	Commander in chief, Pacific
CIP	Counterinsurgency Plan
CMH	Center of Military History, Washington, D.C.
CNO	Chief of Naval Operations
COC	Combat Operations Center
CRS	Congressional Research Service
CTZ	Corps Tactical Zone [I–IV Corps]
DDEL	Dwight D. Eisenhower Library, Abilene, Kans.
DDRS	*Declassified Documents Reference System*
DMZ	Demilitarized Zone
DRVN	Democratic Republic of Vietnam [north]
FMFPac	Fleet Marine Force, Pacific
FRUS	*Papers Relating to the Foreign Relations of the United States*
FY	Fiscal year
GVN	Government of Vietnam [south]
HCAS	U.S. Congress, House, Committee on Armed Services
JCS	Joint Chiefs of Staff
JCSM	Joint Chiefs of Staff Memorandum
JFKL	John F. Kennedy Library, Boston, Mass.
JIC	Joint Intelligence Committee

JSPC	Joint Strategic Plans Committee
JSSC	Joint Strategic Survey Committee
JWGA	Joint War Games Agency
LBJL	Lyndon B. Johnson Library, Austin, Tex.
MAAG	Military Assistance Advisory Group
MACV	Military Assistance Command, Vietnam
MAF	Marine Amphibious Force
MCHC	Marine Corps Historical Center, Washington, D.C.
MEB	Marine Expeditionary Brigade
MHI	Military History Institute, Carlisle Barracks, Pa.
NATO	North Atlantic Treaty Organization
NIE	National Intelligence Estimate
NLF	National Liberation Front
NSA	National Security Agency
NSAM	National Security Action Memorandum
NSC	National Security Council
NYT	*New York Times*
OMB	Office of Management and Budget
OPLAN	Operations Plan
P & O	Plans and Operations Division, U.S. Army
PAVN	People's Army of Vietnam [DRVN]
POF	President's Office File
PRC	People's Republic of China
PROVN	Program for the Pacification and Long-Term Development of South Vietnam
RG	Record Group, National Archives, Washington, D.C.
RRU	Radio Research Unit
RVN	Republic of Vietnam [south]
RVNAF	Republic of Vietnam Armed Forces
SA	Systems Analysis Division, U.S. Pentagon
SCFR	U.S. Congress, Senate, Committee on Foreign Relations
SDC	Self-Defense Corps
SEATO	Southeast Asia Treaty Organization
SVN	South Vietnam
TERM	Temporary Equipment Recovery Mission

Abbreviations

UPA	University Publications of America
USARPAC	U.S. Army Pacific Command
VC	Viet Cong
VNA	Vietnamese National Army [RVN]
VN C.F.	Vietnam Country File
WNRC	Washington National Records Center, Suitland, Md.

1

Introduction:
Losing Battles and Winning Wars

> You put your bombers in, you put your conscience out.
> You take the human being and you twist it all about
> So scrub my skin with women
> Chain my tongue with whisky
> Stuff my nose with garlic
> Coat my eyes with butter
> Fill my ears with silver
> Stick my legs in plaster
> Tell me lies about Vietnam.[1]

Although two decades have passed since U.S. combat soldiers left Indochina, Americans are still telling lies about Vietnam. The ink was hardly dry on the 1973 peace accords when President Richard Nixon, with the help of Ross Perot, exploited the national furor that they had created over alleged prisoners of war remaining in Vietnam to justify their violations of the recently signed treaty and their refusal to make peace with the North Vietnamese.[2] Shortly thereafter, the United States rejected normalizing relations with the Socialist Republic of Vietnam because, as America's "human rights" president, Jimmy Carter, explained, "the destruction was

---

1. "To Whom It May Concern," by Adrian Mitchell, in Laurence Coupe, " 'Tell Me Lies about Vietnam': English Poetry and the American War," in Alf Louvre and Jeffrey Walsh, eds., *Tell Me Lies about Vietnam: Cultural Battles for the Meaning of the War* (Philadelphia, 1988), 167–8.
2. See Bruce Franklin, *M.I.A., or Mythmaking in America* (New Brunswick, N.J., 1993); Edward Herman and Noam Chomsky, *Manufacturing Consent: The Political Economy of the Mass Media* (New York, 1988), chapter 5; Noam Chomsky, *Year 501: The Conquest Continues* (Boston, 1992).

mutual."[3] By 1980, Ronald Reagan and the "New Right" were
making huge electoral gains by pledging to "make America strong
again" and, toward that end, set out to convince the country that
the U.S. war against Indochina had been a "noble cause."[4]

Since then, the lies of Vietnam have created a great deal of political capital for politicians of all stripes, soldiers trying to vindicate
themselves, and opportunist scholars. Throughout the past decade
or so, defenders of the U.S. role in Vietnam have argued that America's defeat was not the result of an illegitimate intervention or
military shortcomings but rather a failure of will because national
leaders, principally President Lyndon B. Johnson, had forced the
troops to "fight with one hand tied behind their backs," a charge
cleverly reiterated by George Bush as he unleashed American air
power against Saddam Hussein in January 1991.[5] In fact, the allegedly liberal media, so despised by advocates of the war, have by
and large accepted such versions of the war.[6]

Indeed, the specter of Vietnam has continued to haunt American
political life and culture to this day. President Ronald Reagan repeatedly invoked the national weaknesses of the Vietnam era to
justify the massive defense buildup of the 1980s, with the attendant

3. Carter press conference, 24 March 1977, transcript in *New York Times* (hereafter *NYT*),
   25 March 1977, 10; on the contradictions between Carter's rhetorical commitment to
   human rights and the practice of his administration with regard to South and Central
   America, the Philippines, East Timor, Korea, southern Africa, and Iran, see Noam
   Chomsky and Edward S. Herman, *The Washington Connection and Third World Fascism: The Political Economy of Human Rights* (Boston, 1979), 14, 34, 37–8, 70, 145,
   170–3, 191, 230, 245, 270, 290–6; Chomsky, *Year 501,* 43, 100, 120, 146–8, 254–5,
   268; Gabriel Kolko, *Confronting the Third World: United States Foreign Policy, 1945–
   1980* (New York, 1988), 247, 262, 269–75, 283–9; Gaddis Smith, *Morality, Reason, and
   Power: American Diplomacy in the Carter Years* (New York, 1986), 7–8, 50–5, 102–3,
   185, 189.
4. Reagan in *NYT,* 19 August 1980, 1.
5. Bush in *Washington Post,* 20 January 1991, D1.
6. Perhaps the best example of the conservative attack on the media is Peter Braestrup, *Big
   Story: How the American Press and Television Reported and Interpreted the Crisis of Tet
   1968 in Vietnam and Washington* (Boulder, Colo., 1977). Despite Braestrup's contention
   that the media undermined the war effort through its unduly critical and pessimistic
   reporting, the Army's official history of press relations during Vietnam shows that, until
   Tet 1968, American reporters essentially reiterated the official government line with little
   deviation; see William Hammond, *Public Affairs: The Military and the Media, 1962–
   1968* (Washington, D.C., 1988); see also Daniel C. Hallin, *The "Uncensored War": The
   Media and Vietnam* (New York, 1986), and Herman and Chomsky, *Manufacturing Consent,* especially chapter 5; Noam Chomsky, "The United States and Indochina: Far from
   an Aberration," in Douglas Allen and Ngô Vinh Long, eds., *Coming to Terms: Indochina,
   the United States, and the War* (Boulder, Colo., 1991): 161–88.

dire economic consequences that are visible today. Invoking America's past war, Caspar Weinberger, U.S. secretary of defense in the 1980s, explained that "we must never send Americans into battle unless we plan to win."[7] To avoid "another Vietnam," the Reagan and Bush administrations time and again used overwhelming force against small states, such as Grenada, Libya, Panama, or Iraq, or engaged in so-called covert operations, most notably in El Salvador, Nicaragua, Angola, and Afghanistan, both to avoid Vietnam-type military embarrassments and to preempt the large-scale public protests that had marked the later years of the Indochina intervention. At the same time, American culture, as demonstrated by the popularity of the "Rambo" interpretation of Vietnam, reflected the view that craven politicians, the liberal media, and disloyal protesters had caused the U.S. failure in Indochina.[8]

Political realignments caused by Vietnam are still evident today as well. Even though John F. Kennedy and Lyndon B. Johnson, the presidents who initiated and escalated the war against Vietnam, were both Democrats, that party has somehow become vulnerable to charges that it is weak on national defense issues, if not disloyal, and that it does not reflect the cultural values of "mainstream" Americans.[9] During the 1992 presidential campaign, that whole process climaxed as the Democratic nominee, Bill Clinton, had to fend off repeated allegations of draft dodging because he had failed to serve in the military and had publicly opposed the war. Rather than frame his decision as a necessary response to an illegitimate war, Clinton dodged and stalled, thereby obfuscating what was arguably the most noble political act of his career. Even now, as Commander in Chief Clinton deliberates over the use of American

---

7. Weinberger in *Washington Post*, 12 November 1984, 14.
8. On the relationship between the legacy of Vietnam and U.S. aggression in the 1980s, see Walter LaFeber, "The Last War, the Next War, and the New Revisionists," *democracy* 1 (1981): 93–103; and Marilyn Young, "This Is Not a Pipe," *Middle East Report* (July–August 1991): 21–4. On the role of popular culture, especially the Rambo movies, in cultivating public ideas about Vietnam, see Franklin, *M.I.A.*, 150–9, and Walter Hixson, " 'Red Storm Rising': Tom Clancy Novels and the Cult of National Security," *Diplomatic History* 17 (Fall 1993): 599–613, especially 604 and 612; Chomsky, *Year 501*, and "The United States and Indochina: Far from an Aberration."
9. On the political impact of Vietnam, see Thomas Byrne Edsall and Mary D. Edsall, *Chain Reaction: The Impact of Race, Rights, and Taxes on American Politics* (New York, 1991), especially chapters 3–5.

force in Bosnia, Somalia, Haiti, and elsewhere, references to Vietnam are omnipresent.[10]

This book, then, is a response to the legacy of Vietnam, a war that former President Richard Nixon charged had been "misremembered" in the mid-1980s.[11] Nixon was right, but it was he and other defenders of the war whose memory is suspect on several counts. But rather than challenge the entire revisionist view of Vietnam as a noble effort undermined at home, a task that would collectively require considerations of virtually every political, military, and economic decision taken during the war, I will here focus on the role of U.S. military leaders in critically analyzing the American experience in Vietnam and on the political interplay between civilian and service officials in that era.

There are four interrelated themes that inform my work and comprise the body of this study: military recognition of the parlous nature of war in Vietnam and criticism of the U.S. role there; civilian responsibility for decisions to fight in Indochina; political maneuvering between civilian and military leaders over the war; and interservice division over the commitment to and strategy used in Indochina.

Military Criticism. Put simply, U.S. military leaders were wary of intervention in Vietnam from 1945 forward and, once committed there, were deeply divided over and offered candid and often pessimistic analyses of American prospects in the war. Beginning in the early 1950s, many of the more influential military officials of the period warned against fighting in Vietnam and, even after hundreds of thousands of U.S. troops were deployed there, held a realistic, and often bleak, outlook about the war.

Since then, many American officers have charged that craven politicians, particularly Lyndon Johnson and Secretary of Defense Robert Strange McNamara, unduly limited their ability to fight the enemy. In reality, service leaders from the top down – chairs of the Joint Chiefs of Staff (JCS), commanders in Vietnam, service chiefs

10. In just over two weeks in late 1993, the *Washington Post* published articles invoking the memory of Vietnam in current discussions of the War Powers Act (16 October, A18; 22 October, A26; 23 October, A5); military–media relations (17 October, C1); and Somalia (6 October, A1 and A12; 8 October, A22).

11. Richard Nixon, *No More Vietnams* (New York, 1985), 9.

of staff, field advisors – always recognized that the war in Vietnam was not going notably well and that the Vietnamese Communists were militarily and politically superior to the representatives of the fictive state of South Vietnam (SVN) to which the United States had attached its hopes.

Political Responsibility. Political leaders, however, had decided to extend containment, which in the case of Vietnam amounted to rollback, to Indochina, in the first instance to restore Asian capitalism and then to maintain their credibility as guardians of the world political economy. As Bruce Cumings pointed out in his brilliant study of the origins of the Korean War, "presumably 'conservative' military figures dragged their feet" while "liberal" political leaders expanded American participation in the Korean and Vietnamese conflicts.[12] Throughout the 1950s and 1960s, however, those officers charged with conducting the war never shared the internationalist perspective of civilian officials. American officials were more concerned with developing military Keynesianism than with global economic policies, and they believed that maintaining institutional power and acquiring appropriations remained their principal mission. John Foster Dulles, secretary of state during the 1950s, in fact charged that the military was in the habit of making "maximum [budget] demands for the deliberate purpose of shifting the decision [for defense policy] to the political branch."[13] Once

---

12. "The disagreements," Cumings adds, "were not really substantive, but about departmental prerogative and budget lines." Such considerations, to be sure, were involved in civil–military disputes over defense policy. But, at least with regard to Vietnam, the military based its dissent or criticism on larger factors as well, including its overall conception of national strategy and the political costs and benefits that the services might incur or gain from entering into the Vietnam conflict. In the end, the military, which had reservations about the war, reflected a much broader understanding of Vietnam than did the civilians who sent U.S. troops to Indochina, which is not to say that either was well aware of political and cultural conditions driving the Vietnam War. Bruce Cumings, *The Origins of the Korean War*, volume II, *The Roaring of the Cataract* (Princeton, N.J., 1990), 59; see also James Donovan, *Militarism U.S.A.* (New York, 1970), 120–31. On the origins of the U.S. anti-Communist commitment to Vietnam, see, among others, Lloyd Gardner, *Approaching Vietnam: From World War II through Dienbienphu* (New York, 1988); Gabriel Kolko, *Anatomy of a War: Vietnam, the United States, and the Modern Historical Experience* (New York, 1985); and Andrew Rotter, *The Path to Vietnam: Origins of the American Commitment to Southeast Asia* (Ithaca, N.Y., 1987).
13. On the importance of gaining appropriations to the military's mission, see, among others, James Gavin, *War and Peace in the Space Age* (New York, 1958), 150–79, 248–65; A. J. Bacevich, *The Pentomic Era: The U.S. Army between Korea and Vietnam*

committed to battle in Vietnam, American forces also pursued a civilian-directed strategy – attrition and massive firepower – because political leaders wanted to end the war as quickly as possible without endangering their domestic agenda.

Civil–Military Acrimony. Given such divergent purposes, civil–military affairs, manifested in the arena of domestic politics, came to have a powerful impact on the U.S. approach to war in Vietnam. The military had a realistic vision of the risks of war in Indochina and there were uniformed naysayers for various categories – the decision to intervene, constant escalation, the strategy of attrition and air war, and tactics. Notwithstanding such reservations, American military representatives understood the limits of bad news that could be forwarded to Washington and so went along with the political decisions for intervention and, in due course, asked for more of it. Like other participants in the policy-making process, as Morton Halperin has suggested, the military ultimately equated national security with its own organizational interests.[14]

In so doing, American officers – who always recognized the White House's desire to conclude the war successfully and at the least cost to its political program at home *and* were always concerned that the military would be held accountable for any failures in Vietnam – consistently shifted the burden for political and military decisions onto Presidents Kennedy and Johnson, who had initiated and expanded the commitment despite military reservations. In time, American generals in Saigon and Washington began requesting the very measures, including the activation of Reserves,

(Washington, D.C., 1986), 16–21; Douglas Kinnard, *President Eisenhower and Strategy Management: A Study in Defense Politics* (Lexington, Ky., 1977), 21–7; Lawrence J. Korb, *The Joint Chiefs of Staff: The First Twenty-five Years* (Bloomington, Ind., 1976), 107; Gabriel Kolko, *The Roots of American Foreign Policy* (Boston, 1969), 30–47; Richard Barnet, *Roots of War: The Men and Institutions behind U.S. Foreign Policy* (New York, 1972), 165–6; Dulles in Ronald W. Pruessen, "John Foster Dulles and the Predicaments of Power," in Richard Immerman, ed., *John Foster Dulles and the Diplomacy of the Cold War* (Princeton, N.J., 1990), 27. More pointedly, Dean Acheson, as Bruce Cumings notes, had "an easy and hearty contempt" for American officials, usually military leaders, who ignored world political economy in their considerations of national security. Bruce Cumings, "'Revising Postrevisionism,' or, The Poverty of Theory in Diplomatic History," *Diplomatic History* 17 (Fall 1993): 539–69.

14. I would like to thank Gabriel Kolko for helping develop my ideas on this point. See also Morton Halperin, *Bureaucratic Politics and Foreign Policy* (Washington, D.C., 1974), 121.

national mobilization, and totally unhindered escalation, that the White House wanted to avoid and would never authorize, thus making civilians even more responsible for forcing young men to fight with a hand tied behind their backs, as various service representatives and their allies would later suggest. As such, the military had actually created during the war the revisionist argument that self-imposed political limits caused the American failure in Vietnam.[15]

Interservice Disputes. Such political maneuvering was not confined to just the armed forces' relationship with the civilian establishment. There was great conflict within the military as well. In particular, Marine leaders and other "dissident" officers protested the Army-dominated strategy of massive firepower, attritional warfare, and air power, at times venomously.[16] By attacking American strategy in Vietnam – and again the Marines, something akin to junior members of the defense establishment, stand out – such dissidents could offer alternative approaches to the war, most popularly counterinsurgency or pacification, and accrue political currency, and hopefully budget appropriations, when the wisdom of their criticism became clear to officials in Washington. Indeed, General James Gavin, a respected military figure from World War II to the 1970s, indicted the entire JCS system because the various chiefs of staff remained more concerned with the particular interests of their services than with the need for unified and coherent

15. Not long after the U.S. withdrawal from Vietnam, various conservative military officers, politicians, and scholars – stung by the public disdain and attendant political crises spawned by the war – began to publish memoirs and books to justify their role in Indochina. Essentially arguing that the United States had intervened in Vietnam for the right reasons, to forestall Communist victory, and that the American military could have triumphed if only political leaders had unleashed it, these revisionists put forth their new version of Vietnam with facility and effectiveness, so much so that by 1980 candidate Reagan could publicly call Vietnam a noble cause, an opinion that would have likely been derided only a few years earlier. Among the early revisionists, the best examples include William Childs Westmoreland, *A Soldier Reports* (Garden City, N.Y., 1976); Ulysses S. Grant Sharp, *Strategy for Defeat: Vietnam in Retrospect* (San Rafael, Calif., 1978); Guenter Lewy, *America in Vietnam* (New York, 1978); and Norman Podhoretz, *Why We Were in Vietnam* (New York, 1982).
16. Probably the best-known example of military criticism of the war was Army Colonel John Paul Vann, the subject of Neil Sheehan's award-winning *A Bright Shining Lie: John Paul Vann and America in Vietnam* (New York, 1988). Vann, however, was one of a much larger and quite significant group of officers to question the war in harsh terms, and one of the purposes of my study is to thoroughly develop that theme.

military planning, and he even suggested that the government establish a senior military advisory board, composed of past service leaders, to replace the Joint Chiefs. General David Shoup, who opposed the growing U.S. commitment to Vietnam as Marine Corps commandant in the early 1960s and became an outspoken foe of the war later in the decade, moreover argued that the various services intervened in Indochina principally to gain the resources and promotions endemic to wartime.[17]

Taken together, these themes demonstrate that U.S. military leaders never felt compelled to fight a major war in Vietnam, yet accepted obligations there as part of a political battle for power at home. Once committed by civilian leaders, U.S. officers continued to lament the difficulties facing their troops in Indochina and for the most part were not particularly sanguine about the odds for success in the war. Within the military itself, a virtual civil war occurred as many ranking officers virulently attacked the U.S. strategy of firepower and attrition. And political factors, including control of the historical legacy of Vietnam, conditioned the way the war was conducted to a principal degree from the outset of the U.S. commitment. Although Robert McNamara has gained great notice, and vilification, for his admission that he knew the war was unwinnable but continued it nonetheless, the United States, in the final analysis, suffered a military loss that most leading officials could see coming years before the liberation of Saigon in 1975.[18]

Although I believe that most military leaders held realistic views of the peril and prospects of war in Vietnam, service officials did not have a uniform or homogenious outlook on the conflict. There was great diversity, and often division, within the armed forces in their response to Vietnam. In order to provide clarity and brevity, and avoid unnecessary repetition, I have developed five categories into which I have placed various military responses to Vietnam: dissenters, doubters, critics, politicos, and true believers. Although

---

17. Gavin, *War and Peace in the Space Age*, 257–62; David Shoup, "The New American Militarism," *Atlantic Monthly*, April 1969, 51–6; on Gavin's and Shoup's specific criticism of Vietnam, see Robert Buzzanco, "The American Military's Rationale against the Vietnam War," *Political Science Quarterly* 101 (Winter 1986): 559–76.
18. Robert S. McNamara with Brian VanDeMark, *In Retrospect: The Tragedy and Lessons of Vietnam* (New York, 1995).

these typologies provide a structure with which to study military approaches to Vietnam, they are nonetheless artificial constructs – not canon – so it will not be unusual to see ranking officers shift from one group to another, sometimes chameleon-like, as they adapted to the dynamics of events and policy, groped for solutions to the war, or played politics for institutional benefit.

Dissenters. Though never more than a minority of U.S. officers, several powerful and respected military leaders of the postwar era – especially Generals Matthew B. Ridgway, James Gavin, and David Monroe Shoup – rejected outright the notion that the United States could play a constructive military role in Indochina and so opposed entry into Vietnam from within the defense establishment in the 1950s and then publicly criticized the war in the 1960s. These officers, along with others such as General J. Lawton Collins, Army chief of staff during the Korean War, and Admiral Harry D. Felt, the Pacific commander in the early 1960s, believed that Vietnam was peripheral to American security concerns and that U.S. troops could not effectively fight against guerrillas in Indochina, especially when allied to a corrupt and politically unstable regime, whether it be French-dominated or indigenous, in southern Vietnam.[19]

Doubters. Like the dissenters, many officers questioned the growing U.S. commitment to Vietnam, but, given their positions within the military, were charged with conducting U.S. affairs there and thus ignored their own reservations in order to execute policy. Thus J. Lawton Collins, Admiral Felt, and General Lionel McGarr, the chief of the Military Assistance Advisory Group (MAAG) in Saigon in the early 1960s, offered highly critical appraisals of the

19. Throughout this book I will make frequent reference to "southern Vietnam" and "northern Vietnam," or "the south" and "the north," to distinguish between the geographic enemies partitioned at the seventeenth parallel. Vietnam was historically a single country, with the southern half, the Republic of Vietnam (RVN), artificially created at the Geneva Conference in 1954 by the United States. From that point on, the struggle in Vietnam revolved around the very issue of who constituted the legitimate government of that country. Thus to call the southern section "South Vietnam" conveys the status of nationhood where it is not established. As Gabriel Kolko points out in addressing this very issue, "RVN" is a "heuristic description" – albeit one that I do use – while southern attempts to call itself the "Government of Vietnam" (GVN) had "neither a legal nor a historical basis." Kolko, for the sake of convenience, uses "South Vietnam" as a geographic description, but I believe that "southern Vietnam" is a more precise and historically legitimate term. See Kolko, *Anatomy of a War,* xii–xiii.

U.S. role in Vietnam, but also acquiesced in the political decision
that the Republic of Vietnam (RVN) had to be saved.

Critics. Perhaps the most intriguing, and important, group, the
critics offered a harsh, and at times prescient, analysis of the war,
one they could have used to oppose publicly any commitment or
escalation in Vietnam. Some of the best-known and influential officers of the period – including Maxwell Davenport Taylor, the
Army chief of staff in the 1950s and JCS chair in the Kennedy years;
Harold K. Johnson, Army chief from 1964 to 1968; Wallace M.
Greene, Jr., the commandant of the Marine Corps from 1963 to
1967; Victor H. Krulak, the Marines' Pacific commander throughout the mid-1960s; and John Paul Vann, Army colonel and media
star whose critiques of the war became well known and
controversial – understood that political chaos in the RVN was
making anti-Communist progress impossible, that the presence of
American soldiers and the attendant firepower was counterproductive, and that a new approach to fighting in Vietnam was needed.
Despite their influence, however, their alternative strategies –
mostly an emphasis on counterinsurgency tactics and even more
massive air attacks – were not politically viable or militarily feasible. Civilian leaders in Washington thus dismissed or ignored them
for the most part.

Politicos. Undoubtedly the most influential group, the highest-
ranking officers of the Vietnam era simultaneously made war and
played politics. This group includes the officers mentioned in the
"critics" category (with the exception of Vann, who was in Vietnam in a civilian capacity by the mid-1960s) as well as the JCS
chair, Earle Wheeler; the U.S. commander in Vietnam, William
Childs Westmoreland; and the Pacific commander, Admiral U. S. G.
Sharp. These officers clearly understood the problems inherent in
Vietnam and always offered candid appraisals of the problems and
prospects in the war, yet advocated, often stridently, escalation of
the air war and the deployment of more ground troops, principally
for political reasons. Given their awareness of the uncertain, if not
bleak, chances for success, these officers consistently requested the
very measures – massive reinforcement, activation of Reserves, mobilization, total air war – that the White House would never authorize. In so doing, the military scored political points at civilian

expense and effectively pinned responsibility for the U.S. loss in Vietnam onto America's civilian leaders, where it belonged.

True Believers. Although all American officers professed their faith and optimism in the ability of U.S. forces to win in Vietnam, not as many seemed to actually expect success to be forthcoming in a timely fashion. Among those who genuinely expected the United States to prosecute the war successfully in Vietnam were Westmoreland, Sharp, General Paul D. Harkins, Westmoreland's predecessor in Saigon, and General William DePuy, deputy commander of the Military Assistance Command, Vietnam (MACV), in the mid-1960s. For the most part, these officers, who did recognize the military peril and political stakes involved in Vietnam, nonetheless were publicly confident of ultimate victory. When, time and again, America's corrupt ally or imposing enemy caused a U.S. setback in the war, the credibility of these officers eroded, although it was not until the 1968 Tet Offensive that the full magnitude of their errors was obvious enough for the U.S. media to detail.

The military's divisive and inconsistent approach to the war offered prima facie evidence that the American failure in Vietnam was essentially unavoidable. But the armed forces, though deeply divided over Vietnam, agreed on the need to protect service interests against civilian control. Thus, at times in the Vietnam era, the military's behavior seemed erratic, desperate, or paranoid, but American officers did not suspect their civilian bosses during the 1950s and 1960s without reason. Indeed, even before the full-scale U.S. intervention in Vietnam, heated civil–military disputes had become part of the American political structure, and, during the Eisenhower and Kennedy years in particular, the services seemed to be losing influence and funding. As America went to war in Indochina, then, U.S. officers tried to pin down the White House about the extent and nature of war in Vietnam, while Kennedy and Johnson and their advisors expected the military to find some way to win the war before civilians would have to experience the political fallout from a long campaign in a remote country. Clearly, a workable strategy was simply not possible when irresponsible civilians and politicized generals ignored the policy implications that they themselves had identified and generated. Politics, in the form of civil–military relations, thus became a determining factor in the American approach to Vietnam as leading officials, uniformed and otherwise, hoped to avoid leaving their fingerprints on the coming disaster half a world away.

As one studies the evolution of military thinking on Vietnam over *la longue durée,* many such items coagulate and form vital historical patterns. For our present purposes, three interrelated concepts – armed forces' dissent against or criticism of civilian foreign policy, increasing military involvement in politics, and strained civil–military relations – will historically elucidate the four themes of this book, and thus require further examination. Despite frequent preconceptions of the military as a hawkish institution whose leaders clamor for war, U.S. service officials have held diverse views on defense issues and were often less inclined to urge military responses to international conflict in the cold war era.[20] Such military temperance was evident, for instance, right after World War II as the JCS produced studies on the Soviet Union challenging the increasingly popular view that Stalin was irrevocably committed to revolution and expansion. While various diplomatic officials were counseling President Harry S Truman to use force against the USSR in a dispute over base rights in the Dardanelles and Aegean and to block a claim to Trieste by Yugoslavia, ranking service officials urged negotiations and concessions. At the same time, the chiefs expressed "little strategic interest" in Korea, and would even consider withdrawing American forces from the peninsula should the situation become too volatile. Not surprisingly, then, the armed forces recommended noninvolvement during the June 1950 deliberations over U.S. intervention in Korea, and during crises in Formosa (1955), Hungary and Egypt (1956), Lebanon (1958), the Congo (1960), Berlin (1961), North Korea (1968), and Jordan (1970).[21]

20. Richard K. Betts, *Soldiers, Statesmen, and Cold War Crises* (Cambridge, Mass., 1977); Halperin, *Bureaucratic Politics and Foreign Policy,* 60–1; and Melvyn P. Leffler, *A Preponderance of Power: National Security, the Truman Administration, and the Cold War* (Stanford, Calif., 1992), 14. For more critical observations about the role of the military during the Vietnam era, see John Kenneth Galbraith, *How to Control the Military* (New York, 1969); and Erwin Knoll and Judith Nies McFadden, eds., *American Militarism 1970* (New York, 1969).
21. Leffler, *Preponderance,* 51, 75, 78; Cumings, *Origins of the Korean War,* 629–33; D. Clayton James with Anne Sharp Wells, *Refighting the Last War: Command and Crisis in Korea, 1950–1953* (New York, 1993), 133; Korb, *Joint Chiefs of Staff,* 134.

Although imbued with and proud of its "can do" ethic, the military in the cold war era has been just as likely to exhibit the "can't do" spirit. Given such military caution, it was not unusual to find America's civilian policy makers urging a more activist martial role than U.S. officers. As a result, Dean Acheson, the secretary of state at the outbreak of war in Korea, heaped scorn upon the armed forces' judgment. Service chiefs, he complained, "do not know what they think until they hear what they say"; once they make up their minds, however, "the Pope has spoken, and they are infallible."[22] Throughout the 1950s and 1960s, as U.S. involvement in Vietnam grew, but without tangible success, the military would become more critical of the war and the civil–military dialectic would intensify accordingly, leading to greater political conflict.

Such political disputes were nothing new either. Military leaders had become more politically minded in the years after World War II. Although American officers have cultivated the image of loyal servants to their civilian bosses, generals, admirals, and other top brass have always been concerned with affairs outside of the military sphere. So while Maxwell Taylor had the temerity to assert that the Army "respects its civilian leadership and abstains from any involvement in politics," Harry Truman more correctly observed that the average American officer "learns of his dependence on 'politics' from the moment he solicits his first application blank for a service academy."[23] That convergence of military and political considerations also expanded dramatically in the Vietnam era and became an epistemological legacy of the war. As defense budgets soared and the United States pursued a militarized foreign policy, American chiefs engaged in political maneuvering and, at times, battles over greater appropriations for their particular service, more resources and new technological systems, expanded missions, and an increased role in formulating basic defense policy.

22. Acheson quoted in Cumings, *Origins of the Korean War,* vol. II, 629–31. During the Formosa crisis, Army chief Matthew Ridgway was especially vehement in opposing a military response; see Dwight Eisenhower, *The White House Years: Mandate for Change, 1953–1956* (Garden City, N.Y., 1963), 462.
23. Taylor in Kolko, *Roots,* 35; Truman in Jack Raymond, *Power at the Pentagon* (New York, 1964), 174–5. Matthew B. Ridgway also pledged noninvolement in politics during his tenure as Army chief of staff, pointing out that he was willing to fight for his service's interests until civilian officials made policy, at which point, he noted, "they could expect completely loyal and diligent execution of those decisions." In Kolko, *Roots,* 35.

Although both interservice and civil–military acrimony reached new, and eventually crisis, proportions in the Vietnam era, such conflicts had been growing since the United States embarked on the path toward empire and created a corporate state at the turn of the twentieth century and were thereafter a fundamental part of the American political structure.[24] Throughout World War II and the early cold war years, as the military emerged as a power in its own right, dissent from civilian leadership became ever more common and the armed forces increasingly gained more autonomy and political clout. As such, military criticism during the Vietnam War was part of a shifting battleground in the ongoing fight between service and civilian officials.

Interservice conflict and military involvement in political affairs had been apparent even before the United States entered World War II as the Army and Navy feuded over the propriety and degree of support to be given to Britain. Such division continued well into the war as Navy officers championed a "Pacific First" strategy against the Army's emphasis on the ground defense of Europe.[25] As the war ended, with the United States established as the dominant world power, American officials believed that they had to expand and reorganize the armed forces in order to meet the needs of a militarized foreign policy. Some influential Americans, notably Republican stalwarts Herbert Hoover and Robert Taft, warned against intensifying the cold war in large part because they feared that the armed forces would exploit its new, expanded role in defense considerations to gain undue influence and political power. Such concerns were not considered viable, however, and after much wrangling among military and political leaders, including an effort to abolish the Marine Corps and the creation of an independent Air Force, Congress passed the National Security Act in 1947, establishing a unified Department of Defense and the Central Intelligence Agency (CIA), and officially sanctioning the JCS as the nation's ranking military body. But since then, the JCS, as former

---

24. On the military's role in the politics of imperialism, see Leonard D. White, *The Republican Era: A Study in Administrative History, 1869–1901* (New York, 1958), 134–74; and David Healy, *US Expansionism: The Imperialist Urge in the 1890s* (Madison, Wis., 1970), 144–58.
25. Mark Perry, *Four Stars* (Boston, 1989), 1–4.

Assistant Defense Secretary Lawrence Korb put it, "has been a consistent source of irritation to the men for whom it worked."[26]

Indeed, the 1947 defense reorganization spawned more serious controversies. Navy officers, fearing that they were losing influence and appropriations to the new Air Force, immediately challenged the new service over control of nuclear weapons, the development of the B-36 strategic bomber, construction of a naval supercarrier, and the size of the Marines. The services negotiated their differences throughout 1948, culminating in the so-called Key West and Newport Agreements, but the political conflict remained unresolved. Within a year, however, the Air Force gained a major victory as Truman and his new defense secretary, Louis Johnson, hoped to cut defense spending and thus canceled the Navy's supercarrier, but simultaneously decided to fund the B-36 and give the Air Force responsibility for delivering nuclear weapons. As Navy officers saw it, their chief of naval operations (CNO), Louis Denfeld, had caved in to Air Force demands. Thus began the "Revolt of the Admirals," in which Navy representatives publicly became involved in political matters to a greater extent than ever before. Ultimately, several ranking officers quit the Navy to protest Truman's decisions and the insurgent admirals forced Denfeld to resign.[27] To Louis Johnson, the Naval dissidents were conducting a "campaign of terror" against the new military establishment, while the Air Force secretary, Stuart Symington, wondered whether the rebellious admirals were trying to seize control of military decisions from civilian leaders.[28]

The interservice friction and civil–military skirmishing that

26. Harry S Truman, *Memoirs*, volume 2, *Years of Trial and Hope* (Garden City, N.Y., 1956); Lawrence J. Korb, *The Fall and Rise of the Pentagon: American Defense Policies in the 1970s* (Westport, Conn., 1979), 112–15; Gordon Keiser, *The US Marine Corps and Defense Unification, 1944–1947: The Politics of Survival* (Washington, D.C., 1982); Victor Krulak, *First to Fight: An Inside View of the U.S. Marine Corps* (Annapolis, Md., 1984); Perry, *Four Stars*, 6–7; Michael J. Hogan, "Foreign Policy, Partisan Politics, and the End of the Cold War," in Michael J. Hogan, ed., *The End of the Cold War: Its Meanings and Implications* (New York, 1992), 229–43.

27. Perry, *Four Stars*, 11–19; Allen Millett, *Semper Fidelis: The History of the United States Marine Corps* (New York, 1982), 472–3; Leffler, *Preponderance*, 44, 105, 325; In Truman's version of the admiral's revolt, he ousted Denfeld to restore discipline; see Truman, *Memoirs*, 53.

28. Robert Donovan, *Tumultuous Years: The Presidency of Harry S Truman, 1949–1953* (New York, 1982), 105–13.

characterized the admirals' revolt only became worse as the United States intervened in a civil war in Korea. In the first instance, the military was "extremely reluctant" to send ground forces into combat there, and it remained opposed to such measures up to Truman's decision to deploy troops on 30 June 1950. Even then, Omar Bradley, also the JCS chair, and other ranking Army officers – including J. Lawton Collins, Matthew Ridgway, and Albert Wedemeyer – were wary that the president and his commander, Douglas MacArthur, would widen the war and probably prompt Chinese intervention. That precise scenario occurred in October as MacArthur moved his units north of the thirty-eighth parallel, a decision that Bradley considered "drastically wrong."[29] MacArthur, however, continued to escalate the war that fall, initially with Truman's authorization, thus prompting the JCS to call for his removal. By early 1951, as the commander in Korea was publicly criticizing Truman for seeking a cease-fire rather than military victory, the president believed that the very survival of his administration was at stake and so decided to fire MacArthur in April on the advice of leading civilian and military figures.[30]

MacArthur returned from Korea a national hero, however, thus giving Truman a political black eye. Even though Generals Bradley, Collins, and George Marshall, then serving as secretary of defense, supported Truman's decision in testimony before the Senate, MacArthur was able to use the hearings effectively to pillory the "defeatism" inherent in Truman's limited war. With the MacArthur controversy, the military had become a fully politicized institution. The commander's removal had prompted not only a civil–military crisis but also sparked major schisms within the military itself, and had challenged the young JCS system as well. In the end, and despite MacArthur's political appeal, the new military command organization did survive, and the bureaucratization of the armed forces was nearing completion. The alliance between civilian and military leaders, uneasy in any case, would become more problematic in a short time.[31]

29. Cumings, *Origins of the Korean War*, 629–33, 713; Callum MacDonald, *Korea: The War before Vietnam* (New York, 1986), 25–6, 34.
30. Dean Acheson, *Present at the Creation: My Years at the State Department* (New York, 1969), 521; MacDonald, *Korea*, 92–8; Cumings, *Origins of the Korean War*, 629–33, 713.
31. MacDonald, *Korea*, 99–104; Perry, *Four Stars*, 43–6.

Ironically, relations between the White House and military became more strained and politicized as General of the Army Dwight Eisenhower assumed the presidency. Committed to balancing the budget and limiting Soviet defense options, Eisenhower thus adopted the "New Look" defense policy, essentially a reliance on America's nuclear superiority and on the Air Force's ability to deliver atomic weapons, with a corresponding reduction in other defense systems.[32] Eisenhower accordingly proposed cutting defense funding by almost 20 percent – from over $42 billion to about $34 billion – in his first budget, thereby invoking the ire of various service leaders, especially Army Chief of Staff Matthew Ridgway, who publicly and harshly condemned the New Look. Such civil–military tension escalated throughout the Eisenhower years, causing the president to lament the armed forces' "legalized insubordination." Upon Ridgway's retirement, Eisenhower, seeking a new Army chief with views "in accord with those of the president" regarding strategic doctrine, chose Maxwell Taylor, but he too challenged the New Look's reliance on nuclear weapons and its limited appropriations for his service. By the end of the decade, Ridgway, Taylor, and General James Gavin, perhaps the Army's brightest rising star, had all quit the armed forces and publicly rebuked the administration's defense policy.[33]

By the late 1950s and early 1960s, even the Air Force began to fear that the advent of unmanned missiles would obviate the need for manned bombers and in time saw itself, as the Navy had in the 1940s and the Army had just a few years earlier, in a "fight for existence." Eisenhower nonetheless continued to assert his control over defense policy and the budget process. In the "most spectacular legislative battle" of 1958, the president reorganized the Defense Department to weaken the roles of the JCS and service chiefs in the chain of command and downgrade the status of the service secretaries, instead giving the defense secretary the authority to transfer orders directly to field commanders. As Eisenhower saw

32. Eisenhower, *Mandate for Change*, 445–58.
33. Dwight Eisenhower, *The White House Years: Waging Peace, 1956–1961* (Garden City, N.Y., 1965), 356; Kinnard, *Strategy Management*, 23–7, 32–5, 41–2; Bacevich, *Pentomic Era*, 16–18; on military criticism of Eisenhower's defense policy, see Matthew Ridgway, *Soldier: The Memoirs of Matthew B. Ridgway* (New York, 1956); Maxwell Taylor, *The Uncertain Trumpet* (New York, 1959); Gavin, *War and Peace in the Space Age*.

it, the JCS's "greatest task was to work corporately in support of
the president and secretary of defense" whereas the service secretaries "should not be interested in matters of strategic planning."[34]

Such measures, inevitably, plunged civil–military affairs ever
more deeply into politics. As chief of staff, Taylor became the consummate political general, cultivating ties on Capitol Hill with influential Democratic senators like John F. Kennedy of Massachusetts and Stuart Symington of Missouri.[35] In fact, the military in
general, especially the Air Force, began to forge an informal alliance with the Democrats to protest the Eisenhower defense program, especially after the president continued to hold the line on
military spending following the Sputnik scare of 1957 and major
Democratic gains in midterm elections the following year. Lyndon
Johnson of Texas, head of a Senate subcommittee on military preparedness investigating American defense posture in the wake of
Sputnik, facilitated the military's battles against the White House
by staging hearings at which he and other Democrats gave military
leaders the opportunity to score Eisenhower over the "missile gap"
and the need for greater appropriations. After one officer had
bashed the New Look before the Johnson subcommittee, a Pentagon reporter observed that his testimony "had probably helped
the Democrats more than several speeches by their candidates" for
the presidency. "You get the idea, don't you," the general replied.[36]

Not coincidentally, Symington, Johnson, and Kennedy competed
for the 1960 presidential nomination, running against the
Eisenhower military legacy in the process. Kennedy, eventually
elected in November, had especially trumpeted the need for a new
defense program, one in large measure shaped by Maxwell Taylor.
The past Army chief, tired of seeing, in his opinion, his service

34. Eisenhower in Kinnard, *Strategy Management,* 89–93; Eisenhower, *Waging Peace,* 244–
    53; Korb, *Fall and Rise of the Pentagon,* 112–17; Deborah Shapley, *Promise and Power:
    The Life and Times of Robert McNamara* (Boston, 1993); Vincent Davis, *The Admirals
    Lobby* (Chapel Hill, N.C., 1967), 228–34.
35. Richard Aliano, *American Defense Policy from Eisenhower to Kennedy: The Politics of
    Changing Military Requirements, 1957–1961* (Athens, Ohio, 1975), 90–1, 231; Perry,
    Four Stars, 69; Douglas Kinnard, *The Certain Trumpet: Maxwell Taylor and the Ameri-
    can Experience in Vietnam* (New York, 1991), 37–54.
36. Aliano, *American Defense Policy,* 109–15, 264, quotation on 84; Raymond, *Power at
    the Pentagon,* 186; James E. Hewes, Jr., *From Root to McNamara: Army Organization
    and Administration, 1900–1963* (Washington, D.C., 1975), 301–2; Perry, *Four Stars,*
    82–3; Kinnard, *Strategy Management,* 90–1; Davis, *The Admirals Lobby,* 228–34.

downsized, denigrated in budget considerations, and ill-prepared for ground war, contended that the Eisenhower doctrine of massive nuclear retaliation to enemy provocation left the United States with no room to respond to localized or limited conflicts, especially in the emerging political battlegrounds of the Third World.[37] Kennedy agreed and accordingly latched onto Taylor's policy of "flexible response," namely a sizable increase in Army forces to prepare that service to fight nonnuclear battles, including wars of counterinsurgency against Communist guerrillas. Kennedy's victory was also, by inference, Taylor's triumph and it demonstrated the power of military leaders to engage effectively in political matters. Indeed, the Kennedy–Taylor alliance marked a new phase in civil–military relations, one in which the armed forces' role in defense policy formulations far surpassed that of a generation earlier.

The military, in the aftermath of World War II, had been transformed from a relatively small, supporting institution in U.S. foreign policy to a bureaucratized, political force vying for appropriations, influence, and power.[38] With the intervention into and subsequent expansion of the American commitment to Vietnam, those changes in the military's mission and political role, and the legacy of interservice battles and civil–military ill will, would increasingly bear on the U.S. war in Indochina, leading to both military failure and political crisis.

In what illustrates the persistence of tension in civil–military relations, the standing of the armed forces, which seemed to be on the rise in 1961, had already peaked and would soon reach its lowest levels in the postwar era as service influence over policy and strategy, and even some operational control, began to wane.[39] The first sign of trouble in the eventual estrangement between the Kennedy administration and American service officials came less than three months after inaugural day as the president suffered an embarrassing political defeat at the Bay of Pigs in Cuba, and tried to shift blame for the fiasco onto the military. At the same time the new management techniques of Robert McNamara and the intrusion of his "whiz kids" into the Pentagon rankled armed forces

37. Taylor, *Uncertain Trumpet.*
38. Aliano, *American Defense Policy,* 100.
39. Betts, *Soldiers, Statesmen, and Cold War Crises,* 6.

representatives, who believed that the new civilian officials rightly belonged in an "ivory tower" and were unduly interfering with military prerogatives.[40]

McNamara, though publicly claiming that there was no split between civilian and military leaders regarding the administration of the Pentagon or defense policy, nevertheless felt compelled to clamp down on media representatives who had reported on the military's dissent. At the same time, the armed forces were alarmed by the secretary's tendency to centralize more military authority in the Pentagon and his increased moves toward service "unification." Eventually, many service officials began to complain about McNamara's vanity and intolerance, and others more stridently attacked his "reign of fear" at the Defense Department. As many senior officers saw it, a "meek subservience" to the secretary was the best avenue for promotion. Navy officials in particular challenged McNamara's leadership, principally because he had begun to question the potential effectiveness of aircraft carriers – and, in effect, all surface warships – in the event of general war against the Soviet Union.[41]

By the time American forces began to pour into Indochina on a large scale and fire shots in anger at the Vietnamese Communists, civil–military relations had been irrevocably soured over the course of a generation of conflict and political maneuvering. The impact on the American experience in Vietnam over the coming decade would be little short of explosive. After a long and intensive period of civil–military disputes, reasonable deliberation, let alone cooperation, on defense concerns was unlikely, and, accordingly, war in Vietnam became inevitable. Even in the early stages of intervention, military and political leaders – with an eye toward history – were considering ways to avoid responsibility for any shortcomings in the American effort. As the U.S. role grew, and prospects remained static, political and service officials scurried for cover.

By 1967 members of the JCS were talking about resigning en masse to protest Lyndon Johnson's handling of the war, which would have amounted to a U.S. version of the *golpe de estado* that

40. Shapley, *Promise and Power,* 104; Davis, *The Admirals Lobby,* 232–9, 245.
41. See sources cited in previous note.

Americans expected out of banana republics, but not industrial behemoths. With the 1968 Tet Offensive, which made it numbingly obvious to American elites that the United States could not "win" in Vietnam, military officials subtly forced the White House to deny a request for massive reinforcement and thereby effectively liquidated their adventure in Vietnam. At that point, senior American officers began to rewrite the war to suit their own purposes, which, to be fair, virtually everyone connected with the war did anyway. In the meantime, as presidents, secretaries, and generals played politics, millions of soldiers, civilians, and children of all hues died in Indochina.

The impact of Vietnam on civil–military affairs, and thus on U.S. national security policy, cannot be understated. As a result of their long-term struggle with civilian officials over the decision to intervene and the conduct of the war in Vietnam, military leaders have become increasingly, and effectively, engaged in the political process over the past generation. U.S. service chiefs have created, inculcated, and exploited a legacy of Vietnam that has led to greater power in the years since the war ended. Indeed, it is not hyperbolic to suggest that the military has demonstrated virtual veto power over aspects of U.S. foreign and military policy. In the aftermath of Vietnam, military leaders began to challenge openly the White House's decision-making prerogative, especially during the Carter years, and at the same time military officials – especially retired Admirals Elmo Zumwalt and Thomas Moorer – associated with the Committee on the Present Danger actively facilitated the Reagan campaign's attacks on the Democratic Party.[42]

Since then, the military, despite the vast array of weapons gained from its huge budgets in the Reagan years, rejected combat intervention in Central America in the mid-1980s, instead developing so-called low-intensity conflict to destabilize governments at a lower cost to the United States.[43] Ranking officers, if journalist Bob Woodward is to be believed, were wary of, if not opposed to, going

---

42. Perry, *Four Stars*, 293.
43. Michael T. Klare and Peter Kornbluh, eds., *Low-Intensity Warfare: Counterinsurgency, Proinsurgency, and Antiterrorism in the Eighties* (New York, 1988); General Edwin Simmons interview in *NYT*, copy in Marine Corps Historical Center (MCHC), Washington, D.C., Oral History section.

to war against Panama and Iraq, and ultimately agreed to do so because they could use overwhelming force against much weaker enemies.[44] Even then, General H. Norman Schwarzkopf, commander of U.N. forces in the Persian Gulf War, publicly charged that civilian "hawks" – whom he accused of having a "John Wayne mentality" – pressured him for an early land war.[45]

Schwarzkopf and other military leaders have maintained a high profile since the war and their retirements. Both he and General Colin Powell, the JCS chair from 1989 to 1993, became virtual national heroes, were frequently mentioned as potential candidates for high office, and signed million-dollar contracts for their memoirs. News broadcasts and talk shows all seem to include some retired general as a paid expert on national security affairs, thereby giving the military even more influence in molding both elite and public opinion on defense issues. In fact, armed forces prestige has grown so much that Bill Clinton, in his campaign to pass the North American Free Trade Agreement, even trotted out the recently retired General Powell to endorse the pact, although it had no evident ramifications for military issues.[46]

Indeed, under Clinton, the draft dodger–cum–commander in chief, the military has arguably achieved its greatest power in the postwar era. It has opposed, publicly, any deeper American involvement in Bosnia, Somalia, or Haiti. Despite rampant talk of a "peace dividend" to meet domestic needs now that the cold war in Europe is over, the services have successfully staved off all but minimal cuts in their budget allocations. And, in a repudiation of civilian control over military matters on par with MacArthur's four decades earlier, the JCS simply rejected a Clinton proposal to open the services to entry by acknowledged gays and lesbians.[47] It may be that homophobia in the military prompted the chiefs' response to the president's plan, but it is just as likely that armed forces leaders saw an opportunity to score political points against Clinton by exploiting an issue that lacked broad public support. By focus-

44. Bob Woodward, *The Commanders* (New York, 1991).
45. *NYT,* 20 September 1992, 1, 10.
46. *NYT* and *Washington Post,* 6 November 1993, 1.
47. On the military's more recent challenges to the White House, see Russell F. Weigley, "The American Military and the Principle of Civilian Control from McClellan to Powell," *Journal of Military History* 57 (October 1993): 27–58.

ing on allowing homosexuals in the services, U.S. officers effectively diverted the issue of budget cuts from the spotlight and, by mobilizing powerful allies in Congress, the media, and among the public, demonstrated their political clout to a chief executive who had yet to prove his bona fides as commander in chief.[48]

Ever since Vietnam, according to Colin Powell, military leaders "have learned the proper lessons of history, even if some journalists have not."[49] In this context Powell was specifically referring to the need to avoid another "Vietnam" in Bosnia. Unspoken, however, was the clear recognition that the military – at various times and to varying degrees – can tell its civilian superiors what to do. Today's headlines concerning civil–military affairs – whether they discuss budgets, interventions, or the ouster of cabinet officials – form a continuum with the developments of the Vietnam era. During those years that the United States engaged in war in Indochina, American officials, uniformed and civilian, changed the way defense policies were made and wars were fought. Although various individuals recognized the peril of involvement in Vietnam, institutional considerations held sway and American soldiers were sent to Asia to destroy a country while their bosses fought for power in Washington. American military leaders may never have mastered Vietnam, but they have gained influence, power, and appropriations since then – all after losing a war.

48. Competing doctrines of foreign policy, Bruce Cumings has pointed out, lack meaning unless linked to constituencies within and without the state. "Constituencies generate doctrines," he notes, "and doctrines generate constituencies." Although Cumings's observation was specifically relevant to the cold war, it is just as true today. Cumings, "Revising Postrevisionism."
49. Powell in *NYT,* 8 October 1992, A35.

2

Prologue to Tragedy: U.S. Military Opposition to Intervention in Vietnam, 1950–1954

[W]hen the day comes for me to face my Maker and account for my actions, the thing I would be most humbly proud of was the fact that I fought against, and perhaps contributed to preventing, the carrying out of some hare-brained tactical schemes which would have cost the lives of thousands of men. To that list of tragic accidents that fortunately never happened I would add the Indo-China intervention.

Matthew B. Ridgway[1]

Although American leaders in the following decade would establish Vietnam as the central battlefield in the global cold war, U.S. military officials in the 1950s consistently opposed expanded commitments to and intervention in Indochina. Indeed, throughout the early part of that decade, the armed forces worked against military involvement in the First Indochina war more than any other institution, in or out of government. From 1950 to 1954, when the Truman and Eisenhower administrations made a series of irrevocable commitments to the French and then native anti-Communist elements in southern Vietnam, the Joint Chiefs of Staff (JCS), its various committees, respective service leaders, and other senior officers working in government voiced serious misgivings about intervention in Indochina, with Army officers in particular opposed to such measures. In light of U.S. limits and priorities, they explained, an expanded role in Vietnam would damage the national interest.

1. Ridgway, *Soldier*, 278.

To press their case against involvement in Vietnam, military dissenters presented a complex yet well-developed case against involvement in Indochina based on comprehensive and interrelated
political, economic, and military factors. Above all, service leaders
rooted their opposition to war in their conception of grand strategy. Given America's expanded commitments, especially in Europe,
at the outset of the cold war, J. Lawton Collins, Hoyt Vandenberg,
James Gavin, Matthew Ridgway, and other officers believed that
the United States simply did not have the resources to get involved
in areas of peripheral significance such as Indochina. Ironically,
military and civilian leaders reached divergent conclusions although they analyzed Vietnam from similar premises. The military's
"Eurocentricity" – to use George McT. Kahin's term – led it to see
war in Indochina as a dangerous diversion from America's primary
responsibilities in Europe, while, simultaneously, civilian officials
with "Europe First" principles saw involvement in Vietnam as essential to gaining French support in the Atlantic alliance.[2]

Both diplomatic and service officials decried the repressive nature of French rule in Indochina, but at the same time feared possible Communist moves in Western Europe, particularly France, even
more. Washington civilians, more myopic than their military counterparts, also saw Ho Chi Minh, the Nationalist-cum-Communist
leader of the Democratic Republic of Vietnam (DRVN), as little
more than a myrmidon of Joseph Stalin, so they equated Vietnamese independence with a victory for the Soviet Union. Accordingly, Presidents Harry S Truman and Dwight Eisenhower were
reluctant to pressure Paris too firmly about the need for political
reform in Vietnam, maintained steady levels of funding to France
throughout the early 1950s, and actually urged the Vietnamese to
temper their pleas for political concessions from the French. Indeed
the French themselves understood that they would not "win" the

2. George McT. Kahin, "The United States and the Anticolonial Revolutions in Southeast
Asia," in Yonosuke Nagai and Akira Iriye, eds., *The Origins of the Cold War in Asia*
(New York, 1977), 338–61; Walter LaFeber, "Roosevelt, Churchill and Indochina,
1942–1945," *American Historical Review* 80 (December 1975): 1277–95; Christopher
Thorne, "Indochina and Anglo-American Relations," *Pacific Historical Review* 45 (Feb-
ruary 1976): 73–96; George Herring, "The Truman Administration and the Restoration
of French Sovereignty in Indochina," *Diplomatic History* 1 (Winter 1977): 97–117; and
Gary Hess, "The First American Commitment in Indochina: The Acceptance of the Bao
Dai Solution, 1950," *Diplomatic History* 2 (Fall 1978): 331–50.

war but hoped to hold on long enough to improve their bargaining position in any negotiations with the Communists.[3] Nonetheless, American civilian officials were still urging Paris to stay the course in Vietnam.

Military officials, however, recognized the peril of intervention in Indochina, and they also defined the national interest more narrowly than did the civilian establishment. In the early years of cold war, U.S. policy makers accepted global commitments which assumed that American resources, soldiers, and national will were abundant, if not limitless.[4] At the same time the armed forces harbored serious reservations about their ability to counter communism everywhere that it appeared, and were more concerned about solidifying their own role in the defense policy-making process. Thus the debate over Indochina policy was also a duel over the nature of the national interest, the relationship between American resources and objectives, and bureaucratic prerogative.

Such considerations of commitments and limits led the military to oppose intervention in Vietnam during the Truman administration and even more strongly after 1953, when President Dwight Eisenhower introduced the New Look, called for reductions in military spending, and thereby began a major imbroglio between the White House and armed forces. By then, the services also believed that budget considerations made any large-scale involvement in Vietnam impractical, that the United States would need British cooperation in Indochina, and that American forces should not be expected to protect unilaterally the French position there. With this recognition of American limits and priorities, military leaders not only rejected a combat role in Vietnam but also called into question the very idea of *global* containment which was fueling the cold war.[5]

3. David L. Anderson, *Trapped by Success: The Eisenhower Administration and Vietnam, 1953–1961* (New York, 1991), 12–13, 23, 67–8; George McT. Kahin, *Intervention: How America Became Involved in Vietnam* (Garden City, N.Y., 1987), 37–52; George S. Eckhardt, *Command and Control, 1950–1969* (Washington, D.C., 1974), 8–9.
4. See, for instance, John Lewis Gaddis, *The Long Peace: Inquiries into the History of the Cold War* (New York, 1987); and Melvyn Leffler, *Preponderance of Power*, and "The American Conception of National Security and the Beginnings of the Cold War, 1945–48," *American Historical Review* 89 (April 1984): 356–78.
5. For varying interpretations of containment and the U.S. conception of national security, see John Lewis Gaddis, *Strategies of Containment: A Critical Appraisal of Postwar American National Security Policy* (New York, 1982); Daniel Yergin, *Shattered Peace: The*

Dissenters within the military also understood that the objective conditions in Indochina militated against U.S. intervention there, and rejected involvement in Vietnam for four interrelated reasons. First, the military recognized that the First Indochina War had deep, indigenous roots. Native distrust and hatred of the repressive French colonial administration, and, in turn, the absence of effective native anti-Communist leadership, had created an inchoate political environment that Ho Chi Minh had exploited to Communist advantage. Next, American officers recognized that Ho and General Vo Nguyen Giap, the commander of Viet Minh forces, enjoyed great popular support throughout Vietnam and possessed the military capacity to conduct both guerrilla and conventional warfare over extended areas and a long period of time. Third, the People's Republic of China (PRC), and, to a lesser degree, the Soviet Union would benefit strategically from the diversion of U.S. resources to Indochina, an area of ancillary importance, and they would moreover exploit U.S. intervention as a propaganda weapon among anticolonial Asians. Finally, American generals realized that involvement in an Asian war of national liberation-cum-revolution could create intense and possibly insurmountable problems for their conventionally trained and technologically oriented soldiers.

The military's reservations about involvement in Indochina were already apparent at the end of World War II. With White House agreement American military chiefs did not include Southeast Asia within the U.S. sphere of interest. More directly, Major Allison Thomas, head of an intelligence mission to Vietnam, and General Philip Gallagher, U.S. advisor to Guomindang occupation forces in northern Vietnam, actively lobbied for American contacts with Ho and sympathized with the nationalist, albeit leftist, Viet Minh, with Gallagher "confidentially" wishing that Ho's northern followers "could be given their independence."[6]

Origins of the Cold War and the National Security State (Boston, 1977); Gabriel Kolko and Joyce Kolko, *The Limits of Power: The World and United States Foreign Policy, 1945–1954* (New York, 1972). On Eisenhower's conception of national security, see Richard H. Immerman, "Confessions of an Eisenhower Revisionist: An Agonizing Reappraisal," *Diplomatic History* 14 (Summer 1990): 319–42.

6. Commanding General, U.S. Forces, India-Burma Theatre, memorandum to War Department, Commanding General, U.S. Forces, China Theatre, and Commanding General,

America's most respected service leader, General George C. Marshall, who served as secretary of state from 1947 to 1949 and then secretary of defense from 1950 to 1951, likewise doubted that the United States or France could thwart the Vietnamese independence movement. In 1947 Marshall scored a French proposal to restore Emperor Bao Dai, an exiled playboy living on the Riviera, to the throne because it implied that the West had to "resort [to] monarchy as a weapon against communism." A year later he lamented that French forces "have no prospect" of success in Vietnam. Rather than demonstrate influence, Marshall anticipated, the Indochina war "will remain a grievously costly enterprise, weakening France economically and all the West generally in its relations with Oriental peoples."⁷ In July 1949 the chiefs, in policy paper JCS 1992/4, produced their most striking summation of the perils of interference in Indochina. The "widening political consciousness

U.S. Army Liaison Section in Kandy, Ceylon, 11 September 1945, CRAX 27516, Records of the Joint Chiefs of Staff, Record Group 218, Chairman's File, Admiral Leahy, 1942–48, National Archives, Washington, D.C. (hereafter RG 218, with appropriate filing information); Gallagher, Hanoi, to General R. B. McClure, Kunming, 20 September 1945, in Gareth Porter, ed., *Vietnam: The Definitive Documentation of Human Decisions* (Stanfordville, N.Y., 1979), I:77–8, doc. 41. See also Report on Office of Strategic Services' "Deer Mission" by Major Allison Thomas, 17 September 1945, and memorandum for the record: General Gallagher's Meeting with Ho Chi Minh, 29 September 1945, doc. 40, and Porter, *Vietnam,* I:74–7, I:80–1, doc. 44; Kahin, *Intervention,* 14, 438; and U.S. Congress, House Committee on Armed Services, *United States–Vietnam Relations, 1945–1967: Study Prepared by the Department of Defense,* 12 vols. (Washington, D.C., 1971), book 1, I.C.3, C-66-104 (hereafter HCAS, *USVN Relations* with appropriate volume and page designations).

7. Marshall telegram to Caffery in Paris, 13 May 1947, in Porter, *Vietnam,* I:145–6, doc. 101; Marshall telegram to Caffery, 3 July 1948, ibid., I:176–7, doc. 118. See also Marshall telegram to Reed, 17 July 1947, ibid., I:156–7, doc. 104. It became standard practice for the military to question any large commitment to Vietnam. In JCS studies of national security priorities in 1947, Southeast Asia was consistently ranked at the bottom, while officials in the Navy and War Departments more specifically recognized Ho Chi Minh's overtures to the United States and realized that he was not a puppet of Stalin. Leffler, *Preponderance of Power,* 148, 166.

Foreign military leaders recognized the Western dilemma in Vietnam as well. The supreme allied commander in Southeast Asia, Admiral Lord Louis Mountbatten of Britain, understood that combined British-Indian forces could disarm Japanese forces still in Indochina in a short while, but also recognized that his forces would then have "less and less good excuse" for remaining in Vietnam. "In fact," Mountbatten admitted, "we shall find it hard to counter the accusations that our forces are remaining in the country solely in order to hold the Viet Namh [*sic*] Independence Movement in check." Accordingly, Mountbatten urged the continued use of Japanese forces to maintain order in Indochina. SACSEA (Mountbatten) memorandum to Chiefs of Staff, 2 October 1945, SEACOS 500, RG 218, Chairman's File, Admiral Leahy, 1942–8.

and the rise of militant nationalism among the subject people,"
they understood, "cannot be reversed." To attempt to do so, the
JCS presciently argued, would be "an anti-historical act likely in the
long run to create more problems than it solves and cause more
damage than benefit." [8]
Although key military leaders held well-established views concerning the dangers of involvement in Vietnam in mid-1949, they
soon would be thrown on the defensive by a wave of international
events that intensified the cold war, including Mao Zedong's proc-
lamation of the PRC, the formation of the North Atlantic Treaty
Organization (NATO), the successful test of a Soviet atomic bomb,
and, at home, the development by the National Security Council of
NSC 68, which envisioned a huge American military buildup to
pursue containment policies globally. Under the weight of these
events, the Truman administration inflated the importance of previously peripheral areas such as Vietnam and began to accelerate
aid to those places. Thus the JCS, despite Army Chief of Staff J.
Lawton Collins's warnings against a "primarily military effort" in
Indochina, followed the White House's lead and recommended aid
there to "check . . . the influence of the USSR in Asia." On 3
February 1950 Truman recognized Bao Dai's government and, just
months later, NSC 64, which pressed for "all practicable measures"
to protect Indochina, and then NSC 68 further expanded the U.S.
commitment to Vietnam.[9]
Though not discounting the perceived threat of Indochinese
communism, American officers expressed caution, doubt, and concern regarding an extended commitment to Vietnam. An ad hoc
JCS committee warned that the introduction of military advisors
into Indochina would identify the United States with colonialism
and the Americans and the French could thus "expect little success
in opposing Communism irrespective of the sincerity of their ef-

8. JCS 1992/4, "U.S. Policy toward Southeast Asia," 9 July 1949, 092 Asia to Europe, case
   40, Records of the U.S. Army Staff, Record Group 319 (hereafter RG 319, with appropriate filing information).
9. Chief of Staff, Army, memorandum to JCS, RG 218, CCS 452 China (4-3-45); Ronald
   Spector, *Advice and Support: The Early Years of the U.S. Army in Vietnam, 1941–1960*
   (New York, 1985), 99. See also JCS 1721/42, 17 December 1949, RG 218, CCS 452
   China (4-3-45); NSC 68, "United States Objectives and Programs for National Security,"
   14 April 1950, in John Lewis Gaddis and Thomas Etzold, eds., *Containment: Documents
   on American Policy and Strategy: 1945–1950* (New York, 1978).

forts." A report by the Army Plans and Operations (P & O) division more pointedly criticized U.S. policy, advocating assistance to France only "consistent with other global commitments of higher priority and short of [the] commitment of . . . combat forces . . . in Indo-China." The P & O pessimistically estimated that the Viet Minh would drive the French out of Indochina on the basis of popular support alone, not Chinese assistance. Ho enjoyed the support of 80 percent of the Vietnamese people, Army planners reported, yet 80 percent of his followers were not Communists. Such indigenous appeal, as well as limited PRC support, virtually assured Viet Minh success.[10]

The president overcame such misgivings and, in early March, approved a $15 million, essentially military, aid package to Indochina. In May, encouraged by Secretary of State Dean Acheson, Truman appropriated another $10 million in military assistance and then created an economic aid mission to Indochina. At the same time, war broke out in Korea and State Department officer John Melby and General Graves Erskine returned from Indochina and urged intensified efforts there, convincing the administration even more of the need to contain Asian communism. Nonetheless, both Army intelligence and the Joint Intelligence Committee (JIC) reported that the Viet Minh was growing in size and effectiveness, while the JCS warned that a military solution to this "internal security problem" was not possible and wanted France to understand that U.S. troops would not be committed to Indochina.[11]

10. Report by the Ad Hoc Committee of Major General R. E. Duff, USA, Captain W. O. Floyd, USN, Major D. D. Duff, USAF, to the JCS, "Program of Assistance for the General Area of China," JCS 1721/43, 16 January 1950, RG 218, CCS 452 China (4-3-45), section 7; Plans and Operations position paper, "U.S. Position with Respect to Indochina, 25 February 1950," RG 319, G-3 091 Indochina TS.
11. JCS 1992/22, "Estimate of the Indochina Situation," 11 September 1950, RG 319, G-3 091 Indochina, TS. See also *The Pentagon Papers: The Defense Department History of United States Decisionmaking on Vietnam, Senator Gravel Edition,* 5 vols. (Boston, 1971), 1:65–6 (hereafter cited as *Pentagon Papers: Gravel* with appropriate volume and page designations); Department of State release, 25 May 1950, ibid. 370–2, doc. 6; John Melby, "Vietnam – 1950," *Diplomatic History* 6 (Winter 1982): 97–109; Joint MDAP Survey (Melby-Erskine) Mission report, 24 August 1950, RG 218, CCS 092 Asia, BP 1; JIC report to JCS, "Estimate of the Indochinese situation," JCS 1992/22, 25 August 1950, RG 218, CCS 092 Asia (6-25-48), section 5; JCS memorandum for Secretary of Defense, 7 September 1950, JCS 1992/29, 7 October 1950, RG 218, CCS 092 Asia (6-25-48), section 6.

Barely a month later, the JCS added that the Viet Minh now numbered 92,500 regular forces and about 130,000 guerrillas, and was also developing task forces of 3,000 to 5,000 troops for conventional warfare. Given such size and organization, Giap's forces had the military capacity to move freely throughout most of Indochina, support the resistance in French-occupied areas, continue to harass lines of communication, and even seize French border outposts. Accordingly, the chiefs, in response to NSC pressure for intervention, maintained that "the U.S. will not commit any of its armed forces to the defense of Indochina against overt foreign aggression or *augmented internal Communist offensives.*" The Joint Strategic Plans Committee (JSPC) also saw no reason for the United States to consider committing its forces to a "series of inconclusive peripheral actions which would drain our military strength and weaken . . . our global position." Collins was more blunt. "France will be driven out of Indochina," he prophesied, and was "wasting men and equipment trying to remain there."[12]

Despite such dire warnings the Truman administration committed over $130 million in additional funding and matériel to Vietnam by late 1950. Apparently emboldened by the American assistance, French leadership appointed World War II hero Jean de Lattre de Tassigny to command its forces in Indochina with instructions to prosecute the war vigorously. French hopes then rose dramatically as de Lattre's forces successfully repulsed Viet Minh offensives at Vinh Yen and Mao Khe, north of Hanoi, and in June gained an impressive victory at Phat Diem in the Hong River delta, some eighty miles southeast of Hanoi.[13]

American service dissenters were not so impressed with these "glorious victories," as de Lattre had described them. Recognizing the limits on American resources and the continued strength of the

12. Annex 2, JCS 1992/34, "Military Situation in Indochina," 17 October 1950, RG 319, G-3, 091 Indochina TS; JCS memorandum to Secretary of Defense, "Draft Statement of U.S. Policy on Indochina for NSC Consideration," 18 October 1950, RG 330, CD 092 Indochina 1950, Records of the Office of the Assistant Secretary of Defense for International Security Affairs(emphasis in original); JSPC 958/5, "U.S. Military Measures in Southeast Asia," RG 218, CCS 092 Asia (248), section 9; U.S. Minutes of U.S.–U.K. Political–Military Conversations, 26 October 1950, U.S. Department of State, *Papers Relating to Foreign Relations of the United States, 1950* (Washington, D.C., 1976), 3:1696 (hereafter cited as *FRUS* with appropriate year, volume, and page designations).
13. Spector, *Advice and Support,* 136–9, map on 138.

Viet Minh, the JSPC and JCS insisted that if the French requested even air or naval support "they will have to be told point blank that none will be committed." The United States "has no intention" of supplanting French efforts in Indochina, Assistant Army Chief for P & O Maxwell Taylor ironically affirmed, "either at the present or in the future." Army planner General Robinson Duff added that any increased commitments to Asia would damage America's capacity to defend "our primary strategic area, Western Europe." Such misgivings were well founded, as Army intelligence showed. Despite French success the Viet Minh continued to grow and was now disposed to attack "virtually any part" of the French perimeter in the north.[14]

Such military reservations, however, did not go unchallenged as political and military officials such as Donald Heath, the ambassador to Saigon, General Francis Brink, the commander of the U.S. Military Assistance Advisory Group (MAAG), David Bruce, the ambassador to Paris, and Admiral Arthur Radford, the commander in chief of Pacific forces (CINCPAC), remained sanguine about American prospects in Vietnam and pressed Washington to "exert every care" to check communism there. Most U.S. military leaders, however, were more firmly opposed to war in Indochina, in large measure due to the U.S. experience in Korea. Ranking military officials had initially opposed the introduction of ground troops into Korea in June 1950. With hopes for a decisive victory dashed by the next year, the military realized that the outlook for Vietnam was little better. To the JIC, it was clear that U.S. intervention in

14. The Viet Minh, by early 1951, totaled 120,000 regular forces, a one-third increase in six months, and had rearmed four infantry divisions in Tonkin. Army Intelligence Staff Study, "Probable Viet Minh and/or Chi Com Courses of Action in Indochina," 24 April 1951, RG 319, G-3 091 Indochina. See also JSPC report to JCS, "U.S. Military Measures in Southeast Asia," JCS 1992/57, 23 February 1951, RG 218, CCS 092 Asia (6-25-48), section 11; JSPC report to JCS, "Military Staff Talks on Defense of Indo-China," JCS 1992/58, 3 March 1951, RG 218, CCS 092 Asia (6-25-48), section 11; General Maxwell Taylor memorandum for Collins, "Indochina," 27 March 1951, RG 319, G-3 091, Indochina TS; Duff, G-3, memorandum to Chief of Staff, USA, "Action to Assure Effective Allies in the Case of a Major War in the Far East," 15 May 1951, RG 319, G-3 092 Asia TS. General Sidney Spalding, a contributor to NSC 68, had complained earlier that U.S. attempts to bolster the French position in Vietnam ran counter to overall American defense objectives. Spalding "question[ed] the wisdom" of pressing France to do more in Indochina. "Western Europe," he stressed, is "still the key." General Sidney Spalding memorandum for General Burns, 19 December 1950, RG 330, CD 092 Indochina 1951.

Barry University Library
Miami *Fl* *33161*

Indochina "would involve political and military disadvantages and costs similar to those sustained in Korea." Ironically, an early conclusion to the war on the peninsula would actually diminish American prospects in Vietnam. In the event of a Korean armistice, the PRC would be free to transfer 340,000 forces from North Korea and 330,000 from Manchuria to Indochina, while the Americans would still have to maintain troops and matériel in South Korea.[15] Not surprisingly, then, the JCS rejected the French contention that Korea and Indochina were but separate fronts in "one war" against Asian communism and, with de Lattre visiting Washington in September 1951, urged against further aid to France "to cover what is substantially an internal budget deficit of another country."[16]

Again, though, the military lost a political battle as the French commander won increased aid and a public relations success. The JCS nonetheless cautioned that the United States was "becoming engaged in war" itself by supporting the French against the "indigenous Vietminh armed forces." The chiefs also continued to resist the idea of involvement in Vietnam during a meeting with State Department officials on 21 December, just after the Viet Minh had routed French forces at Hoa Binh, west of Hanoi. Air Force Chief of Staff Hoyt Vandenberg, while not urging intervention, wondered whether the United States was "prepared to let Southeast Asia go?" Collins, however, pointed out that the "loss" of Indochina would not prompt its neighbors to fall like dominoes to communism. The JCS chair Omar Bradley moreover doubted that "we could get our public to go along with the idea of our going into Indochina in a

15. JIC report to JCS, "Effect of a Cease-Fire in Korea on Chi Com Capabilities in Southeast Asia," JIC 529/6, 16 August 1951, RG 218, CCS 092 Asia (248), section 16. See also *FRUS, 1951*, 6:433–7, 443–4; Spector, *Advice and Support*, 142; on the relationships between Vietnam policy and the Korean War, see Enclosure "D," JCS 1992/58, 3 March 1951, RG 218, CCS 092 Asia (248), section 11; see also Army Intelligence Staff Study, cited in note 14; JIC report, "Estimate of Indochinese Situation," JCS 1992/86, 10 July 1951, RG 319, G-3 091 Indochina TS; JIC 529/7, 27 August 1951, RG 218, CCS 092 Asia (248), section 16; G-3, Plans Division, memorandum to General Jenkins, "U.S. Policy with Respect to Indochina in the Event the Korean War Ends," 1 October 1951, RG 319, G-3 091 Indochina TS.

16. JCS memorandum for Secretary of Defense (Lovett), "Combat Operations in Indochina," 19 November 1951, RG 218, CCS 092 Asia (248), section 19. See also sources cited in note 15; Joint Strategic Survey Committee (JSSC) memorandum to JCS, "Additional Aid to Indochina," JCS 1992/91, 30 August 1951, RG 319, G-3 091 Indochina TS; JSSC memorandum to JCS, "Combat Operations in Indochina," JCS 1992/12, 10 November 1951, RG 319, G-3 091 Indochina TS and 091.3 (MDAP) Indochina 1951.

military way." Collins agreed and concluded that "we must face the probability that Indochina will be lost." In the meantime the JSPC warned that even limited involvement in Vietnam "could only lead to a dilemma similar to that in Korea, which is insoluble by military action."[17]

Throughout 1952, as the Truman administration – already bearing one-third of the cost of France's war – increased its assistance to Vietnam, political and military officials continued to joust over American policy in Indochina. NSC 124/2, officially adopted in June, saw Southeast Asia as an area of vital interest to the United States and contemplated military intervention to support friendly governments. Ambassador Heath and General Brink rejected the "over pessimistic" intelligence reports recently received from Vietnam, while Dean Acheson suggested that a naval blockade or air attacks might be needed to prevent PRC intervention in Vietnam.[18] Military dissenters, however, continued to distance themselves from such bellicose suggestions, and so neither political nor military leaders seriously considered combat intervention at this time. The JCS, as Defense Secretary Robert A. Lovett wrote to NATO Commander Dwight Eisenhower, remained "unanimously opposed to the commitment of any troops" to Indochina. The chiefs, in fact, even refused to transfer funding for other Asian nations to Vietnam because such aid reductions would "jeopardize . . . the U.S. military position in the Far East." With regard to the situation in Vietnam, incoming MAAG Chief General Thomas Trapnell could only lament that "the enemy retains the initiative."[19]

17. See JCS and JSSC memoranda cited in note 16 above; Substance of Discussion of State-JCS Meeting at the Pentagon Building, 21 December 1951, *FRUS,* 1951, 6:568–70; and JSPC memorandum to JCS, "Conference with France and Britain on Southeast Asia," JSPC 958/58, 22 December 1951, RG 218, CCS 092 Asia (248), section 20.
18. NSC Staff Study on United States Objectives and Courses of Action with Respect to Communist Aggression in Southeast Asia, 13 February 1952, *Pentagon Papers: Gravel* 1:375–81, doc. 10; Heath to Department of State, 5 April 1952, *FRUS,* 1952–4 (Washington, D. C., 1982), 13:99; Dean Acheson, *Present at the Creation: My Years at the State Department* (New York, 1969), 861.
19. Lovett memorandum to Eisenhower, 3 January 1952, *Declassified Documents Reference System,* 81, 36A (hereafter *DDRS* with appropriate year and document designations); Bradley, CJCS, memorandum for Secretary of Defense, "Supplemental FY 52 MDAP for Indochina ($30 Million)," RG 330, CD 091.3 Indochina 1952; Trapnell to Collins, 20 December 1952, RG 330, CD 091.3 Indochina 1953. See also Chief of Staff, USA, memorandum, "The U.S. Position to Be Taken at the 5-Power Ad Hoc Meeting," RG 218, CCS 092 Asia (248), section 24.

In early 1953, however, new President Dwight Eisenhower and Secretary of State John Foster Dulles, who had attacked Truman and Acheson during the 1952 campaign for being soft on communism, seemed likely to reverse the deteriorating situation in Vietnam and substantially increase the U.S. commitment or even intervene there. But the new administration tempered any desire to take a military role in Vietnam because of the New Look's reliance on nuclear weapons to cut military spending and balance the budget. Thus the Republicans continued to press the French and native armies to retain dominant responsibility for their war in Indochina.[20]

Not only did the New Look mark a shift in defense policy, but, because of Eisenhower's goal of balancing the budget via reductions in military spending, it also prompted a breakdown in civil–military relations that would have serious repercussions for the U.S. experience in Vietnam. Though the military signed off on the president's goals of reallocating resources within the armed services and emphasizing nuclear deterrence and air defense, various officers, especially Army Chief Matthew Ridgway, balked at cutting the defense budget. Thus began a series of public disputes between the armed forces and Eisenhower over national security policy and, within that context, the U.S. approach to Vietnam. Not surprisingly, Ridgway would become the president's greatest critic on both issues while the new JCS chair, Admiral Arthur Radford, a "ruthless partisan and outstanding bureaucratic infighter," would do Eisenhower's bidding within the military on both budgets and Indochina.[21]

Undoubtedly, some service officials rejected intervention in Vietnam principally because the New Look and its reliance on nuclear weapons made war in the jungles of Indochina impossible. But it was also evident that conditions inside Vietnam were simply not suitable for American involvement. As Air Force General and JCS director Charles Cabell explained, "terrain difficulties, the guerrilla

20. William Conrad Gibbons, *The U.S. Government and the Vietnam War: Executive and Legislative Roles and Relationships, Part I: 1945–1961*, Prepared for the Committee on Foreign Relations, United States Senate (Washington, D.C., 1984), 120–9; Spector, *Advice and Support*, 167–9.
21. Kinnard, *Eisenhower and Strategy Management*, 21–4.

nature of Vietminh operations, and the political apathy of the population preclude decisive consolidation of areas cleared of Vietminh, unless . . . physically occupied by friendly forces." Such a commitment, Cabell concluded, "is beyond the capabilities of the friendly strength."[22]

Military conditions in Vietnam thus had not changed appreciably in the first months of the Eisenhower administration. The U.S. military found the new French strategy – the Letorneau plan, a three-phase program to end the war by 1955 – preferable to continued stasis, but even France's biggest booster, Admiral Radford, recognized the Western disadvantage in Vietnam. The Viet Minh, he understood, was committed to national liberation, had superior intelligence, could conduct guerrilla operations freely, and could rely on PRC support. More stridently, J. Lawton Collins charged that French Commander Raoul Salan was a "second-rater," while Hoyt Vandenberg wondered whether the United States was "pouring money down a rathole" in Vietnam. The Air Force chief was particularly alarmed because he believed that France was the keystone to European security and thus "the Indochina thing has to be settled before NATO will work."[23]

When General Giap's incursion into Laos in mid-April seemed to confirm the blunt assessments of Collins and Vandenberg, Eisenhower and Dulles sent the caustic, bellicose General John "Iron Mike" O'Daniel to study the situation in Vietnam. They also pressed the French to appoint a more aggressive commander, with Henri Navarre the agreed-upon choice. Despite U.S. military analyses that offered a bleak forecast for the French at that time, O'Daniel, the White House, and the Congress were all buoyed by

22. Cabell in memorandum, Assistant Secretary of State for Far East Affairs (Allison), to Secretary of State, 28 January 1953, *FRUS,* 1952–4, 13:366–9. Cabell, as the JCS and Army had done repeatedly earlier, recognized the difficulties involved in a principally guerrilla war in Indochina, which contradicts Ronald Spector's assertion that the U.S. military underestimated the strength and ability of Viet Minh guerrillas and consistently urged a greater use of firepower against them. Spector, *Advice and Support,* 167–9.
23. Collins and Vandenberg in Substance of Discussion of State-JCS Meeting at the Pentagon Building, 24 April 1953, *FRUS,* 1952–4, 13:496–503. See also JCS 1992/214, 10 April 1953, "Proposed French Strategic Plan for the Successful Conclusion of the War in Indochina," RG 218, CCS 092 Asia (248), section 398; for further detail on Radford's recognition of Viet Minh strengths, see CINCPAC memorandum to CNO, "Evaluation of Military Operations in Indochina," 18 April 1953, RG 218, CCS 092 Asia (248), BP part 9.

the so-called Navarre concept, which envisioned immediate local attacks to be followed by a general offensive in the fall, and also by French premier Joseph Laniel's transfer of some political authority to Indochinese states to "perfect" their independence. To American officials, such measures indicated that the French were seriously attempting to correct the military and political problems plaguing their efforts in Indochina. As a result, Washington appropriated an additional $785 million in military assistance to Vietnam in 1953.[24]

The JCS endorsed the fait accompli of additional aid, but questioned the optimistic views that prompted it. At a joint meeting with diplomatic officials, the chiefs doubted that the French would improve and, in what had already become their mantra, rejected any combat involvement in Indochina because of commitments elsewhere, the need to maintain the strategic reserve, budgetary limits, and deteriorating conditions inside Vietnam. General Collins pointed out that a campaign in Indochina would be worse than that in Korea. Any U.S. forces could expect a "major and protracted war. . . . Militarily and politically we would be in up to our necks." But he also understood that he spoke "from a military point of view" and that the JCS's judgment was not decisive. Stating the obvious, he conceded that "if our political leaders want to put troops in there we will of course do it."[25]

The National Security Council (NSC) did want to put troops into Vietnam, citing Indochina as an area of vital strategic importance that the United States should defend with military forces if needed in NSC 162/2, authorized in October 1953. Perhaps the NSC was eager to intervene because, inside Vietnam, the politicomilitary situation had reached a turning point. In October, the frustrated Vietnamese National Congress threatened to withdraw from the French Union, while simultaneously Viet Minh forces routed units

---

24. National Intelligence Estimate (NIE) 91, "Probable Developments in Indochina Through Mid-1954," 9 June 1953, *FRUS, 1952–4*, 13:592–602; JSSC report to JCS, "Possible Military Courses of Action in Indochina," JCS 1992/227, 22 June 1953, ibid., 615–18; U.S. Joint Mission to Indochina of General John O'Daniel report, HCAS, *USVN Relations*, book 9, 69ff.; *Pentagon Papers: Gravel*, 1:77–87.
25. Substance of Discussion of State-JCS Meeting at the Pentagon Building, 10 July 1953, *FRUS, 1952–4*, 13:648ff.

of the Vietnamese National Army at Bui Chi in Tonkin. Against that backdrop O'Daniel returned to Vietnam in early November to evaluate the French performance. The general reported that Navarre had made considerable progress and could expect real success within a year. Felix Stump, the new CINCPAC, Robert Carney, the new Navy chief of staff, and Ridgway, the new Army chief, questioned O'Daniel's optimism, however, contending that victory was not possible given the indigenous resentment against and weak leadership of the French.[26]

A Special Intelligence Estimate, which the JCS and the three services coordinated with the CIA, was even more gloomy regarding the U.S. future in Indochina. American involvement had given the PRC license to intervene in Southeast Asia to "liberate Indochina from American imperialism." Should the United States assume a combat role in Vietnam, the climate and terrain, along with native rejection of Western interference, could lead to "a long and indecisive war" that "could be exploited politically." In time, "the U.S. and Vietnamese will to fight might be worn down." Even if Franco-American forces could defeat the Viet Minh, Giap's forces could regroup, continue guerrilla operations, and force the United States to maintain a military role in Vietnam "for years to come."[27] The JSPC and the JCS added to that blunt report in December with their most detailed planning assessment to date. Any U.S. contribution to the war would have to be huge, including 200,000 ground troops, 4,000 military trainers, 6 infantry divisions, several air wings, and a number of naval craft, as well as new base construction. Such a commitment could cost billions of dollars and would thereby drain logistic reserves and delay aid to NATO and other Army units, all during a drawdown at home. It would also force major production increases and, most important, would require

26. U.S. Military Mission to Indochina report, 19 November 1953, JSPC 958/136, 7 December 1953, RG 218, CCS 092 Asia (248), section 51; CNO memorandum to JCS, "Comments by CINCPAC on Progress Report on Military Situation in Indochina," 4 December 1953, RG 218, CCS 092 Asia (248), section 51; Memo, Chief of Staff, Army (Ridgway), on O'Daniel Report, 19 December 1953, RG 218, CCS 092 Asia (248), section 51.
27. Special Estimate: "Probable Communist Reactions to Certain Possible U.S. Courses of Action in Indochina through 1954," 18 December 1953, *Pentagon Papers: Gravel,* I:429–34, doc. 19.

increased draft calls, extended terms of service, and a recall of reservists.[28]

At the same time that military officials were rejecting calls for more involvement in Vietnam, political skirmishing between the armed forces and White House was growing. In an early 1954 speech, Dulles called for a policy of "maximum deterrent at a bearable cost," which the secretaries of defense and the treasury, Charles Wilson and George Humphrey, correctly understood to mean that air power would be the dominant element in U.S. strategy. Ridgway, already fighting Eisenhower's Indochina policy, attacked the New Look with even greater virulence, arguing that the Army ground soldier was still the key to successful military action.[29] Civilian and military leaders were thus engaged in two battles by 1954, one over their fundamental mission and budgets, and the other concerning Vietnam.

While American officials debated such issues, the battle in Indochina reached its denouement. In late November 1953, Navarre's forces occupied the village of Dien Bien Phu in northwest Vietnam to use as a garrison from which to conduct conventional operations with twelve battalions, artillery, and air support. In December, however, Giap laid siege to Dien Bien Phu. Navarre clearly had blundered, and by early 1954 the Viet Minh had isolated French forces in that remote village on the Laotian border.[30] In Washington, Dulles and other diplomatic officials advocated using the relief of Dien Bien Phu as a pretext for committing American forces to Vietnam, a position with which defense representatives at an 8 January 1954 NSC meeting strongly disagreed. Admiral A. C. Davis, director of the Pentagon's Office of Foreign Military As-

---

28. JSPC 958/41, "Review of U.S. Policy toward Southeast Asia," 21 December 1953, RG 218, CCS 092 Asia (248), section 52; JCS 1992/262, 24 December 1953, RG 218, CCS 092 Asia (248), section 53.

29. Kinnard, *Eisenhower and Strategy Management,* 25–7. Ironically, while Dulles was pointing out the need for economical defense, the United States was suffering from its first recession of the Eisenhower years, created in large part by the reductions in military spending, a condition downplayed by the White House. Anthony S. Campagna, *The Economic Consequences of the Vietnam War* (Westport, Conn., 1991), 6.

30. For background on the politicomilitary importance of Dien Bien Phu and U.S. reaction, see Spector, *Advice and Support,* 182–3; George Herring and Richard Immerman, "Eisenhower, Dulles, and Dienbienphu: 'The Day We Didn't Go to War' Revisited," *Journal of American History* 71 (September 1984): 343–63.

sistance, warned that the "involvement of U.S. forces in the Indochina war should be avoided at all costs." American officials "should not be self-duped into believing the possibility of partial involvement – such as 'naval and air units only.' One cannot go over Niagara Falls in a barrel only slightly." U.S. leaders had to understand, the admiral plainly insisted, "that there is no cheap way to fight a war, once committed."[31]

The NSC balked, optimistically arguing that a Communist victory in Indochina was not likely, but anomalously clamoring for U.S. intervention to stem the disintegration there. Army P & O, however, rejected its arguments and also found "grave implications" in a French request for flying crews and maintenance personnel because "if fulfilled, the U.S. will be participating in actual operations." Even France's advocate Admiral Radford lamented that the Air Force had sent two hundred mechanics to Indochina though it needed them at home.[32] Radford additionally conceded that the Viet Minh had several military advantages over the French, including more mobility, greater efficiency with fewer forces, familiarity with the terrain, and, crucially, indigenous support; the PRC, the JCS chair conceded, sent "a very small amount" of matériel to Ho monthly, only about one thousand tons. The JCS further recognized that the Viet Minh still held the military initiative and had successfully identified itself with "freedom from the colonial yoke and with the improvement of the general welfare of the people." Even so, American policy makers such as Dulles, Radford, and

31. Other Pentagon officials also balked at plans to intervene. "The commitment of U.S. forces in a 'civil war' in Indochina," one defense representative charged, "will be an admission of the bankruptcy of our policy re[garding] Southeast Asia and France, and should be resorted to only in extremity." *Pentagon Papers: Gravel,* 1:89–90.

32. Discussion at 181st Meeting of the National Security Council, 21 January 1954, *DDRS,* 85, 001801; NSC 5045, "U.S. Objectives and Courses of Action with Respect to Southeast Asia," 16 January 1954, *Pentagon Papers: Gravel,* 1:437, doc. 20; G-3 Study, "Further U.S. Assistance in the Indochina War Short of Committing U.S. Armed Forces," 12 January 1954, RG 319, G-3 091 Indochina; General Charles Bonesteel, (Office of ASD/ISA), memorandum for the record, "Meeting of President's Special Committee on Indochina," 29 January 1954, 30 January 1954, HCAS, *USVN Relations,* book 9, 240–4. General Walter Bedell Smith, the undersecretary of state, added that the introduction of more mechanics or trainers into Vietnam could "create . . . the impression that we were backing into the war in Indochina." Radford and Bedell Smith in Executive Sessions of the Senate Committee on Foreign Relations, 83rd Cong., 2d sess., 16 February 1954, 6:112.

Undersecretary of State Walter Bedell Smith continued to press for combat intervention to rescue the French at Dien Bien Phu.[33]

Such analyses served as prologue to the decisive spring 1954 debate over intervention. Despite recognizing the troubled military situation, Radford continued to press for intervention, even pledging such action to French military representatives. While the admiral also confided to Dulles that "we must stop being optimistic about the situation," he nonetheless urged the president to "be prepared to act promptly and in force possibly to a frantic and belated [French] request . . . for U.S. intervention." Toward that end Radford, on 31 March, convened the JCS to propose direct American intervention in Vietnam.[34]

Ridgway led the opposition, emphatically dissenting from the chair's recommendation. In the first place, he believed that only Eisenhower or Dulles, not the JCS chair, had the authority to raise the issue of intervention. For Radford to do so, the Army chief rather naively argued, "would be to involve the JCS inevitably in politics." With regard to conditions on the ground, Ridgway found America's capacity to affect the outcome at Dien Bien Phu "altogether disproportionate to the liability it would incur," which included a "greatly increased risk of general war." Marine Commandant Lemuel Shepherd bolstered Ridgway's dissent, finding "no significant promise of success" in American intervention. As the commandant saw it, the United States could either accept failure or send ground troops into Vietnam. Though America could "ill afford" the former, Shepherd did "not believe that the other is a matter which we should even consider under present circumstances."[35]

33. JCS Paper, "The Situation in Indochina," 7 February 1954, RG 218, CCS 092 Asia (248), section 57; Radford in Executive Session (see note 32). See also O'Daniel Mission report, 5 February 1954, HCAS, *USVN Relations,* book 9, 246–58; *Pentagon Papers: Gravel,* 1:90–1; HCAS, *USVN Relations,* book 1, II.B.1, B-6.
34. Ely memorandum for Radford, 23 March 1954, and Radford memorandum for Eisenhower, "Discussion with General Ely Relating to the Situation in Indochina," 24 March 1954, RG 218, CCS 091 Indo-China (March 1954). See also HCAS, *USVN Relations,* book 9, 288–91; memo of telephone conversation between secretary of state (Dulles) and chair of the JCS (Radford), 24 March 1954, *FRUS, 1952–4,* 13:1151; Radford, chair, JCS, to chief MAAG Indochina Trapnell, NR:JCS 959075, 29 March 1954, RG 218, Chair's File, Admiral Radford, 1953–7, CCS 091 Indo-China (1953); Radford memorandum for secretary of defense, 21 March 1954, RG 218, Chair's File, Admiral Radford, 1953–7, CCS 091 Indo-China (1953).
35. Like Ridgway, Shepherd warned that air support, being promoted as a panacea by some

Such JCS opposition, however, did not end the debate over intervention. To the secretary of state, the JCS was too concerned with the possibility of atomic war against the PRC or Soviet Union and was paying too little attention to its "political" or "defensive" options in Indochina. Dulles and Radford also continued to press allies and politicians to support the French presence in Indochina, largely because of Eisenhower's insistence that he would not intervene unilaterally or without congressional approval. In fact, the president, writing to the U.S. commander in Europe, General Alfred Gruenther, condemned the "astonishing proposals for unilateral American intervention in Indo-China." Gruenther's own "adverse opinion" of military action in Vietnam "exactly parallels mine," Eisenhower wrote. If the war in Indochina was to continue, he observed, the bulk of ground forces would have to come from France while "additional forces should come from Asiatic and European troops already in the region."[36]

General Albert Wedemeyer, the president's friend and past U.S. commander in China, supported the views of Eisenhower and Gruenther. Wedemeyer congratulated the president for his restraint during the Dien Bien Phu crisis, agreeing that native forces should be responsible for any combat in Vietnam because of Asian resentment against any Western presence. Yet, both a special presidential committee on Indochina and the NSC weighed in on the side of intervention. General Graves Erskine, chair of Eisenhower's committee, found it imperative that "the Western position in Indo-China . . . be maintained and improved by a military victory," even if, the Security Council added, the war expanded beyond the Indochinese theater.[37]

elements of the Washington defense establishment, would be "an unprofitable adventure . . . without important effect on the fortunes of the soldier on the ground." Ridgway and Shepherd memoranda for the JCS, 2 April 1954, RG 218, Radford Chair's File, Admiral, 1953–7, CCS 091 Indo-China (April 1954); documents also in Papers of Matthew Ridgway, Military History Institute (MHI), Carlisle Barracks, Pa., box 30 (hereafter cited as Ridgway Papers, MHI, with filing information).

36. Pruessen, "Dulles and the Predicaments of Power," 27; Eisenhower to SAC-EUR (Gruenther), 26 April 1954, *DDRS*, 76, 30G. In an interview conducted ten years after the Dien Bien Phu crisis, Eisenhower continued to defend his decision against intervention. "[T]o fight against guerrillas is very difficult because guerrillas can always fade away and then come back to fight again. There's no way of getting hold of them and getting them by the throat." Eisenhower Oral History, 25, Dulles Oral History Project, Seeley Mudd Library, Princeton University.

37. Wedemeyer to Eisenhower, 12 May 1954, Dwight D. Eisenhower Library, Abilene,

Ridgway again dampened such enthusiasm for intervention. He pointed out that the Army would have to commit at least seven divisions to fight in Vietnam, even with air and naval support or the use of atomic weapons. Bolstered by the report of a technical survey team, he added that Vietnam lacked adequate port and bridge facilities, that monsoons would limit military operations, and that the local communications system was too primitive to support an American presence there. Even if engineers could build up ports and airfields to handle the influx of U.S. troops, standard Army units were "too ponderous" for combat in Vietnam, a land "particularly adapted to the guerrilla-type war" at which the Viet Minh had been so successful. The Army chief stressed, moreover, that the PRC, not Ho and Giap, represented the more viable threat to U.S. interests in Asia. Accordingly, a combat commitment in Vietnam would amount to a "dangerous strategic diversion" of limited U.S. military power to a "non-decisive theater to the attainment of non-decisive local objectives." Ridgway reported such findings to the president in a late May briefing and he believed that "to a man of [Eisenhower's] military experience its implications were immediately clear."[38]

Ridgway may have been overly optimistic though, because the president, Dulles, Radford, and O'Daniel continued to look for ways to increase the American stake in Vietnam. The JCS made it clear, however, that intervention at Dien Bien Phu would not be a " 'one-shot' affair," but rather a "continuing logistic supply requirement" for America's Far East forces and it would ultimately

Kansas, White House Central Files, Office Files, box 862, folder 181-C, Indo-China (hereafter cited as DDEL, with filing information); Special Committee Report on Southeast Asia – Part II, 5 April 1954, *Pentagon Papers: Gravel,* 1: 472–6, doc. 32; NSC Action 1074-A, 5 April 1954, HCAS, *USVN Relations,* book 9, 298–332.

38. Army position on NSC Action 1074-A, n.d., HCAS, *USVN Relations,* book 1, II.B.1, B-10, book 9, 333; Chief of Staff, USA, memorandum to JCS, 6 April 1954, *FRUS, 1952–4,* 13:1269–70; Ridgway quoted in Robert Asprey, *War in the Shadows: The Guerrilla in History* (Garden City, N.Y., 1975), 817–18; Ridgway interview with Maurice Matloff, 2–6, MHI. See also JCS memorandum for Secretary of Defense, "Indochina," 8 April 1954, RG 218, CCS 092 Asia (248) section 62; *Pentagon Papers: Gravel* 1:93; Chief of Staff, U.S. Army, memorandum to JCS, "Reconnaissance of Indochina and Thailand," JCS 1992/359, 14 July 1954, 15 July 1954, RG 218, CCS 092 (248), section 75; Ridgway, *Soldier,* 276; Richard H. Immerman's recent Bernath Lecture would seem to confirm the validity of Ridgway's observation. See "Confessions of an Eisenhower Revisionist."

involve U.S. troops in direct military operations, create increasing demands for reinforcement, risk American casualties, and possibly provoke Chinese intervention. Thus the "real question" attending the debate over Dien Bien Phu was whether the United States would "commence active participation by [American] forces in the Indo-china war." By early May 1954 military opponents of intervention clearly held the upper hand. Other concerns, such as rearming the Federal Republic of Germany, were of principal interest to service officials; the French garrison at Dien Bien Phu was doomed; and U.S. officials were headed to the conference on East–West affairs in Geneva that would partition Vietnam along its seventeenth parallel and provide for timely elections to unify the country. Eisenhower could find no allies willing to join in bailing out France, and, except for Radford, the chiefs had rejected all pleas to begin an American version of the Vietnam war.[39]

Throughout the first months of 1954 the military had coordinated a strong campaign against intervention. Though concerned with the ramifications of Communist success in Vietnam, most officers understood that the political and military environment in both America and Indochina militated against U.S. prospects in Southeast Asia. General Thomas Trapnell, past MAAG commander, typified the American military dilemma regarding Vietnam. Though an advocate of holding the line against the Viet Minh, Trapnell recognized that Ho was the most respected leader in Vietnam and that Indochinese communism had attracted intellectuals, peasants, and urban workers alike. Ho and Giap, moreover, directed an experienced force with about 300,000 troops, including one artillery and six infantry divisions, engineers, and numerous support units. The Viet Minh, Trapnell added, had developed effec-

39. JCS memorandum for Secretary of Defense, "French Request for Additional Aid," 27 April 1954, RG 330, ASD/ISA, 091 Indochina, May–December 1954. See also Secretary of Defense memorandum to the Service Secretaries and JCS, 15 April 1954, Porter, *Vietnam*, I:537–8, doc. 312; *Pentagon Papers: Gravel*, 1:100–6, 129; HCAS, *USVN Relations,* book 1, III.A.2, A-16-17; DulTe 12, Paris to Secretary of State, 24 April 1954, *DDRS,* 81, 361B; Spector, *Advice and Support,* 211; Eisenhower, *Mandate for Change,* 354–5; *FRUS,* 1952–4, 13:1431; Rolf Steininger, "John Foster Dulles, the European Defense Community, and the German Question," in Immerman, *Dulles and the Diplomacy of the Cold War,* 87; on the Geneva Conference, see Richard Immerman, "The United States and the Geneva Conference of 1954: A New Look," *Diplomatic History* 14 (Winter 1990): 43–66.

tive regional militia, possessed a "tremendous capability" for mobility and endurance, and was skilled in political and psychological indoctrination. Believing that time – and U.S. and French public opinion – was on their side, Vietnamese Communists were conducting "a clever war of attrition." Trapnell believed that the United States should resist the Left in Asia, but he insisted that a "military solution to the war in Indochina is not possible."[40]

The Army's assistant chief for planning, General James Gavin, corroborated that assessment in a hundred-page report on Vietnam commissioned by Ridgway. Waging war in Indochina, Gavin found, would require transferring vast amounts of resources from other programs in more important parts of the world. The Army would also have to extend its terms of service for active personnel, activate reservists, and increase draft calls. In addition, the services would also need to reopen military bases and increase material production for Indochina, which ran contrary to New Look budget policy. Worse, Gavin estimated that American troops would suffer about 28,000 casualties monthly. And, of course, he reminded his superiors, the Viet Minh remained a formidable military force.[41]

Even into mid-1954, Eisenhower and Dulles still sought multilateral action to stem the Communist advance in Vietnam and had not yet dismissed a combat role there. The JCS again moved to block any plans for intervention, limited or otherwise. Any involvement, the chiefs explained, "would continue and expand considerably even though initial efforts were indecisive." In time, the United States would have to commit additional naval and air units, "and extensive ground forces to prevent the loss of Indochina." The JCS also rejected an offer by Syngman Rhee to send troops to Vietnam. South Korean involvement would, "in effect, constitute U.S. intervention," by proxy, which was a steep price to pay to save a country "devoid" of vital resources and in an area that was "not a decisive theater" in Asia. Defense Secretary Charles Wilson, presumably putting forth the JCS's views, argued that the most desirable course

---

40. General Thomas Trapnell comments at debriefing, 3 May 1954, HCAS, *USVN Relations,* book 9, 406–20.
41. Supplement to Outline Plan for Conducting Military Operations in Indochina with United States and French Union Forces, Spring (April–May) 1954, RG 319, G-3 091, Indochina TS (5 April 1954) FW 23/5.

of action in Vietnam was to "get completely out of the area. The chances of saving any part of Southeast Asia were . . . nothing." Gavin was more succinct as he echoed General Omar Bradley's analysis of Korea in asserting that an American military commitment to Vietnam "involves the risk of embroiling the U.S. in [the] wrong war, in the wrong place, at the wrong time."[42]

Such views held sway in 1954. American forces did not intervene in Indochina, although neither did the United States dissociate itself from Vietnamese affairs. To the contrary, political leaders immediately began to assume the French role in Vietnam while military dissenters continued to question the wisdom of U.S. policy. Specifically they were concerned about political instability in the south, about sending a U.S. military training mission to Vietnam, and about involving the United States in a collective security arrangement for Southeast Asia. So far as the first reservation was concerned, most military leaders rejected fighting in Indochina because of the constant political turmoil in Saigon associated with Bao Dai and then his American-picked successor Ngo Dinh Diem. Even prior to the Geneva armistice, the JCS conceded that any settlement of the French–Vietnamese conflict "based upon free elections would be attended by the almost certain loss of [Indochina] to Communist control."[43]

Supporters of the southern regime recognized such weaknesses as well. Colonel Edward Geary Lansdale, head of an intelligence mission to Saigon in 1954–5, found that the Viet Minh, following Mao's axiom that guerrillas needed grass-roots support as fish needed water, had "exemplary relations" with the villagers. By contrast, southern soldiers had become "adept at cowing a popula-

42. JCS 1992/334, "Military Situation in Tonkin Delta," 7 June 1954, RG 218, CCS 092 Asia (248), section 71; JCS 1992/348, "Rhee Offer of One Corps for Commitment in Indochina," 29 June 1954, RG 218, CCS 092 Asia (248), section 73; Wilson in 215th Meeting of National Security Council, 24 September 1954, Whitman File – NSC Series, box 6, DDEL; Gavin, G-3, memorandum for Chief of Staff, USA, "Military Implications of Cease-Fire Agreements in Indochina," 22 July 1954, RG 319, G-3 091 Indochina. See also JCS memorandum for Secretary of Defense, sub: Additional Aid for Indochina, 24 June 1954, RG 330, ASD/ISA 091 Indochina, May–December 1954.
43. JCS 1992/287, "Preparations of Department of Defense Regarding Negotiations on Indochina for the Forthcoming Geneva Conference," 11 March 1954, RG 218, CCS 092 Asia (248), section 59. See also JCS memorandum for Secretary of Defense, 12 March 1954, HCAS, *USVN Relations,* book 9, 266–70. On the inevitability of Communist victory in any elections in Vietnam, see Kahin, *Intervention,* 53, 450.

tion into feeding them [and] providing them with girls." An Army study corroborated such views, noting that Ho and Giap could count on about 340,000 soldiers, with about one-fourth of those active *below* the partition line.[44] By late 1954, it was clear to the JCS that Vietnam's internal political situation was "chaotic" and that Diem's government could not even guarantee the loyalty of its military forces. Without native support and sacrifice, the chiefs warned, "no amount of external pressure and assistance can long delay complete Communist victory in South Vietnam." The military's analysis of Vietnamese politics thus pointed out that government stability was a prerequisite to military credibility. It also made clear – despite later, specious claims that the DRVN "invaded" the south – that the Second Indochina War had deep indigenous roots indeed.[45]

General J. Lawton Collins, sent to Vietnam as Eisenhower's special representative in December 1954, also understood that internal turmoil, not outside aggression, was destroying southern Vietnam. Appalled by Diem's authoritarian ways and failure to challenge the various sects involved in southern political and economic affairs, Collins recognized as well that the Viet Minh "have and will retain the capability to overrun Free Vietnam if they wish." He even suggested that U.S. withdrawal, although the "least desirable" option, "may be the only sound solution."[46] Diem, however, rescued his position in April 1955 by beating back the sects' challenge to his leadership, at which point Eisenhower and Dulles decided to stick with him over the long haul.[47] By October 1955, when Diem be-

44. Lansdale Team's Report on Covert Saigon Mission in 1954 and 1955, *Pentagon Papers: Gravel*, 1:573–83, doc. 95; G-3 Staff Study, "Long-Range (Through FY 56) for Development of Minimal Forces Necessary to Provide Internal Security for South Vietnam," 2 November 1954, RG 319, G-3 091 Indochina.
45. JCS 1992/412, "Indochina," 5 November 1954, RG 218, CCS 092 Asia (248), section 86. On right-wing revisionist claims that Ho Chi Minh's forces invented the National Liberation Front in the south and "invaded" the RVN, see, inter alia, Podhoretz, *Why We Were in Vietnam*, 44–6, 174–5; and Lewy, *America in Vietnam*, 15–18.
46. Collins to Dulles, 20 January 1955, *DDRS*, 78, 295A; Collins to Dulles, 13 December 1954, HCAS, *USVN Relations*, book 1, IV.A.3, 20–2. Many of Collins's reports from Vietnam can be found in *FRUS, 1955–7* (Washington, D.C., 1985), 1:200–370. See also David Anderson, "J. Lawton Collins, John Foster Dulles, and the Eisenhower Administration's 'Point of No Return' in Vietnam," *Diplomatic History* 12 (Spring 1988): 127–47.
47. To Eisenhower and Dulles, it was Collins, not Diem, who might have to be replaced. During a meeting with the president in early March 1955, Eisenhower told Dulles to

came president in an election that would have embarrassed a Chicago alderman, the Republic of Vietnam (RVN) was officially established and the United States was heading toward war in Vietnam.[48]

The military had also long been critical of plans to establish a training mission in Indochina. As Dien Bien Phu fell, Ridgway rejected plans for such a program because American trainers would be in the "invidious position" of bearing responsibility for inevitable failures over which they had no control. He also established preconditions, never met by the French or southern Vietnamese, for the development of any training mission, including full independence for the states of Indochina, American control over indigenous forces, and political stability in southern Vietnam. Without such measures, the JCS cautioned, it was "hopeless to expect a U.S. military mission to achieve success."[49] Communist troops were "laying the groundwork for a strong, armed dissident movement" in the south, Gavin and General Paul Adams concluded, and it would be dangerous to put American trainers in the middle of an imminent "civil war," which might well provoke greater intervention by the Soviets and the Chinese.[50]

---

consider replacing Collins with Maxwell Taylor and suggested that a special law be developed to allow the general to serve as special ambassador without giving up his military rank. Taylor, however, became the Army chief shortly thereafter, while Collins was replaced by Elbridge Durbrow, who became ambassador to the RVN. Dulles's Memorandum of Conversation with the President, 7 March 1955, White House Memorandum Series, John Foster Dulles File, folder: Meetings with the President (7), DDEL.

48. Anderson, *Trapped by Success,* chapters 5 and 6.
49. F. W. Moorman memorandum to Gavin, "Indochina," 11 May 1954, RG 319, CS 091 Indochina; JCS 1992/367, "U.S. Assumption of Training Responsibility in Indochina," 3 August 1954, RG 218, CCS 092 Asia (248), section 77; Spector, *Advice and Support,* 223. See also HCAS, *USVN Relations,* book 1, III.A.2, A-19–20; Cable, CH MAAG to DEPT AR, 20 June 1954, NR: MG1750A, RG 218, CCS 092 Asia (248), section 72; HCAS, *USVN Relations,* book 1, IV.A.3, 7–9, and book 10, 701–2; Gavin and Adams to Ridgway, "U.S. Policy toward Indochina," 10 August 1954, RG 319, G-3 091 Indochina. For background on military criticism regarding training, see HCAS, *USVN Relations,* book 2, IV.A.4, 2–5; Brink to General Reuben Jenkins, Office of Assistant Chief of Staff, G-3, Department of Army, 16 April 1952, 091 Indo-China 1952, RG 218, Chair's File, General Bradley; memorandum of conversation, Director PPS (Nitze), 12 May 1952, *FRUS,* 1952–4, 13:141–4; JSPC memorandum to JCS, "Report of U.S. Joint Military Mission to Indochina," JCS 1992/246, 3 November 1953, RG 218, CCS 092 Asia (248), section 48; Admiral Davis memorandum to Nash, "U.S. Military Advisors in Indochina," 27 November 1953, RG 330, 012.2–742 Indochina.
50. Gavin and Adams to Ridgway, "U.S. Policy toward Indochina," 10 August 1954, RG 319, G-3 091 Indochina.

The JCS additionally estimated that training could cost about $440 million, which would push the total U.S. bill in Indochina for 1954 to over $1 billion at the same time that the Army was brawling with Eisenhower over defense spending at home. Because of that financial burden and continuing political instability, the chiefs contended that military support of Vietnam was a "low priority" program that should not "impair the development of effective and reliable allied forces elsewhere." Dulles, however, found the JCS's cost estimates "excessive" and attacked its tentative approach to the training issue. Ultimately, then, the chiefs acquiesced to a training mission because "political considerations are overriding." As Gavin later recalled, "we in the Army were so relieved that we had blocked the decision to commit ground troops to Vietnam that we were in no mood to quibble" over training.[51] It is not likely that the military could have done otherwise.

Nor would the armed services wage a political battle over U.S. participation in a collective security arrangement for Southeast Asia either. Although the JCS was not unresponsive to plans for collective action against communism in that region, it held "serious misgivings" that they might "imply commitments which the United States would not be able to meet." Accordingly, the chiefs insisted that any treaty to which the United States was a party make no commitment to fund or maintain indigenous armies or agree to deploy U.S. forces to defend other signatories. The JCS specifically balked when Dulles proposed that a coalition of nations protect Vietnam in the event of external aggression, while training the Vietnamese to maintain internal security. Thus the military held its ground when Thailand and the Philippines sought a U.S. commitment for the defense of other member nations.[52]

The final pact establishing the Southeast Asia Treaty Organization (SEATO) reflected such concerns. Admiral Davis, a Pentagon

---

51. JCS memorandum to Secretary of Defense, "Retention and Development of Forces in Indochina," 22 September 1954, RG 218, CCS 092 Asia (248), section 83; JCS memorandum to Secretary of Defense, 22 September 1954, "U.S. Assumption of Training Responsibilities in Indochina," HCAS, *USVN Relations*, book 2, IV.A.4, 2–5; James Gavin, *Crisis Now* (New York, 1968), 49. See also secretary of state to secretary of defense, 11 October 1954, *FRUS, 1952–4*, 13:2132–5.
52. JCS 1992/375, "Report of Joint U.K.-U.S. Study Group on Southeast Asia," 6 August 1954, RG 218, CCS 092 Asia (248), section 77A; *Pentagon Papers: Gravel*, 1:212, 216–18; HCAS, *USVN Relations*, book 1, IV.A.1, A-14–15, 22.

representative at the inaugural conference, found the "consultative" U.S. role outlined in the pact "consistent in its military implications with [JCS] positions." U.S. political and military leaders had thus sent mixed signals regarding their interests in Asia. The secretary of state, as the *Pentagon Papers* authors observed, wanted to "put the communists on notice that aggression would be opposed"; the JCS on the other hand "insisted that the United States must not be committed financially, militarily, or economically" to intervention in Southeast Asia. Despite Dulles's bellicose rhetoric, the final treaty manifested the military's reservations regarding collective action more than it did any American desire to roll back communism in Asia.[53]

Rather than simply execute American policy in Indochina, the JCS, the Army, and various officers staged an offensive of their own against intervention. While other scholars have correctly cited British reluctance and Franco-American difficulties in the American decision against war in Vietnam, it seems that the military's opposition was crucial as well. Even if the president did not explicitly credit Ridgway and other dissenters, it is clear that Eisenhower and his top officers similarly recognized the peril of intervention in Indochina, at least in early 1954. Without a "proper political foundation" in Vietnam, the president later wrote, "this war in Indochina would absorb our troops by the division." Of course, the military had been sounding such themes since the end of World War II and, as Richard Immerman has observed, the decision against intervention was consistent with Eisenhower's military background and his concept of national security. Indeed, it is difficult to imagine that the military's dissent did not influence the president. From mid-1954 onward, however, Eisenhower and his successors ignored or dismissed virtually every reservation concerning Vietnam that service leaders had put forth, with tragic yet – as Matthew Ridgway and others understood – predictable consequences. Indeed, as Gen-

53. HCAS, *USVN Relations,* book 1, IV.A.1, A-14–15, 22–5; JSPC directive, 31 January 1955, "Concept and Plans for the Implementation, If Necessary, of Article IV, I, of the Manila Pact," JSPC 958/232/D, RG 218, CCS 092 Asia (248), section 3. See also sources cited in note 52, and Gavin and Adams for Chief of Staff, USA, "U.S. Policy toward Indochina," August 1954, RG 319, G-3 091 Indochina.

eral Gavin observed, by 1954 Vietnam was already becoming a "swamp-ridden jungle Moloch with an insatiable appetite for aircraft, arms, and other military supplies."[54]

In the end American service leaders did not determine policy, but repeatedly had to respond to faits accomplis and adapt their views to suit political imperatives. Time and again U.S. officers tried to stave off the pressure to intervene, only to acquiesce in civilian decisions to increase the commitment to Vietnam. Nonetheless the military had sounded a prescient warning on Vietnam, and had indicted the national security state as envisioned in NSC 68 as well. Officers in the early 1950s stressed that they did not possess the resources or capabilities to become engaged on every front and so North America, Europe, and certain areas in Asia – Japan, Taiwan, Thailand, the Philippines – all merited greater priority in defense policy considerations than did Southeast Asia. In its conception of grand strategy, a commitment in Indochina was not a reasonable end given America's limited means, nor were conditions in Vietnam suitable for U.S. involvement. Whereas civilians might wage cold war at all points on the globe, the military, demonstrating its "can't do" spirit, had a more restricted analysis of the national interest.

Government leaders, however, ignored the military's clear and detailed warnings about the danger of war in Vietnam. They did not rush blindly into Indochina or get mired in a quagmire once there, but simply ignored knowledgeable counsel and consciously expanded their commitment to the RVN. Indeed the very factors that service leaders of the 1950s cited to argue against intervention – economic constraints, the relatively low priority accorded to Indochina, political instability, the indigenous appeal of the enemy, the perils of jungle warfare – became even greater barriers to success in the following decade and directly led to U.S. failure in the Vietnam War. There is no irony; the system did not work.[55]

---

54. Eisenhower in editorial note, *FRUS, 1952–4* 13: 2167–8. See also Herring and Immerman, "Eisenhower, Dulles, and Dienbienphu"; Ambrose, *Eisenhower*, 176; Immerman, "Confessions of an Eisenhower Revisionist"; Gavin, *Crisis Now*, 41. On Eisenhower's commitments to Vietnam after his decision against intervention, see Immerman, "The United States and the Geneva Conference."

55. See David Halberstam, *The Best and the Brightest* (New York, 1972); Daniel Ellsberg, *Papers on the War* (New York, 1972); and Leslie H. Gelb with Richard K. Betts, *The Irony of Vietnam: The System Worked* (Washington, D.C., 1979).

America's military leaders had different, more limited conceptions of national security than did the civilian foreign policy establishment. More concerned with fostering military Keynesianism in Washington than with communism in Vietnam, service leaders saw little reason to squander limited resources in Indochina. Administration officials, however, had an exaggerated sense of American capabilities and saw Vietnam as an important theater in the cold war because of the need to maintain French fealty in NATO and build a new capitalist order in Asia.[56] Within that framework, taking a stand in Vietnam became unavoidable. Civilian officials thus discounted the service leaders' military advice in the pursuit of more extensive goals. The generals may have acted in what they thought was the national interest – or at least in the interest of their respective services – but civilian leaders had a truly internationalist perspective.

With America's political and service leaders approaching Indochina from fundamentally different viewpoints in the early 1950s, the stage was set for the next two decades of destruction and despair in Vietnam. Military leaders, despite their consistent efforts to crush the Communist enemy, retained their reservations about the war and were frequently and irreconcilably divided over the U.S. commitment and strategy in Vietnam. Politics in Saigon and Washington would determine the nature of the war as much as events on the battlefield. And civil–military relations would progressively deteriorate and accordingly erode the U.S. effort in Vietnam. By the mid-1950s, then, America was trying both to prepare for and to avoid war in Vietnam.

56. Kolko, *Anatomy of a War;* Gardner, *Approaching Vietnam;* Rotter, *The Path to Vietnam;* Kahin, "The United States and Anticolonial Revolutions"; Robert M. Blum, *Drawing the Line: The Origin of the American Containment Policy in East Asia* (New York, 1982); William Borden, *The Pacific Alliance: United States Foreign Economic Policy and Japanese Trade Recovery, 1947–1954* (Madison, Wis., 1984); Michael Schaller, "Securing the Great Crescent: Occupied Japan and the Origins of Containment in Southeast Asia," *Journal of American History* 69 (September 1982): 392–414.

3

Preparing for and Avoiding War: Military Affairs and Politics in Vietnam and the United States, 1955–1960

Strategy has become a more or less incidental by-product of the administrative processes of the defense budget.

Maxwell Davenport Taylor[1]

From the Collins mission and Diem's successful response to the sect crisis in April and May 1955 to the end of the Eisenhower presidency, Vietnam was not a primary concern to U.S. policy makers, who focused their attentions instead on areas of greater importance such as Europe, Japan, China, and the Middle East.[2] Nevertheless, after the Geneva partition of Vietnam, the creation of SEATO, and the establishment of a U.S. Army training mission to Vietnam, the American commitment to Diem was unmistakable and irrevocable. As a result, America's military leaders began to take a more optimistic approach to affairs in Vietnam, apparently reversing their earlier views about the dangers of war in Indochina.

These appearances were somewhat deceptive, however; the change in military thinking was not as profound as it seems at first glance. To be sure, the new MAAG commander, General Samuel Williams, was as optimistic and deaf to criticism as his predecessor, O'Daniel, had been. Williams ignored both Diem's repressive ways and the need to train the southern Vietnamese army to fight a guerrilla war. With U.S. acquiescence, Diem organized his army not to fight the Communist enemy so much as to maintain his own

1. Taylor, *Uncertain Trumpet*, 121.
2. The most comprehensive, although not interpretively creative, treatment of Eisenhower's foreign policy is Stephen Ambrose, *Eisenhower: The President* (New York, 1984).

authority.[3] Other military leaders, however, continued to debate military policy in Vietnam. Although dissenters such as Generals Ridgway and Gavin would retire in the mid-1950s, most military representatives continued to doubt the need for or wisdom of greater involvement in Indochina. Many, serving as a link to the dissenters of the early 1950s and later critics within the services, openly challenged the U.S. approach to Vietnam. They continued to believe that political stability in the RVN was a prerequisite for effective American action and that Vietnamese, not American, troops would have to be responsible for any combat against the Viet Minh or the northern army (the People's Army of Vietnam, or PAVN). Still others began to recognize the importance of domestic politics in developing strategy for and making war in Vietnam, and civil–military relations became an even more significant factor in U.S. defense policy. Indeed, political developments in the United States growing out of the New Look helped lay the groundwork for the U.S. experience in Vietnam in the succeeding decade.

Military leaders continued to hold strong misgivings about a U.S. role in Vietnam in 1955. Echoing J. Lawton Collins's analysis, the Joint Strategic Plans Committee (JSPC) found it "apparent that if the 1956 elections are held, the Communists will probably emerge victorious." Radford and the JCS still saw Indochina as just "an important part of Southeast Asia which merits limited U.S. support in the implementation of national policy."[4] Into May 1955, the chiefs, who did see Diem offering the "greatest promise" of stability, continued to hold reservations about the RVN leader and his army. The RVN's Armed Forces (RVNAF) could offer no more than "token resistance" to enemy aggression and its loyalty to the Ngos was "open to question" in any event. But from such premises, which had been put forth repeatedly since 1950, U.S. service leaders now concluded that the support of an "outside military force,"

---

3. BDM Corporation, *A Study of Strategic Lessons Learned in Vietnam* (McLean, Va., 1980), volume 6, book 1, 1-19 to 1-20; Kolko, *Anatomy of a War*, 90.
4. JSPC report to JCS, 17 January 1955, JCS 1992/438, "Reconsideration of U.S. Military Program in Southeast Asia," RG 218, CCS 092 Asia (248), section 2; Radford memorandum to Secretary of Defense, 21 January 1955, "Laotian Force Levels," RG 218, CCS 092 Asia (248), section 2.

presumably either American or SEATO, would be needed to ensure the RVN's stability and territorial integrity.[5]

Yet the Americans still assumed that the Vietnamese themselves would be responsible for their own defense. During deliberations over the size of the southern Army – initially called the Vietnamese National Army (VNA) and later known as the Army of the Republic of Vietnam (ARVN) – military officials in Washington and Saigon were pressing for an expansion of the VNA so that U.S. intervention, then being advocated by the NSC, could be avoided.[6] American officials originally had hoped to establish a 100,000-man Vietnamese army in 1955, but soon saw that more forces would be needed both to provide internal security and to resist outside aggression. In August 1955 the outgoing MAAG chair, O'Daniel, argued that the RVN was "at the critical point in its fight for freedom," and pressed Washington to fund a 50,000-troop increase in Diem's army. Given the Viet Minh's organization, skills, and size – Ho and Giap now had approximately 367,000 forces, up 26,000 from mid-1954, with their battle corps increased to 250,000 from 147,000 – the VNA would eventually need about a quarter-million troops, coupled with popular support of the Diem regime, to defend the south adequately.[7]

The JCS expressed similar concerns in greater detail in September. Although confident of their ability to repel an attack from the DRVN, or even to unify Vietnam under anti-Communist rule, the chiefs recognized that such a commitment would have to include large elements of naval, air, and ground forces. Given the VNA's problems and the low priority of Vietnam in strategic considerations, however, the JCS incredibly urged nuclear strikes against the Communists. Without atomic weapons, the chiefs explained, the United States would have to provide "greater forces than . . . would be justified" given the relative unimportance of Indochina.[8]

5. JCS 1992/460, 9 May 1955, "Indochina (Vietnam)," RG 218, CCS 092 (248), section 8; see also HCAS, *USVN Relations*, book 10, 971–3.
6. Deputy Assistant Secretary of State for Far Eastern Affairs (Sebald) to Secretary of State, 8 June 1955, *FRUS, 1955–7*, 1:436–8.
7. CH MAAG telegrams to CINCPAC, 11 August 1955, RG 218, CCS 092 Asia (248), section 10; see also CINCPAC telegram to OSD 11 August 1955, ibid., and Spector, *Advice and Support*, 262–8.
8. JCS 1992/479, 9 September 1955, "U.S. Policy in the Event of a Renewal of Aggression in Vietnam," RG 218, CCS 092 Asia (248), section 11.

Such recommendations also reflected interservice rivalries, over both defense budgets and Vietnam policy, and showed just how unlikely successful military involvement would be. The Army and Marines, looking to regain past influence and funding, believed that an effective response in Vietnam would require an effort comparable to that in Korea, which would be impossible under New Look policy in any event. Moreover, since they would be responsible for any ground combat, they contended that any successful intervention would depend on the "military energy and solidarity of the Vietnamese" themselves. Air Force planners, on the other hand, saw an opportunity to boost their service role and so maintained that successful intervention would depend on the "swift intervention of U.S. forces" and the use of atomic bombs. Without nuclear weapons, the Air Force believed, Vietnam would be overrun by the Communists "before sufficient U.S. strength could be brought to bear."[9]

That debate over U.S. policy in the autumn of 1955 was important for two reasons. First, it sent the mixed message that the military was sanguine about its ability to intervene in Vietnam, but even more reluctant to commit valuable resources there. It also revealed that intramilitary division over policy and appropriations would be a crucial factor in war planning throughout the U.S. involvement in Indochina. On top of those developments, military doubters continued to recognize that political instability continued to plague the south, with Diem having "no intention of tolerating an election he cannot win."[10] The new MAAG chair, General Williams, despite his predecessor's continued enthusiasm, arrived in Saigon to find the American effort in shambles. Some officers had spent a year in Vietnam without traveling outside of Saigon, he complained. "You can well imagine," he wrote to a fellow officer, "how little they knew of the problems of the fellows in the field. Many of them could not have cared less."[11] Even Radford, the

---

9. See sources in previous note; see also Spector, *Advice and Support*, 270–1.
10. Admiral Edwin T. Layton, Deputy Director for Intelligence, Joint Staff, memorandum for Director Joint Staff, 22 December 1955, "Emerging Pattern – South Vietnam," RG 218, CCS 092 Asia (248), section 17.
11. Despite plentiful evidence to the contrary, O'Daniel termed allegations that Diem was a dictator "nonsense," gave a positive appraisal of the VNA's development, and called for more U.S. assistance. R. E. Hoey, Far East division, to Mr. Kocher, PSA, 2 March 1956,

RVN's biggest booster among the chiefs, returned from a January 1956 trip to Vietnam to report a "much worse picture of the situation" there than he had earlier observed.[12]

Given such appraisals, U.S. officials in early 1956 looked for new ways to increase their role in Vietnam in order to stem the disintegration in the south. As a first step, the JCS, MAAG, and State Department – in order to increase the U.S. training contingent above the 342-man ceiling established at Geneva without expressly repudiating the agreement – established the Temporary Equipment Recovery Mission (TERM), an organization of about 350 U.S. military logistics experts and civilian technicians from other SEATO countries.[13] Military leaders, however, held few illusions that the TERM would solve the myriad problems of Vietnam. General Alonzo Fox, a Pentagon official concerned with the deepening American commitment in the RVN, discouraged the Army from requesting excessive numbers of advisors. At the same time an Air Force study found the VNA in dire shape. Most southern officers were "not fully trained or qualified," while only 30 percent of field-grade and a mere 10 percent of senior officers could be considered competent for their positions.[14] The United States thus faced a double-edged sword regarding the TERM: it had to guard against an expansive commitment, yet the VNA desperately needed more help. Such dilemmas would not be resolved during the war.

An Army staff study of the VNA supplemented the Air Force

"General O'Daniel's Appearance before the House Foreign Affairs Committee, 29 February 1956," Record Group 59, General Records of the Department of State, 751G.00/3-256 (hereafter cited as RG 59 with appropriate filing information); Williams to Admiral George W. Anderson, Chief of Staff, CINCPAC, 28 March 1957, Samuel T. Williams Papers, box 2, folder 17, MHI.

12. 274th Meeting of the National Security Council, 26 January 1956, Ann Whitman File, NSC Series, DDEL; see also Donovan to Eisenhower, 5 February 1956, and Dulles to Eisenhower, 10 February 1956, Whitman File, Dulles-Herter Series, box 5, Dulles February 1956 (1), DDEL.

13. Anderson, *Trapped by Success*, 135–6; Spector, *Advice and Support*, 260–2; William Sebald, Far East division, State Department, to Mr. Murphy, 5 March 1956, "Views of DOD of Military Personnel Requirements for Free Viet Nam," RG 59, 751G.00/2-1756.

14. Memorandum of Conversation, General Fox, OSD/ISA, and William Sebald, Acting Assistant Secretary, Far East division, State Department, 23 March 1956, "Temporary Equipment Recovery Mission," RG 59, 751G.5/3-2356; Colonel R. D. Wentworth, Deputy Secretary, USAF, to CINCPAC, 6 March 1956, "Training of Southeast Asian Non-Communist Military Leaders," RG 218, CCS 092 Asia (6-25-48), section 21.

findings and added that the officer corps was often insubordinate and more concerned with politics than war. American officers had to "admit in all sincerity that we do not have all the necessary elements to contain [the enemy] much less defeat him." General Williams nonetheless did little to address such problems, while his predecessor, O'Daniel – retired but still active in matters relating to Vietnam – continued to tell anyone who would listen that Diem was popular and that the VNA's reorganization was going well. Yet O'Daniel also admitted that the Communists were so popular that it would be "suicidal" for Diem to agree to national elections. He thus urged U.S. leaders to maintain a strong presence in Vietnam, "which may be necessary for as much as 25 years."[15]

Other military officials were not so enthused about such a long-term commitment. Although some remained optimistic about their ability to contain communism in Indochina, various generals continued to assume that the VNA would have to be responsible for any combat. Even in the spring and summer of 1956, when the NSC directed the JCS to examine its capability to intervene in Vietnam, the military was split over the nature and extent of any U.S. combat role in Indochina. The JCS chair, Radford, and CNO Admiral Arleigh Burke both assumed that the ARVN would successfully take control of all of Vietnam while U.S. participation would be limited to advising and to providing air and naval support. On the other hand, the CINCPAC, Stump, and the MAAG chair, Williams, both envisioned a large-scale American commitment and an invasion across the seventeenth parallel likely.[16]

Such deliberations spoke directly to the issue of the U.S. training policy, and thus the ARVN's mission. Williams, influenced by Ridgway's aggressive tactics in Korea, anticipated large-scale ground combat and again argued that Diem's army would have to be enlarged and trained for conventional operations, despite the guerrilla nature of the insurgency. Though he agreed that the southern Vietnamese, backed by other Asians, would have to repel Ho and Giap, the MAAG chair also worried that the Viet Minh outnum-

15. Spector, *Advice and Support*, 278–9, 282; O'Daniel, "A Brief concerning the Situation in Vietnam," 27 March 1956, Whitman File, International Series, box 50, folder: Viet Nam (2), DDEL.
16. Anderson, *Trapped by Success*, 137–9.

bered the VNA by a two-to-one ratio and lamented that "large-scale Asiatic support would not appear to be forthcoming." In the event of hostilities, Williams estimated that VNA forces north of Da Nang would "unquestionably be badly mauled" but that if Diem reinforced that area the Communists would simply bypass it. Ironically, the ever sanguine MAAG leader also provided a laundry list of VNA disadvantages in any war against the Viet Minh: Ho and Giap could not be expected to attack without thorough planning and infiltration along protected routes; enemy morale would be bolstered by claims that Diem was a "puppet" of "Western colonialists"; the ARVN command would be unable to communicate with field units; and the rainy season would thwart established plans to attack northward via Laos. In effect, then, the VNA's lack of skill and experience put it at an even greater disadvantage than its numerical inferiority. At least two U.S. divisions would be needed to contain the Viet Minh, Williams assumed, but the development of a much larger and stronger indigenous ground force remained the key to successful warfare in Vietnam.[17]

Questions over the size of the southern army naturally led to considerations of its mission. In late 1954, U.S. leaders had envisioned the VNA's role as simply providing and maintaining security within Vietnam south of the seventeenth parallel.[18] The JCS, however feared that such a "single mission concept" for the VNA would eventually force American troops to assume responsibility for preventing the northern Communists from expanding into the RVN. The U.S. military, for the duration of the war, would not resolve the ensuing dilemma over whether to focus on local defense in southern Vietnam or to exercise massive retaliation against the DRVN. In addition, U.S. officers continued to see Vietnam as a peripheral interest, devoid of decisive objectives, yet contemplated using nuclear weapons in Indochina. As a result, American leaders constantly expanded the U.S. mission to cover such ambiguous and seemingly contradictory planning concepts. SEATO responsibilities, the French withdrawal, and Diem's constant pressure also

17. CH MAAG, Vietnam, telegram to CINCPAC, 9 June 1956, RG 218, CCS 092 Asia (248), section 23; on Army planners' views, see Spector, *Advice and Support*, 271–3.
18. Secretary of State to Secretary of Defense, 11 October 1954, HCAS, *USVN Relations*, book 2, IV.A.4, 10–15.

served to enlarge the U.S. role in Indochina, while in the Pentagon
military planners were using the example of Korea – a huge conventional war – to prepare for combat in Vietnam.[19]

Such factors led the MAAG to create the Vietnamese armed
forces in the image of the U.S. Army, with an emphasis on superior
technology and weaponry and a corresponding neglect of paramilitary and counterinsurgency (CI) capabilities. As noted, many JCS,
MAAG, and Pentagon planners expected the ARVN to have a principally defensive mission, delaying external aggression until outside, presumably U.S., forces intervened.[20] Williams, over the objections of the RVN's military staff and U.S. embassy officials,
accordingly organized the ARVN to include seven conventional
divisions while disbanding many field and light divisions and territorial regiments.[21] Owing to such conventional thinking, the
MAAG commander essentially ignored any training for pacification. He assumed that internal conflicts would be handled by the
Vietnamese Civil Guard (CG), national police to be trained by the
CIA and advisors from Michigan State University. As Williams saw
it, instruction in counterinsurgency would divert the ARVN from
its more important conventional duties. "A division on pacification
goes to pieces fast," Williams believed. As guerrillas went under-
ground, the ARVN troops would "start sitting around . . . and go
to pot."[22]

Despite such planning for conventional warfare, other military
officials were not prepared to give Williams carte blanche to build
up the ARVN. In May 1956, Admiral Stump forwarded Williams's
request to expand the Vietnamese army to 170,000 soldiers with
his "non-concurrence," while Radford, meeting with Diem in July,
gave "no encouragement whatever" to his overtures for a troop

19. Ibid.
20. Ibid., Spector, *Advice and Support,* 273.
21. BDM, *Strategic Lessons,* volume 6, book 1, 1-19 to 1-20.
22. Williams quoted in Spector, *Advice and Support,* 320; on the Michigan State role in
    training, see Anderson, *Trapped by Success,* 141–9, and, for a critical view, the April
    1966 issue of *Ramparts.* The MAAG was also critical of the Michigan State advisory
    group. In a memorandum to General Williams, MAAG Colonel James I. Muir com-
    plained of an "unusually frustrating afternoon" he had spent with that group, conclud-
    ing that the Michigan State people knew "no more about the civil guard than we do –
    perhaps not as much." Muir to Williams, 10 December 1957, "Interim Report, Civil
    Guard Study," Williams Papers, box 2, folder 122, MHI.

increase. Into September, in fact, CINCPAC and JCS representatives were more concerned about reducing the size of the ARVN than adding 20,000 forces to it.[23] Caught between the political commitment to ensure an anti-Communist southern state in Vietnam and New Look restrictions on U.S. involvement, the military simultaneously prepared for a huge conventional war in Indochina, assumed that indigenous armies would be responsible for combat, and then rejected attempts to build up the ARVN to accomplish a task that was beyond its capabilities in any case. With such incoherent planning, the failures of 1975 could have been anticipated two decades earlier.

In truth, the JCS did have a sense of the dilemmas it could face in Vietnam. Surely, military leaders remembered how Ridgway, Collins, and others had fought against intervention in the early 1950s. So when NSC 5612 claimed in August 1956 that the loss of Southeast Asia would "destroy" the balance of power in Asia, the chiefs rejected such alarmist language, instead predicting merely "adverse" consequences to U.S. security in that area. The original grandiose statement, the JCS argued, improperly implied that the United States could or should establish an "equipoise of power in Asia."[24] Just three months later, the chiefs again rejected State Department proposals to earmark U.S. forces for Southeast Asia as done with NATO, insisting that U.S. leaders should not develop strategy with SEATO signatories, but only discuss methods of providing support "without making a specific commitment of forces."[25]

From Saigon, the MAAG forwarded an equally ambivalent view of conditions in Vietnam. Although satisfied with the American effort and convinced of the need to maintain forces, MAAG officials also understood that "extreme nationalism and anti-Western feeling can not be far below the surface." Maintaining a large num-

---

23. Daniel Anderson, Counselor of Embassy, to Department of State, 6 September 1956, RG 59, 751G.5/9-656, #76; Kattenburg, Southeast Asia division, State Department, to Kocher and Young, 14 September 1956, "CINCPAC Briefing on MDA Program for Viet Nam, FY 57–8, at the Pentagon, September 13," RG 59, 751G.5-MSP/9–1456.
24. 295th Meeting of the National Security Council, 30 August 1956, Whitman File, NSC Series, DDEL.
25. JCS memorandum for the Secretary of Defense, 16 November 1956, "U.S. Force Commitments to the SEATO," HCAS, *USVN Relations*, book 10, 1096–7.

ber of U.S. forces was thus "a potential source of offense to Vietnamese sensibilities." Accordingly, the U.S. presence should be limited to "absolute needs" while "discretion and circumspect behavior is a *must*." Despite his apparent satisfaction with the situation, even Williams hoped to "resist pressure to increase American personnel" in Vietnam, in part by employing foreign nationals instead of U.S. representatives where possible.[26]

Again O'Daniel offered contrast, if not comic relief, to the military's cautious views. During an autumn 1956 visit to Vietnam, the past MAAG chief believed that the RVN was "entirely pacified and secure," but admitted that its forces lacked proper equipment and were "relatively small and woefully weak," had been "inadequately trained for modern war," and were "particularly weak in their command structure and in technical know-how."[27] With such reports, it seems, military officials were trying to win support in Washington for additional resources. Similarly, just months later, Admiral Stump – citing such "discouraging changes" in Vietnam as Viet Minh expansion to 275,000 regular troops organized in eighteen divisions, increased Communist infiltration, and DRVN neutralization of Laos and Cambodia – also asked Dulles to augment the MAAG beyond the 342 advisors and additional TERM personnel then in the RVN.[28]

Pessimism or political manipulation aside, U.S. and Vietnamese leaders still assumed that the ARVN would have to carry the burden of a ground war. Diem's brother and counselor, Ngo Dinh Nhu, meeting with American diplomatic and military officials in April 1957, understood that it would be undesirable to rely on U.S. troops "since this would be, after all, a civil war."[29] Accordingly, Diem again asked for authorization to increase his army to 170,000

26. CS Bulletin, MAAG, n.d., Williams Papers, box 1, folder 138, MHI, emphasis in original.
27. Memorandum of Conversation between Robertson and O'Daniel, 25 September 1956, "Viet Nam," RG 59, 751G.00/9–2556, C/S, AMK.
28. Samuel Williams, Remarks at USOM Meeting, 4 October 1956(?), Williams Papers, box 1, folder 134, MHI; CINCPAC to Secretary of State, 19 March 1957, RG 59, 751/G.5, MSP/3–1857. During visits with National Security Advisor Dillon Anderson and Army Chief of Staff Maxwell Taylor, Diem reinforced Stump's views and again requested more U.S. aid. Anderson to Secretary of State, 30 March 1957, RG 59, 751G.00/3–3057, #2957.
29. Memorandum of Conversation, 5 April 1957, "Military Aid for Viet-Nam," RG 59, 751G.5 MSP/4–557.

troops in order to meet the Communist challenge. And again American leaders, worried that such a military buildup would deflect attention from the need to create a viable economy and social structure in the RVN, rejected his pleas.[30]

Although the debate over the size of the ARVN and of the U.S. advisory group in Vietnam seemed to focus on budgetary constraints, Viet Minh capabilities, and Vietnamese economic development, the unarticulated factor behind the Ngos' requests for more troops was the desire to strengthen their grip on the political process in the RVN. Diem's and Nhu's repressive ways are so well known that they need no discussion here.[31] Maintaining a large and loyal military was essential to Diem's plans to retain power. Indeed, the RVN's alarmist reports about Ho's designs on the south had little credibility, but gave Nhu and Diem a justification for seeking more U.S. support. General Tran Van Don, an aide to the RVN leader, admitted to General Fox that the RVN had no evidence of any Viet Minh buildup or plans to attack across the seventeenth parallel. Don also conceded that both the PRC and the Soviet Union gave limited aid to the DRVN, and that the RVN's intelligence apparatus, not coincidentally dominated by minority Catholics loyal to the Ngos, was less than adequate.[32]

At the same time, Admiral Stump, General Williams, and U.S. Ambassador Elbridge Durbrow met with Diem and suspected that he might be exaggerating Vietnam's internal, "terrorist" threat in order to preempt any U.S. aid reduction and to bolster his plans to raise another 20,000 more troops for the ARVN.[33] By October, Durbrow and Williams understood that Diem would not enact any of the agricultural or economic reforms that were needed to provide stability in the south. Facing the prospect of American aid cuts,

---

30. Anderson to Secretary of State, 6 May 1957, "Re. Diem's Proposed Agenda of 3 May," RG 59, 751G.11/5–657.
31. See, among others, Kahin, *Intervention;* Kolko, *Anatomy of a War;* and Marilyn Young, *The Vietnam Wars: 1945–1990* (New York, 1991). The best-developed discussions of Diem's repression and corruption in the 1960s are Sheehan, *A Bright Shining Lie,* and David Halberstam, *The Making of a Quagmire* (New York, 1990).
32. Captain W. M. Kaufman, U.S. Navy, Memorandum of Conversation, 13 May 1957, RG 59, 751G.11/5–1357.
33. Durbrow to State Department, 26 September 1957, "Conversation with President Ngo Dinh Diem, September 16 1957," Foreign Service Despatch 106, RG 59, 751G.00/9–2657.

they believed, Diem had most likely decided that he needed a strong, loyal military machine to maintain his rule.[34] According to Ronald Spector, Williams was less critical of Diem than Durbrow, but there is little doubt that the Army, Navy, and Air Force attachés shared the ambassador's view. Williams believed that the U.S. team in Saigon should avoid criticizing Diem in order to maintain his cooperation and confidence, and he maintained, as always, that the RVN was properly focusing its attention and resources on military planning over economic development.[35]

By late 1957, it is clear, U.S. policy in Vietnam had assumed the characteristics that would continue for the duration of the American experience there. Despite their increasing awareness of Diem's repression, the ARVN's weaknesses, the Viet Minh's strengths, and politicomilitary constraints at home, U.S. service leaders kept insisting that they could build a credible military establishment in the south and contain communism in Vietnam. The authors of the *Pentagon Papers* would later refer to this as the non sequitur approach to military policy making. From the mid-1950s onward, the military would time and again report on the myriad obstacles to progress in Vietnam, yet would always conclude that success would be achieved. Although Williams, other officers, and many scholars who write about these years stress the U.S. military's optimism about its future in Vietnam,[36] the truth is that many American service leaders had realistically evaluated the shortcomings of the RVN and did not feel compelled to intervene in combat there during the Eisenhower administration. Even if they were not as rejectionist as the dissenters had been, these doubters and critics still had little stomach for war in Vietnam.

Indeed, the situation on the ground was worsening. By mid-1958 MAAG intelligence estimated that Ho and Giap could now rely on about 270,000 regular troops and 235,000 paramilitary forces, which would gain the military initiative at the outset of any conflict

---

34. Durbrow to State Department, 8 October 1957, "Conversation with President Ngo Dinh Diem on October 1, 1957," Foreign Service Despatch 115, RG 59, 751G.00/10–857.
35. Spector, *Advice and Support*, 304–5; Durbrow to State Department, 5 December 1957, "Evaluation Report of Vietnam: December 1957," Foreign Service Despatch 191, RG 59, 751G.00/12–557.
36. See, for example, Spector, *Advice and Support*, and Anderson, *Trapped by Success*.

and could effectively conduct both conventional and "subversive" operations in the south.[37] Meanwhile, the JCS dismissed a Navy proposal to establish a military mission in Southeast Asia because of more important commitments elsewhere. As Ridgway later noted, the Army in the 1950s had so many obligations – in NATO, SEATO, and other pacts – that it could never have met them all.[38] Making matters worse, intelligence operatives in the Pacific Command reported that the RVN's Self-Defense Corps (SDC) and Civil Guard (CG) were not combat-effective even though they were supposed to maintain internal security and were subsidized with over $6 million annually. The paramilitary units were unable to free the ARVN for combat and, in the *Pentagon Papers* analysts' words, were "confusingly organized, inadequately equipped, poorly trained, and badly led – even when compared with ARVN."[39]

Such critical evaluations were not coincidental, for the MAAG had virtually ignored counterinsurgency in its training activities. MAAG reports from 1955 to 1959 were essentially silent on the issue of irregular warfare. In fact, in March 1959 MAAG officers complained that the ARVN was diverting troops and equipment to pacification and security missions – presumably to satisfy Diem's and Nhu's political objectives – to the detriment of "formal training programs." And although those programs did little to train paramilitary units, the MAAG expected the CG to "eventually assume complete responsibility for the internal security of the nation."[40]

As Williams was preparing the ARVN to counter and reverse any encroachment by Hanoi, Eisenhower appointed a special committee, headed by retired General William Draper, to evaluate U.S.

---

37. HCAS, *USVN Relations,* book 2, IV.A.5, tab 4, 18–19.
38. JCS 1992/671, 1 August 1958, JCS memorandum to CNO, "Establishment of a Nucleus for a U.S. Military Mission for Southeast Asia," RG 218, CCS 092 Asia (248), section 40; Ridgway interview with Clay Blair, #4, pp. 42–4, MHI. O'Daniel, of course, continued to wax optimistic about Diem and the RVN. See Elting to State Department, 26 July 1958, Foreign Service Despatch 28, RG 59, 751G.00/7–2658, and O'Daniel to Senator H. Alexander Smith, 20 November 1958, Smith Papers, box 121, Seeley Mudd Manuscript Library, Princeton University.
39. HCAS, *USVN Relations,* book 2, IV.A.4, 17–23.
40. Ibid. Maxwell Taylor, Army chief of staff during this time, later asserted that the question of the type of training for the ARVN never arose in JCS deliberations over Vietnam, but that U.S. military leaders "unconsciously" trained the ARVN in the U.S. image. Maxwell Taylor Oral History, interviewed by Ted Gittinger, 1 June 1981, interview 2, 2–4, Lyndon B. Johnson Library, Austin, Tex. (LBJL).

foreign aid programs. The subcommittee on Southeast Asia, chaired by former National Security Advisor Dillon Anderson and including General Collins and Colonel Lansdale, urged limited U.S. objectives and roles in that area. U.S. military assistance, committee members contended, should contribute to internal security against Communist "subversion" and support only the "minimal" forces required to meet outside aggression. Thus, the U.S. representatives advocated, in contrast to General Williams, training and equipping the CG and other paramilitary forces to eventually replace ARVN units in internal security tasks.[41]

The proposed budget for fiscal year (FY) 1960, however, included reductions in aid to Vietnam, which Collins and Durbrow feared would kill efforts to improve the CG. General Collins, whose views on Diem and the ineffectiveness of the ARVN had not changed much from 1955, questioned the need for Saigon to maintain 150,000 troops. Such a force, he claimed, would drain resources needed for economic development. A smaller force would protect such programs without diminishing security, as the ARVN was not capable of waging war against the north anyway. Eisenhower, however, again stood by Diem despite the general's charges. As Dillon Anderson, whose own analysis was similar to Collins's, reported, the president was determined to continue his support of the RVN, but also had no intention of intervening in combat there: "[H]e wasn't going to do it. Either there or anywhere else on the continent of Asia."[42]

Eisenhower's sentiment was certainly appropriate, for the military was not offering a rosy view of U.S. prospects in that area. General Ridgway, the administration's foremost public critic, reminded the media that any war in Indochina would have to be fought in rugged terrain where "air power in a combat role would be almost useless."[43] In a mid-1959 evaluation of U.S. policy in the

41. "Summary of Paper on Southeast Asia," Draper Committee, box 2, folder: Committee Meetings – Sixth – 24–6 February 1959 (2), DDEL.
42. Anderson, *Trapped by Success,* 178–9; Dillon Anderson Oral History (Columbia Oral History Project), 27–31, DDEL; "Background Country Study as to Vietnam," Draper Committee Study, 27 February 1959, Eisenhower Library, White House Central Files, Confidential File, Subject Series, box 40, folder: Mutual Security and Assistance [1959] (6), DDEL.
43. Ridgway's answers to *New York Journal American* interview, 9 September 1959, Ridgway Papers, box 32, MHI.

Far East, the JCS again recognized that indigenous problems, not Moscow- or Beijing-directed subversion, were fueling discontent in Asia. Even non-Communist areas on that continent were "characterized by inter- and intra-national stresses and strains that almost defy solution by orderly processes." In those areas, including Indochina, nationalism, "fed by residual resentments against European colonialism," inhibited cooperation with the United States. Accordingly, American leaders could not expect their policies to be sympathetically received unless they offered Asians some positive benefit rather than only stressing the negative goal of containing communism. Complicating such problems, most American allies were more concerned with matters affecting Europe and NATO, and thus offered little support to the United States in Southeast Asia.[44]

Circumstances inside Asia were none too favorable either. In a November 1959 summary of the situation in Vietnam, the MAAG reported that the ARVN had made little or no progress in addressing its problems over the past five years. It was still plagued by an unclear command and control structure; a politically motivated officer corps; inadequate internal security planning due to the "virtually non-existent capabilities" of the CG and SDC; insubordinate and irresponsible behavior at both the field and command levels; and poor logistics and technological support. Despite such concerns, a U.S. Army Command and General Staff College report from mid-1960 proclaimed, apparently in all seriousness, that the ARVN was now ready to "march to Hanoi."[45]

Such bravado notwithstanding, the JCS admitted that the RVN's armed forces were "inadequately trained and organized," and U.S. Army officials lamented the ARVN's inability to effectively counter

44. JCS memorandum for Deputy Assistant Secretary of Defense for NSC Affairs and Plans, 14 July 1959, "U.S. Policy in the Far East," HCAS, *USVN Relations,* book 10, 1211–35; see also testimony of Defense Secretary Neil McElroy, General John Guthrie of the Pentagon's International Security Affairs division, and Senators Mike Mansfield and Frank Church in U.S. Congress, Senate, Committee on Foreign Relations [SCFR], *Mutual Security Act of 1959,* 86th Cong., 1st Sess., 1959, 228, 267, 301–3.

45. HCAS, *USVN Relations,* book 2, IV.A.1, 17–23; U.S. Marine advisors working with the Vietnamese marine corps similarly complained that its "defensive psychology" was threatening the American effort to create a credible fighting force. Robert H. Whitlow, *U.S. Marines in Vietnam: The Advisory and Combat Assistance Era, 1954–1964* (Washington, D.C., 1977), 23–4.

the enemy's guerrilla tactics. Since 1955 the MAAG had prepared the ARVN along conventional, big-unit lines, but in early 1960, as Diem put it, the RVN was engaged in "all-out guerrilla war with the Viet Cong," Diem's derisive term for the Viet Minh.[46] Accordingly, the JCS and CINCPAC agreed that counterinsurgency training for the ARVN was now imperative. Other U.S. officials, however, had been calling for such measures much earlier. General I. D. White, the Army's Pacific commander, had written to Army Chief Lyman Lemnitzer in 1957 that U.S. strategy for Vietnam, which focused on countering invasion from the north, was "unrealistic" because it ignored the principal role of "guerrilla warfare." Vietnamese officials, invoking the French experience in the First Indochina War, too recognized the need for locally recruited, mobile forces, and Diem allegedly "lectured" U.S. military representatives that he needed troops well versed in CI tactics to fight the Viet Cong (VC).[47] General James Collins, Jr., who later wrote the U.S. Army's history of the ARVN, agreed, finding that the Vietnamese army's "organization was too centralized and its equipment too heavy to counter the rapid growth of the guerrilla war."[48]

Other officers continued to criticize U.S. policy for political reasons. Admiral Stump asked Admiral Harry D. Felt, the incoming CINCPAC, to let Lansdale visit Saigon to persuade Diem to open up the political process. Without such liberalization, Stump expected the RVN leader to subject himself to criticism "to the extent that he may have a blowup equal to that in Korea." Stump added that Eisenhower had recently told him, "as he has many times in the past," that political stabilization was especially important because the Ngos were alienating themselves further from the southern population.[49] Such critiques of the situation in Vietnam did not sway the MAAG commander. In mid-1960 Williams continued to insist that the ARVN was trained and equipped for both conven-

46. JCS telegram to CINCPAC, 30 March 1960, HCAS, *USVN Relations,* book 2, IV.A.4, 1.1; CS, USA, memorandum for JCS 24 March 1960, "Anti-Guerrilla Training for Vietnam," JCS 1992/791, 24 March 1960, RG 218, 9155.3/4060, Vietnam [15 February 1960].

47. BDM, *Strategic Lessons,* volume 6, book 1, 1-19-1-31.

48. James Lawton Collins, Jr., *The Development and Training of the Vietnamese Army, 1950–1972* (Washington, D.C., 1975), 127.

49. Stump to Felt, 23 May 1960, Edward Geary Lansdale Papers, folder: 1133, Hoover Institution on War, Revolution, and Peace, Palo Alto, Calif.

tional and CI operations and that the southern soldiers enjoyed "the same foot mobility as the Viet Cong guerrillas."[50]

Williams, however, also recognized that the ARVN's performance was abysmal. A resurgence of enemy activity in Military Region V, south of Saigon, had made the situation "rather tight" there. The VC would attack sharply, draw Vietnamese troops into battle, and then "disappear into thin air when they came along." Simultaneously, the insurgents were able to strike CG posts and kidnap some village officials "with apparent ease and at will." In the delta, the ARVN's 32d Regiment was particularly hard-hit, with the enemy killing about thirty troops in a sixty-minute fight, destroying several buildings, and capturing a large number of ARVN weapons. "The brazenness of this attack shocked the Vietnamese to the roots," Williams admitted; "in that respect," he added, looking for a silver lining, "the attack may have been a good thing." Given such performances by the Vietnamese military, the MAAG commander concluded, it was necessary to "sabotage" Diem's plans to establish a separate force of 10,000 commandos because it would remove what good officers he had from the Army.[51]

As U.S. leaders deliberated over such concerns, the situation in Vietnam continued to worsen. Intelligence reports indicated that enemy numbers in the south were still rising and that the ARVN was unable to deal with either main-force VC units or smaller guerrilla bands.[52] Finally, then, the Americans decided to train the RVNAF in counterinsurgency. Admiral Felt stressed that the MAAG had to train southern troops to maintain local security "on a continuing basis" while simultaneously earning the allegiance of the people via programs to improve their political, economic, and

50. Williams to Durbrow, 1 June 1960, in BDM, *Strategic Lessons,* volume 6, book 1, 1-35 to 1-36.
51. Williams to General Samuel Myers, 20 March 1960, Williams Papers, box 2, folder 75, MHI; see also BDM, *Strategic Lessons,* volume 6, book 1, 2-4 to 2-5.
    General Lionel McGarr, slated to replace Williams as MAAG chair, also scored Diem's proposals. In a commissioned study of the RVNAF, his deputies concluded that Diem "continues to organize military units outside the aegis, and contrary to the advice, of the U.S. MAAG." Such units, the Command and General Staff College report asserted, were of "questionable value," drained the ARVN's "best people" from U.S.-supported units, and, still worse, would require additional American support. HCAS, *USVN Relations,* book 2, IV.A.5, tab 4, 82-3.
52. HCAS, *USVN Relations,* book 2, IV.A.5, tab 4, 43–51.

social welfare. American advisors, he claimed, were reorganizing southern forces "so they are not built in the image of U.S. divisions, but are being built to do a job in their own country." Unlike Europe, where general war was possible, "brush fire, or limited wars" could break out in Indochina and could "be kept limited by their political objectives." As Felt put it, the "maintenance of internal security is not a purely military job."[53]

Lionel McGarr, Williams's replacement as MAAG chair in 1960, used similar language to emphasize the need for CI skills within the ARVN. Defeating the insurgency in the south, the incoming MAAG leader argued, hinged on the military's capability to protect villagers from Communist attack. The VC held the initiative, and to get it back the RVN had to develop better intelligence about its foe and create what McGarr called an "anti-guerrilla guerrilla." The conventionally trained ARVN was too inflexible and slow to thwart the insurgency in the south, he noted, and the MAAG's "conventional" thinking was "too often geared to highly sophisticated weapons systems, complex logistics, stylized or rigid tactics, and vulnerable lines of communication."[54]

McGarr thus recommended an overhaul of the RVN's armed forces. Waxing philosophical, he asked his officers to be "creative" and to develop a new approach to the war which should synthesize "the usable portions of history, the closely coordinated military and political concepts of our enemy, and the application of both conventional and unconventional warfare." He also urged that the government transfer the CG out of the Department of Interior, which was under the Ngos' political control, to the RVN Department of Defense, modify the ARVN's structure to establish clear lines of command and control, and streamline the military's bureaucracy. The MAAG commander, however, did not seem optimistic. VC military success "can happen here – it is our job to prevent

53. Felt quoted in Edward J. Marolda and Oscar P. Fitzgerald, *The United States Navy and the Vietnam Conflict,* vol. II: *From Military Assistance to Combat, 1959–1965* (Washington, D.C., 1986), 93–4; Felt in *Mutual Security Act of 1959,* 6, 11.
54. McGarr, Information, Guidance and Instructions to MAAG Advisory Personnel, 10 November 1960, "Anti-Guerrilla Guerrilla"; McGarr directive, "Implementing Actions for Anti-Guerrilla Operations," 15 November 1960, both in Vietnam Country File, National Security File, box 193, folder: Vietnam, 4/24/61, McGarr Presentation, John F. Kennedy Library (hereafter cited as VN C.F., NSF, JFKL with appropriate box and folder titles).

it. At present, better use of resources is Vietnam's only readily available solution – and it is at best a marginal one."[55]

McGarr's frankness offered a stark contrast to his predecessor's reporting on the war in Vietnam. Under Williams, a MAAG official later charged, "there was a tendency to report things optimistically . . . people held back a little bit in reporting anything wrong because they feared that it would reflect on them adversely." More pointedly, a U.S. trainer at a late 1959 MAAG conference was "shocked to hear some advisers reporting on a world I had never seen." But when Colonel Russell M. Miner, a senior advisor in the northern RVN, admitted that most ARVN units, including those he had trained, "couldn't really punch [their] way out of a paper bag," his report "blew the lid off" the conference and left Williams "absolutely incensed."[56]

The MAAG chair's efforts to present a sanguine view of the war notwithstanding, military officials in Washington tended to be doubters and critics. The CNO, Arleigh Burke, a strident hawk in the 1960s, believed that neither Eisenhower nor anybody else "had any intention of committing troops to either South Vietnam or Laos."[57] Lemnitzer, the Army chief and later JCS chair, observed that the military always expected to limit its role in Vietnam to military assistance and advisory groups because military leaders such as Eisenhower and MacArthur insisted "that we should not get engaged in a land battle on the continent of Asia."[58] J. Lawton Collins agreed, adding that he did not "know of a single senior commander that [*sic*] was in favor of fighting on the land mass of Asia."[59] And General Lewis Fields, a Marine representative on the Joint Staff from 1958 to 1960, noted that the JCS "didn't think the United States should get involved in that conflict. It's a morass, it's a swamp." Vietnam, Fields lamented, "just grabs you up and takes so much effort – to accomplish what?"[60]

55. See sources cited in previous note.
56. General Charles Symroski and Lt. Colonel L. B. Woodbury in Spector, *Advice and Support*, 294–5.
57. Burke Oral History (Columbia Oral History Project), 165–72, DDEL.
58. Lemnitzer Oral History (Columbia Oral History Project), 46–8, DDEL.
59. Collins interview at Combat Studies Institute, Army Command and General Staff College, 14, MHI.
60. Fields Oral History, 251, MCHC.

Despite such sentiments, American leaders turned Vietnam into a symbol of the cold war and progressively increased the U.S. stake there. Although military leaders in Saigon and Washington presented an ambivalent view of their prospects in Indochina, American aid continued to flow to a country that was led by the authoritarian Ngo family and that had an ill-prepared army without a credible mission. Although American leaders saw problems with the RVN, 78 percent of U.S. aid to Diem from 1956 to 1960 went into the military budget, while only 2 percent was allocated to health, housing, and welfare programs.[61]

Though claiming to want to avoid American intervention in Indochina, U.S. leaders, by feeding Diem's and Nhu's addiction to power, guns, and money, made it inevitable. As the Ngos received more resources from the United States they became even more arbitrary and authoritarian and, in turn, unpopular. Ultimately, American "advisors" would enter Vietnam to prop them up. Despite reports from Saigon that stressed the confusion and contradiction inherent in the American policy in Vietnam, military and political leaders never advocated the type of "agonizing reappraisal" that might have led to a different policy. U.S. military officials consistently recognized the enemy's strength as an indigenous force in the south, the fatal weaknesses of Diem and the ARVN, and the questionable priority of Indochina in national security considerations, yet they continued to accentuate whatever positive characteristics they could detect or invent in the RVN. By late 1960, when McGarr presented his bleak report on Vietnam and decided to emphasize counterinsurgency, John Kennedy of Massachusetts was awaiting inauguration as president, and the American role in Vietnam was about to expand markedly.

Kennedy's ascendancy is thus a fitting segue not only to a consideration of his policies in Vietnam, but also to the political developments that helped propel him into the White House and that gave him material for the script he would write on Vietnam. Although not discussed in studies of Vietnam in the late 1950s, political events at home played a major role in defining the eventual U.S. commitment to Indochina. In particular, budget battles emanating

---

61. Anderson, *Trapped by Success,* 133.

from the New Look, interservice rivalries, and political debates over the theory of limited war created the conditions under which America would enter combat in Vietnam, against the Communists and, given the military's internal disagreements, seemingly against itself.

Throughout the Eisenhower years, the JCS and White House engaged in a virulent and eventually public debate over defense policy and spending. At the same time, the military services fought among themselves over both the limited resources available in New Look budgets and the type of military strategy that would best serve the interests of their respective branches. Ironically, the results of those battles, including increased defense spending, a reassertive military in the 1960s, and the military doctrine of flexible response, laid the groundwork for both war in Vietnam and for subsequent military criticism of that very war. Under the New Look and its concomitant doctrine of massive retaliation, Eisenhower allocated a lion's share of resources to the Air Force, which, with its capability to deliver nuclear weapons, presumably would deter enemies and wage war more cost-effectively. As Army Chief Maxwell Taylor saw it, however, the inflexible New Look offered "only two choices, the initiation of general war or compromise and defeat."[62] Thus the Army, stung by shrinking allocations and fearing for its institutional integrity, if not existence, pressed for a flexible defense capability to wage "limited" or nonnuclear war, principally in the Third World. The alternative strategy, which Taylor called "flexible response," caught Kennedy's attention and facilitated his intervention into Vietnam. It also led, however, to virulent division between the services over the military strategy that the Army, which dominated the Military Assistance Command, Vietnam (MACV), during the war, would pursue.

In similar fashion, the budget battles and political ill will between the civilian and military leadership, and among the services themselves, prompted American generals to overcome their misgivings about war in Vietnam in order to reassert their institutional importance and lay claim to greater allocations and more influence in national security policy making. Having felt Eisenhower's wrath in

62. Aliano, *American Defense Policy*, 37, 107–8; Taylor, *Uncertain Trumpet*, 5–7.

the 1950s, the military came to see intervention in Vietnam as a way to maintain its institutional power vis-à-vis U.S. political leaders, as well as a means to expand the mission of the respective services.[63]

The military's feud with Dwight Eisenhower and his defense secretary, Charles Wilson, has been well documented and does not require a detailed elaboration here.[64] Although the New Look promised not only security but economy, the military was not enthused about Eisenhower's plans. The Army and Navy resented the Air Force's ascendancy (it would receive 46 percent of defense appropriations between 1952 and 1960), the military in general complained of diminishing appropriations, and service leaders, as Maxwell Taylor explained, feared that the president was turning the JCS into an essentially political body loyal to him.[65] Although Taylor's lament was disingenuous – the military and he himself had long been involved in politics – the 1950s did mark a transitionary phase in military affairs. As the military became more bureaucratized, civil–military relations became even more politicized and difficult.[66] By the end of the Eisenhower presidency, some of America's best-known Army leaders – including Ridgway, Gavin, and Taylor – had publicly broken with the administration's defense policies, leading the president to complain that the military's behavior bordered on treason.[67]

The Army especially challenged Eisenhower's conception of national security. Ridgway, the chief of staff from 1953 to 1955, balked when appropriations for his service dropped from $16 to $9 billion and when ordered to reduce troop strength from 1.5 to 1

---

63. The most comprehensive treatment of the military's involvement in politics is Mark Perry's *Four Stars* (Boston, 1989), see chapters 1–3 for this period.
64. See, inter alia, Ambrose, *Eisenhower;* Perry, *Four Stars;* Kinnard, *The Certain Trumpet;* Douglas Kinnard, *The Secretary of Defense* (Lexington, Ky., 1980); Korb, *The Joint Chiefs of Staff;* Bacevich, *The Pentomic Era;* Taylor, *Uncertain Trumpet;* Ridgway, *Soldier;* Gavin, *War and Peace in the Space Age.*
65. Korb, *Joint Chiefs of Staff,* 109; Taylor, *Uncertain Trumpet,* 20–1.
66. On the late 1940s political battles, see Demetrios Caraley, *The Politics of Military Unification* (New York, 1966). For the Marine Corps' perspective, see Gordon W. Keiser, *The US Marine Corps and Defense Unification, 1944–1947: The Politics of Survival* (Washington, D.C., 1982). On MacArthur and Korea, see Burton Kaufman, *The Korean War: Challenges in Crisis, Credibility, and Command* (Philadelphia, 1986); see also Aliano, *American Defense Policy,* 100.
67. Ambrose, *Eisenhower,* 515–16; Aliano, *American Defense Policy,* 135.

million by fiscal year 1956. Such dramatic cuts, the general complained, "would so weaken the Army that it could no longer carry out its missions."[68] Defense Secretary Wilson nonetheless ordered the Army staff to make the reductions and adjust to the New Look's budget realities. Ridgway in turn retired after just two years as chief and blasted the president's defense policy in a highly publicized memo to Wilson.[69] More pointedly, a senior officer retiring at the same time told Ridgway he was "convinced that if present trends continue the Army will soon become a service support agency for the other armed services."[70]

Other officers shared such fears that the military in general, and the Army particularly, had become ill prepared to ensure the national security. In 1956 General Gavin, head of Army research and development and charged with developing an anti–ballistic missile defense system, the Redstone, complained that the Navy and Air Force had forced their less successful missile programs on the Pentagon to the detriment of Army efforts.[71] Before a congressional committee the general also criticized the New Look and warned that the use of atomic weapons would have "catastrophic effects." In response, Undersecretary of State Herbert Hoover, Jr., charged that Gavin's testimony had "made the orderly conduct of our foreign relations almost impossible." To Treasury Secretary George Humphrey, such criticism was motivated by money. "If you gave a nickel to anybody," he complained, "the Army had to have a lot more." In turn, Lyndon Johnson, head of a Senate subcommittee investigating U.S. military posture, charged that the administration was using "rubber-hose tactics" to silence Gavin. The general, for his part, took early retirement and refused appointment as NATO commander to show his disgust with the New Look.[72]

Taylor's program of flexible response rescued the Army, however. Rather than rely on ponderous units backed by massive fire-

---

68. Ridgway, *Soldier,* 288.
69. Ridgway to Wilson, 27 June 1955, reproduced in *Soldier,* 323–32.
70. Quoted in Bacevich, *Pentomic Era,* 20.
71. Gavin, *War and Peace in the Space Age,* 14–16; Ambrose, *Eisenhower,* 428–9; Perry, *Four Stars,* 77–9; Aliano, *American Defense Policy,* 118–19.
72. 290th Meeting of the National Security Council, 12 July 1956, Whitman File – NSC Series, DDEL; Humphrey in Kinnard, *Eisenhower and Strategy Management,* 72; Johnson in *NYT,* 8 January 1958, 10.

power, the general urged the development of smaller and more mobile groups that could fight against Soviet-supported insurgencies in the Third World. Taylor's analysis thus had a double advantage for him and the Army. It correctly anticipated that the superpowers would compete in the developing countries – not against each other directly – in the 1960s, thereby gaining notice from U.S. policy makers. And it gave his service the primary role in defense policy formulations. In the 1950s, as Lieutenant Colonel A. J. Bacevich explained, Army soldiers had "lamented a perceived loss of status and esteem in the eyes of their countrymen"; the Army was represented by Beetle Bailey, the Air Force by Steve Canyon. Perhaps a bit paranoid, Army officers feared becoming little more than an "auxiliary service," to be used for "ceremonial purposes while the Air Force girds its loins to fight our wars."[73] Taylor's plan offered redemption and photo opportunities. Having lost the battles over the budget and control of nuclear weapons, the Army could recoup its influence with flexible response and counterinsurgency.[74]

Therein also lay the roots of war. The Army, as Ridgway had pointed out during the Dien Bien Phu crisis, was not capable of intervening with its conventional forces in Indochina. Taylor's program, on paper at least, not only made limited wars in Third World environments possible, but also promised success. The Army, as it saw events, had suffered under Eisenhower's budget cuts while the Air Force had gained political and economic primacy. To aspiring politicians like Kennedy and Johnson, who had exploited the military's critique of the New Look for their own political purposes, Vietnam would became a test case for the new military doctrine.

At the same time, however, the Army would find old habits hard to break. Having been reinvigorated by Kennedy's election (and in

73. Bacevich, *Pentomic Era*, 20–1.
74. On the political–military battles over the budget and strategy, see the sources listed in note 64. Some political leaders also suggested that reductions in appropriations to the U.S. military should be matched by cuts in assistance to other areas. Senator Hubert Humphrey pointed out that 60 percent of American aid to the Far East went to Taiwan, Korea, and Vietnam, and he suggested that U.S. leaders reexamine such programs in light of budget constraints. SCFR, *Mutual Security Act of 1959*, 492.

some cases rehabilitated: Taylor returned as the president's military advisor and then JCS chair, and Gavin became ambassador to Paris), the Army still was not terribly eager to fight in Vietnam or to change its mission to emphasize CI. Having gained a strategic victory in battle on the Potomac, the Army did not hunger for war on the Mekong, or for an overhaul of its traditional approach to combat. In the final analysis, flexible response was essentially a political, not military, doctrine, used to score bureaucratic points for the Army at home but ineffective on the battlefields of Indochina. Thus it was virtually the exact type of Army that fought in Vietnam as had in Korea a decade earlier, limited-war theory notwithstanding.

But the political conditions under which Americans fought had changed markedly. Civil–military relations had been badly strained in the years between World War II and Vietnam. Political and service leaders would henceforth view each other warily and, during the Vietnam War, would develop policy with politics as well as military needs in mind. The services, led by doubters and critics on Vietnam but mindful of the feuds over budgets and mission in the 1950s, would be vigilant in securing and protecting resources and influence for their respective branches. As a result, U.S. soldiers in Vietnam entered a war to defend an unworthy regime, which they were unlikely to win, with distrustful politicians and generals leading them, and without any coherent strategy for success.

4

Pinning Down the President: JFK, the Military, and Political Maneuvering over Vietnam, January– October 1961

It is inappropriate for any members of the Defense Department to speak on the subject of foreign policy.

Robert Strange McNamara[1]

In 1956 Senator John F. Kennedy saw the Republic of Vietnam as the "cornerstone of the Free World in Southeast Asia." Diem's regime, he boasted, "is our offspring, we cannot abandon it."[2] Four years later, while campaigning for the presidency, Kennedy charged that Dwight Eisenhower had not confronted communism vigorously enough, and he promised a new, activist military program for America, invoking Generals Taylor, Ridgway, and Gavin to add credibility to his criticism that massive retaliation had not provided security against American enemies.[3] Just months later, in his inaugural address, the new commander in chief pledged to "pay any price, bear any burden, meet any hardship, support any friend, oppose any foe, to assure the survival and the success of liberty."[4]

Despite Kennedy's adversarial world view and strident cold war rhetoric,[5] many recent studies have cleared him of responsibility for the U.S. commitment to and subsequent aggression in Vietnam.

1. McNamara in Raymond, *Power at the Pentagon*, 174.
2. Kennedy in Young, *Vietnam Wars*, 58–9.
3. Maxwell D. Taylor, *Swords and Plowshares* (New York, 1972), 180; Hewes, *From Root to McNamara*, 299–300.
4. Kennedy in U.S. Government Printing Office, *Inaugural Addresses of the Presidents of the United States from George Washington 1789 to John F. Kennedy 1961* (Washington, D.C., 1961), 267–70.
5. On Kennedy as the consummate cold warrior, see the various essays in Thomas G. Paterson, ed., *Kennedy's Quest for Victory: American Foreign Policy, 1961–1963* (New York, 1989).

Filmmaker Oliver Stone, historian John Newman, and former CIA operative Fletcher Prouty, among others, have contended that the young president had decided by late 1963 to quit Vietnam, reverse the cold war, and challenge the political power of the military-industrial-intelligence complex at home. Amid such pacifism, a militaristic cabal led by the JCS and the CIA decided to do away with Kennedy and go to war in Vietnam.[6] Although such revisionism can be lucrative, it is demonstrably absurd. Between January 1961 and November 1963 John Kennedy daily confronted a growing crisis in Vietnam and increasingly staked U.S. credibility and treasure there. Whereas about 1,000 military advisors had been deployed in January 1961, over 16,000 were stationed in Vietnam at the time of the president's assassination. Whereas Eisenhower had given the MAAG principally a training mission, Kennedy began a war of aggression, complete with air power, helicopters, napalm, crop destruction, and defoliation.[7] And whereas Indochina had once been a "peripheral" interest, Kennedy made it the centerpiece of the cold war, the place where America would draw the line against world communism. Without question, Kennedy

6. Stone's movie, *JFK,* began the most recent rehabilitation of Kennedy in 1991. John Newman's book, *JFK and Vietnam* (New York, 1992), and Fletcher Prouty's *JFK: The CIA, Vietnam and the Plot to Assassinate John F. Kennedy* (New York, 1992), have both been released in connection with Stone's film in an attempt to add scholarly credibility to his accusations about the conspiracy to kill Kennedy because of his dovish policies on Vietnam. Among earlier, mainstream, defenders of Kennedy see, for example, Hugh Sidey in *Time,* 14 November 1983, 69. Of course, the classic apology for Kennedy's foreign policy remains Arthur M. Schlesinger, Jr.'s *A Thousand Days* (New York, 1965). Curiously, as Noam Chomsky has recently pointed out, the original, 1965 edition of Schlesinger's work deals with Vietnam in a rather matter-of-fact fashion. But as time went on and it was clear that the war was a disaster, Schlesinger, in *Robert Kennedy and His Times* (New York, 1978), contended that Kennedy was poised to withdraw from Vietnam after the 1964 election. In 1992, in a favorable review of Newman's book in the *NYT Book Review* (29 March 1992, 3, 31), Schlesinger goes even further, contending that he has always put forth the JFK withdrawal thesis. See Noam Chomsky, *Rethinking Camelot: JFK, the Vietnam War, and US Political Culture* (Boston, 1993), and "Vain Hopes, False Dreams," *Z Magazine* 5 (October 1992): 9–23. For further criticism of the Stone-Newman view of Kennedy, see the exchanges, particularly Alexander Cockburn's, in the *Nation,* 6–13 January 1992, 20 January 1992, 9 March 1992, and 18 May 1992. The best criticism of Kennedy's policy can be found in Kahin, *Intervention;* Kolko, *Anatomy of a War;* and Lawrence J. Bassett and Stephen E. Pelz, "The Failed Search for Victory: Vietnam and the Politics of War," in Paterson, *Kennedy's Quest for Victory,* 223–52.

7. On Kennedy's 1962 escalation, see Chomsky, "Vain Hopes"; Young, *The Vietnam Wars;* Kahin, *Intervention;* and Sheehan, *A Bright Shining Lie.*

had planted, then fertilized, the seeds of disaster in Vietnam during his thousand days in the White House.

Although Kennedy's responsibility for war in Vietnam is clear, the military's role in intervention is less so. Its response to White House policy on Vietnam from 1961 to 1963 was variously ambivalent, critical, or even inchoate. Clearly U.S. military leaders did not respond to the prospects of intervention as dissenters like Ridgway, Collins, Gavin, and others had a decade earlier. But neither did ranking military figures – including CINCPAC Harry D. Felt, MAAG Chair Lionel McGarr, and Marine Commandant David Shoup – behave according to the hawkish caricature that many liberal critics have developed over the years.[8] Most officers in Washington and Saigon in fact tended to be critics and politicos who recognized the perilous situation in Vietnam, were never eager for combat, understood the various obstacles to success, and were aware of the domestic political implications of warfare in Indochina. Yet, within two and a half years, they had overcome their reluctance to intervene and had begun to pursue a military solution in Vietnam. At the same time, service leaders recognized that U.S. prospects in Vietnam were uncertain and that an American combat role could not ensure success. By November 1963, then, the U.S. military – obedient to if not totally in concert with Kennedy's political objectives – was involved in a war in Vietnam that would serve neither U.S. nor Vietnamese interests.

Kennedy's intervention in Vietnam was affected by a crisis half a world away. Less than one hundred days into his presidency, he sanctioned an attack against Fidel Castro's revolutionary government in Cuba by U.S.-trained, Miami-based Cuban terrorists. Castro's army routed the invaders at the Bay of Pigs, and Kennedy, despite what the Cuban émigrés thought he had promised, failed to provide air or naval support to the anti-Castro forces. The Cuban

8. See the sources in note 6, as well as Peter Dale Scott, *The War Conspiracy* (Indianapolis, Ind., 1972); Galbraith, *How to Control the Military;* and Knoll and McFadden, *American Militarism 1970.* Two works that are also highly critical of the military, but more sophisticated and balanced than Schlesinger, Newman, et al., are Andrew F. Krepinevich, Jr., *The Army and Vietnam* (Baltimore, 1986); and Cecil Currey (Cincinnatus), *Self-Destruction: The Disintegration and Decay of the United States Army during the Vietnam Era* (New York, 1981). George McT. Kahin's *Intervention* and Marilyn Young's *Vietnam Wars* are also critical of the military's approach to Vietnam during the Kennedy years.

government had barely subdued the attack when recriminations for the fiasco began to fly around Washington, especially between the administration and the military. The humiliation of the Bay of Pigs spurred Defense Secretary Robert Strange McNamara to lose trust in the JCS and assume a larger role in military planning, developments that would have an enormous impact on policy making for Vietnam.[9]

The president was most disappointed with the JCS, which, he believed, had only cursorily reviewed the Bay of Pigs plans and had not forthrightly expressed its serious reservations about them. The military, Kennedy feared, would try to blame him for their failure.[10] "I hope you kept a full account of that," the president told his advisor and biographer Arthur Schlesinger after the Bay of Pigs affair. "You can be damn sure that the CIA has its record and the Joint Chiefs theirs. We'd better make sure we have a record over here."[11] To undercut the armed forces' position, Kennedy even authorized journalist Arthur Krock to report that the chiefs had guaranteed success against Castro, "as in Guatemala" in 1954, and that the president had "lost confidence" in his military advisors.[12]

Kennedy also feared that his interests were not being adequately represented in military decisions and so brought Maxwell Taylor out of retirement to head a commission to investigate the Cuban affair. The subsequent findings were just what the president wanted. The chiefs, Taylor reported, had given the White House the impression that they favored the assault and expected success, thereby prompting Kennedy to initiate the attack against Cuba.[13] Taylor had thus given Kennedy a credible reason to blame the holdover brass from the Eisenhower era for his problems. "My God," he lamented, "the bunch of advisers we inherited." After the

9. According to McNamara's deputy Roswell Gilpatric, the secretary "became so disenchanted with the military advice he got" after the Bay of Pigs debacle, "that he insisted on examining the basic data himself." The chief lesson he had learned in April 1961, McNamara told Schlesinger, was "do your own work. Don't rely on advice from anybody." Quotations in Shapley, *Promise and Power*, 115–16; see also Henry L. Trewhitt, *McNamara: His Ordeal in the Pentagon* (New York, 1971), 97–8.
10. Theodore S. Sorenson, *Kennedy* (New York, 1965), 305–6; Schlesinger, *Thousand Days*, 290–7.
11. Schlesinger, *Thousand Days*, xi.
12. Arthur Krock, *Memoirs: Sixty Years on the Firing Line* (New York, 1968), 369–71.
13. Taylor, *Swords and Plowshares*, 188–9; Sorensen, *Kennedy*, 607; Perry, *Four Stars*, 114–17.

Bay of Pigs, Schlesinger added, the president saw the JCS, and CIA, as "soft spots" in his administration and "would never be over-awed by professional military advice again."[14] The chiefs too resented the political aftermath of the Cuban debacle. Of all the civilian and military officials involved in the planning for Cuba, none was as critical as Marine Commandant David Shoup, who explained later that once Kennedy had decided to invade the island, the chiefs "were just trying to help him do what . . . had been approved by giving people, material, training help, and God knows what else." There was "complete unanimity" among military people, he added, that the plan "had one very poor chance of success."[15]

Taylor's report on civil–military relations – which urged "direct and unfiltered" military advice to the president – thus angered the JCS. To the chiefs Taylor was now an "outsider" who was exploiting the Bay of Pigs situation to promote his own views on strategy, especially flexible response, to the president and was scapegoating the armed forces in the process. From that point on Taylor was Kennedy's most trusted military advisor and, in October 1962, became the new JCS chair. The general's reemergence notwithstanding, the president's relations with the military would remain strained after the events of April and May 1961. As Taylor himself admitted, "this unhappiness with the Chiefs hung like a cloud over their relations with the President after the Bay of Pigs episode."[16]

14. Schlesinger, *Thousand Days*, 290–7.
15. Shoup, however, did not believe that the Taylor report was specifically aimed at placing blame for the Bay of Pigs on the military instead of Kennedy. David M. Shoup Oral History, John F. Kennedy Library, 17–25. Shoup, Ted Sorenson later recalled, was probably Kennedy's favorite chief, the only JCS holdover after Kennedy brought his own people into the Pentagon in 1962. Sorenson, *Kennedy,* 607; Shoup is somewhat famous – or infamous, depending upon one's perspective – for his strident criticism of the war in the later 1960s, but among Marines his opposition to the Bay of Pigs plans is still highly regarded. During the spring 1961 preparations Shoup brought a transparent map of Cuba to a planning meeting and laid it over the United States map to show just how large the island was and how difficult it would be to subdue it. For effect, Shoup then took an overlay with a small red dot on it and laid it on top of the other maps. Shoup explained that the dot represented the size of the island of Tarawa, site of a Pacific battle in World War II where the commandant had earned the Medal of Honor, and where, Shoup reminded, "it took us three days and eighteen thousand Marines to take it." Halberstam, *Best and Brightest*, 85.
16. Taylor, *Swords and Plowshares*, 187–9; see also Perry, *Four Stars*, 114–17; Lewis Sorley, *Thunderbolt: General Creighton Abrams and the Army of His Times* (New York, 1992), 178–9.

Indeed, Kennedy's disenchantment with the military in the aftermath of the Cuban episode cannot be understated. The White
House and armed forces had enjoyed a short-lived honeymoon
before the events of April 1961 soured civil–military relations
badly, if not irrevocably. As the president and his chiefs made policy
on Vietnam, memories of the fallout from the Bay of Pigs could not
remain far below the surface. From the outset of the Kennedy
presidency, through the 1968 Tet Offensive, which ended any
American hopes of success in the war, the White House and armed
services would always approach Vietnam with an emphasis on politics at home as well as military needs on the battlefield. Service
leaders, who had done battle against Eisenhower over the New
Look just a few years earlier, had initially looked with favor upon
Kennedy, who had run as the consummate cold warrior in 1960
and who had told his defense secretary to develop military requirements without regard to arbitrary budget ceilings. But the armed
forces began to flood the Pentagon with requests for more resources, raising the ire of the "whiz kids" and, coupled with the
effects of the Cuban affair, leading to greater suspicion between
civilian and military leaders.[17]

No relationship was as strained as that between McNamara and
the JCS. The new secretary and his staff of RAND Corporation
alumni and university types saw the chiefs as just one of the many
resources available to them in defense planning, and their self-
confidence, if not arrogance, unnerved American officers. Making
matters worse, McNamara restructured the budgeting system to
base appropriations on particular missions or objectives, not on the
military's evaluation of overall needs, and he attempted to keep
service officials on a short leash by ordering them not to reveal any
policy differences in public, and enforcing that directive by sending
Pentagon representatives to monitor any testimony by JCS members before Congress. In response, military leaders began to feed
their frustrations with McNamara to various senators and representatives and also local officials in districts that relied on military
spending. The new defense secretary, as soon as he took office, thus

17. Alain C. Enthoven and K. Wayne Smith, *How Much Is Enough? Shaping the Defense
    Program, 1961–1969* (New York, 1972), 325; Shapley, *Promise and Power*, 104.

found himself at odds with the armed forces and influential members of Congress.[18]

Because of such growing ill will between the military and civilian establishment, service officials, who recognized the obstacles to success in Vietnam and the political imperatives driving Kennedy's policy there, would thus follow the president's aggressive lead on Indochina policy, despite their reservations. In fact, the military took the president at his word with regard to Vietnam so, while Kennedy sought to achieve victory against the Communists while keeping U.S. costs down, the military, more wary of political leaders than ever, would seek an expanded war in order to make the president accountable for his commitment to Vietnam.

The Bay of Pigs and its aftermath not only helped to condition the military's response to Vietnam, but put added pressure on the White House for a foreign policy success as well. After the failure to oust Castro, as George McT. Kahin points out, Kennedy had been "hoist with the petard of his own campaign charges" that the Eisenhower administration was soft on communism. So he had to take a stand elsewhere. Walt Whitman Rostow, counselor of the Department of State and chairman of the Policy Planning Council, likewise told McNamara and Secretary of State Dean Rusk that "clean-cut success in Vietnam" might ease the political tension created by the Bay of Pigs failure. From Saigon, the MAAG chief, General McGarr, also noted the White House's "strong determination" to stop the "present deterioration [of] US prestige" after the events of April 1961.[19] Given the president's commitment to contain communism anywhere, Vietnam might very well have become a national security priority in any case, but the Cuban misadventure, along with a political setback in Laos at the same time, made it

18. Kinnard, *The Secretary of Defense,* 84; Korb, *The Joint Chiefs of Staff,* 118–20; Hewes, *From Root to McNamara,* 307–10; Kolko, *Anatomy of a War,* 144; Raymond, *Power at the Pentagon,* 179–80, 281–3; Donovan, *Militarism U.S.A.,* 118, 126; John Taylor, *General Maxwell Taylor: The Sword and the Pen* (New York, 1989), 275.

19. Kahin, *Intervention,* 127; Rostow to McNamara, Rusk, and Dulles, 24 April 1961, "Notes on Cuba Policy," in Laurence Chang and Peter Kornbluh, eds., *The Cuban Missile Crisis, 1962: A National Security Archive Documents Reader* (New York, 1992), 16–19 (I would like to thank Bill Walker for bringing this document to my attention); McGarr to Felt, 10 May 1961, *FRUS,* Vietnam, 1961 (Washington, D.C., 1988), 129. The *FRUS* volumes for 1961–63 are separated into four volumes – vol. 1: 1961, vol. 2: 1962, vol. 3: January–August 1963, and vol. 4: August–December 1963. I will hereafter refer to them by year number, with appropriate filing information.

imperative for him to justify his cold war credentials by preserving America's "offspring," the RVN.

As Kennedy assumed office, however, Vietnam was not the principal focus of his foreign policy considerations. In fact, at a 19 January transition meeting, the outgoing president considered Laos, where a corrupt, American-backed government verged on collapse, rather than Vietnam to be the key to anti-Communist success in Southeast Asia.[20] Kennedy first dealt with Vietnam in late January, when he met with his advisors to discuss Edward Lansdale's recent mission there. The Air Force general, a specialist in psychological warfare who was also a close friend of Diem, had returned from a two-week tour of the RVN with an alarming view of the situation. His "grim views," shared by both Vietnamese and U.S. intelligence as well as by Diem himself, gave the president his first "sense of the danger and urgency of the problem in Vietnam," according to Rostow.[21]

As Lansdale saw it, the RVN could do "no more than postpone eventual defeat" without a dramatic turnaround in morale and a national mobilization for war.[22] During a 28 January meeting to

20. Christian Herter, Memorandum for the Record, 19 January 1961, Post-Presidential, Palm Desert-Indio File, box 10, folder: Kennedy, J. F., 1962, DDEL; likewise, General Earle Wheeler, who would be Army chief of staff and JCS chair for the better part of the Vietnam War, briefed Kennedy on defense policy at Eisenhower's direction before the 1960 election and only cursorily discussed the situation in Laos and Southeast Asia in general. Wheeler Oral History, 6–7, JFKL; Fred I. Greenstein and Richard H. Immerman, "What Did Eisenhower Tell Kennedy about Indochina? The Politics of Misperception," *Journal of American History* 79 (September 1992): 568–87.

21. Rostow to McGeorge Bundy, 30 January 1961, VN C.F., box 193, JFKL.

22. Lansdale's memorandum to the Secretary of Defense (Gates), 17 January 1961, can be found in the Papers of Edward G. Lansdale, Hoover Institution Archives, Palo Alto, Calif., folder 1376 (hereafter cited as Lansdale Papers with appropriate filing information), and HCAS, *USVN Relations,* book 2, IV.A.5, tab 4, 66–77, and book 11, V.B.4 (book I), 1–12. See also Felt to Lansdale, 10 December 1960, Lansdale to General Erskine, 9 January 1961, and Lansdale to Gates and Douglas, 12 and 14 January 1961, all in Lansdale Papers, folder 1376. Lansdale, although prone to hyperbole, correctly noted that the people of Vietnam had progressed materially with U.S. support "but are starting to lose the will to protect their liberty." He was wrong to equate liberty with loyalty to the autocratic Diem gang, but, in an analysis ironically similar to that of radical historian Gabriel Kolko, he understood that the American presence was fundamentally altering the nature of Vietnamese society and culture, a condition that would continue to engender resentment against the U.S. role there throughout the 1960s. See sources cited already and Kolko, *Anatomy of a War.* For more information on the Lansdale mission, see Congressional Research Service (CRS), *The U.S. Government and the Vietnam War: Executive and Legislative Roles and Relationships, Part II, 1961–1964,* Prepared for the Committee on Foreign Relations, U.S. Senate (Washington, D.C., 1984), 11–13; Kahin, *Intervention,* 129–30.

discuss Cuba and Indochina, Lansdale and others stressed the need for immediate action to stem the Communist insurgency in southern Vietnam.[23] The DRVN, under pressure from its southern cadre to intensify the war against Diem, had just approved the establishment of the National Liberation Front (NLF) in order "to overthrow the dictatorial . . . Diem clique, lackeys of the U.S. imperialists, to form a . . . coalition government in south Vietnam, to win national independence and . . . to achieve national reunification."[24]

The Lansdale mission and formation of the NLF, as well as a Soviet pledge to support "wars of liberation" in the Third World, thus compelled Kennedy to respond, and on 30 January he approved the Counterinsurgency Plan (CIP) for Vietnam. The president, prompted by Taylor's doctrine of flexible response, saw counterinsurgency as the means to defeat the VC short of total war. American officials had been working on the CIP since the previous year, and McGarr, as noted in the previous chapter, had questioned the MAAG's failure in the 1950s to train the ARVN to handle the Communist insurgents.[25] The CIP recommended that the United States fund increases of 20,000 troops in the ARVN (to 170,000) and 36,000 forces in the CG (to 68,000). It would also increase subsidies to Diem by another $42 million, to be added to the $225 million annual contribution already being made to the RVN. In return for such support, Diem would be expected to reform his government's autocratic political structure, or aid could be withheld.[26]

Despite approval of the CIP, many American officials had reservations about the plan. The president himself wondered why such

23. Summary Record of a Meeting, the White House, 28 January 1961, *FRUS*, Vietnam, 1961, 13–15; M. Bundy to McNamara, Rusk, and Allen Dulles, 29 January 1961, and Rostow to M. Bundy, 30 January 1961, VN C.F., NSF, box 193, JFKL.
24. In Kahin, *Intervention*, 115.
25. Paper Prepared by the Country Team Staff Committee, 4 January 1961, "Basic Counterinsurgency Plan for Viet-Nam," *FRUS*, Vietnam, 1961, 1–12; HCAS, *USVN Relations*, book 2, IV.A.5, tab 4, 86–7, and book 11, V.B.4 (book I), 14–16; Young, *Vietnam Wars*, 75–6; CRS, *Government and Vietnam*, 13–16. In addition to McGarr's November 1960 reports on guerrilla warfare (see last sections of Chapter 3, the MAAG developed a guidebook on "Tactics and Techniques of Counter-Insurgent Operations," n.d., VN C.F., NSF, box 204, folder: Vietnam, MAAG, Counterinsurgency, parts I–VII, JFKL.
26. See sources cited in previous note; see also Joint State-Defense-ICA Message, 3 February 1961, VN C.F., NSF, box 193, JFKL.

increases in the ARVN were needed if, as military officials in Saigon reported, the VC had only about 10,000 guerrillas in the south. Admiral Felix Stump, the CINCPAC in the mid-1950s, complained that officials from the State Department and Pentagon had not taken Lansdale's concerns about the insurgency seriously enough. Lansdale, after meeting with McNamara, found the defense secretary "very hard to talk to [about CI]. Watching his face as I talked, I got the feeling that he didn't understand me." Army Chief of Staff George Decker simply challenged the need for CI, telling Kennedy that "any good soldier can handle guerrillas." And McGarr himself urged that the White House reconsider its proposal to withdraw aid to Diem if political liberalization was not forthcoming.[27]

McGarr's ambivalent views on CI would come to typify the U.S. military approach to Vietnam. The MAAG chief had alternately advocated, then questioned, the emphasis on counterguerrilla warfare.[28] In the same way, other military leaders, beginning during the April 1961 Laos crisis and continuing to 1963, would put forth similarly ambivalent proposals regarding the need for or wisdom of deploying U.S. combat troops to Vietnam. The Laos issue began to boil over at the precise time that acrimony between civilian and military officials over the Bay of Pigs would reach its peak. At a 27 April meeting with the JCS, Kennedy first raised the idea of putting troops into Laos to prop up the shaky regime, then being pressured by Communist Pathet Lao guerrillas moving on Vientiane.

27. Record of 28 January Meeting, *FRUS*, Vietnam, 1961, 14; Kennedy to Lemnitzer, 5 February 1961, JFK Library, President's Office File, Countries File, Vietnam, box 128, folder 9 [hereafter cited as POF, CF, VN with appropriate filing information]; Stump in Cecil Currey, *Edward Lansdale: The Unquiet American* (Boston, 1988), 226; Lansdale in CRS, *Government and Vietnam War*, 11–13; Decker in Douglas Blaufarb, *The Counterinsurgency Era: U.S. Doctrine and Performance* (New York, 1977), 80; McGarr to Director of Military Assistance, Office of Assistant Secretary of Defense, 3 March 1961, *FRUS*, Vietnam, 1961, 43–4.

28. To Andrew Krepinevich, McGarr only paid "lip service" to the need for counterinsurgency, like most military leaders in Washington and Saigon at the time. Citing McGarr's statement that "we will 'out conventional' the unconventionalists," Krepinevich argues that the MAAG leaders had no intention of pursuing a strategy any different than that of his predecessor, General Williams. Krepinevich, though correct in part, exaggerates the case against McGarr. The MAAG commander did stress CI more than other military officials at the time, as evidenced by his late 1960 studies on CI. And McGarr's emphasis on CI was credible enough to get him ousted as the MAAG leader in late 1961 in favor of General Paul D. Harkins, who pursued a strictly conventional strategy in Vietnam. Andrew Krepinevich, *The Army and Vietnam* (Baltimore, 1986), 57–8.

The chiefs, while stressing that intervention was a political decision and that they would carry out whatever course the president chose, did not encourage U.S. combat in Laos. As Roger Hilsman, the director of the State Department's bureau of intelligence and research, explained, it was a "shibboleth" among the JCS that American forces should "perhaps never again . . . fight any kind of war on the ground in Asia."[29] Accordingly, the chiefs told Kennedy that he would have to support a huge troop commitment to defend Laos, between 60,000 and 140,000 troops, and authorize U.S. military commanders to employ nuclear weapons in the event of PRC intervention. The military also shocked the president by informing him that such a sizable deployment would unduly drain troops from Europe amid the Berlin crisis while the strategic reserve at home was becoming dangerously low.[30] By this time, however, Kennedy was reluctant to even consider the military's proposals. Had it not been for the recriminations after the Bay of Pigs, the president noted, he "might have taken this advice seriously."[31]

The military itself was split over intervention, with Generals Decker and Shoup, the chiefs of the services most likely to see combat in Laos, pointing out the logistical, tactical, and health problems inherent in a jungle war there and warning that Mao or other Asian Communists could open another front against the West elsewhere in the region. As Shoup put it, the military was mostly interested in "finding some way to stop [the Laos imbroglio] and get out." For his part, Decker "thought that there was no good place to fight" in Southeast Asia, though he hoped to hold onto as much of Indochina as possible. Only the Navy and Air Force chiefs, Arleigh Burke and Curtis LeMay, whose troops would fight at a distance and suffer limited casualties, were more amenable to intervention.[32]

29. Roger Hilsman, *To Move a Nation: The Politics of Foreign Policy in the Administration of John F. Kennedy* (Garden City, N.Y., 1967), 129.
30. Kahin, *Intervention*, 127, and Young, *Vietnam Wars*, 78, offer the 60,000 troop figure, while the Congressional Research Service history, *Government and Vietnam*, 26, states that the JCS wanted between 120,000 and 140,000 forces. See also Sorenson, *Kennedy*, 645.
31. Kennedy in Schlesinger, *Thousand Days*, 339.
32. Shoup Oral History, 10–11, JFKL; Decker in Memo of Conversation, 29 April 1961, "Laos," HCAS, *USVN Relations*, book 11, 62–6; Sorenson, *Kennedy*, 644–5; Marolda and Fitzgerald, *U.S. Navy and Vietnam*, 69–71; Hilsman, *To Move a Nation*, 142–55.

Kennedy thus was left to accept the establishment of a coalition government in Laos that included the Pathet Lao as a major partner. As a result, the president's anti-Communist reputation came under further attack as Republican congressional leaders and former Vice-President Richard Nixon rushed to charge him with defeat in Southeast Asia.[33] Clearly, April 1961 had not been a good month for the new administration, with the Cuban and Laotian situations casting a pall over U.S. foreign policy and damaging the president's credibility. In May 1961, then, Kennedy and his advisors would begin to consider seriously American military intervention in Vietnam and set the country onto the path toward full-scale war in Indochina over the course of the next decade.

Throughout the early 1961 deliberations, Kennedy consistently took a hard line regarding the need to make a stand in Vietnam. After just ten days in office Kennedy told his special assistant for National Security Affairs, McGeorge Bundy, to study U.S. policy in Indochina, where "we must be better off in three months than we are now," and he established a special Presidential Task Force on Vietnam to develop a program to do just that.[34] On 1 March, Rusk told the embassy in Saigon that the "White House ranks [the] defense [of] Viet-Nam among [the] highest priorities [of] US foreign policy," with Kennedy especially afraid that the RVN could not survive over the two-year period anticipated for the CIP to become effective.[35] By the end of the month, McGeorge Bundy wanted the newly appointed ambassador, Frederick E. Nolting, Jr., to hurry to Saigon, for Kennedy was "eager indeed that [Vietnam] should have the highest priority for rapid and energetic action."[36] Throughout May, as the foreign policy establishment debated, the president repeatedly emphasized his commitment to stop the VC. Indeed, the JCS chair, Lyman Lemnitzer, told McGarr that "Kennedy was ready to do anything within reason to save Southeast Asia."[37]

The military also recognized the political factors driving Ken-

33. Kahin, *Intervention*, 132.
34. Rostow memorandum to M. Bundy, 30 January 1961, *FRUS*, Vietnam, 1961, 19.
35. Department of State to Embassy, Saigon, 1 March 1961, ibid., 40.
36. CRS, *Government and Vietnam*, Vietnam, 33.
37. McGarr to Felt, 6 May 1961, *FRUS*, Vietnam, 1961, 89.

nedy's position on Indochina and thus sought to pin down the president on what his objectives in and commitment to the RVN would involve. Lemnitzer, during a trip to Southeast Asia, feared that the White House would repeat its vacillating approach to Laos, "which can only lead to the loss of Vietnam." But, the JCS leader wondered, would Kennedy seek to maintain a pro-American RVN, and if so, would he take military action in a timely manner or "quibble for weeks and months" over policy, funding, and Vietnamese political problems? The current "marginal and piecemeal efforts" would have to stop if the United States was to reverse the insurgents' success in Vietnam, as Lemnitzer saw it.[38]

After meeting with Lemnitzer, McGarr informed Admiral Felt that the JCS chair and Kennedy both "have repeatedly stated [that] Vietnam is not to go behind [the] Bamboo Curtain under any circumstances, and we must do all that is necessary to prevent this from happening." Moreover, the MAAG chief stressed, "they both state this is a primarily military problem" and that officials in Saigon should not be restricted by the Geneva accords, budgetary constraints, or red tape in obtaining military support. The politicians, McGarr said, needed to get the MAAG off of its "short leash."[39] Given such views, there seems little question that George McT. Kahin correctly observed that "from the early months of his presidency Kennedy sought a military solution in Vietnam, and he soon began to militarize the direct American intervention that Eisenhower had initiated."[40]

The military's approach to Indochina was a bit more nuanced than Kennedy's. Various service leaders had debated the merits of a CI strategy, resisted intervention in Laos, recognized the VC's strength in the south and Diem's shortcomings, and, in the aftermath of the Bay of Pigs, began to view the president with suspicion. But various critics and politicos also thought that Kennedy should increase the size of the ARVN and CG and unleash American military personnel in Vietnam as well.[41] Service officials, it seems, were

38. Lemnitzer to JCS, 6 May 1961, *FRUS*, ibid., 126.
39. McGarr to Felt, 10 May 1961, ibid., 129.
40. Kahin, *Intervention*, 129.
41. See "Draft Notes of First Meeting of the Presidential Task Force on Vietnam, the Pentagon, 24 April 1961," *FRUS, Vietnam, 1961*, 77–80; "A Program of Action to

thus hedging their bets on Vietnam. Lemnitzer, McGarr, and others, though worried about expanding the war, were not considering bolting from Vietnam and they also recognized that the president had attached the greatest importance to success against communism there. So, as the debate over Vietnam in May would show, the military was not clamoring for combat, but would follow Kennedy's lead in order to make the White House accountable for any commitment to Indochina.

The Washington policy debate over Vietnam in May 1961 offers a fascinating picture of the decision-making process and an effective counterargument to those who contend that the military coerced the president into war. Most works point out that the JCS urged Kennedy to deploy troops to rescue Diem at this point, thereby setting into motion the interventionist U.S. approach to Vietnam.[42] Recognizing Kennedy's political will, the chiefs did urge the dispatch of U.S. troops to Vietnam, but simultaneously continued to point out flaws in Diem's government and army, to admit the VC's increasing infiltration into the south and their inability to stem it, to show a grasp of the political implications of Caucasian interference in Indochinese affairs, and to cite the possibility of PRC intervention in response to a large American presence in Southeast Asia. The military, politically minded and still trying to pin down Kennedy on the nature of the commitment he envisioned, was clear on the significant task ahead of it in Vietnam, and not unduly optimistic about its future there. In fact, about half of the MAAG officers in Vietnam were pessimistic about the future and believed that Diem would have to be ousted if the RVN was to achieve the political stability needed to challenge the VC.[43]

Prevent Communist Domination of South Vietnam," 1 May 1961, *FRUS*, *Vietnam*, *1961*, 93–115 and at VN C.F., NSF, box 193, folders: Vietnam, 4/25/61–4/31/61 and Vietnam, 5/1/61–5/2/61, JFKL.

42. See, inter alia, Kahin, *Intervention*, 132; Krepinevich, *The Army and Vietnam*, 58–9; CRS, *Government and Vietnam War*, 39–40.

43. Trapnell in "Summary Report of Laos-Viet-Nam Task Force Meeting of March 27, 1961," VN C.F., NSF, box 193, folder: Vietnam 1/61–3/61, JFKL.
    At the same time, Theodore Sorensen, a trusted presidential advisor, stressed the need for social, economic, and political reform and wondered "whether [deploying U.S.] forces in Viet-Nam (shaky) and Thailand (doubtful regime) [will] commit [the] U.S. to areas we might otherwise regard as no better a place to fight than Laos." Untitled, handwritten note, presumably from Sorensen, 27 April 1961, Theodore Sorensen Papers, box 55, folder: Vietnam 1954, 4/27/61, JFKL; see also Durbrow telegram to Secretary of State, 12 April 1961, VN C.F., NSF, box 193, JFKL.

Robert W. Komer, a CI advocate on the NSC staff, further complained that "the average MAAG officer is simply not suited for the type of war we're going to have to fight (Lansdale is well aware of this)."[44] Military plans for Indochina, he added, seemed to rely on "forces too large and unwieldy for early action" because the purpose of deploying U.S. troops "is *not* to fight guerrillas." Accordingly, Komer was "not convinced" that Kennedy should send forces to Vietnam, though some type of U.S. military "presence" would be needed.[45] Dean Rusk also opposed the use of combat troops in Vietnam at that time, urging both intermittent increases in the MAAG to avoid attention on America's moves and further study of the troop question.[46]

Before considering the troop issue, then, Kennedy's advisors were noncommittal at best about the future U.S. role in Vietnam. At the 4 May meeting of the Presidential Task Force on Vietnam, however, Deputy Defense Secretary Roswell L. Gilpatric directly posed the troops question with JCS representative General Charles Bonesteel, III, who admitted that the chiefs had assessed possible deployments to Laos, but "not specifically" to Vietnam.[47] Responding to a question from Ambassador to Thailand Kenneth T. Young on the U.S. ability to choke off Communist infiltration, Bonesteel doubted that the Vietnamese or American military could seal off a 1,500-mile-long border. In turn, Young wondered why the United States was pouring hundreds of millions of dollars into Vietnam if it could not accomplish the fundamental task of keeping the VC out of the south. Young's criticism then gave the general an opening to call again on the president to determine the U.S. role in Vietnam. To Bonesteel, the "central point" was to discover "how

---

44. Komer added that the White House would have to create a viable political system in the south to avoid a situation like that in Korea, where, eight years after that war ended, the United States was still trying to develop a stable political system in the south. Komer memorandum to Rostow, 28 April 1961, "Comments on Program of Action for Vietnam," VN C.F., NSF, box 193, JFKL.
45. Komer to M. Bundy and Rostow, 4 May 1961, VN C.F., NSF, box 193, folder: Vietnam 5/3/61–5/7/61, JFKL, and in *FRUS, Vietnam, 1961,* 123.
46. Robert Levy, JCS Representative, Memorandum for the Record, 5 May 1961, HCAS, *USVN Relations,* book 11, 67–8.
47. General Bonesteel was one of the more respected members of the military establishment in 1961. A Rhodes scholar, Bonesteel served as a key advisor to Assistant Secretary of War John McCloy after World War II and was relied upon heavily for advice on German matters by Secretary of War Robert Patterson in the late 1940s. Leffler, *Preponderance of Power,* 29, 118, 152.

seriously are we to take the objective" of the task force report, namely preventing a Communist takeover in the south. "If we are to take this seriously," he observed candidly, "we should recognize that it posed a major requirement for very sizeable force commitments." The JCS thus needed a statement of "real national intent" before developing any troop proposals.[48]

Bonesteel thus had made it explicit that the JCS would be following Kennedy's lead, not pushing the president to intervene. It is also possible that the military never wanted to place combat troops into Vietnam and, to avoid another Cuban-type episode, made clear its reservations up front with the expectation that the president would have to seek an alternative to American war there and thus absolve the services for any unpopular decisions on Indochina in the future. The White House, however, still, and perhaps contradictorily, hoped to achieve anti-Communist success while limiting its commitment to the RVN. In National Security Action Memorandum (NSAM) 52, drafted on 6 May and authorized five days later, the president augmented the MAAG's training mission and increased funding for the RVNAF. If needed, the White House was also prepared to send "task forces" of engineer, medical, and health units both to help the Vietnamese fight against the VC and to improve their lives, and as a symbol of America's "willingness" to defend the RVN.[49]

The JCS now wanted to do more. "Assuming that the political decision is to hold Southeast Asia outside the Communist sphere," the chiefs maintained, "U.S. forces should be deployed immediately to South Vietnam." Such a commitment, military leaders hoped, would preempt the need for more combat troops later by deterring the DRVN or PRC from intervening in Vietnam, releasing the ARVN from static defense positions to conduct CI operations, increasing the American training function, providing a nucleus if the war did spread, and indicating America's anti-Communist resolve

---

48. Even Walt Rostow, whose hawkishness on Vietnam would be unparalleled in time, cautiously noted that "we must be honest in assessing the ability of U.S. military power to be effectively employed against the VC." Draft Memorandum of Conversation of Second Meeting of the Presidential Task Force on Vietnam, 4 May 1961, *FRUS,* Vietnam, 1961, 115–23.
49. NSAM 52 Draft, 6 May 1961, NSF, Meetings and Memoranda, boxes 328–30, folder: NSAM 52, Vietnam, JFKL; NSAM 52 Final Copy, 11 May 1961, HCAS, *USVN Relations,* book 11, 136–54.

throughout Asia. Accordingly, the chiefs recommended that McNamara urge Diem to request American forces during his up-coming visit with Vice-President Lyndon B. Johnson in Saigon.[50]

Diem, and Ambassador Nolting, however, feared that a larger U.S. military presence would revive anticolonial, and thus anti-Diem, sentiment, and so they were not receptive to the vice-president's offer of troops and a bilateral defense treaty. Upon his return to Washington, Johnson informed the president of Diem's rejection and assumed that the troop issue was resolved. But that view, as the *Pentagon Papers* analysts pointed out, was "not very emphatically passed on [by Kennedy] to subordinate members of the Administration," most likely because the president himself wanted to keep the option of deploying forces to Vietnam alive. Accordingly, both Lansdale and McGarr, among others, continued to look for ways to get Diem to accept more American military personnel.[51]

Admiral Felt, however, "strongly opposed" U.S. troop deploy-ments, especially because he feared that American forces would usurp Vietnamese responsibilities and that, in the absence of any DRVN intervention in the south, the United States would be seen as the aggressor in the war. Felt also pinpointed the dilemma that Kennedy and the military had created. Limited war in Vietnam "would commit the U.S. to another Korea-type support and as-sistance situation." Once American forces intervened, "we can't pull out at will without damaging repercussions." The admiral's policy, as one of his staff officers explained, was to "help the Viet-namese get organized, get trained, [be] given the military equipment to fight their own war, but to keep U.S. troops out of that country."[52]

50. JCS memorandum to Secretary of Defense, 10 May 1961, RG 218, CCS 9155.3/9108, Vietnam (27 April 1961), section 3, part 1; *Pentagon Papers: Gravel*, 2:48–9, 65–6; JCS to CINCPAC, 11 May 1961, John Newman Papers, JFKL. The John Newman Papers is a collection of the documents which Newman used in writing *JFK and Vietnam*. It had just arrived at the JFK Library when I worked there in July 1992 and had yet to be processed. At the time the documents were organized chronologically in large binders, so my citations will list the document and date.

51. *Pentagon Papers: Gravel*, 2:55–9; Lansdale memorandum for Gilpatric, 18 May 1961, "U.S. Combat Forces for Vietnam," HCAS, *USVN Relations*, book 11, 157–8; Nolting telegram to Rusk, 18 May 1961, VN C.F., NSF, box 193, JFKL; Kahin, *Intervention*, 132–3.

52. Felt was also opposed to the JCS call for troops because many units would be transferred from CINCPAC to the MAAG, so he argued that "there is not sufficient justification to

Although Felt was an outspoken opponent of an American troop commitment to Vietnam, his views in some ways represented mainstream military thought. Military critics, along with doubters like Felt and McGarr, continued to decry conditions inside Vietnam, recognize the enemy's strength and potential, and firmly warn against deploying U.S. combat troops to Indochina. Recognizing Kennedy's wishes, however, they also expected the United States to "support the entire effort" to save Diem's state "in money, equipment and supplies."[53] Diem himself, who had not been responsive to Johnson's offer a month earlier, now wanted increased assistance, asking Kennedy on 9 June to subsidize a 100,000-man expansion in his armed forces, up to 270,000.[54]

American officials had recognized the RVN leader's shortcomings but had also made clear the U.S. commitment to Vietnam, and so Diem's request put the administration on the spot for a decision. As Lyndon Johnson, who had called Diem "the Winston Churchill of Southeast Asia" during his visit in May, told an associate "shit, man, he's the only boy we got out there." Though not as blunt as the vice-president, Walt Rostow was "distinctly uneasy about . . . Viet-Nam and the grasp of our men there upon it," and he thus urged the president to send Taylor to Indochina to study the Diem troop request.[55] The general did not tour Vietnam at this time, but did recommend that Kennedy consider a 30,000-troop increase in the RVNAF, to 200,000, while studying the issue further.[56] Roswell Gilpatric agreed with Taylor's 30,000-force proposal, but Rostow, more tentative on Vietnam than would be expected, thought that

tie up forces which are now assigned to me." Felt and Rear Admiral Henry L. Miller, in Marolda and Fitzgerald, *U.S. Navy and Vietnam*, 104–9.

53. "MAAG Response to Vice President Johnson's Request for a Statement of the Requirements to Save Vietnam from Communist Aggression," May 1961, John Newman Papers, JFKL.

54. Diem to Kennedy, 9 June 1961, HCAS, *USVN Relations*, book 11, 167–73; Taylor, *Swords and Plowshares*, 220.

55. Johnson in Halberstam, *Best and Brightest*, 167; Rostow to the President, 21 June 1961, "Next Steps in Viet-Nam," VN C.F., NSF, box 193, folder: Vietnam, 6/19/61–6/30/61, JFKL; Editorial Note, *FRUS*, Vietnam, 1961, 185.

56. Taylor to Kennedy, 29 June 1961, "Reply to Diem's Request for a 100,000 Man Increase in the Army of Viet-Nam," VN C.F., NSF, box 193, folder: Vietnam, 6/19/61–6/30/61, JFKL.

the MAAG recommendation for 100,000 additional troops in the RVN "sounds like desperation."[57]

Again facing an ambivalent response on Vietnam from his advisors, Kennedy asked for further study of the issue. At this point Maxwell Taylor, whom the president had appointed as the White House military representative on 1 July and who would become, in General Shoup's words, "the military part of . . . Kennedy's mind," began to play a primary role in Vietnam policy.[58] Looking to "limit . . . U.S. troop participation" in Southeast Asia while native forces conducted operations, Taylor immediately criticized SEATO planning that would rely on outside forces to defend the RVN.[59] As other critics and politicos had done over the preceding months, the general also pointed out that it was difficult to consider future moves in Vietnam without a statement of the U.S. objectives and military mission in Vietnam.[60]

Indeed, officers with differing views on Vietnam – including Felt, McGarr, and the Joint Chiefs – all seemed troubled by the idea of funding another 100,000 soldiers for Diem, especially when 90 percent of the RVN's forces were used mainly to prop up the Ngo regime. Such a measure, they feared, could entangle the United States more deeply in the war in Vietnam. As General Phillip Davidson, later U.S. intelligence chief in Vietnam, observed, the "truth is that in this summer of 1961, nobody in Washington or Saigon seems to have thought seriously of using American troops to *fight* the Viet Cong." U.S. personnel, "if brought in at all," would train or relieve the RVNAF from passive security duties.[61]

57. Gilpatric to Rusk, 3 July 1961, *FRUS,* Vietnam, 1961, 197–8; Sterling Cottrell, Director of Vietnam Task Force, to Walter McConaughey, 8 July 1961, "Vietnam," ibid., 202 and in VN C.F., NSF, box 193, JFKL.
58. Memorandum of Conversation with General Clifton, by Bromley Smith, 3 July 1961, VN C.F., NSF, box 193, folder: 7/1/61–7/4/61, JFKL; Taylor, *Swords and Plowshares,* 197; Shoup Oral History, JFKL, 28.
59. U. Alexis Johnson to Rostow, 8 July 1961, NSF, Regional Security, SEA, box 231, folder: SEA, General, 6/1/61–7/20/61, JFKL; on SEATO's plans for Vietnam, see *FRUS,* Vietnam, 1961, 243[n3], 331.
60. "General Taylor's Suggestions for Pentagon Planning – Accepted by General Lemnitzer," 15 July 1961, NSF, Regional Security, SEA, box 231, folder: SEA, General, 6/1/61–7/20/61, JFKL.
61. On the military's response to the troop request, see Lansdale to Taylor, 21 July 1961, "Vietnam Force Increase," *FRUS,* Vietnam, 1961, 237–8; Col. Edwin F. Black to Ros-

The president, however, was more intensely committed to supporting the RVN than was the military, especially after Nikita Khrushchev had seemed so intransigent on the Berlin issue at Geneva in June. "That son of a bitch won't pay any attention to words," Kennedy remarked about the Soviet leader, "he has to see you move." "Now we have a problem in making our power credible," he then told *New York Times* reporter Scotty Reston, "and Vietnam looks like the place" to correct it.[62] Accordingly, the White House authorized the 30,000-troop increase for Diem and instructed military and diplomatic advisors to develop an overall strategic plan to control the subversion in southern Vietnam.[63] With the military's reluctance to enter combat well established but with his credibility on the line after the Bay of Pigs, the Laos settlement, and the Khrushchev meeting, Kennedy had to deal with competing interests regarding Vietnam. Ultimately, the president would decide to seek victory despite his access to candid evaluations of the situation in Vietnam, first by expanding his support of the Diem regime and, when that failed, by effectively Americanizing the war in 1962.

Various appraisals of the war in mid-1961 gave Kennedy clear proof of the parlous situation facing the United States in Indochina. Taylor found VC infiltration up by 300 percent since 1960, and the embassy called the Communist insurgents "the most powerful guerrilla force in the world" and expected them to begin to target American military personnel.[64] Given its size and disposition of forces in the RVN, plus PAVN support in the north, McGarr

tow, 27 July 1961, "The Situation in South Vietnam," VN C.F., NSF, box 193, folder: Vietnam, 7/27/61–7/31/61, JFKL, and in *FRUS, Vietnam, 1961,* 244–5; Lemnitzer to McNamara, 3 August 1961, ibid., 258; Lemnitzer to McNamara, 18 August 1961, HCAS, *USVN Relations,* book 11, 239–40. Phillip Davidson, *Vietnam at War: The History, 1946–1975* (New York, 1991), 293.

62. Kennedy in Schlesinger, *Thousand Days,* 391; in CRS, *Government and Vietnam War,* 48.
63. NSAM 65, 11 August 1961, "Joint Program of Action with the Government of Viet-Nam," HCAS, *USVN Relations,* book 11, 241–2; see also Nolting to Rusk, 8 August 1961, VN C.F., NSF, box 194, JFKL.
64. Taylor to Kennedy, 18 September 1961, *FRUS, Vietnam, 1961,* 304–5. See also Cottrell to Rusk, 1 September 1961, "Internal Security in Viet-Nam, January–June 1961 (Precis of Saigon's D-83 of August 22, 1961)," VN C.F., NSF, box 194, folder: Vietnam, 9/61, JFKL; Nolting to Rusk, 12 June 1961, VN C.F., NSF, box 193, folder: Vietnam, 6/3/61–6/8/61, JFKL; Robert Johnson to Rostow, 14 June 1961, "Recent Indications of Possible VC Attacks on American Personnel," ibid., folder: Vietnam, 6/13/61–6/19/61.

warned that the VC was capable of conducting both clandestine operations in the RVN as well as large-scale attacks "at times and places of his choosing."[65] In late September the VC did just that, assaulting ARVN posts at Quang Nam, Quang Ngai, and Da Nang. McGarr saw those actions in the 1st Corps Tactical Zone (CTZ, or I Corps), coupled with impressive enemy progress in II and III Corps, as the opening blows in an expanded VC campaign in the south.[66] Military critics not only recognized the VC's strengths, but were aware of the RVNAF's deficiencies as well. A U.S. Army study of the ARVN revealed the same major weaknesses that had been evident for years already, including inexperienced leadership, excessive politicization, inadequate logistics and technical support, poor morale, and combat ineffectiveness.[67] McGarr, in an otherwise upbeat report, further scored the ARVN's counterinsurgency performance in mid-1961 because it did not integrate political, social, economic, and psychological measures. "Permanent pacification . . . can never be accomplished by military sweeps . . . alone," the MAAG chair stressed.[68]

Colonel Robert Levy, a JCS staffer who had just returned from Vietnam, had a more grim assessment. In addition to the VC's

65. The enemy, the MAAG chair reported, had over thirty battalions, sixty-three company-type units, and ten thousand additional political and support personnel dispersed throughout the south. McGarr to Felt, 1 September 1961, "First Twelve Month Report of Chief MAAG, Vietnam," VN C.F., NSF, box 194, folder: McGarr Information Folder for Rostow, 10/28/61, JFKL; McGarr to Felt, 10 September 1961, *FRUS, Vietnam, 1961*, 296–8; McGarr to Felt, 25 September 1961, NSF, VN C.F., box 194, folder: 9/61, JFKL.
66. McGarr to Felt, 21 September 1961, VN C.F., NSF, box 194, folder: 9/61, JFKL, and in *DDRS,* R, 74B; see also SNIE 53-2-61, 5 October 1961, HCAS, *USVN Relations,* book 11, 291–4. William Jorden of the Policy Planning Staff in the State Department also warned fellow policy makers that "we delude ourselves" by assuming that the VC effort in the south primarily involved the movement of units across borders. The enemy was relying heavily on local recruiting for the bulk of its organization, and it was increasing infiltration at the same time. Jorden to Taylor, 27 September 1961, *FRUS, Vietnam, 1961,* 310–14. For purposes of military command and organization Vietnam was divided into four Corps Tactical Zones moving north to south. I Corps was northernmost, beginning right below the DMZ; II Corps was below that, encompassing the vast central highlands; III Corps included the Saigon area; and IV Corps was southernmost, in the Mekong delta area.
67. Chief of Staff, U.S. Army, Report, 1 July 1961, "Order of Battle Summary – Vietnam (South)," VN C.F., NSF, box 193, folder: Vietnam, 7/1/61–7/4/61, JFKL; see also Major Millett's views in Robert Johnson to Rostow, 7 July 1961, "Meeting of Task Force on Viet Nam on July 5, 1961," ibid., folder: Vietnam, 7/5/61–7/13/61.
68. McGarr to Nolting, 13 July 1961, VN C.F., NSF, box 193, JFKL, and *DDRS,* R, 73D.

growing prowess, Levy warned that Diem did not trust his Air Force leaders and that there was poor coordination among the various RVNAF services. Though hopeful that U.S. forces could "lick the Viet Cong problem" if given time, he feared that, if the rebels conducted a full-scale guerrilla effort, "Viet Nam will not be able to manage the problem." Despite such obvious problems, Levy lamented, the RVN had so far failed to appreciate its situation and had not developed an overall plan to deal with the insurgency.[69] Colonel Wilbur Wilson, the senior U.S. Army advisor in II Corps, added that a good many of the ARVN's already "dangerously low" infantry units had suffered so many casualties in September that they were less than 50 percent combat-effective.[70]

So it was amid an increasingly grave situation that the White House developed its plans for Vietnam. The lack of planning before that point indicated both the military's relative indifference toward Vietnam and the obstacles Kennedy would face as he sought victory there. The president himself already recognized the reluctance "of many distinguished military leaders to see any direct involvement of U.S. troops in that part of the world," but asked for military preparations for Vietnam nonetheless.[71] Taylor agreed on the need to develop an overall response to communism in Southeast Asia, but "was not convinced" that "a truly feasible military plan" existed.[72] The JCS too sensed the urgency of the situation in the RVN but its response offered little that was new. As Lemnitzer explained, the chiefs' planning would seek "to minimize U.S. military involvement" while requiring "a maximum effort from the indigenous forces." Short of a DRVN attack across the seventeenth parallel, American forces would just serve as trainers and act as an emergency reserve. Native soldiers would have to contain the principal problem, VC infiltration, "without any significant involvement of American troops," because that was likely to generate PRC inter-

69. Robert Johnson to Rostow, 22 September 1961, "Meeting of the Viet Nam Task Force on Wednesday, September 20, 1961," VN C.F., NSF, box 194, folder: 9/61, JFKL.
70. Wilson to General Dinh, CG, II Corps, 25 September 1961, "Strength of Infantry Units," Wilbur Wilson Papers, 1961 Memoranda to CG II Corps, MHI.
71. M. Bundy Memorandum of a Discussion, the White House, 28 July 1961, *FRUS, Vietnam, 1961*, 252–4.
72. Taylor to Kennedy, 11 August 1961, "Military Plan for Southeast Asia," NSF, Regional Security, SEA, box 231A, JFKL.

vention in return.[73] From the Pacific, Admiral Felt again stressed his opposition to any U.S. troop introduction into Indochina. A naval blockade, which some officers advocated to reduce infiltration, would be a "belligerent act," as the CINCPAC saw it, so the "best course" was still to develop the RVNAF's capabilities to defend its own country.[74] The courses advocated by Taylor, the JCS, and Felt would all take time, however, and other U.S. officials were pressing Kennedy for immediate action. At the very time that the JCS chair sought to "minimize" U.S. involvement, the chiefs also contended that the "time is now past when actions short of [outside] intervention . . . could reverse the rapidly worsening situation." Nolting, expecting the VC to attempt a final drive on the RVN in the near future, warned Washington that "if [the] situation substantially worsens" in Vietnam, the United States "will be faced with the alternatives of sending . . . forces into SVN or backing down." Deterioration on the battlefield and poor morale throughout the south, the State Department agreed, required "emergency actions within 30 days." Accordingly, the White House stepped up its training role and increased aid deliveries to the south.[75]

The military's approach to Vietnam at this point seemed quite inchoate, if not cynical. While assuming that the southern Vietnamese, not Americans, would actually fight the VC, the chiefs also urged the White House to avoid undue preoccupation with the Berlin crisis because Southeast Asia was "now critical from a military viewpoint." As a result, the president should consider "additional mobilization to maintain our strategic reserve," a dramatic gesture with political risks for Kennedy that could not have escaped the chiefs.[76] Only days later, however, the JCS tempered its views again, dismissing a Rostow proposal for a SEATO army of 25,000 troops to prevent infiltration along the Vietnam–Laos border be-

---

73. Taylor to Kennedy, 12 August 1961, "Meeting on Southeast Asia, August 11, 1961," NSF, Regional Security, SEA, box 231A, JFKL.
74. Marolda and Fitzgerald, *U.S. Navy and Vietnam,* 119–20.
75. Nolting to State Department, 18 September 1961, *FRUS,* Vietnam, 1961, 301–4; Chester Bowles, Undersecretary of State, to Embassy, Vietnam, 22 September 1961, ibid., 306–8.
76. JCSM 704–61, 5 October 1961, "Planning for Southeast Asia," HCAS, *USVN Relations,* book 11, 295–6. On Berlin, see Frank Costigliola, "The Pursuit of Atlantic Community: Nuclear Arms, Dollars, and Berlin," in Paterson, *Kennedy's Quest for Victory,* 24–56.

tween the demilitarized zone (DMZ) and Cambodia. Such a patrol would be vulnerable to DRVN or PRC assault, difficult to supply, thinly spread across several hundred miles, and would "be attacked piecemeal or by-passed at the Viet Cong's own choice." The JCS, while rejecting alternative plans to put in troops along the seventeenth parallel itself, did, however, recommend the establishment of a 20,000-man force in the central highlands, even though it would create a "substantial" risk of intervention by Ho or Mao. The Soviet Union, the chiefs also recognized, could stage diversionary operations in Berlin, Korea, or Iran to counter U.S. moves in Southeast Asia.[77]

Nonetheless, William Bundy, deputy assistant secretary of defense for international security affairs, and Rostow believed that "it *is* really now or never" to stop the VC. Nolting sent along more bad news about the enemy's success and ally's deficiencies and added that "we badly need official guidance on Washington['s] thinking re[garding] sending US forces to SVN."[78] Although aware of the White House's resolve to win in Vietnam, the president's advisors had sent mixed signals regarding America's policy and prospects there. Thus Kennedy, on 11 October, announced that General Taylor and Rostow would head a mission to Vietnam to evaluate the war and consider the feasibility of U.S. military intervention or "other alternatives in lieu of" combat forces.[79] Kennedy assumed that the "initial responsibility" for the war rested with "the people and government" of Vietnam. Taylor apparently took those views seriously, noting that the U.S. force structure was not sufficient to both meet its obligations in NATO and Berlin and also implement military plans for Vietnam. He then placed the burden

77. JCS to Taylor, 9 October 1961, "JCS Study of Operations in South Vietnam," VN C.F., NSF, box 194, folder: Vietnam, 10/4/61–10/9/61, JFKL; JCSM 716–61, 9 October 1961, "Concept of Use of SEATO Forces in Southeast Asia," HCAS, *USVN Relations*, book 11, 297–9, and *Pentagon Papers: Gravel*, 2:73–9; see also Paper Presented by Vietnam Task Force, "Concept for Intervention in Viet-Nam," 11 October 1961, VN C.F., NSF, box 194, folder: Vietnam 10/1/61–10/3/61, JFKL, and *FRUS*, Vietnam, 1961, 340–2.
78. Bundy to McNamara, 10 October 1961, "Viet-Nam," HCAS, *USVN Relations*, Book 11, 312; Nolting to Rusk, 9 and 10 October 1961, VN C.F., NSF, box 194, folder: Vietnam 10/4/61–10/9/61, and 10/10/61–10/11/61, JFKL.
79. *Pentagon Papers: Gravel*, 2:79–80; Lemnitzer to Felt, 13 October 1961, *FRUS*, Vietnam, 1961, 362–3.

of decision on Kennedy's shoulders. "The capital question," as the general saw it, "is whether additional forces should be mobilized now or the limitation of our military capabilities in Southeast Asia accepted as a permanent fact."[80]

The White House and military, it seems, were maneuvering to force each other into accountability for Vietnam. In spite of his fervent commitment to save Diem, the president, aware of the military perils of war in Vietnam, called on the feeble RVNAF rather than U.S. troops to stop the enemy. For its part, the armed forces frankly pointed out America's questionable ability to affect the deterioration in the south but also called for intervention in concert with Kennedy's political goals. This much was clear even before Taylor left for Vietnam. Just below the surface of Vietnam policy making, however, the specter of civil–military contention was growing larger.

In a thorough and incredibly candid analysis of the political and military factors that were conditioning U.S. policy in Indochina, McGarr revealed that the type of political acridity so evident during the New Look era and Bay of Pigs tangle was also characterizing and dragging down the American experience in Vietnam. The MAAG chief, moving beyond the usual military behavior of accepting the assumptions of policy and trying to find practical solutions to them, even if disagreeing with civilian decisions, actually questioned the assumptions driving the U.S. role in Indochina not only from a military perspective but from a political viewpoint as well. To McGarr, it was clear that the military was at odds with the State Department, embassy, and Vietnam Task Force appraisals and recommendations for Vietnam. Their reports of deterioration in the south and the urgent need for action from Washington, McGarr wrote to Lemnitzer, were "written primarily for high level civilian consumption to cover [the] State Department with paper in the eventuality that the situation here goes from bad to worse." Recent bleak reports had merely "point[ed] up dangers . . . of which we were already well aware and previously reported." Diplomatic offi-

---

80. Kennedy to Taylor, 13 October 1961, HCAS, *USVN Relations*, book 11, 327; Taylor to Kennedy, 11 October 1961, "Discussion of Southeast Asia Planning," *FRUS, Vietnam, 1961*, 336–7.

cials, McGarr complained, had only just started "reading their mail" and learning the details of the war.[81]

Clearly McGarr feared that the civilian establishment would try an end run around the military in Saigon so, "for the protection of the Armed Forces of the United States and specifically the Army which runs MAAG Vietnam," he wanted Lemnitzer to see his unfiltered judgment of the "presently worsening situation here." State Department officials, McGarr believed, were overlooking past mistakes and "basic differences of opinion between them and the military" in Vietnam. Both Foggy Bottom and the embassy, he added, had ignored or opposed the need to build up the ARVN and develop the CIP, and it was only "Kennedy's pronouncements on Vietnam as well as Vice-President Johnson's visit here, not to mention increasing Viet Cong pressure, [that] made [the RVNAF increase] imperative." Worse, the RVN's leaders, also bypassing reluctant U.S. military officials, now "feel they can get anything they want, regardless of MAAG recommendations, by going through the Ambassador to top American levels." While McGarr was not as pessimistic as he had a right to be, he did see a "slimmer and slimmer" chance to "pull this one out of the fire." Aware of the political factors involved in developing Vietnam policy, the MAAG chief concluded with striking honesty that "as I am jealous of the professional good name of our Army, I do not wish it to be placed in the position of fighting a losing battle and being charged with the loss."[82]

McGarr's views may be as close as one comes to finding a "smoking gun" on the politics of Vietnam in the Kennedy years. In his report the MAAG chief had crystallized the major factors that were dooming the U.S. experience in Vietnam. Not only clearly recognizable battlefield deterioration – caused principally by an imposing enemy as well as a deficient ally – but, just as important, domestic political brawls would make it virtually impossible for America to meet its objectives in Vietnam. It was against this backdrop that

81. McGarr to Lemnitzer, 12 October 1961, *FRUS,* Vietnam, 1961, 347–59. McGarr was referring to Joint State-Defense Message 337, 22 September 1961, ibid., 306–8.
82. See sources in previous note. Ironically, McGarr has been essentially ignored in all major works on Vietnam, but, with the publication of the *FRUS* volumes on Vietnam, the MAAG chief's insight and worries about the war are clear.

Taylor toured Vietnam and Kennedy committed U.S. soldiers and treasure to an impending disaster in Vietnam. Exacerbating such politicomilitary tension, reports out of Vietnam offered a bleak picture as various critics scored the ARVN's loyalty and competence. Although engaged in a guerrilla war, Marine General Victor H. Krulak, a CI expert, lamented that, in both the United States and Vietnam, "nobody knew anything" about counterinsurgency. A Marine major who had just visited Vietnam further told Rostow that about 90 percent of the RVNAF was not even engaged in fighting the VC, its command and control structure was inadequate, and the MAAG had "no sense of urgency," not even putting in a forty-hour workweek. Nonetheless, he believed that the Vietnamese could contain the enemy with just U.S. advisory, logistic, and technical support.[83]

Admiral Felt, the commander with overall responsibility for the area in which any combat would take place, dispelled even that level of optimism. During a Taylor stopover in Hawaii, the CINCPAC again opposed an expanded American commitment to Vietnam in strong terms. The admiral, who had earlier joined McGarr in rejecting the transfer of U.S. jet aircraft to the RVN, offered Taylor a litany of the disadvantages inherent in any combat role in Vietnam. Felt told Kennedy's military representative that using U.S. troops in Indochina would "stir up [a] big fuss throughout Asia about [the] reintroduction of [the] forces of white colonialism" into Vietnam, could provoke intensified Communist aggression, might prompt the NLF to establish an alternative government somewhere in the south, and would lead to a long-term commitment with U.S. soldiers "likely to be forced into varying forms of military engagement with [the] VC." Before deploying combat troops, Felt concluded, the United States should exhaust

---

83. Wilson to McGarr, 18 September 1961, "Anti-Guerrilla School, Army Officers, Vietnam"; Timmes to Wilson, 19 October 1961, "Improved Intelligence"; Wilson to McGarr, 5 October 1961; and Wilson to McGarr, 15 October 1961, "Organizational Requirements for Success in the Conduct of the Pacification Campaign in Vietnam," all in Wilson Papers, 1961 Memoranda to Chief MAAG, Chief Army Section, MHI; Krulak Oral History, 188, MCHC; Commander Worth Bagley, Memorandum for the Record, 12 October 1961, "Conversation with Major Taylor, USMC, in regard to his Views on the Military Situation in South Vietnam," VN C.F., NSF, box 194, folder: Vietnam, 10/12/61–10/15/61, JFKL.

the range of alternatives "which will not kick off war with Communist China."[84]

By October 1961 Kennedy's service leaders were not pressing him into war and, had the president so desired, he could have invoked military criticism of the RVN to back away from a commitment and immunize himself against charges of being soft on communism. Given their reactive approach and reluctance to fight, it is probable that American officers would not have complained so long as the civilian leadership did not try to deflect blame onto them, as had happened after the Bay of Pigs. But after nine months in office with no foreign policy achievements of note and his credibility at stake, Kennedy was committed to firm action to maintain the RVN.[85] Taylor's evaluation, then, reflected both strains in official U.S. thinking on Vietnam. The general, prompted by officers in Saigon, urged the president to deploy troops to Vietnam under the guise of a logistical task force in the Mekong delta, which had been recently ravaged by floods and which was also a VC stronghold. Taylor also recommended that the White House send more aviation and helicopter units to Vietnam, offer more funding to develop CG and SDC forces, and establish a "limited partnership" with Diem by offering more aid in exchange for political reform.[86]

Taylor's interventionist response, however, did not really square with his bleak assessment of the situation in Vietnam, and his reports seemed filled with non sequiturs more than reasoned analysis. The general recognized the VC's buildup and success, the ARVN's command and intelligence inadequacies and passive defense, and the political mess that the Ngos had created. Even more the military representative was aware of the peril involved in sending troops to Vietnam. At home the strategic reserve was too weak to tolerate further depletion to a "peripheral area" where

---

84. Nolting to Rusk, 13 October 1961, VN C.F., NSF, box 194, folder: Vietnam, 10/12/61–10/15/61, JFKL; Felt to JCS, 20 October 1961, ibid., folder: Vietnam, 10/20/61–10/26/61; Felt in HCAS, *USVN Relations,* book 2, IV.B.1, 102, *Pentagon Papers: Gravel,* 2:80–4, and Marolda and Fitzgerald, *U.S. Navy and Vietnam,* 126–8.
85. On the foreign policy setbacks of 1961 and their impact on Kennedy's subsequent actions, see the essays in Paterson, *Kennedy's Quest for Victory.*
86. *Pentagon Papers: Gravel,* 2:88–92, 137; Taylor to Department of State, 25 October 1961, *FRUS,* Vietnam, 1961, 427–9. McGarr initially brought up the flood relief idea to Taylor; see McGarr to Felt, 23 October 1961, ibid., 424–5.

U.S. forces would be "pinned down for an uncertain duration."
Once in Indochina, the American presence would "increase tensions and risk escalation into a major war in Asia." If initial deployments did not produce results, "it will be difficult to resist the
pressure to reinforce" and, should the United States want to eliminate the insurgency in the south, "there is no limit to our possible
commitment," unless Kennedy authorized attacks against Hanoi
itself.[87]

But Taylor also believed that the introduction of a logistics task
force was imperative to reverse the "present downward trend of
events" by boosting Vietnamese morale, improving the ARVN, and
serving as a deterrent to future Communist moves. He also "had no
enthusiasm for the thought of using U.S. Army forces in ground
combat in this guerrilla war" where the large American units would
have to maneuver and fight in a jungle environment. The general
found it "noteworthy," however, that the forces he was proposing
for Indochina would not be charged with clearing VC out of the
south, which would continue to be "the primary task of the
[RVNAF] for which they should be specifically organized, trained,
and stiffened" by U.S. advisors.[88] McGarr and Lansdale also
stressed the need to develop the ARVN's counterinsurgency
capabilities, a job allegedly begun several years earlier. "Just adding
more things, as we are doing at the present," Lansdale lamented,
"doesn't appear to provide the answer that we are seeking."[89]

Many of the president's other advisors, including many civilians,
thought otherwise. McNamara, Rusk, the Bundys, Gilpatric, Rostow, and Komer, as well as the Joint Chiefs, actually wanted to
expand on Taylor's proposal for an 8,000-man flood relief force.
On 1 November Rusk warned against a "major commitment [of]
American prestige to a losing horse." Days later, however, he agreed
with McNamara and the chiefs that Vietnam would not survive
without U.S. troop support on a "substantial scale," that an even-

87. Taylor to Kennedy, 1 November 1961, HCAS, *USVN Relations*, book 11, 337–42;
    Pentagon Papers: Gravel, 2:84–92.
88. See sources cited in previous note; see also Taylor, *Swords and Plowshares*, 238–9, 243;
    Halberstam, *Quagmire*, 69; Kinnard, *Certain Trumpet*, 96–104.
89. Lansdale to Taylor, 23 October 1961, "Unconventional Warfare," and McG. Bundy to
    McNamara, 30 October 1961, both in *FRUS*, Vietnam, 1961, 418–20 and 447–56;
    Currey, *Unquiet American*, 236–9.

tual force of 205,000 with reserve mobilization might be required, and that Kennedy ought to preserve the RVN and commit "whatever . . . combat forces may be necessary to achieve this objective." McGeorge Bundy did not go quite so far. Citing Felt's critical views, he was wary of an expanded commitment but nonetheless urged the president to deploy limited forces, about a division, for military operations, not morale boosting, in the south.[90]

Taylor, however, continued to advance his relatively temperate views. His naval aide, Lieutenant Commander Worth Bagley, again stressed that Taylor designed his troop plans to reassure the south of U.S. resolve, "not . . . to accomplish any positive military task other than . . . self-defense." American forces, Taylor and Bagley added, would not "get mired down in an inconclusive struggle" because they had not envisaged "any positive military objective." The general and his aide nonetheless understood that the Rusk-McNamara call for "substantial forces" indicated that Taylor's "lower-tone approach . . . is not viable."[91]

Taylor in October 1961 might have played the type of critical role Ridgway had during the Dien Bien Phu crisis in May 1954. To be sure, he was as aware of the peril of war in Indochina as was his predecessor as Army chief, yet the White House military representative did not heed his own warnings about intervention. Although recognizing the morass in the RVN and the prospects of initial troop movements into Vietnam snowballing into a large-scale, long-lived commitment, Taylor wanted to send troops camouflaged as flood relief personnel. Perhaps he earnestly wanted to preserve a non-Communist state in an admittedly peripheral area, or he simply lacked the courage to express his convictions forcefully. More likely, however, the politically minded general knew what his patron in the White House wanted to hear and

90. Komer to McG. Bundy, 31 October 1961, "The Risks in Southeast Asia," NSF, Regional Security, SEA, box 231a, JFKL; *Pentagon Papers: Gravel*, 2:104–9; William Bundy Memorandum for the Record, 6 November 1961, McNamara to Kennedy, 5 November 1961, Notes by the Secretary of Defense, 6 November 1961, Rusk to President, 7 November 1961, McNamara to Kennedy, 8 November 1961, all in *FRUS*, Vietnam, 1961, 532–61; Notes of a Meeting, the White House, 11 November 1961, 12:10 P.M., *FRUS*, Vietnam, 1961, 577–8; McG. Bundy to Kennedy, 15 November 1961, Theodore Sorenson Papers, box 55, folder: Vietnam, 5/9/61–10/1/63, JFKL; Kahin, *Intervention*, 134–7.
91. Bagley to Taylor, 7 and 9 November 1961, *FRUS*, Vietnam, 1961, 555–7 and 569–70.

tailored his response accordingly, but with enough reservations to deflect blame if the situation in Vietnam fell apart. George McT. Kahin, whose work on the Vietnam war is unparalleled, is only partly correct in observing that "in sending out his most hawkish advisors, Kennedy presumably expected them to come up with hawkish recommendations, and that is clearly what he got."[92]

Within the Kennedy administration there would be a good many civilians far more hawkish than Taylor, and the president in November did not firmly decide which side he would join. Kennedy thus rejected the McNamara-Rusk-JCS call for a big commitment, Taylor's logistics force, and negotiations based on the 1954 Geneva settlement, as proposed by Ambassador-at-Large Averell Harriman. At a 15 November NSC meeting, the president's angst on the troop issue was noticeable. Unlike Korea in 1950 or Berlin in 1961, enemy action in Vietnam was "more obscure and less flagrant." Kennedy "could even make a rather strong case against intervening in an area 10,000 miles away against 16,000 guerrillas with a native army of 200,000, where millions had been spent for years with no success." Rusk, McNamara, Lemnitzer, and McGeorge Bundy were not so reflective, however, and the president, whose critical ruminations amounted to little more than devil's advocacy, "returned the discussion to the point of what will be done next in Viet Nam rather than whether or not the U.S. would become involved."[93] Although the White House did not send combat troops, Kennedy authorized the transfer of two fully operational helicopter companies to Vietnam, increased the number of U.S. advisors, and allowed Air Force trainers to participate in operations against the VC. By December he had sent about 2,200 "advisors" to the RVN, an increase of nearly 300 percent from January of that year.

---

92. Kahin, *Intervention*, 136.
93. Notes on National Security Council Meeting, Washington, D.C., 15 November 1961, 10 A.M., *FRUS*, Vietnam, 1961, 607–10; see also W. Bundy Memorandum for the Record, 6 November 1961, ibid., 532–4. Marilyn Young asserts that, at the NSC meeting, Kennedy, "facing the full measure of his own doubts, . . . had turned away." I do not believe, however, that those doubts stemmed from Kennedy's personal fear of intervention so much as from the contradictory and often negative reports out of Vietnam. See *Vietnam Wars*, 81. Lawrence Bassett and Stephen Pelz likewise credit the president for backing down in November by telling the chiefs that troops were a "last resort" for Vietnam. "The Failed Search for Victory," 238.

In his first ten months as president, John Kennedy moved Vietnam from a secondary foreign policy consideration to a centerpiece of the cold war. With his credibility on the line after he was unable to displace Castro or prevent Pathet Lao success early on, the president determined that he would confront growing Communist insurgencies in places such as southern Vietnam "regardless of the cost and regardless of the peril." Indeed, "no greater task faces this country or this administration," Kennedy told newspaper editors in April.[94] If the United States did not protect "small and weak" countries such as the RVN and Laos from Communist attack, "the gates will be opened wide" for insurgency elsewhere, he warned.[95] To Maxwell Taylor, the Kennedy commitment to Vietnam was so clear that he did not even consider whether the preservation of the RVN was in the national interest during his October trip. The White House had already decided that it was.[96]

The military, therefore, had to react to Kennedy's policy and approached Vietnam from different, and often contradictory, angles. While accepting the need to develop a capacity for antiguerrilla warfare in the ARVN, U.S. personnel in fact created a conventional army. American officers admitted that they could do little to choke off enemy infiltration, but kept expanding the RVNAF to do that, usually at the expense of village security. Some service leaders – Taylor, Felt, and Shoup, most notably – questioned the expanding American commitment, but most generals simply deferred to the White House. And while virtually every military official of significance rejected any type of U.S. combat role in Vietnam, they declined to press for disengagement, or even a more temperate approach to the war, and thus helped create the conditions that would lead to American intervention. Although aware, as Taylor had warned, that the pressure to reinforce could become irresistible once American personnel were in the country, military officials continued to raise the ante in Vietnam, with American advisors, troops, and treasure as their chips.

94. President Kennedy's Address to American Society of Newspaper Editors, 20 April 1961, *Pentagon Papers: Gravel*, 2:801–2.
95. President Kennedy's Address to the United Nations, 26 September 1963, Statements by President Kennedy on Vietnam, n.d., National Security File, Memos to the President, Walt Whitman Rostow, box 8, folder: volume 6, 11–20 June 1966 [2 of 2], LBJL.
96. Taylor Oral History (2), 4–5, LBJL.

As the policy-making dialectic progressed throughout 1961 it became clear that the president and his defense secretary, among others, were committed to effective action in Vietnam. Kennedy had invested, and lost, a good deal of political capital in the Caribbean, Europe, and Indochina and desperately wanted a cold war victory. U.S. military leaders, however, responded to different factors. Politically hardened after several years of civil–military feuds, the brass wanted to pin down Kennedy on his Vietnam policy and make him responsible for it. At no time before the Taylor mission was there any consensus in the armed forces regarding increased levels of support to the RVNAF or the need for, or desirability of, U.S. military action in Vietnam. In fact, many, maybe most, generals had been shaped by the Eisenhower-era military response to Indochina and thus recognized the dangerous nature of the conflict and wished to avoid combat. And, as McGarr's remarkably insightful October analysis had shown, the military understood the political implications of failure in Indochina as well. But the president's own political considerations fueled policy and a major U.S. role in Vietnam became a fait accompli by the time Kennedy pledged a "sharply increased joint effort" to rescue Diem's state in NSAM 111, which he authorized on 22 November 1961.[97]

Over the course of the following twenty-four months that effort would continue to increase but become even less "joint" as U.S. military personnel took on increasing responsibilities and turned the Vietnamese conflict into an American war. November 1961 may well have been Kennedy's last best chance to avoid intervention, but he instead chose to go to war, with an uncertain future and reluctant military lined up behind him.

97. NSAM 111, 22 November 1961, *FRUS*, Vietnam, 1961, 656–7.

5

The Best and Worst of Times: The U.S. War against Vietnam, October 1961–November 1963

General, I don't think you understand. I didn't come for a briefing. I came to tell you what we have decided.

Alain Enthoven[1]

Having decided to maintain and increase the American commitment to the RVN but defer on combat troop deployments, John Kennedy would spend the next two years of his presidency, and his life, groping for an effective response to the southern rebellion and political turmoil in Saigon. Despite political and military problems recognized by all, the president would authorize an 800 percent increase in U.S. advisors to Vietnam, extend American participation in operations against the VC, begin to consider troop withdrawals because of perceived improvements in the fight against the insurgency, and ultimately help coordinate the overthrow of the Diem government. By November 1963, the United States would be well on its way toward creating and intervening in a major war in Southeast Asia.

At the same time, U.S. military officials would express conflicting views regarding Vietnam policy. Service leaders generally supported the president's expansion of the American role in Vietnam, especially after Kennedy replaced holdover military leaders with his own generals and because of the president's embrace of military Keynesianism, with projected defense budget increases of $17 billion over five years.[2] Optimism grew within military circles with

1. Enthoven, one of McNamara's "whiz kids" and director of Systems Analysis in the Pentagon, to a U.S. general in Germany, in Trewhitt, *McNamara*, 12–13.
2. Campagna, *Economic Consequences of Vietnam*, 7.

General Paul Harkins's arrival in Saigon in 1962, just as U.S. resources were pouring into the RVN and American aircraft appeared to be containing the VC. Even critics of the U.S. role fell in line and supported the growing commitment despite the many problems that remained apparent to them. Indeed, U.S. officers continued to recognize that the VC was stronger and committed to conducting long-term, attritional warfare that could not be defeated with a conventional military response. They continued to lament the incessant political repression and chaos in Saigon, and, in the case of John Paul Vann and others, the politicization and incompetence of the RVNAF. And, whatever their opinion of the wisdom or risks of intervention, virtually every American military official assumed during this period that the United States would not send combat forces into battle in southern Vietnam.

Politics also continued to play a significant part in decision making as military representatives remained suspicious of White House intentions and still hoped to pin down Kennedy regarding his policy for Vietnam. Such political conflict became quite overt as various civilian and service leaders worked together to oust Lionel McGarr as the MAAG chair, thereby invoking the general's warning that the military was going to be blamed for the U.S. failure in Indochina. At the same time, Pentagon civilians began to conduct defense policy more assertively, especially during the Cuban Missile Crisis, which added tension to the already strained relationship between the politicians and the generals.

The U.S. military remained internally divided over Vietnam policy as well. Continuing a trend that would ultimately prove disastrous, American officers engaged in internecine bureaucratic warfare over the organization and mission of any U.S. force that might be committed to Vietnam. While the various services fought over control of the war in Saigon and the type of strategy to be employed against the VC – and ultimately for power and influence at home – U.S. military personnel already in the field in the RVN were seriously divided over whether General Harkins's conventional approach could succeed in a conflict that seemed to demand a counterinsurgency approach. In the end, though, effective anti-guerrilla action would take too long. Heretics like Lionel McGarr and John Vann would be ignored or dismissed. Washington seemed to want a war in Vietnam, and U.S. military officials provided it.

Although Kennedy may have rejected the deployment of combat forces to Vietnam after Taylor's visit, he had not wavered at all in his commitment to the RVN. The president, rejecting calls for negotiations, asserted that "if we postpone action in Vietnam to engage in talks with the Communists, we can surely count on a major crisis of nerve in Viet-Nam and throughout Southeast Asia. The image of U.S. unwillingness to confront Communism – induced by the Laos performance – will be . . . definitely confirmed. There will be panic and disarray." As Kennedy saw it, the stakes in Vietnam were higher than ever. "If we negotiate now – while infiltration continues – we shall in fact be judged weaker than in Laos, for in that case we at least first insisted on a cease-fire."[3] As a result of Kennedy's position, the military would pursue a more activist policy in 1962, and would continue to follow the White House's lead on Vietnam.

But military critics also continued to recognize just how badly conditions in Vietnam had deteriorated. In his year-end report McGarr estimated that VC strength in the south had continued to rise, a trend which, "if continued, can be fatal," and that the enemy now controlled or influenced about 60 percent of the RVN.[4] Worse, the RVN had made "little or no progress in developing an overall plan" for the war. In addition to those problems on the ground, the military understood the constraints to be imposed on U.S. policy. As McNamara explained, the chiefs would have to adjust to a "perennially unclear political framework and to a policy that for overall national reasons sets limits on military action." The defense secretary did, however, reassure them that they would be

3. Kennedy to McNamara and Rusk, 14 November 1961, in Kahin, *Intervention*, 137–9. Kennedy took the language of this memo precisely from a memo Rostow had written to him on the same day, in *FRUS*, Vietnam, 1961, 601–3; see also Kinnard, *Certain Trumpet*, 100–3.
4. MAAG, Vietnam, to JCS, 8 November 1961, "South Vietnam Operations Plan and Border Control Plan," RG 218, JCS 1961, CCS 9155.3/9105 Vietnam (8 November 1961); Outline, Chief MAAG, Vietnam, 1961, *DDRS*, 78, 361B.

given "considerable scope" in conducting military affairs in Vietnam and that the Pentagon was willing to press the White House for more resources as they saw fit.[5]

In mid-December, at a meeting with military leaders in Honolulu, McNamara was more assertive. He informed the generals that the White House had decided to "pursue the Viet Nam affair with vigor and that all reasonable amounts of resources could be placed at the disposal of the commanders in the area."[6] Even so, the consensus at Honolulu was that "there's not likely to be any gimmick which will win the war for us. While air and naval action [can] contribute, it's mainly a ground force problem." McNamara – who lamented that the United States was "stuck" with Diem, should not expect him to reform, and would have to do its best regardless of political chaos in the RVN – also informed the chiefs that Kennedy was still not prepared to send combat forces to Vietnam.[7] Meanwhile, reports from critics in the field continued to emphasize the RVNAF's problems and admit, as Wilbur Wilson wrote to McGarr, that "no significant gains are being made against the Viet Cong."[8]

Such bleak conditions helped create serious impediments to military planning, and by December 1961, the armed forces had yet to develop any strategy for Vietnam. In November, Felt had expressed "a great deal of skepticism" about proceeding into Vietnam without adequate plans, and he charged that "the intent is to develop tactical plans before a sound strategic concept."[9] Felt had indeed touched upon a central dilemma in the U.S. military's approach to Vietnam. After training the ARVN to fight a conventional war

5. McNamara to Felt and McGarr, 28 November 1961, *FRUS, Vietnam,* 1961, 679–80.
6. Notes of Colonel Howard Burris, Vice-President's Military Aide, at 19 December 1961 NSC Meeting, in Editorial Note, *FRUS, Vietnam,* 1961, 746–7.
7. General T. W. Parker, Special Assistant to the Chair, JCS, to Lemnitzer, 18 December 1961, *FRUS, Vietnam,* 1961, 740–1. Like McNamara, John Kenneth Galbraith, U.S. Ambassador to New Delhi, believed that reform was impossible with Diem in charge in the south. But while the defense secretary saw that as requiring more American resolve, Galbraith saw it as proof of the need to disengage from Vietnam. Galbraith to Kennedy, 21 November 1961, HCAS, *USVN Relations,* book 11, 410–18.
8. Wilson to McGarr, 26 December 1961, "Personnel, Intelligence Training, and Operational Matters of Interest, II Corps," Wilson Papers, 1961 Memoranda to CH MAAG, CH USASEC, MHI; Wilson to General Timmes, CH USASEC, 31 December 1961, "Intelligence Mobile Training Team," Wilson Papers, 1961 Memoranda to CG II Corps, MHI.
9. Felt to McGarr, 4 November 1961, RG 218, JCS 1961, CCS 9155.3/9105, Vietnam (8 November 1961).

throughout the late 1950s, the MAAG – a dedicated follower of prevailing fashion – shifted to emphasize counterinsurgency with Kennedy's emergence. But U.S. officials were deeply divided over whether the Americans ought to develop CI capabilities in fact, or continue to fight the kind of wars they had experienced during World War II or in Korea. By late 1961 and early 1962, the military would elect to rely on firepower and attrition to gain victory, while the centerpiece of American CI policy, the Strategic Hamlets program, would become a famous failure.

It seemed clear to many Americans in Vietnam that the ARVN was incapable of quashing the insurgency and a new approach was needed. In Saigon, McGarr was convinced that Diem had to accept the new CI doctrine and reorganize the RVNAF command and control structure.[10] The southern leader, however, feared losing his grip over the ARVN and was wary of such MAAG recommendations. He thus latched onto a proposal developed by a British CI expert, Robert Thompson, who had gained experience in suppressing a Communist rebellion in Malaya, to stop the VC with minimal U.S. military interference. Thompson, unlike most American officers, argued that rural political turmoil, rather than the VC, was the biggest threat to stability in the south. It followed then that Diem ought to provide economic development to outlying areas and provide security with police forces instead of only trying to destroy the enemy.[11]

The Americans reacted to Thompson's proposals sharply. Lemnitzer believed that the Briton's experience in Malaya was not relevant to Vietnam and that the VC insurgency had already developed "far beyond the capability of police controls." The JCS chair was also suspicious of Thompson's motives because of recent "indications that the British, for political reasons, wish to increase their influence in this area and are using the Thompson mission as a vehicle."[12] McGarr likewise scored the Thompson plan for emphasizing security in the densely populated Mekong delta instead of

10. McGarr report, 25 October 1961, *DDRS*, R, 75A.
11. Thompson to Diem, 11 November 1961, HCAS, *USVN Relations*, Book 11, 345–58; *Pentagon Papers: Gravel*, 2:139–43.
12. Lemnitzer to Taylor, 12 October 1961, "Counterinsurgency Operations in South Vietnam," *Pentagon Papers: Gravel*, 2:650–1, and HCAS, *USVN Relations*, book 11, 324–6.

"War Zone D" – a VC stronghold about twenty miles northwest of Saigon, also known as the "Iron Triangle" – and for urging that police rather than military forces provide village security. The MAAG chief, aware that Washington wanted to see results in Vietnam, also charged that it would take too long for Thompson's plan to become effective.[13]

McGarr and Felt, however, agreed with the Thompson group that the situation "is critical, with the peak of the crisis possible at any moment." The CINCPAC again stressed that "an over-all operational plan defining responsibilities, tasks and priorities must be produced."[14] Rather than developing a comprehensive plan, however, Diem and his American patrons hoped that the establishment of Strategic Hamlets – "safe areas" to which peasants would be transferred to deprive the VC of recruits and support – would alter the course of the war.[15] In contrast to the military, the White House saw the program as the "principal operational vehicle" by which the CI doctrine would be "translated into reality." That reality, however, was never achieved and by late 1963 the RVN abandoned the counterproductive Strategic Hamlets program after it had facilitated VC recruitment and done more harm than good for the Vietnamese.[16]

The debate over strategy in general also claimed McGarr as a victim. The MAAG chief from September 1960 to July 1962, McGarr is barely a footnote in most studies on Vietnam, but his outlook on the politics of the war and U.S. prospects in Vietnam is singularly enlightening and essential to understanding Kennedy's policy toward Indochina. As the ranking U.S. officer in Saigon, McGarr understood the politicomilitary morass in Diem's state and his reaction to it offers a clear contrast to the White House's appraisals of Vietnam. Although imbued with what Andrew Krepinevich calls the Army's "Concept" – the traditional reliance on firepower and conventional strategy – McGarr seems to have been among those military leaders who did pay more than lip service to

13. *Pentagon Papers: Gravel*, 2:140–1.
14. Felt to JCS, 5 December 1961, "Activities of the Thompson Group," RG 218, JCS 1961, CCS 9155.3/9105/3360, Vietnam (9 August 1961).
15. Still the best work on rural politics and strategic hamlets is Frances FitzGerald, *Fire in the Lake: The Vietnamese and the Americans in Vietnam* (New York, 1972).
16. *Pentagon Papers: Gravel*, 2:455; FitzGerald, *Fire in the Lake*; Kahin, *Intervention*.

developing capabilities for political warfare and counterinsurgency in the RVN. He also understood the political stakes involved in Vietnam policy making at home.[17] Thus, his virtual ouster as military leader in Vietnam in early 1962, engineered by various U.S. officials, mostly civilian, indicates that CI, although a successful public relations strategy at home with green beret–clad soldiers at the Special Forces school at Fort Bragg, would not be seriously pursued in Vietnam.

Washington had begun to question McGarr's role in Vietnam before the Taylor mission, with Dean Rusk asking Nolting whether he was "the right man for the job" in early October. The ambassador, while admitting that relations between Diem and the MAAG were strained, expressed confidence in the commander but urged Taylor to study the situation while in Saigon.[18] Taylor's views on McGarr were apparent immediately; on 24 October he excluded the MAAG chief from a meeting scheduled with Diem and U.S. representatives.[19] By mid-November, Rusk, McNamara, and McGeorge Bundy were intent on reorganizing the U.S. military in Vietnam to supersede McGarr. Bundy, agreeing with the secretaries of state and defense, urged that a "military man" take over the war in Vietnam, with Nolting as a "complement" but not the "head man" there. McGarr, Bundy observed, "has been inadequate" and must be replaced. Consequently, McNamara instructed the JCS to develop plans for a new command structure in the RVN and to recommend a senior officer to assume control of it.[20]

The chiefs replied that the CINCPAC should run the war, because all of Southeast Asia, not just Vietnam, was at stake. Still trying to pin down the White House and Pentagon, they again

17. There were many more officers who, like McGarr, would stress the need for pacification in the RVN. Among the more notable were John Paul Vann and several Marine leaders who were virtually at war with U.S. commanders Paul Harkins and William Westmoreland throughout the war. For more development of this aspect, see Robert Buzzanco, "Division, Dilemma, Dissent: Military Recognition of the Peril of War in Viet Nam," in Dan Duffy, ed., *Informed Dissent: Three Generals and the Vietnam War* (Chevy Chase, Md.: Vietnam Generation/Burning Cities Press, 1992), 9–37; Sheehan, *A Bright Shining Lie.*
18. Nolting to Department of Defense, 6 October 1961, *FRUS, Vietnam,* 1961, 326–8.
19. McGarr to Lemnitzer, 24 October 1961, *FRUS, Vietnam,* 1961, 425–7. On Taylor's "unfavorable impression" of McGarr, see also Taylor Oral History (2), 14–15, LBJL.
20. McGeorge Bundy to Kennedy, 15 November 1961, *FRUS, Vietnam,* 1961, 605–7; McNamara to Lemnitzer, 13 November 1961, ibid., 589–90.

noted that any changes in the command structure had to be preceded by "clearly defined United States objectives that will be pursued in South Vietnam." Rostow, however, more directly responded to the issue, telling the president that the United States was wasting its money on "choppers and other gadgetry" unless "we . . . get a first class man out there to replace McGarr."[21] Lansdale and Samuel Williams, McGarr's predecessor, also weighed in against the MAAG chief. Although the war had worsened, Lansdale wrote to Williams, "your successor seems to be fighting it with memos," and thus had lost his influence among the RVN's leaders. Williams added that recent rumors had indicated that Kennedy, McNamara, the ARVN's generals, and MAAG officers had all lost confidence in McGarr and someone was needed to "ride herd" on the RVNAF.[22] Rather than focus on the *job* to be done in Vietnam, civilian leaders thought that finding the right *man* for it was the essential ingredient to success.

Under such circumstances, McGarr's days as the military's top man in Vietnam were numbered. Lemnitzer informed him on 23 December that, while the chiefs were "completely satisfied" with his performance, his civilian counterparts in Washington wanted to begin a "new era" in U.S.–RVN relations, which meant establishing a new command structure in Vietnam.[23] The new organization, the U.S. Military Assistance Command, Vietnam (MACV), would stress the role of U.S. assistance rather than advice, as embodied in the MAAG, and would give the American commander in Saigon the "controlling voice" on both U.S. and Vietnamese military matters. McGarr and the MAAG would thus be subordinate to the new four-star commander.[24] Felt and Rusk, however, objected to the JCS reorganization. Both believed that the CINCPAC should coordinate the U.S. military effort for all of Southeast Asia, with Rusk insisting that the ambassador retain overall authority for U.S. activities in the RVN. Thus the Pacific commander of the Navy, the service with the most limited role in Vietnam, would run the war,

21. JCS 2343/46, 22 November 1961, "South Vietnam," RG 218, JCS 1961, CCS 9155.3/9105 Vietnam; Rostow to Kennedy, 6 December 1961, Newman Papers, JFKL.
22. Lansdale to Williams, 28 November 1961, *FRUS,* Vietnam, 1961; 687–9; Williams to Lansdale, 10 December 1961, Lansdale Papers, box 42, folder 1182.
23. Lemnitzer to McGarr, 23 December 1961, *FRUS,* Vietnam, 1961, 758–60.
24. See source in previous note, and McNamara to Rusk, 18 December 1961, ibid., 745.

much to the chagrin of the other branches. Such wrangling over command arrangements would continue to haunt the military throughout the war.[25]

From Saigon, McGarr criticized the new structure and the overall American approach to Vietnam. The MAAG commander, admitting that he was "professionally and personally disappointed," lamented that his "frank periodic reports" had not yet prevented civilian policy makers from trying to solve "a very unconventional situation in a basically conventional manner." The civilian demand for large-scale military success without corresponding political-economic-psychological planning, McGarr charged, had forced the RVNAF to take military action for which it was ill-prepared and which proved counterproductive. The reorganization, he added, gave Diem "virtual veto power over . . . proposed measures required to win." In one of the greater ironies of the war to that point, McGarr, a conventionally trained Army commander, had attacked the Kennedy administration, supposedly imbued with the doctrines of flexible response and counterinsurgency, for ignoring the need to develop the RVNAF's capabilities for antiguerrilla war. "Permanent results require long range coordinated action on all fronts and defeat of insurgencies historically takes years," the MAAG chief reminded Lemnitzer. The emergence and triumph of the MACV over the MAAG, Bruce Palmer later charged, was a major mistake, as it signaled that the United States, in emphasizing its assistance to Saigon, would overlook its primary military mission, namely the development and training of native forces.[26]

If the McGarr coup alone was not indicative of the civilian establishment's preparations to escalate the U.S. commitment in Vietnam, the announcement of the new commander surely was. Although Roger Hilsman and others wanted Kennedy to appoint General William P. Yarborough, head of the Special Forces school, or another officer with CI experience to command the MACV, the president in February 1962 chose Paul D. Harkins, an old tank commander and protégé of Maxwell Taylor and a true believer on

25. George S. Eckhardt, *Command and Control, 1950–1969* (Washington, D.C., 1974), 26–7; Kolko, *Anatomy of a War*, 143–4.
26. McGarr to Lemnitzer, 27 December 1961, *FRUS, Vietnam, 1961*, 765; BDM, *Strategic Lessons*, volume 6, book 1, 2–25 and 2–37, n. 39.

Vietnam.[27] Harkins, an unimaginative but politically connected general, essentially ignored training for CI warfare and adopted a strategy based on the traditional Army concepts, namely attritional warfare designed to destroy the enemy's army. As Harkins envisioned it, the CG and SDC would provide security while the ARVN would smash VC main-force units. The MACV commander, and Taylor, believed that technological superiority could decide the war in America's favor. They especially stressed the U.S. advantage in airmobility, anticipating that the ARVN could call in air support to flush out the VC guerrillas and then destroy them.[28] But the Vietnamese forces, as the military had repeatedly pointed out since the 1950s and as McGarr had just charged, were neither trained for nor competent to assume such tasks.

With Harkins in and counterinsurgency downplayed, the U.S. military began to confront the VC aggressively and progressively Americanize the war. Yet military critics continued to warn of the perils of that approach. Howard Burris, the vice-president's military aide, warned that America could expect huge losses and a ten-year war in Southeast Asia.[29] From Hawaii, the U.S. Army's Pacific Command (USARPAC) added that the NLF could be on the verge of establishing a provisional government in the south and that the Communists could launch "battalion-strength operations anywhere in South Vietnam at times and places of their own choosing."[30] The JCS essentially agreed, admitting that a slight decrease in insurgent activity "in no way indicates a diminishing capability of the VC [to] mount larger scale attacks at any time."[31]

27. Gilpatric Memorandum for the Record of a Meeting with the President, Palm Beach, Fl., 3 January 1962, *FRUS,* Vietnam, 1962 (Washington, D.C., 1991), 3–4; Lemnitzer to Felt, 6 January 1962, ibid., 14–16; Terms of Reference for Senior United States Military Commander in Vietnam, 12 January 1962, ibid., 35–6; Memorandum by Maxwell Taylor, 13 January 1962, ibid., 37.
28. Hilsman, *To Move a Nation,* 426; Bassett and Pelz, "The Failed Search for Victory," 241.
29. Burris to Lyndon Johnson, 16 March 1962, *DDRS,* 78, 456C.
30. USARPAC Intelligence Bulletin, February 1962, Newman Papers, JFKL. John Newman contends that Kennedy had not received information regarding the USARPAC's bleak reports; since they were "unclassified," this seems highly unlikely. Newman, *JFK and Vietnam,* 228.
31. JCS to McNamara, 13 January 1962, JCSM-33–62, RG 218, JCS 1961, 9155.3/9105, Vietnam; JCS to White House for Taylor, 21 January 1962, *DDRS,* R, 76H.

McGarr, still MAAG chief, continued to forward his candid evaluations on the war. Writing to Lyndon Johnson, the MAAG chief rejected the "attractive idea [of] quick and spectacular military victories" that had, unfortunately, gotten the upper hand over a sustained, long-range, realistic approach. While supportive of U.S. aid increases to the RVN, McGarr reminded the vice-president that Diem continued to run the show in the south and could not be relied upon to prosecute the war vigorously. "In providing the GVN [Government of Vietnam, i.e., the RVN] the tools to do the job," the MAAG chief thus warned, "we must not offer so much that they forget that the job of saving the country is theirs – only they can do it."[32] Commandant Shoup also had reservations about the expanding American role in Vietnam, only deploying a helicopter squadron, task unit Shufly, to Soc Trang, eighty-five miles southwest of Saigon at the direction of the JCS.[33]

Perhaps more telling than the views of the USARPAC, McGarr, and Shoup was the report of the JCS's Joint War Games Control Group – which conducted a war game on Vietnam, Sigma I-62, in February. The game pitted officials representing the "Red" (NLF) and "Blue" (U.S.) governments – the RVN was apparently not deemed a necessary participant – and the results could not have been reassuring. The Blue representatives admitted that the NLF had a "tremendous head start" in covert warfare, and that civic action (CI) programs in the south would not show results until the RVN stopped VC infiltration. The simulated U.S. response thus involved a huge commitment, including air strikes against the DRVN and a U.S. Marine attack across the seventeenth parallel. Such a commitment, Blue officials recognized, would prompt PRC intervention and require changing the U.S. political objectives in Vietnam. The Red officers understood that the American team was impatient and would not allow appropriate time for civic action

32. "While the VC retains the capability to launch attacks at the time and place of his choosing," the MAAG chair explained to Felt, "available information indicates [that] acts of terrorism, sabotage and propaganda," which Harkins's strategy would not hamper, "will form the main effort for the VC for the immediate future." McGarr to CINCPAC for Taylor, 6 January 1962, VN C.F., NSF, box 195, folder: Vietnam, 1/6/62–1/12/62, JFKL, and *DDRS*, R, 76E; McGarr to Johnson, 22 February 1962, *DDRS*, 76, 33H.
33. Whitlow, *Marines in Vietnam, 1954–1964*, 57–8.

programs to develop, while the threat of DRVN or Chinese intervention would temper American action. Maybe the situation was best summed up by the game director, who observed that "it appears that Red wanted to win without a war while Blue wanted not to lose also without a war."[34]

Other officials, however, became true believers as U.S. matériel began to pour into the RVN. Beginning in January 1962 the White House had deployed Army helicopter companies, fixed-wing aircraft, a troop carrier squadron with aircraft operating out of southern Vietnam and the Philippines, reconnaissance planes, air control personnel, equipment for crop defoliation, Navy mine sweepers, and more advisors, and it approved the use of napalm against the VC. While thus expanding the American role, the chiefs nevertheless continued to insist that they still planned to build up the RVNAF to fight the war itself, even though they were prepared to request U.S. combat troops if conditions continued to worsen.[35] In early 1962, however, the American helicopters and chemical weapons sent the VC reeling.[36] Both the MACV commander and Nolting agreed that a "spirit of movement" was finally noticeable due to the American military's contributions to the RVN.[37]

Apparently emboldened by such optimism, visiting Attorney General Robert F. Kennedy assured officials in Saigon that "we are going to win in Viet-Nam. We will remain here until we do win."[38] To make certain that his brother's prophecy came true, the president himself directed the Joint Chiefs to develop contingency plans to save the RVN should present efforts prove inadequate.[39] The JCS chair also reaffirmed the American commitment, charging that

34. Sigma I-62 Final Report, 26 February 1962, NSF, Regional Security, SEA, box 232, folder: Southeast Asia . . . War Game, JFKL.
35. Talking paper for Chair, JCS for Meeting with President, 9 January 1962, "Current U.S. Military Actions in South Vietnam," *Pentagon Papers: Gravel*, 2:654–9; on crop warfare, see McGarr to Felt, 3 February 1962, VN C.F., NSF, box 195, folder: Vietnam 2/62, JFKL; on helicopters, see Lemnitzer to Kennedy, 17 February 1962, Newman Papers, JFKL; on possible drawbacks to defoliation, see McGarr to Felt, 3 February 1962, *FRUS*, Vietnam, 1962, 90–2.
36. Hilsman, *To Move a Nation*, 442–4.
37. Memorandum for the Record, 23 February 1962, "Trip to Hawaii – Third Secretary of Defense Conference on Vietnam," Newman Papers, JFKL.
38. *NYT*, 19 February 1962, 1.
39. General Chester V. Clifton, President's Military Aide, to McGeorge Bundy, 29 March 1962, *FRUS*, Vietnam, 1962, 283.

negotiations with Ho, as urged by Ambassador to India John K. Galbraith, would put the United States in the position of reneging on "what is by now a well-known commitment to take a forthright stand against Communism in Southeast Asia." Citing Kennedy's and McNamara's pronouncements on Vietnam, he stressed that America would support Diem and the Vietnamese "to whatever extent may be necessary" to eliminate the VC.[40]

In early 1962 the military had apparently little reason to question such a commitment, in large part because reports on the war from Saigon were becoming more positive. The period between the introduction of American aircraft, napalm, and defoliants into Vietnam and the end of 1962 may have been the military high point of the U.S. war in Vietnam as Harkins's reliance on firepower and technology kept the VC off balance and caused tremendous damage to the insurgency.[41] In fact optimism ran so high that Kennedy, in July 1962, rejected another Harriman proposal for negotiations to establish a coalition government and hold free elections in the south, even though the NLF had agreed to talks. The president feared that Ho's followers would eventually control any state created out of joint talks and, as Lawrence Bassett and Ste-

---

40. Lemnitzer to McNamara, 13 April 1962, JCSM-282–62, *Pentagon Papers: Gravel*, 2:671–2.
41. For sanguine views of the war, see, inter alia, General William Rosson Memorandum for the Record, "Briefing for Mr. William Bundy . . . , 1 March 1962," Newman Papers, JFKL; Hilsman Memorandum for the Record, 19 March 1962, "Visit with General Paul Harkins and Ambassador Nolting – 17 March 1962," Hilsman Papers, box 3, folder 8, JFKL; JCS to CINCPAC, 21 March 1962, Newman Papers, JFKL; Lemnitzer to McNamara, 30 March 1962, VN C.F., NSF, box 196, folder: Vietnam, 3/29/62–3/31/62, JFKL, and in *DDRS*, 76, 331; Hilsman to Taylor, 31 March 1962, Hilsman Papers, box 3, folder 8, JFKL; Lucius D. Battle, Special Assistant Secretary of State, to McG. Bundy, 18 April 1962, "Status of Actions with Respect to South Viet-Nam," VN C.F., NSF, boxes 202–3, folder: Vietnam, Status Reports 4/14/62–7/11/62, JFKL; Thomas W. Davis Memorandum for the Record, "Minutes of the Meeting of Special Group (CI), 19 April 1962," NSF, Meetings and Memoranda, box 319, folder: Special Group (CI), 1/61–6/62, JFKL; Department of Defense Paper, "Visit to Southeast Asia by Secretary of Defense, 8–11 May 1962," *FRUS*, Vietnam, 1962, 379–87; "Status Report on Southeast Asia," Prepared by Task Force Southeast Asia, Department of State, 27 June 1962 and 11 July 1962, both in VN C.F., NSF, boxes 202–3, folder: Vietnam, Status Reports, 4/4/62–7/11/62, JFKL; General Decker Statement in General Dodge to General Clifton, 8 or 9 July 1962, VN C.F., NSF, box 196, folder: Vietnam, 7/7/62–7/10/62, JFKL; Harkins Memorandum for the Record, 18 July 1962, "Meeting at Gia Long Palace, Saigon," Newman Papers, JFKL; "Record of the Sixth Secretary of Defense Conference, Camp Smith, Hawaii, July 23, 1962," *FRUS*, Vietnam, 1962, 546–56.

phen Pelz observed, Kennedy "preferred to seek victory, rather than accept defeat, however much disguised or delayed."[42]

Notwithstanding the heightened commitment and attendant optimism of early 1962, many American officers continued to point out serious problems in the RVN and hedge their bets on the necessity or viability of a U.S. combat commitment. Admiral Felt pointed out that main-unit VC forces, enjoying the support of a "significant segment" of the rural population, would seek "a prolonged form of attritional warfare" that could not "be defeated by purely military means."[43] The USARPAC's intelligence report for March – candidly titled "Guerrilla War Drags on in South Vietnam" – confirmed such views. Communist strategy, it explained, "is not designed to achieve total victory . . . but to force a political settlement through . . . military pressure, subversion, and propaganda."[44] Burris and Bagley, the military advisors to Lyndon Johnson and Maxwell Taylor, added that a thousand ARVN desertions monthly, coupled with battle losses and political instability, had made improvements in the southern military situation unlikely.[45] Such pessimism was apparently widespread. Generals William Rosson and William Yarborough, recently returned from a tour of Southeast Asia, during which Harkins said that defeat of the VC was "at hand," found "almost universal skepticism" away from MACV headquarters in Saigon.[46]

---

42. Bassett and Pelz, "The Failed Search for Victory," 240.
43. Felt to JCS, 22 February 1962, *FRUS*, Vietnam, 1962, 167–70. On the need to focus on political rather than just military measures, see also Victor Krulak, JCS Special Assistant for CI, to Gilpatrick, 26 March 1962, "Civic Action in Vietnam," *FRUS*, Vietnam, 1962, 276–9.
44. USARPAC Intelligence Bulletin, March 1962, John Newman Papers, JFKL.
45. Burris to Johnson, 30 March 1962, "VC Activity," *FRUS*, Vietnam, 1962, 284–5; Burris to Johnson, 16 April 1962, "Threats to Diem," ibid., 330–1; Bagley to Taylor, 18 April 1962, "GVN Responsiveness," ibid., 333–4.
46. Krepinevich, *Army and Vietnam,* 76–7. Around that same time, the noted military historian General S. L. A. Marshall, after a briefing in Saigon during which Harkins boasted of U.S. helicopters moving ARVN troops to various flashpoints, warned the MACV commander, "you know it will not work. Right now Charly [soldiers' slang term for VC] is making himself furtive and hard to find." Once the VC recognized U.S. tactics, Marshall added, it would expose itself to draw the helicopters into areas near its base camps, where "ambush will follow ambush." Marshall in W. Scott Thompson and Donaldson D. Frizzell, eds., *The Lessons of Vietnam* (New York, 1977), 48. Marine advisors in the south likewise recognized the VC's effective antihelicopter tactics; see Whitlow, *Marines in Vietnam, 1954–1964,* 69–70.

In his report after returning Rosson decried the continuing absence of an effective CI strategy. The RVNAF, junior officers told him, was still poorly trained and too passive, civic action was "disorganized and fragmented," and the U.S. command structure required "reorganization and simplification." Although Rosson did not appear discouraged, his report, as the record of his briefing reads, "did not present a picture which would give rise to optimism." The Army staff in Washington, however, paid little attention to his analysis, although, as Andrew Krepinevich observes, it had served notice of an "emerging revolt" by field advisors against Harkins's strategy and optimism.[47]

Despite understanding the problems they faced in Vietnam, American service officials seemed to put politics above military conditions and continued to follow Harkins's lead on Vietnam strategy, in large part because Kennedy was publicly committed to the RVN. The United States "cannot desist in Viet-Nam," the president asserted at an April news conference, even as the number of American casualties in the RVN continued to rise.[48] Nonetheless, throughout June and July 1962 various military officials continued to submit candid evaluations of the VC's military successes and increasing attacks on economic targets, rising infiltration into the south, and continued deficiencies in the Strategic Hamlets program.[49] Perhaps because of such frank assessments the military, despite its outward optimism and belligerence, was not unduly eager for combat.

Roger Hilsman, in fact, charged that armed forces leaders were tying the president's hands on Indochina policy. In mid-1962, amid continued turmoil in Laos and Vietnam, Kennedy and his chiefs considered possible military responses. Although the president and

47. H. H. Gardner Memorandum for the Record, "Meeting of the Special Warfare Group (Focal Point) for 4 May 1962," Newman Papers, JFKL; Krepinevich, *Army and Vietnam*, 76–7.
48. President Kennedy's News Conference, 11 April 1962, *Pentagon Papers: Gravel*, 2:810.
49. See Wilson to General Dinh, 8 July 1962, "VC Activity in Kontum Province," Wilson Papers, Folder: CH Army Sec – CG-II Corps, 1 January–31 July 1962, MHI; USARPAC Intelligence Bulletin, June and July 1962, Newman Papers, JFKL; John McCone, DCI, to Kennedy, "Viet Cong Ambush of Military Convoy," n.d., POF, CF, VN, box 128a, folder 3, JFKL; Whitlow, *Marines in Vietnam, 1954–1964*, 69–70; Hilsman to Rusk, 16 July 1962, Hilsman Papers, box 3, folder 8, JFKL; Rostow to Kennedy, 17 July 1962, "Next Steps in Viet-Nam," VN C.F, NSF, box 193, JFKL.

secretary of state, among others, wanted to deploy U.S. troops to the area – in Rusk's case into the DRVN – Hilsman and NSC staff member Michael Forrestal worried "that the military was going to go soft" in its approach to Indochina. The chiefs, he complained, "beat their chests until it comes time to do some fighting and then [they] start backing down." General Decker, acting JCS chair at the time, had drawn up a list of possible courses of action – including negotiations, diplomatic approaches to the Soviet Union, or committing SEATO defense forces – which Hilsman called "the damndest collection of mush and softness I have seen in a long time." Because of this weakness, he believed, "of course the President was in no position to do the military moves he wanted." Kennedy was thus "boxed in" because the military had put forth only limited measures for Indochina and Kennedy "hasn't decided enough to deter the Communists but he has decided more than enough to get into all sorts of political trouble . . . at home."[50]

Kennedy would soon find such political trouble, in both Vietnam and at home, in the person of John Paul Vann. Two of the classic works on the Vietnam War – David Halberstam's *The Making of a Quagmire* (1965) and Neil Sheehan's more recent and compelling *A Bright Shining Lie* (1988) – have thoroughly covered Vann's ideas and impact, so his story does not require a full retelling here. But it is necessary to take account of his insights on Vietnam, both because they widely diverged from established U.S. policy and because of the attention he received, principally from Halberstam's reports in the *New York Times*.

Lieutenant Colonel Vann was the advisor to the ARVN's 7th Infantry Division, operating in the northern Mekong delta. For the better part of a decade after his arrival in Vietnam in early 1962 – as

50. Hilsman Memorandum, 9 May 1962, Hilsman Papers, box 2, folder 6, JFKL. This document, a hectically written, somewhat stream-of-consciousness effort, was untitled, but a close reading indicates that Hilsman, who referred to himself in the third person singular throughout, was the author; Hilsman also quoted in Stephen E. Pelz, "Documents: 'When Do I Have Time to Think?' John F. Kennedy, Roger Hilsman, and the Laotian Crisis of 1962," *Diplomatic History* 3 (Spring 1979): 22. It is indeed ironic that Hilsman would criticize the military's alleged softness in Indochina in May 1962, for the JCS – urging a military emphasis in Vietnam – had criticized his "Strategic Concept for South Vietnam," which had viewed the insurgency as a primarily political problem and urged a program of civic action. Hilsman report, "A Strategic concept for South Vietnam," 2 February 1962, *FRUS*, Vietnam, 1962, 73–90; "Memorandum of a Discussion at Department of State–Joint Chiefs of Staff Meeting," 9 February 1962, ibid., 113–16.

an officer and then a civilian official – Vann would concern himself with making the Vietnamese responsible for their own war and with challenging the MACV strategy in Vietnam. To Vann, the ARVN's passivity and Harkins's lavish use of air power and artillery had led to indiscriminate bombings of peasant hamlets and other brutalities against the people of the RVN, which in the end facilitated VC and NLF recruiting and propaganda. Vann's pleas about such problems to MACV headquarters, however, fell on deaf ears and when, in September, he briefed incoming JCS Chair Maxwell Taylor, Harkins consistently "presented views and/or overrode key points" that the dissident colonel tried to present.[51] Thus Halberstam would write on 20 October that "the closer one gets to the actual contact level of the war, the farther one gets from official optimism." A "high American officer" cited in the *New York Times* report added that he thought that "this war is being officially reported to look good on short-range progress reports . . . [but] some basic things just aren't being corrected and I don't know if we're in a position to correct them."[52]

In mid-1962, however, Washington maintained its sanguine outlook on the war. McNamara, citing "tremendous progress" and aware of the tenuous nature of public support for a long-term commitment to Diem, directed the chiefs to develop plans to build up the RVNAF to the point where the United States could begin to phase out the use of American personnel in Vietnam.[53] The Pentagon and White House thought such action was feasible in no small part because Harkins had assured the defense secretary that "there is no doubt we are on the winning side." The commander, in fact, estimated that it would only take about a year for the MACV to get the ARVN, CG, and SDC fully operational and engaged against the VC "in all areas." McNamara, not quite so optimistic, told Harkins to assume that it would take three more years "to bring the VC in SVN under control."[54]

51. Sheehan, *Bright Shining Lie,* 50, 57, 67, 94, 97–100, 106–7, 110–12; Halberstam, *Quagmire,* 144.
52. Halberstam, *Quagmire,* 149–50.
53. Hilsman's "Summary Assessment," 10 June 1962, HCAS, *USVN Relations,* book 12, 469–80; *Pentagon Papers: Gravel,* 2:162–4.
54. Record of the Sixth Secretary of Defense Conference, 23 July 1962, *FRUS,* Vietnam, 1962, 546–60.

Notwithstanding such planning, John Vann was not alone among military officials in expressing reservations about the war, even as optimism was peaking in the later months of 1962. Several American officers, after touring Vietnam, had expressed varying degrees of pessimism. Diem had retained "absolute control" over his armed forces, to the point of refusing to arm certain units for fear that the weapons could be used against his regime in a coup attempt, they reported. The ARVN itself was "pervaded by apathy," and was "equally proficient," one officer sarcastically observed, "at attacking an open rice field with nothing in it and . . . at quickly by-passing any heavily wooded area that might possibly contain a few VC." Summing up the visit, the officer believed that "the military and political situation in South Vietnam can be aptly described by four words, 'it is a mess.' "[55]

The MACV itself found that the number of VC-initiated attacks and infiltration continued to rise, with a confirmed 1,600 to 1,800 guerrillas entering the south in recent months, more than offsetting increased VC casualties. The Army's Pacific command added that the insurgents "almost undoubtedly still retain the initiative and are free to set the pattern of military action." Indeed the VC's capabilities had "not been significantly reduced by GVN offensives; Communist vigor remains undiminished." Harkins admitted that the VC "completely dominate[s] [the] bulk of inhabitants" in the border areas of southern Vietnam and "can move across the border . . . to locations deep within corps area with little or no chance of being detected or [reported]." Even "cautiously optimistic" American officers like the naval attaché in Saigon, Commander Everett Parke, advised that "we must not expect to see a sudden dramatic improvement. We are up against people who are capable of outsitting us and outwaiting us, and unless we make up our minds to . . . get this thing put into long-term perspective, I think we will be deluding ourselves."[56]

55. Officers' reports of August 1962 enclosed in Krulak Memorandum for Chief of Staff, U.S. Army, Chief of Naval Operations, Chief of Staff, U.S. Air Force, etc., 27 December 1962, "Exchange of Counterinsurgency Lessons Learned," Newman Papers, JFKL.
56. VC Order of Battle, 1 August 1962, USARPAC Intelligence Bulletin, August 1962, COMUSMACV to Aug 924, 14 August 1962, Burris to Johnson, 13 August 1962,

The military seemed to be of two minds on Vietnam. While Harkins and other true believers pushed the official line that the RVN could successfully eliminate the enemy in a short time, others had desolate views of the war and urged a long-range perspective. By that time, however, service leaders understood the president's determination to achieve success in Vietnam, and political developments in the fall reinforced their approach to the war. On one hand, Kennedy replaced the Eisenhower holdovers on the JCS, thus ensuring military fealty to his Vietnam policy. At the same time, however, civil–military skirmishing flared up again during the October Missile Crisis when American officers, especially CNO Admiral George Anderson, wanted to respond aggressively to the deployment of missiles in Cuba, but McNamara and the president refused. To the military, the defense secretary again had infringed upon its prerogatives by handing down operational orders, prompting Anderson to complain that "we've been sold out." The resulting limitations on military autonomy created, as Graham Allison described it, "enormous pain and serious friction" between armed forces and civilian leaders.[57]

Even though by later 1962 ranking officers were more loyal to Kennedy, anomalously, the relationship between service and political leaders was becoming more adversarial. With regard to Vietnam, these two currents converged to strengthen the U.S. commitment to the RVN, either out of true conviction or in an effort to make Kennedy more accountable for the imbroglio in Indochina. It should not seem surprising, therefore, that the incoming JCS chair, Maxwell Taylor – who had consistently expressed his own reservations about Vietnam and on that very day heard Vann's biting remarks on the war – nonetheless met with Nhu, Nolting, and Harkins on 11 September and was "much encouraged" by the progress in Vietnam since his October 1961 visit. He observed that the situation "resembled that which usually exists during any war.

"Determination of South Vietnam Build-up," all in Newman Papers, JFKL; Parke in Marolda and Fitzgerald, *U.S. Navy and Vietnam,* 266; see also officers' reports on CI, August 1962, in Krulak to Wheeler, etc., 27 December 1962, also in Newman Papers.
57. Anderson in Taylor, *The Sword and the Pen,* 270; Graham Allison, *Essence of Decision* (Boston, 1971), 128; Raymond, *Power at the Pentagon,* 286; Kinnard, *The Secretary of Defense,* 80.

There is a period during which an impasse exists, and then, suddenly, a sudden surge to victory."[58]

In his official report, filed on 20 September, Taylor added a sanguine outlook on the war, lauding progress in the Strategic Hamlets program, improved training in the ARVN, better performances from the CG and SDC, reforms in the command and control structure, reduced casualty rates, and greater RVN control over southern territory.[59] But the JCS chair-designate still believed that Berlin and Franco-American relations remained more pressing problems than Indochina and recognized that, inside Vietnam, serious obstacles to success continued to exist. Infiltration remained high, there was "still no coordinated national plan establishing priorities for operations against the VC," and RVNAF intelligence remained inadequate despite U.S. efforts. Taylor, Bruce Palmer later observed, was so closely associated with the president that his "objectivity and independence of mind had to be somewhat compromised." As a result, he appeared "to be ambivalent on the basic issues of Vietnam."[60]

Just as Taylor returned to Washington, David Shoup, the only chief to retain his position after Kennedy's reorganization of the JCS, arrived in Vietnam. The commandant "came back an expert," he sarcastically observed later, but his evaluation at the time was not optimistic. He especially criticized the Strategic Hamlets program, which was dislocating rural Vietnamese and thus undermining efforts to win the allegiance of the people. The Vietnamese marine corps, which was being trained by the U.S. Marines, had shown negligible progress as well. Shoup thus continued to oppose U.S. combat entry into the war "with no qualms whatever" and

---

58. Memorandum for the Record, 14 September 1962, "Meeting with Special Advisor to the President of Vietnam, 11 September 1962," *FRUS*, Vietnam, 1962, 636–41. The memo does not indicate the time at which Taylor and Nhu met; Vann had lunch with Taylor and Harkins at 12:30 on 11 September. Sheehan, *Bright Shining Lie*, 97–9; Kinnard, *Certain Trumpet*, 110.

59. Paper Prepared by the President's Military Representative (Taylor), 20 September 1962, "Impressions of South Vietnam," *FRUS*, Vietnam, 1962, 660–3; see also Forrestal to Kennedy, 28 September 1962, "Crop Destruction in Vietnam," VN C.F., NSF, box 196, folder: Vietnam, 9/22/62–9/29/62, JFKL.

60. See sources cited in previous note; Taylor, *Sword and Pen*, 255–6; Bruce Palmer, *The 25-Year War: America's Military Role in Vietnam* (New York, 1985), 20.

believed that such resistance to intervention was the position of "every responsible military man to my knowledge."[61]

Despite substantial aid to the RVN, an October 1962 analysis of the war from Saigon did not offer a promising outlook for the next six months. MACV intelligence lauded RVN improvements and remained optimistic that American air power and weaponry would continue to damage the enemy seriously. As the MACV saw it, the VC "need a significant military victory, or victories, to reestablish their public image and discredit the government forces." Such sanguine views, however, did not flow easily from the intelligence estimate. The enemy, U.S. officers reported, had increased its strength to about 22,000 confirmed main-force units, 120,000 guerrillas, and additional political support personnel; continued to infiltrate about 1,000 guerrillas monthly; and had over 17,000 PAVN troops near the DMZ which could enter the RVN without undue opposition. The MACV also expected VC logistics support and military activity to continue unabated, and thought that insurgent attacks in the northern sectors of the RVN would deal serious military and political blows to the Diem regime.[62] For the remainder of 1962 military reports out of Vietnam sounded similarly ambivalent themes about the war.[63]

Both the JCS chair and USARPAC admitted that the strategic hamlets, though improving, were poorly constructed and defended. By November 1962, Taylor reported, the Vietnamese had

---

61. "And I suspect today they still feel the same way," Shoup added in the 1967 interview. Shoup, Oral History, 35–6, JFKL; Whitlow, *Marines in Vietnam*, 49–53. Unfortunately, Marine archivists were unable to find a copy of Shoup's October 1962 report.

62. MACJ2, 11 October 1962, "Intelligence Estimate, Period October 1962–February 1963," in Task Element 79.3.3.6 Command Diary, 6 November 1962–31 October 1963, MCHC. Also at this time an Australian Army advisor to Harkins, Colonel Francis P. Serong, toured Vietnam and reported "considerable improvement" with a successful conclusion "definitely in sight." Serong added, however, that once the war ended on the battlefield "we will be faced with a political problem by comparison with which the present one will seem mild." Colonel Francis P. Serong Report, "Current Operations in South Vietnam, October 1962," William Childs Westmoreland Papers, folder 498 [2 of 2]: #1 History Backup, 30 March 1962–November 1963, Washington National Records Center (WNRC), Suitland, Md. (hereafter cited as Westmoreland Papers with appropriate filing information).

63. See, for example, General Herbert Powell to Wheeler, 16 November 1962 and 13 December 1962, Newman Papers, JFKL; Wilbur Wilson to General Dinh, 28 November 1962, "Training Estimate of the 42d Infantry Regiment," Wilson Papers, Folder: Memoranda to General Dinh, CG II Corps – 1 August 1962, MHI.

developed less than one-third of a projected 11,000 areas designated as hamlets, with only 600 of those adequately secure and properly administered.[64] The Army's Southeast Asia branch further contended that the VC was "still forcing the [RVN] to fight on the Communists' terms." Additionally, the enemy was arming itself with captured weapons to such an extent that "today, the Viet Cong has a claim on the arsenals of the United States and the Government of South Vietnam." Such developments demonstrated that the VC had successfully met its needs – weapons, equipment, food – from inside the RVN itself. With "minimal and simple" logistics requirements, the VC was "almost completely self-sufficient through in-country procurement."[65]

Field reports from Vietnam, however, showed diminishing VC activity, "growing effectiveness" from the ARVN, and greater hamlet control.[66] The U.S. military was generally pleased with the RVNAF's performance and expansion – ARVN strength had risen to 219,000, the CG to 77,000, and SDC to 99,500 – while the increased U.S. presence in Vietnam, including 11,000 "advisors," 300 aircraft, 120 helicopters, heavy weapons, pilots flying combat missions, defoliants, and napalm, had sent the VC reeling.[67] "The tide has turned" in the highlands, Wilbur Wilson now concluded.[68]

The tide seemed to reverse itself quickly, however. Hilsman and Forrestal, whom the president had dispatched to Saigon, arrived and on 2 January 1963 reported that "things are going much better than they were a year ago," although "not nearly so well as" Harkins and others might suggest.[69] That very day the VC proved that Hilsman's latter observation was true. At Ap Bac in the

64. Taylor to McNamara, 17 November 1962, "Viet Cong Attacks on Strategic Hamlets," *FRUS*, Vietnam, 1962, 736–8; USARPAC Intelligence Bulletin, November and December 1962, Newman Papers, JFKL.
65. U.S. Army Southeast Asia Branch Briefing at Fort Holabird, 29 November 1962, Newman Papers, JFKL.
66. JCS Operations Directorate, Southeast Asia Sitrep 46–62, 14 November 1962, ibid.
67. Bassett and Pelz, "The Failed Search for Victory," 240–1; Collins, *Development and Training*, 29.
68. Wilson to Harkins, 12 November 1962, 13 December 1962, Wilson Papers, Folder: Memoranda to MACV, MHI; see also Wilbur Wilson, 12 January 1963, "Year-End Report of Viet Cong Activity in II CTZ," Wilson Papers, enclosure 32, II CTZ Fact Sheets, MHI.
69. Hilsman Memorandum for the Record, 2 January 1963, *FRUS*, Vietnam, January–August 1963 (Washington, D.C., 1991), 3–5.

Mekong delta, about thirty-five miles southwest of Saigon, the RVNAF, being pressed by American advisors for a victory in a set piece battle, saw a golden opportunity to rout VC forces. With a four-to-one troop advantage and supporting artillery, armor, and helicopters, American observers expected the ARVN's 7th Division to control the field at Ap Bac. The VC, however, dominated the battle that day, inflicting heavy damage on the RVN troops, killing three U.S. advisors, and downing five helicopters. The ARVN failed to use adequately U.S.-provided armored personnel carriers, and refused to engage the enemy for fear of incurring greater casualties. Ap Bac shocked many Americans in Vietnam, yet, as Halberstam wrote at the time, "the only people not surprised are the American advisors in the field." While Harkins and Felt, among others, proclaimed success, John Paul Vann bitterly attacked the ARVN in his after-action report on Ap Bac. As Vann saw it the southern Vietnamese were still poorly trained, afraid to fight, and lacking in battle discipline.[70] The USARPAC likewise criticized the RVNAF and pointed out that the American and Vietnamese losses "will be turned into [a] propaganda weapon and will provide [the] enemy with [a] morale-building victory."[71]

At the same time General Edward Rowny, an old associate of Hilsman then in Vietnam on a special mission to introduce new technology to the Vietnamese, more generally questioned U.S. optimism. A year after reorganization, Rowny reported, the MACV command structure was still troubled, with CINCPAC "trying to run the war even in practical detail." While Harkins was "a good officer and competent" he was "not . . . imaginative and driving, highly motivated or creative." The MACV's saving grace, Rowny believed, was its junior officer corps, most of whom challenged

---

70. Editorial Note, *FRUS*, Vietnam, January–August 1963, 1–2; Halberstam, *Quagmire*, 155–69; the most detailed treatment of Ap Bac is in Sheehan, *Bright Shining Lie*, 203–65. The VC's Ap Bac success should not have been so shocking. A Marine evaluation of helicopter tactics had determined that less than 10 percent of the territory over which U.S. helicopters flew could be considered "safe areas." Commander, Marine Aircraft Group 16 to COMUSMACV, 10 January 1963, "Evaluation of Helicopter Tactics and Techniques Report," Enclosure D#15, in Task Element 79.3.3.6 Command Diary, 6 November 1962–31 October 1963, MCHC.
71. CINCUSARPAC to JCS et al., 4 January 1963, VN C.F, NSF, box 197, folder: Vietnam, 1/1/63–1/9/63, JFKL.

Harkins's strategy and called for more political and civic action programs.[72]

Rowny, who took part in twenty operations during his visit, also criticized the ARVN, as Vann had, for its "considerable delay" in waiting for air strikes, for allowing the VC to escape, and for its brutal habit of capturing or shooting anyone left in a bombed-out village on the grounds of being "suspected VC." While harsh with senior citizens and children, the ARVN soldiers "do not really want to tangle with the enemy" because Diem's prohibition on defeat had led to "excessive caution" among his commanders. Hilsman and Forrestal themselves were guardedly optimistic, concluding that "the war will last longer than we would like, cost more in terms of both lives and money than we anticipated, and prolong the period in which a sudden and dramatic event could upset the gains already made."[73]

Ap Bac and candid reports out of Vietnam notwithstanding, Kennedy and McNamara continued to insist that all was well in Vietnam. As Chester Cooper, an NSC analyst, explained, Washington looked upon Ap Bac as only "an embarrassing trough in an upward-moving curve of government progress."[74] Reports by the CIA, Bagley, and Burris, however, pointed out the VC's growing capability. To Burris the war was an "escalating stalemate," while Bagley warned the JCS chair that no amount of military aid would save Diem unless accompanied by "parallel . . . economic and social reform."[75]

Army Chief of Staff Earle Wheeler, head of a military team that Kennedy sent to Vietnam in late January, offered a brighter view, praising the Strategic Hamlets program as the "single greatest case for . . . encourage[ment]" and lauding improvements in the ARVN,

---

72. Hilsman Memorandum, January 1963, "Conversation with Major General Edward L. Rowny, " *FRUS,* Vietnam, January–August 1963, 7–11; Hilsman, *To Move a Nation,* 454–5.
73. Ibid.; Hilsman and Forrestal Memorandum for the President, 25 January 1963, "A Report on South Vietnam," *Pentagon Papers: Gravel,* 2:717–25, and in *FRUS,* Vietnam, January–August 1963, 49–59.
74. Chester Cooper, *The Lost Crusade: America in Vietnam* (New York, 1970), 199–202.
75. "Current Intelligence Memo Prepared in Office of Current Intelligence, CIA, 11 January 1963," *FRUS,* Vietnam, January–August 1963, 19–22; Bagley to Taylor, 17 January 1963, "South Vietnam," ibid., 30–2; Burris to Johnson, 24 January 1963, "Vietnam," Newman Papers, JFKL.

CG, and SDC. Wheeler understood that the United States had to guard against an "over commitment of forces" but wanted to make the DRVN "bleed a little bit" so urged that the ARVN, with U.S. training, stage a "powerful military endeavor" of "sabotage, destruction, propaganda and subversive missions against North Vietnam."[76] Forrestal immediately challenged Wheeler's analysis, telling Kennedy that a White House meeting with the Army chief "was a complete waste of your time for which I apologize." The "rosy euphoria" of Wheeler's report, Forrestal charged, made effective planning for future action impossible.[77] Harkins, however, had no such planning problems, requesting a further reinforcement of 129 aircraft from CINCPAC. Felt, who had told the chiefs that Harkins's previous request was his last, balked. He pointed out that Washington would interpret such a vast expansion as proof that the RVN "in fact was unable to achieve victory over the VC without a significantly increased US commitment in Viet-Nam."[78]

Felt, however, had joined the bandwagon on Vietnam by early 1963, predicting that victory was likely by 1965, even though "the VC are still everywhere."[79] Harkins too continued his "Alice-in-Wonderland reporting," as George McT. Kahin called it, and by mid-1963 Dean Rusk and others found the United States "turning an important corner" in Vietnam.[80] By contrast, reports from the

76. Wheeler to JCS, January 1963, "JCS Team Report on Vietnam," VN C.F., NSF, box 197, folder: Vietnam, 1/10/63–1/30/63, JKFL; see also Hilsman to Harriman, 2 February 1963, and Wheeler Press Release and Briefing, 4 February 1963, all in Hilsman Papers, box 3, folder 13, JFKL.
77. Forrestal to Kennedy, 4 February 1963, "South Vietnam," *FRUS, Vietnam*, January–August 1963, 97–8.
78. Harkins's request included one squadron of B-26s and one squadron of T-28s – both strike aircraft – and two squadrons of C-123s, three squadrons of L-19s, and one company of Caribous – all transport planes. Nolting agreed with Felt's rejection but told him that, if imperative, transport but not offensive aircraft might be sent to Vietnam. Counselor of Embassy in Vietnam (Melvin Manful) to Director of Vietnam Working Group (Chalmers Wood), 23 January 1963, *FRUS, Vietnam*, January–August 1963, 32–4.
79. For Felt's optimism, see Wheeler Press Conference, 4 February 1963, Hilsman Papers, box 3, folder 13, JFKL; Felt to JCS, 2 March 1963, and CINCPAC to RUEPDA/DIA, 14 March 1963, VN C.F., box 197, folder: Vietnam, 3/1/63–3/19/63, JFKL; Felt to JCS, 22 February 1963, Hilsman Papers, box 3, folder 12, JFKL.
80. Harkins to Diem, 23 February 1963, *FRUS, Vietnam*, January–August 1963, 118–22; Harkins to Felt, 30 March 1963, ibid., 186–9; "Memorandum for the Record of Secretary of Defense Conference, Honolulu, May 6, 1963," ibid., 265–70; Rusk in Kahin, *Intervention*, 143.

field were gloomy with advisors Vann, Wilson, and Daniel Boone Porter, and MACV official General Robert York, among others, raising Harkins's ire with their allegations about the ARVN's reckless attacks on civilians and "favoritism and graft" among local officials.[81]

While contending with such bleak reviews of the war from the field, the MACV leadership had to confront another problem – interservice rivalries – which, over *la longue durée,* would become more grave. As Taylor became the JCS chair, he immediately had to confront serious division within the military establishment. General Curtis LeMay, the Air Force chief of staff, and "the *enfant terrible* of the JCS" as the chair saw it, was concerned with obtaining more jets rather than developing policy while his service in general feared that the Navy's missile submarines were usurping its strategic mission. The Army in fact had superseded the Air Force as the dominant service by 1962, thus bringing to fruition Taylor's design from the previous decade, and was developing further its own aviation assets, much to the chagrin of the other military branches. Taylor, however, remained worried that the Navy was hamstringing his efforts to reorganize the unified commands, particularly CINCPAC, and was dominating his Joint Staff, a body of four hundred advisors who were supposed to offer nonpartisan advice to the chair but in reality promoted their services' positions. Given such internecine struggles, military planning for Vietnam was bound to suffer and McNamara, who skillfully exploited military divisions, could dismiss his officers more easily. Perhaps then Taylor's biographer, and son, was on target in asserting that, by 1962, the service chiefs were "little more than bit players" in the policy-making process."[82]

From the initial deployment of U.S. advisors to Vietnam, a serious interservice feud had developed within the MACV as well. In 1960 Air Force General Theodore Milton criticized McGarr's plans, which were "entirely dominated by classic ground force

81. Krepinevich, *The Army and Vietnam,* 81–2. At the same time Senate majority leader Mike Mansfield returned from a trip to Vietnam warning that the conflict was fast becoming an "American war" and that many problems evident in 1955 still plagued the American effort. Kahin, *Intervention,* 146–7.
82. Taylor, *Sword and Pen,* 275–9; Korb, *Joint Chiefs of Staff,* 115–16.

thinking." At the same time, LeMay charged that the Army, in developing James Gavin's concept of airmobility, was "in effect building another air force for the Army."[83] The February 1962 MACV reorganization also caused acrimony, as the Army and Air Force both opposed CINCPAC's operational authority for the war. LeMay was also at odds with Harkins, whom he considered an "idiot," because few Air Force officers were on the MACV staff and air activities, he charged, were "depreciated in South Vietnam." But when LeMay complained that his representatives could not get past Harkins's chief of staff, Marine General Richard Weede, to discuss air operations, Commandant Shoup shot back that "if Senior Air Force officers in Saigon were not man enough to insist on seeing [Harkins] on a vital issue, we were in greater difficulty there than [I] had thought."[84]

Such division escalated throughout 1962. The Army and Air Force continued to argue over command of the air, with LeMay wanting his commanders to control all aircraft and aviation units in Vietnam, including the Army's, while Army officers insisted that its ground commanders control their aviation assets.[85] The Air Force's director of planning bluntly remarked that "it may be improper to say we are at war with the Army. However, we believe that if the Army efforts [to control strategy and air assets] are successful, they may have a long term adverse effect in the US military posture that could be more important than the battle presently being waged with the Viet Cong."[86] At the same time relations among the Joint Chiefs in Washington were increasingly strained. As LeMay saw it, the chiefs were excluded from the decision-making process because of Taylor's relationship with the president. "We didn't agree with Taylor in most cases," the Air Force chief noted.[87] Nathan Twining, Air Force general and JCS chair from 1957 to 1960, later charged that Taylor's rise to prominence in the Kennedy admin-

83. Milton in Robert Futrell, *The United States Air Force in Southeast Asia: The Advisory Years to 1965* (Washington, D.C., 1981), 54; LeMay in Donald Mrozek, *Air Power and the Ground War in Vietnam: Ideas and Action* (Maxwell Air Force Base, Ala., 1988), 31–6.
84. LeMay in Futrell, *Air Force in Southeast Asia*, 101; "idiot" quotation in Perry, *Four Stars*, 28–9; Shoup in Bagley to Taylor, 26 April 1962, *FRUS*, Vietnam, 1962, 343–5.
85. Eckhardt, *Command and Control*, 37.
86. Quoted in Mrozek, *Air Power and Ground War*, 35–6, 27.
87. LeMay in Perry, *Four Stars*, 126–8.

istration was a turning point in Vietnam policy. Twining "couldn't understand how they [Taylor and Kennedy] were putting so many troops in there." Many other officers, he contended, believed that any U.S. commitment would necessarily escalate. "We got euchered into" intervention based on Taylor's rosy outlooks, the general argued, but "we used to fight with him all the time. This was in the JCS."[88]

Twining's enmity for Taylor ran deep. "I've always felt sorry for him. He must have a hard time living with himself," he maintained. His charges about Taylor's decisive role are exaggerated too, but Twining's analysis does speak clearly to the deep divisions within the military regarding Vietnam. In turn, Air Force leaders came under criticism from the Army. General Rowny told Hilsman that the U.S. Air Force in Vietnam was reluctant to provide close air support for helicopter missions, and was stressing "interdiction" and "retaining command of the air" even though the DRVN had no air power to speak of in the south.[89] Such internecine fighting would continue within the MACV throughout the war and come to a head in early 1968, when, in the aftermath of the Tet Offensive, the Army, Air Force, and Marine Corps were virtually at war against each other, and by which time it was clear that America would not achieve success in Vietnam.

In mid-1963, however, Harkins and his associates were principally concerned with ending the war in Vietnam. Since January of that year he and Felt had been developing plans to augment the RVNAF, eventually to 575,000 forces, and withdraw about 1,000 American military personnel "based on the assumption that the progress of the counterinsurgency campaign would warrant such a move."[90] Obviously the chiefs and MACV believed that conditions

88. The Twining interview was conducted in the later 1960s and his criticism was even more biting. Asked whether Taylor had finally seen the errors of his ways, Twining believed he was "still fighting it," using "subterfuge" to expand the U.S. role in Vietnam. But Taylor was "a smart boy, he ought to be able to see now what's happened. He always goes over there and says they're [U.S. and RVN forces] doing fine. Well, sure . . . but my God, how long does it go on?" Twining Oral History (Columbia Oral History Project), 224–6, 274, DDEL.
89. Ibid.; Hilsman, January 1963, "Conversation with Rowny," *FRUS,* Vietnam, January–August 1963, 7–11.
90. *Pentagon Papers: Gravel,* 2:179–83; see also Felt to JCS, 25 January 1963, "Comprehensive Plan for South Vietnam," *FRUS,* Vietnam, January–August 1963, 35–49;

in the RVN did warrant withdrawal plans. Harkins reported that two-thirds of the projected strategic hamlets had been completed and were providing security to about 8 million villagers in the south.[91] Kennedy partisans would later point to these withdrawal plans as evidence of the president's desire to leave the morass in Vietnam. Kennedy, and McNamara, had planned to reduce the number of American personnel, however, because they anticipated victory, not because they wanted to bolt from a deteriorating war.[92]

Along those lines, Harkins told Taylor that "we have accomplished our part of everything we set out to do after your visit in the Fall of '61 – all except ending the war, and that is not far off if things continue at present pace." All that was needed to finish off the VC, Harkins believed, was the "will and determination of the Vietnamese to win."[93] In Washington, Kennedy's will and determination were not in question. Invoking Mao's victory in China, the president vowed to stand firm in Vietnam and he and his advisors "believe[d] strongly" in maintaining an independent RVN, Kennedy told reporters in July. Disengagement or a reduced commitment, he added, "would mean a collapse not only of South VietNam, but Southeast Asia. So we are going to stay there."[94] Off the record the president was more forthright, telling a journalist that "we don't have a prayer of staying in Vietnam. . . . But I can't give up a piece of territory like that to the Communists and get the American people to reelect me."[95]

Harkins must have sincerely believed that victory was imminent in August 1963. There was, however, plenty of evidence to indicate otherwise. Political turmoil, an increasingly grave problem since Diem became head of state in 1955, reached a crisis stage in

CINCPAC withdrawal plan in appendix to Taylor to McNamara, 20 August 1963, "Summary Report on Eighth Secretary of Defense Conference, Honolulu, 7 May 1963 (Withdrawal of 1,000 U.S. Military from Vietnam)," *FRUS, Vietnam, January–August 1963*, 590–4.

91. Embassy in Vietnam to State Department, 6 July 1963, *FRUS, Vietnam, January–August 1963*, 468–70; see also report by Krulak, ibid., 455–65.
92. For a defense of Kennedy's withdrawal plans, see Schlesinger, *A Thousand Days;* for a convincing refutation, see Chomsky, *Rethinking Camelot.*
93. Harkins to Taylor, 22 August 1963, *FRUS, Vietnam, January–August 1963*, 607–10.
94. President Kennedy's News Conference, 17 July 1963, *Pentagon Papers: Gravel*, 2:824.
95. Quoted in Thomas Paterson, "Introduction: John F. Kennedy's Quest for Victory and Global Crisis," in Paterson, *Kennedy's Quest for Victory*, 3–23.

mid-1963. The RVN president intensified his persecution of Buddhists in the south while his brother, Nhu, angered Americans by making overtures to the NLF about a negotiated, neutralist solution in Vietnam.[96] As acrimony between Diem and the Americans was escalating, politics again entered the fray as John Vann added to Harkins's problems by again challenging the MACV view of the war. By July 1963 Vann's outlook on Vietnam had attracted the attention of Army Generals Harold K. Johnson, Barksdale Hamlett, and Bruce Palmer, who arranged a briefing by Vann to the Joint Chiefs. Taylor and Krulak, however, conspired to cancel Vann's appearance, prompting an "open war" in the JCS. An enraged Vann said that the United States "couldn't win the war," and other chiefs charged that Taylor was covering for his friend Harkins, while Palmer believed that the JCS chair and McNamara were concerned with Kennedy's 1964 election hopes and did not want the likes of Vann rocking the boat.[97]

Despite the attempts to quiet Vann, other advisors continued to follow his example. After a Vietnamese officer briefing Krulak reported that 123 secure hamlets existed in the southern delta, Lieutenant Colonel Fred Ladd informed the Marine general that only 8 could be considered safe – thereby earning Harkins's rebuke for his honesty.[98] Likewise, John Mecklin, the embassy's public affairs officer, received a glowing report from a senior officer at an American outpost in the delta, only to have the MAAG deputy there later confide that the situation was "rapidly deteriorating."[99] Meanwhile in II Corps, Colonel Hal D. McCown, Wilbur Wilson's successor, had accepted Harkins's outlook on the war but his deputy, Colonel Rowland Renwanz, had a markedly different view. While McCown expected eventual victory, Renwanz scored ARVN inactivity, claimed that the Strategic Hamlets program had made little progress, and estimated that it would take as long as six years just to pacify II Corps.[100] Even Wheeler later conceded that "things

96. Kahin, *Intervention*, 143–4, 153–5.
97. Sheehan, *Bright Shining Lie*, 337–41; Perry, *Four Stars*, 128–9; Palmer, *The 25-Year War*, 22.
98. Hilsman, *To Move a Nation*, 499.
99. Mecklin to Lodge, 24 August 1963, *FRUS*, Vietnam, January–August 1963, 621–5.
100. Krepinevich, *The Army and Vietnam*, 82–3.

went to hell in a handbasket" in Vietnam after the political crises of late 1963.[101]

Kennedy, however, stayed the course on Vietnam. During a 2 September interview with Walter Cronkite, the president, while asserting that it was the RVN's war to win or lose and "all we can do is help," did not "agree with those who say we should withdraw. That would be a great mistake. I know people don't like to see Americans to be engaged in this kind of effort . . . but it is a very important struggle even though it is far away."[102] A week later he told Chet Huntley essentially the same thing. Although Americans would get anxious or impatient about Vietnam, withdrawal "only makes it easy for the Communists. I think we should stay."[103]

Krulak held similar views, returning to Washington after four days in Vietnam with an enthusiastic endorsement of Harkins's policies.[104] But the new ambassador to Saigon questioned such optimism. Henry Cabot Lodge "doubt[ed] the value of the answers which are given by young officers to direct questions by generals or . . . ambassadors. The urge to give an optimistic and favorable answer is quite insurmountable – and understandable. I, therefore, doubt . . . that the military are not affected by developments in Saigon."[105] Even Taylor, who was pleased with Krulak's assessment, used a 10 September NSC meeting to reaffirm that "he

101. Wheeler Oral History, 64–6, JFKL.
102. President Kennedy's CBS Interview, 2 September 1963, "Statements by President Kennedy on Vietnam," NSF, Memos to the President, Walt Whitman Rostow, box 8, folder: volume 6, 11–20 June 1966 [2 of 2], LBJL, also in Hilsman Papers, box 4, folder 1, JFKL.
103. Kennedy quoted by Alexander Cockburn in the *Nation*, 9 March 1992, 318; see also President Kennedy's NBC Interview, 9 September 1963, *Pentagon Papers: Gravel*, 2: 827–8.
104. Krulak Report of Trip to Vietnam, 6–10 September 1963, Hilsman Papers, box 4, folder 2, JFKL. Krulak toured Vietnam with State Department official Joseph Mendenhall, whose report to Kennedy was quite bleak, prompting the president's now famous query to him and Krulak: "Were you two gentlemen in the same country?" At that same White House meeting, Harriman called Krulak a "damn fool." CRS, *Government and Vietnam War*, 170–5. In a 1970 interview with Marine historians, Krulak gave a different version of his 1963 approach to Vietnam. Both Kennedy and McNamara, he charged, "had no idea of how absolutely frustrating and enervating such a war would be," while the JCS "individually or collectively did not have any idea about how complex the war would be." Krulak himself said that he did not believe the sanguine reports out of Vietnam. "I was terrified about the war from the very beginning." Krulak Oral History, 194–7, MCHC.
105. Lodge to Rusk, 11 September 1963, *FRUS*, Vietnam, August–December 1963 (Washington, D.C., 1991), 171–4.

would not be associated with any program which included [a] commitment of U.S. Armed Forces."[106]

Weeks later, Taylor himself and McNamara traveled to Vietnam to appraise the war. The JCS chair and secretary of defense accepted Harkins's view of "great progress," recommended that the 1,000-man withdrawal be publicized, and anticipated that the "bulk of U.S. personnel" could be phased out by the end of 1965. But amid the continued crisis in the RVN, with the ARVN attacking Buddhists as well as plotting against the Ngos, Taylor's report, as George McT. Kahin explained, was "replete with ambiguity and inconsistency" regarding its political evaluations.[107] Nevertheless, the White House issued a statement at the same time again affirming its support of and commitment to the RVN.[108]

In the month following Taylor's and McNamara's return, the situation erupted. As the U.S. military tried to prosecute the war and urged continued support of the Ngos, the political turmoil in Saigon intensified daily, culminating in a 1 November coup during which ARVN troops murdered Diem and Nhu. The Diem ouster had thus laid bare Harkins's optimistic outlook on Vietnam, and the VC immediately went on the offensive in November 1963. The MACV commander, and Lodge, however, still expected a "stepped-up campaign against the Viet Cong" and a more rapid conclusion to the war than would have been possible under Diem.[109] The MACV also continued to insist that the ARVN had the situation in the south under control and promised "excellent working relations" between U.S. officials and the new leaders of the RVN, a junta headed by General Duong Van "Big" Minh.[110]

---

106. Memorandum of NSC Meeting in Kinnard, *Certain Trumpet,* 123–4.
107. McNamara and Taylor to Kennedy, 2 October 1963, "Report of the Taylor-McNamara Mission to South Vietnam," VN C.F., NSF, boxes 200–1, folder: Vietnam, 9/18/63–9/21/63 Defense Cables, JFKL; see also Kahin, *Intervention,* 170–1; Taylor to Kennedy, September 1963, "Summary of Military Operations in Vietnam," POF, CF, VN, box 128a, folder 4, JFKL.
108. White House Statement approved by President Kennedy, 2 October 1963, "Statements by President Kennedy on Vietnam," NSF, Memos to the President, Walt Whitman Rostow, box 8, folder: volume 6, 11–20 June 1966 [2 of 2], LBJL.
109. Lodge 949 to Secretary of State, 6 November 1963, VN C.F., NSF, box 198, folder: President/Rusk/Lodge Messages, volume 1 [2 of 2], LBJL.
110. *Pentagon Papers: Gravel,* 2:190; Country Team Review of Situation, November 1963, VN C.F., NSF, box 204, folder: Vietnam, Honolulu Briefing Book, 11/20/63, parts I and II, JFKL.

Not everyone in uniform was so optimistic. In fact, Krulak believed that it was an "implicit syndrome" among officers to send back sanguine assessments of the war, a condition "exacerbated by the fact that the people on the ground themselves did not know the magnitude of the problem which faced them."[111] But at its first meeting after the coup, the JCS observed that Kennedy wanted political stability, not necessarily democracy, in the RVN but that the "next gov[ernmen]t has only [a] 50–50 chance of being any better."[112] Colonel Francis Serong, an Australian Army advisor to Westmoreland who surveyed the military situation in the RVN after the coup, also took a dim view of events in a report forwarded to Harkins. The war "is now running against us – and has been for some months," Serong noted. The RVNAF's rate of operations was dropping while casualties and weapons losses had risen. The VC was strong in all regions, particularly in the Mekong delta, and the PAVN could successfully intervene in I Corps. Although the colonel saw some short-term benefits in ousting Diem, he believed that the RVN political system would not be significantly modified and that personality conflicts would riddle the junta, hamper military operations, and distort national strategy. Serong thus drew up a list of problems still plaguing the war effort, including "The VC growing stronger. A depleted national manpower base. A S[trategic] H[amlets] program which must be made to work. An inferior officer corps. A low morale military component. An open border. Buddhists – and others. A dispirited population. A dictatorship." In concluding, he could only lament that "except for two personalities, very little has changed."[113]

Clearly John Kennedy saw a troubled country and deteriorating war effort when he looked at the RVN in November 1963. With over 16,000 "advisors," costing over $400 million, stationed in Vietnam, the United States was headed toward a major intervention in Indochina. But the young president who had staked so much

111. Victor Krulak Oral History Transcript, interview of June 1970, San Diego, Calif., 195–7, MCHC.
112. Notes on JCS Meeting of 4 November 1963, Harold K. Johnson Papers, box 126, folder: Notes on Meetings of JCS, September–December 1963, MHI.
113. Report by Colonel F. P. Serong to General Harkins, November 1963, "Situation in South Vietnam Following Change of Government," Westmoreland Papers, folder: 498 [2 of 2]: #1 History Backup, 30 March 1962–November 1963.

American credibility and treasure there would not see the impact of his policies. As Kennedy traveled to Dallas on 22 November 1963, there was no evidence indicating that he would renege on his commitment to the RVN, despite the politicomilitary turmoil in the south that was recognizable to all.[114]

In the year preceding the president's assassination – when, not coincidentally, Kennedy appointees Harkins and Taylor began to run the war in Saigon and Washington – the military's reports had become exceedingly positive. But even those generals most sanguine about conditions in the south constantly recognized that serious problems existed in the RVN and assumed that indigenous forces, not American combat troops, should fight the war in Vietnam. At lower levels, especially among U.S. advisors in the field, the critique of the war was more biting, with John Vann, Wilbur Wilson, and so many others offering candid, and at times desolate, observations about the war.

Such division within the military was endemic to U.S. policy making for Vietnam, but is still overlooked in studies of the war. Nearly three decades have passed since Kennedy's death, but his legacy regarding Vietnam is still controversial and open to widely divergent interpretations. But much of Kennedy's record is clear. The young president, especially after political crises in Cuba, Laos, and Vienna, and thus at home, in the early days of his administration, had decided to commit American resources and credibility to defend the RVN to whatever extent necessary. The military's outlook was more ambivalent, but no wiser. Most service leaders did not abandon their fundamental objective of training and expanding the RVNAF to fight against the VC so that U.S. combat troops would not have to do so. Nor were most officers naive or unduly sanguine about U.S. prospects in Vietnam. For the most part mili-

114. Many Kennedy partisans such as Arthur Schlesinger, Jr., and Kenneth O'Donnell assert he was planning to disengage after the 1964 election, but the evidence otherwise is powerful. The best analysis is Chomsky, *Rethinking Camelot*, and "Vain Hopes, False Dreams." Indeed Kennedy's planned speech for 22 November talked of the need to maintain American vigilance against Communist expansion. See President Kennedy's Remarks Prepared for Delivery at the Trade Mart in Dallas, 22 November 1963, *Pentagon Papers: Gravel*, 2:830–1.

tary critics such as Felt, McGarr, and even Taylor, as well as advisors in Vietnam like John Vann or Wilbur Wilson, recognized that the VC's strengths, RVNAF's deficiencies, and political chaos in the south were creating tremendous, possibly insurmountable, obstacles to success. Many military officials also understood that any initial commitment of U.S. forces would inevitably lead to an expanded American effort and combat participation in a drawn-out war.

At the same time the military was badly fragmented in its approach to Vietnam, with Army, Air Force, and Marine generals divided over questions of organization and strategy. The debate over strategy in particular would intensify and undermine American military prospects in Vietnam. While McGarr and many of his advisors seemed to believe in the need to develop the RVN counterinsurgency capabilities and establish a stable political system, MACV leaders chose to employ conventional tactics such as firepower, air support, and attrition to defeat the guerrillas. As General Harkins – whose range of options for strategy in Vietnam ran the spectrum from A to B – took over in early 1962, U.S. forces in Vietnam progressively employed traditional means to destroy the enemy's army, even though the VC was not an "army" in the traditional sense. When others questioned that strategy – McGarr and Vann for instance – Taylor, Harkins, and White House officials silenced those military critics rather than reevaluate the nature of the war and the American role in it.

Indeed, no fundamental reappraisal of the war was ever likely, or maybe even possible. The military had recognized the political imperatives driving Kennedy's policy on Indochina and reacted accordingly. Despite often grave misgivings about the commitment to the RVN, American generals consistently accepted greater responsibility for the war. Some of the brass – Harkins and Taylor, for example – seemed to have truly believed the prevalent optimism in Saigon at times, although the JCS chair especially was aware of the perils of Vietnam and never wavered from his opposition to deploying ground troops there.

Even more, however, Taylor and other generals had seen civil–military relations progressively deteriorate, so much so that the JCS chair had to lobby McNamara just to promise that he would not prevent the chiefs from exercising their statutory right to give advice to the president.[115] Having been burned by the White House in consecutive administrations, military leaders felt it was essential to pin down the administration on the nature of the U.S. commitment to Vietnam and to force the president to be accountable for any decisions on the war. As a result McGarr in 1961 explicitly warned Lemnitzer that America might very well fail in Vietnam and the military could likely be blamed for the loss. While their reports out of the RVN candidly spoke of conditions there, American officers also knew that the White House wanted to hear good news about the war. As it turned out, military assessments of Vietnam were filled with non sequiturs as much as analysis.

For his part Kennedy was well informed and deliberate in making Vietnam policy. Indeed, some of his supporters believe, as John Newman put it, that "the preponderance of evidence strongly suggests that by 1963 Kennedy knew the war was a lost cause."[116] If so, however, the president consciously extended American participation in an inevitable disaster, for his actions up to November 1963 do not indicate any desire to disengage. He kept increasing the size of the U.S. force in Vietnam, authorized more extensive operations against the VC, and never backed off from his commitment to the RVN. Had he wanted to pull back from Vietnam, Kennedy could have cited the military's own doubts about the war to cover himself against the political fallout from such a move. He never chose to do so.

Instead, as Bassett and Pelz observe, the president overrode the reservations of key officials who sought to make the RVN responsible for its own war and "sent in 16,000 advisers, 100 of whom had died by the end of 1963; he sponsored the Strategic Hamlets program; he unleashed a war of attrition against the NLF; and he allowed the military to use napalm, defoliation, and helicopter envelopment tactics."[117] At the time of his assassination, his vice-

---

115. Taylor, *The Sword and the Pen,* 276.
116. Newman in the *Nation,* 18 May 1992, 650.
117. Bassett and Pelz, "The Failed Search for Victory," 250. In a similar vein, Alexander Cockburn attacks apologists of Kennedy: "The real J.F.K. backed a military coup in Guatemala to keep out Arevalo, denied the Dominican Republic the possibility of land reform, helped promote a devastating cycle of Latin American history . . . and backed a Baathist coup in Iraq that set a certain native of Tikrit on the path to power. He

president, Lyndon Johnson, pointed out that Kennedy "had not revised his assessment of our role there or of the importance of South Vietnam to Southeast Asia and our own security. He continued to believe that the conquest of Southeast Asia would have the most serious impact on Asia and us."[118]

For about a year, between Harkins's arrival and the Buddhist uprisings, it appeared that Kennedy's policies might pay off, and the JCS even began to plan for the withdrawal of American personnel from Vietnam. But by late 1963 it was evident that McGarr, Felt, Shoup, Vann, Wilson, and at times Taylor, among others, had earlier and more realistically described conditions in the RVN. Even so, as Taylor himself later admitted, many American officials during the Kennedy years "didn't foresee the toughness and endurance of the North Vietnamese or the ineptitude of the South Vietnamese leaders in unifying their own people and in using the many forms of aid the U.S. would give."[119] Several American officers, however, did anticipate such problems, but the new administration in Washington was committed to continuing the Kennedy legacy, with the maintenance of the RVN a central component of its national security policy.

presided over Operation Mongoose, inflicting terror upon Cuba. At the very moments bullets brought J.F.K.'s life to its conclusion in Dallas, a C.I.A. officer operating firmly within the bounds of Kennedy's policy was handing poison to a Cuban agent in Paris, designed to kill Castro." See the *Nation,* 6–13 January 1992, 7.

118. Lyndon B. Johnson, *The Vantage Point: Perspectives of the Presidency, 1963–1969* (New York, 1971), 61.
119. Maxwell Taylor Oral History, interview by Ted Gittinger, 14 September 1981 (interview 3), 10, LBJL.

6

"Seeing Things Through in Vietnam": LBJ, the Military, and the Growing U.S. Commitment to Vietnam, November 1963–December 1964

Some say we should withdraw from South Viet-Nam, that we have lost almost 200 lives there in the last four years and we should come home. But the United States cannot and must not and will not turn aside and allow the freedom of a brave people to be handed over to communist tyranny.

Lyndon Baines Johnson[1]

As Lyndon Johnson moved into the Oval Office, U.S. policy in Vietnam was in disarray. The events of November 1963 had undermined the optimistic claims of Harkins, Taylor, and others, and the enemy was successfully exploiting the political crisis in the south. Despite those problems, the new president would not deviate from the path that Kennedy had established. With over 16,000 military personnel already deployed, the United States had made a substantial commitment to the RVN, and the American presence would grow exponentially in the coming years. In the course of his first year in the Oval Office, Johnson would authorize covert operations, approve a massive bombing campaign against the DRVN, and prepare to introduce ground combat troops into the conflict. By early 1965, despite many military leaders' reservations, the United States was about to take over the war in Vietnam.

During the first year of his presidency, Johnson expanded the U.S. presence in Vietnam with clear recognition of the deteriorating conditions in the south and the hazards of intervention there. Like

---

1. Johnson's remarks before the American Bar Association, 12 August 1964, in *Vantage Point,* 575.

Kennedy, however, he believed that political factors, both at home and internationally, made it imperative to continue to protect the RVN. Thus predisposed to find an effective antidote to Communist expansion in Indochina, the president rapidly increased America's military stake there. Barely five years later, Johnson's policy was in ruins. American soldiers, firepower, and bombs could not cure the various illnesses of the RVN. Rather than confront the pathology of its condition, Johnson and his advisors, both civilian and military, tried to cure the RVN with the panacea of technological warfare. In the end, the United States destroyed Vietnam in an attempt to save it. Domestically, intervention in Vietnam would undermine Johnson's political agenda, engender mass opposition, rupture the cold war consensus on foreign policy, and further erode America's postwar hegemony.

The Vietnam War would also lead to a grave crisis in civil–military affairs. Relations between America's political and armed forces leaders, who were mistrustful of each other as a result of the New Look, Bay of Pigs, and Vietnam policies in the preceding half decade, would become increasingly strained during the Johnson years. By the mid-1960s U.S. generals and the White House would be at odds over the nature and direction of the war. Although armed forces leaders had endorsed American intervention, they still had no unified approach to Vietnam. Indeed, the military itself would be deeply divided over the conflict – with the MACV, Marines, and Air Force offering fundamentally different views of America's role and strategy in Vietnam – and it would become clear to many officers that success would not be forthcoming in a timely manner and that the president would establish limits to the American war in Vietnam.

Nonetheless, the armed forces would keep pressing Johnson for more resources and the geographical expansion of the war, which the president would always approve to a lesser extent than the brass had proposed. This cycle of military requests and partial authorization would repeat itself time and again. As a result, the military, still recognizing the barriers to preserving the RVN, would then accuse the White House of unduly restraining its ability to wage war. By early 1965, both uniformed and civilian leaders had created a trap for themselves. Though fearing long-term failure in

Vietnam, they were just as reluctant to accept the political responsibility for "losing" Vietnam in the short term. As a result, U.S. service and political leaders would fight against Ho Chi Minh, and among themselves, for the remainder of the Johnson years. At the same time, U.S. officers, at the outset of the war, were creating the "revisionist" critique that American troops had to fight with "one hand tied behind their backs."

Just after taking the oath of office Lyndon Johnson vowed to carry out Kennedy's agenda, and "that meant seeing things through in Vietnam." Just three days later, at a meeting with Ambassador Lodge, McNamara, and military officials, the new executive stressed that he would not "be the President who saw Southeast Asia go the way China went," and afterward told his advisors to "tell those generals in Saigon that Lyndon Johnson intends to stand by our word."[2] Two weeks later Dean Rusk cabled Lodge that the president "has expressed his deep concern that our effort in Viet-Nam be stepped up to [the] highest pitch." Both Rusk and CIA Director John McCone, however, were giving the president bleak assessments of Vietnam, prompting Johnson to express his "serious misgivings" to Lodge. Nonetheless the president downplayed the need for political reform in the RVN because it was so difficult to establish a stable government amid the VC war in the south.[3]

Despite, or maybe because of, such problems, Johnson also signed off on NSAM 273 on 26 November. Prepared under Kennedy, this directive emphasized that America's "central objective" in Vietnam was still to take the actions necessary to prevent Communist victory in the south.[4] Toward that end, the president ap-

2. Johnson, *Vantage Point*, 42; Tom Wicker, *JFK and LBJ: The Influence of Personality upon Politics* (Baltimore, 1973), 205; Johnson in Schlesinger, *Robert Kennedy and His Times*, 726; see also Memorandum for the Record, 25 November 1963, "South Vietnam Situation," Meeting Notes File, box 1, LBJL.
3. Rusk to Lodge, 6 December 1963, VN C.F., NSF, box 198, folder: President/Rusk/Lodge Messages, vol. 1 [1 of 2], LBJL; Johnson, *Vantage Point*, 43–4.
4. Johnson, *Vantage Point*, 45. Peter Dale Scott and others suggest that NSAM marked a clear departure from Kennedy's policy on Vietnam and set the United States on the path to war. The final draft of 26 November, however, was virtually a verbatim copy of earlier efforts, and the commitment to the RVN was precisely the same. Scott, *The War Conspiracy*. For an excellent refutation of Scott's thesis, see Chomsky, "Vain Hopes, False Dreams," 14–15, and *Rethinking Camelot*.

proved Operations Plan (OPLAN) 34-A in December to increase military and political pressure and conduct "punitive or attritional" operations against the DRVN.[5] Such measures had no immediate impact in Vietnam, however. With Lodge sending bleak evaluations of the RVN's politicomilitary performance, the president dispatched McNamara, McCone, and William Bundy, the assistant secretary of state for Far East affairs, to assess the war in Vietnam. The defense secretary's report, as Johnson put it, "was gloomy indeed." The VC was gaining strength and extending control over more area in the south, Communist infiltration was still rising, and the Strategic Hamlets program had shown few returns. McNamara thus feared that "current trends, unless reversed in the next 2–3 months, will lead to neutralization at best and more likely to a Communist-controlled state." The new Minh government, he further complained, was "indecisive and drifting," and without any clear concept of how to run the country or the war.[6]

McNamara, however, failed to mention in his report the principal American grievance against the new regime in the RVN. "Big" Minh and his prime minister, Nguyen Ngoc Tho, had made overtures to the NLF to establish a "government of reconciliation" in the south and at the same time they rejected American proposals to bomb the DRVN and strike VC bases in the south. Throughout January 1964, then, the Pentagon began to actively seek an alternative to Minh's leadership. Not coincidentally, a coup led by General Nguyen Khanh and supported by the MACV and U.S. Department of Defense ousted Minh on 30 January.[7] During the short-lived Minh administration, Harkins, Taylor, and Curtis LeMay had been pressing the White House and RVN leadership to expand the air war – "we should stop swatting flies and go after the manure pile," as the Air Force chief put it – and conduct offensive operations against the VC.[8] Not all U.S. officers, however, were so eager to widen the war. Advisors in Vietnam such as Wilbur Wilson in III

5. CRS, *Government and Vietnam War*, 210.
6. Johnson, *Vantage Point*, 62–3; McNamara to Johnson, 21 December 1963, "Vietnam Situation," *Pentagon Papers: Gravel*, 3:494–6.
7. Kahin, *Intervention*, 185–8, 197; CRS, *Government and Vietnam War*, 210. In a 1969 interview Wheeler said that the U.S. military was "absolutely not" urging the bombing of the DRVN. Wheeler Oral History (1), 22–3, LBJL.
8. LeMay in Perry, *Four Stars*, 142; Kahin, *Intervention*, 185–200.

Corps reported that the VC had "attacked, harassed and taunted GVN forces and the population with relative impunity," and that there was "no indication" that the situation was changing.[9]

In an address at Marine headquarters in late 1963 the incoming commandant, General Wallace M. Greene, Jr., explicitly rejected American participation in the war in Indochina, lamenting that "we're up to our knees in the quagmire [in Vietnam] and we don't seem to be able to do much about it." Greene hoped that the current Marine presence in Vietnam, about 550 troops, would remain low. "Frankly, in the Marine Corps we do not want to get any more involved in South Vietnam because if we do we cannot execute our primary mission," he admitted. With more important commitments elsewhere, he feared that the corps would be overextended in Vietnam. "You see what happened to the French," Greene ruminated, "well, maybe the same thing is going to happen to us."[10] Generals Victor Krulak, who was assuming command of the Fleet Marine Force, Pacific (FMFPac), and Donald Bennett, director of strategic planning for the Army, had similar reservations about expanding the U.S. role in Vietnam, with Bennett later charging that "certainly from September of [19]63 on, the forcing [into war in Vietnam], as far as I could tell, came from the civilian side."[11]

Despite his own misgivings, Krulak recommended that the president, who had directed him to study OPLAN 34-A, put "progressively escalating pressure" on the DRVN to convince it to stop its "aggressive policies" in the south. Krulak's boss, Commandant Greene, had also joined the air war bandwagon and, with LeMay, pressed for expanded operations above the seventeenth parallel. The other service leaders, as Marine General Henry Buse noted,

9. Wilbur Wilson report, 5 December 1963, "Monthly Intelligence Analysis, III Corps Advisory Group, November 1963," Wilson Papers, MHI. Senior Marine advisors similarly criticized the Vietnamese Marine Corps' inability to conduct pacification operations or obtain intelligence. Even worse, Marine statistics showed that VC-initiated incidents for November 1963 had, for the first time, risen above three thousand. Whitlow, *Marines in Vietnam, 1954–1964*, 133–4; Fleet Marine Force, Pacific (FMFPac), U.S. Marine Corps Forces in Vietnam, March 1965–September 1967, Historical Summary, MCHC.
10. Wallace M. Greene, Jr., "A Marine Corps View of Military Strategy," tape #6276, MCHC. This tape, and all others cited from the Marine Corps Historical Center, were transcribed by me.
11. Victor Krulak, Oral History, June 1970 interview, 204, MCHC; Donald Bennett Oral History, section 7, 30–4, MHI.

were "apathetic" about such proposals, but Maxwell Taylor "was holding the whip hand over the chiefs" to make JCS policy conform to his and McNamara's view of the war.[12]

Taylor, writing for the other chiefs, cited Johnson's commitment to the RVN in NSAM 273 and wanted to "make plain to the enemy our determination to see the Vietnam campaign through to a favorable conclusion." To do so, he added, the White House and chiefs might have to assume temporary authority over the ARVN, pressure the RVNAF to do more to stop infiltration, conduct air strikes against the DRVN, or even commit U.S. forces "as necessary in direct actions against North Vietnam."[13] Again, the military prescription for Vietnam did not conform to the reality that its own evaluations had disclosed. Without any such objective strategic analysis, conditions on the ground were not going to improve.

McNamara too seemed to ignore the implications of his appraisals of the war. In his report, which would become NSAM 288, the defense secretary recommended against overt ARVN or U.S. military action against the DRVN, but otherwise accepted the JCS's views and urged the president to reaffirm his commitment to the RVN, continue to fund and supply the RVNAF, and be prepared to retaliate or begin operations against the Communists. Unless the United States could preserve the RVN, NSAM 288 declared, "almost all of Southeast Asia will probably fall under Communist domination."[14] From Saigon, Henry Cabot Lodge endorsed plans to exert pressure against Vietnam above the DMZ both to bring about a cease-fire and to neutralize the DRVN, thereby "turning it into an Oriental Yugoslavia."[15] Walt Rostow more forcefully told Rusk that the United States had to "draw the line in the dust at the borders of South Viet Nam" by moving additional forces into Indochina to block infiltration into the RVN and by threatening Ho

12. CRS, *Government and Vietnam War,* 214–15; General Henry Buse, Oral History, 205–8, MCHC.
13. Taylor to McNamara, 22 January 1964, "Vietnam and Southeast Asia," *Pentagon Papers: Gravel,* 3:496–9; Taylor, *Swords and Plowshares,* 309–12.
14. McNamara to Johnson, 16 March 1964, "South Vietnam," *Pentagon Papers: Gravel,* 3:499–510; Larry Berman, *Planning a Tragedy: The Americanization of the War in Vietnam* (New York, 1982), 32.
15. Lodge to the White House, 20 January 1964, VN C.F., NSF, box 198, folder: President/Rusk/Lodge Messages, vol. 1 [2 of 2], LBJL.

with American retaliation to enforce compliance.[16] The president himself was not so combative, directing Lodge to press Khanh for more aggressive action against the VC but also assuring the RVN of continued American support.[17]

Again, however, American leaders were ratcheting up the war due to the dismal reports coming out of Vietnam. McNamara, Lodge, Felt, Wilson, Marine advisors, the MACV staff, and other military critics variously pointed out the VC's growing strength, the ARVN's continued ineffectiveness, inadequate intelligence, futile pacification efforts, poor morale in the south, and continued political chaos in the RVN. In March, after returning from another tour of Vietnam, McNamara and Taylor told the NSC that conditions had "unquestionably been growing worse." The VC controlled at least 50 percent of the land area in twenty-two of forty-three southern provinces, southern desertion rates and draft evasion had soared, and the enemy was "recruiting energetically and effectively." Between July 1963 and early 1964 the enemy had virtually destroyed the Strategic Hamlets program, while the political chaos in the RVN continued, with thirty-five province chiefs having been replaced since the November coup.[18]

Despite more bad news, the White House remained committed to staying the course in Vietnam, invoking the political fallout for Harry Truman after Mao's victory in China in 1949 to reject Sena-

16. Rostow to Rusk, 13 February 1964, "Southeast Asia," Papers of Paul Warnke – John McNaughton Files, box 7, folder: book 1 – DOS Material, LBJL.

17. Johnson to Lodge, 18 February 1964, VN C.F., NSF, box 198, folder: President/Rusk/Lodge Messages, vol. 1 [1 of 2], LBJL.

18. See Lodge to Rusk, 6 January 1964, VN C.F. NSF, box 198, folder: President/Rusk/Lodge Messages, vol. 1 [2 of 2], LBJL; Felt to Harkins, 8 February 1964, Warnke-McNaughton, box 3, folder: McNTN, VI, Briefing Book, 29 February 1964 (2), LBJL; General Richard Stilwell report, 10 March 1964, "Counterinsurgency Vitalization," Westmoreland Papers, folder 460 [2 of 2]: #3 History File, 20 December 1965–29 January 1966, WNRC; Summary Record of NSC Meeting No. 523, 5 March 1964, "Secretary McNamara's Mission to Vietnam," NSF, NSC Meeting File, box 1, folder: NSC Meetings, vol. 1, tab 4; various Wilbur Wilson evaluations in Wilson Papers, folders: Memorandums for Gen. Khiem (1964), Memo on Leadership Motivation, and May 1964, MHI; Whitlow, *Marines in Vietnam, 1954–1964,* 121; Johnson, *Vantage Point,* 65–6; McNamara to Johnson, 16 March 1964, "South Vietnam," *Pentagon Papers: Gravel,* 3:499–510. The MACV's own weekly reports were consistently frank about the ever deteriorating situation in the RVN throughout 1964. See Records of the Military Assistance Command Vietnam, part 1, The War in Vietnam, 1954–1973, MACV Historical Office Documentary Collection, University Publications of America (UPA), microfilm reel 2 (hereafter cited as MACV Records, part 1, UPA).

tor Mike Mansfield's proposal for a truce and neutralization of the RVN. Politics was already becoming the tail that wagged the dog and, accordingly, the president had limited options with regard to Vietnam policy. "The only thing I know to do," he lamented to Senate Committee on Foreign Relations Chair J. William Fulbright, "is more of the same and do it more effectively." As Johnson saw it, he could not withdraw, neutralize, or send in combat troops that "may be bogged down in a long war against numerically superior North Vietnamese and Chicom forces 100,000 miles from home." The United States would thus continue its current policy of support and training in the RVN.[19]

Other administration members urged the president to do more. At an NSC meeting following McNamara's return from Vietnam, the defense secretary joined Rusk and Taylor in urging Johnson to establish a border control force, retaliate against the north, and develop a "graduated overt military pressure program" against the DRVN. Such measures might not stop the deterioration in the south, Rusk pointed out, but at least would make it easier to deploy "forces which could be used if it were decided later to take the war to North Vietnam." The JCS chair – a critic, politico, and true believer rolled into one – saw the risks inherent in his own proposals. Taylor understood that even limited measures would produce a "strong reaction" in northern Vietnam and could even prompt the PRC to intervene in Indochina. Nevertheless he and the other chiefs supported the McNamara–NSAM 288 plans and urged the Pentagon to prepare for future deployments in the event of American escalation of the war. McNamara added that the costs of his program would be significant, with initial expenditures of about $60 million by the RVN and $30 million by the United States. With such aid, American officials still hoped, they could avoid increasing U.S. troop numbers in the RVN and try to turn over more responsibility to southern forces.[20]

19. CRS, *Government and Vietnam War*, 215–16; Johnson phone conversation with Fulbright in Doris Kearns, *Lyndon Johnson and the American Dream* (New York, 1976), 196–7.
20. Summary Record of the NSC Meeting No. 524, 17 March 1964, "Report of Secretary McNamara's Trip to Vietnam," and Bromley Smith memorandum for the NSC, 16 March 1964, "Memorandum on Viet Nam, dated March 16, 1964," both in NSF, NSC Meeting File, box 1, folder: vol. 1, tab 5, LBJL; see also JCS 5390 to CINCPAC, 18 March 1964, "Planning Actions, Viet Nam," *Pentagon Papers: Gravel*, 3: 510.

Within armed forces circles, however, there was significant division over the nature of any future military action in Vietnam. Harkins and Felt still believed "that it is necessary to kill and destroy; that it is necessary to penetrate; that it is necessary to harass and ambush; that it is necessary to clear and hold."[21] Retired General Douglas MacArthur, perhaps the country's best-known military man, moreover advised the incoming MACV commander, William Childs Westmoreland, "not [to] overlook the possibility . . . that in order to defeat the guerrilla, you may have to resort to a scorched earth policy." To Michael Forrestal of the NSC staff, such observations served as "warning indicators" that American military policy in Vietnam was dangerously misguided. As Forrestal saw it, the MACV's reports on and approach to the conflict, "which places such emphasis on military activities so similar to those which failed the French, suggests a lack of understanding of what the war is about."[22]

Uniformed officials too recognized that the MACV's conventional, firepower-oriented strategy had not worked as its ever optimistic commander had anticipated. With Harkins's retirement scheduled for June 1964, the president in January had appointed Westmoreland to serve as his deputy until assuming the MACV command in a few months, and his arrival raised some officers' hopes that Harkins's approach to the war would be displaced. General Bruce Palmer, the Army's deputy chief of staff for operations, expected Westmoreland to stress improving the advisory effort for

21. CINCPAC to JCS, 26 February 1964, "Tactical Concepts – RVN," Warnke-McNaughton, box 3, folder: McNTN, VI, Briefing Book, 29 February 1964 (2), LBJL.
22. Westmoreland, *A Soldier Reports*, 40. Westmoreland also received some ambivalent opinions from a close source – his father, who wrote that "I hardly know what to think about the situation in Vietnam." Since the war in Indochina had already lasted over a decade, time was on the enemy's side. And, the elder Westmoreland rather presciently recognized, "if I have the public opinion sized up this country would call all of you home and let that country go to [hell]." James Ripley Westmoreland to William Westmoreland, 22 March 1964, Westmoreland Papers, folder 500: #3 History Backup, 17 February–30 April 1964, WNRC. Forrestal's lamentations were actually stronger than he indicated in his memorandum. He asserted that a recent MACV report on Vietnam, although it "does not by itself prove that we have a military staff in Saigon inadequate for the job," at least makes it clear that the military's approach to Vietnam incorrectly relied on conventional strategy. But, he added parenthetically, he could only make that relatively benign observation "at the risk of violent reaction from the uniformed side of the Pentagon." Forrestal to McGeorge Bundy, 30 March 1964, "South Vietnam," Reference File, box 1, folder: Miscellaneous Vietnam Documents, LBJL.

the RVNAF, as John Paul Vann had long emphasized.[23] From Fort Bragg, the commander of the Special Warfare Center, General William Yarborough, wrote to Westmoreland that "I cannot emphasize too greatly that the entire conflict in Southeast Asia is 80 percent in the realm of ideas and only 20 percent in the field of physical conflict." So long as VC guerrillas continued to believe in the virtue of their cause "there can be no peace." "Repeated terrorist acts" would not cause military defeat, Yarborough believed, but "a war can be lost mentally and morally through these means. This . . . is a danger to be guarded against at all costs."[24]

The JCS's Joint War Games Agency (JWGA) likewise pointed out the problems of war in its April 1964 final report of Sigma I-64, another war game concerning Vietnam. The participants, including Taylor, Wheeler, LeMay, Bruce Palmer, John McCone, the Bundys, Michael Forrestal, George Ball, and Chester Cooper, assumed that current U.S. efforts would remain inadequate, but were aware of the peril in an expanded effort as well. Many participants doubted that the VC responded to Hanoi's control to any major degree, instead believing that the northern influence was "mainly psychological and disciplinary, not material." Even those, presumably military officials, who urged pressure against the north to "take the heat off" in the south recognized that there was "little evidence" to suggest that the DRVN would capitulate, while "a small expenditure of iron bombs involves [the] potential commitment of major US forces representing millions of dollars if the DRV *doesn't* fold up." In the meantime, "the problem of winning popular support in South Vietnam *still goes on* with less command attention and perhaps fewer resources available to cope with real RVN domestic problems."[25]

There were also likely to be strong domestic repercussions to U.S. escalation. While Congress would give a "reluctant go-ahead" to U.S. attacks on the DRVN, there would be "moral and legal questions" surrounding such actions aimed at "innocent populations."

23. Palmer to Vann, 14 January 1964, Vann Papers, folder: 1964, MHI.
24. Yarborough to Westmoreland, 26 February 1964, Westmoreland Papers, folder 460 [2 of 2]: #3 History File, 20 December 1965–29 January 1966, WNRC.
25. Final Report and List of Participants, Sigma I-64, April 1964, especially tab D, NSF, Agency File, JCS, box: 30, folder: JCS War Games, vol. 1 [I], LBJL, emphasis in original.

The administration could also expect "obvious difficulties" in gauging the *"extent of Communist involvement* in 'honest' revolutionary movements [the NLF] against despotic regimes [the RVN]." Indeed, the U.S. planners admitted, America's past support of such regimes and the likelihood of doing so again was sure to be a sticky political issue.[26]

Reports from Vietnam were no more positive. Throughout April, May, and June, VC activity was continuing at "high intensity," especially in areas around Saigon and in II Corps. The VC was also mining railway tracks in I Corps and was undermining America's advantage in air power by effectively using anti-aircraft fire in both the far northern and southern provinces of the RVN. Throughout all regions of the south the insurgents were conducting sabotage, harassments, assassinations of local officials, and small-scale combat, all of which seemed to indicate that the RVNAF and Americans were not able to provide basic village security. By June the VC was conducting fewer operations but increasing the size and tempo of its attacks, often engaging its main force units in battalion-sized actions.[27]

The secretary of defense duly reported the worsening conditions in the south at a mid-May NSC meeting. The VC's military influence was rising and, on the political front, the new Khanh government "is fragmented and a religious crisis [with the Buddhists] is brewing." Such conditions of course made effective military action against the Communists unlikely. Reflecting that situation, military leaders proposed mixed responses to the crisis in the RVN. LeMay and Greene urged reconnaissance missions and air strikes against the DRVN, but Taylor, new Army Chief of Staff Harold K. Johnson, and CNO Admiral David McDonald opposed starting the air war at that time. As the JCS chair explained, any U.S. attack against the north would provoke "a strong reaction by the Viet Cong in the south," which the Communists would be able to increase to levels commensurate with American initiatives. Given such assessments, as well as growing congressional criticism of American involvement in Indochina, the president "concluded the

26. Ibid.
27. See USMACV Weekly Military Reports, April–June 1964, MACV Records, part 1, reel 2, UPA.

[NSC] meeting by commenting that even with increased U.S. aid the prospect in South Vietnam is not bright."[28]

Despite Johnson's bleak view, the secretary of defense was proud that critics referred to Vietnam as "McNamara's War," telling reporters that "I think it is a very important war and I am pleased to be identified with it and do whatever I can to win it."[29] Lodge further wanted to make it clear that the United States would not withdraw from Vietnam. Rather "we will enlarge. We intend to stay. We expect to win."[30] Rusk expected the U.S. public to support any expansion of the war and agreed with the need to remain steadfast in Vietnam.[31] Meanwhile, both Bundys put forth hawkish proposals. While William Bundy preferred air strikes against the DRVN, he thought, and Rusk agreed, that "significant US ground forces" might also be needed in the south.[32] His brother McGeorge assumed that American leaders would not tolerate a Communist triumph in Southeast Asia, but also believed that U.S. prospects were bleak "without a decision to resort to military action" and so he called for "selected and carefully graduated military force" against the DRVN.[33]

Not everyone in an official capacity was so belligerent. Michael Forrestal decried the emphasis on military solutions to political problems with the warning that "we are trying to fit our familiar tools and way of doing things to a problem we have never really bothered to analyze."[34] As he was about to assume command of the MACV, General Westmoreland was candid about U.S. prospects in Vietnam, finding his predecessor's prediction that he would reverse conditions within months to be "incredible." The general also "found the thinking in Washington on increasing the American commitment in South Vietnam, possibly to include bombing North

28. Summary Record of NSC Meeting No. 532, May 15, 1964, "Reports by Secretary Rusk and Secretary McNamara," NSF, NSC Meetings File, box 1, folder: vol. 2, tab 4, LBJL; Futrell, *Air Force and Southeast Asia*, 204.
29. *NYT*, 25 April 1964.
30. Lodge to Rusk, 4 May 1964, Lodge to Johnson, 15 May 1964, and Lodge to Rusk, 22 May 1964, all in VN C.F., NSF, box 198, folder: President/Rusk/Lodge Messages, vol. 1 [2 of 2], LBJL; *Pentagon Papers: Gravel*, 3:166.
31. Rusk to Lodge, 21 May 1964, in CRS, *Government and Vietnam War*, 252–4.
32. Vincent Demma, "Suggestions for the Use of Ground Forces, June 1964-March 1965," unpublished manuscript, used at Center of Military History (CMH), Washington, D.C.
33. M. Bundy in CRS, *Government and the Vietnam War*, 256–7.
34. Forrestal to McNaughton, 1 May 1964, DDRS, 78, 129A.

Vietnam and even introducing American combat troops, far more advanced than anything we were considering in Saigon."[35] The president, however, wanted to expand the American role in Vietnam, and so directed his civilian and military advisors to meet at Honolulu in early June to discuss the war.

Lyndon Johnson was already facing a dilemma in Vietnam in mid-1964. Reports from Saigon and the field consistently indicated a worsening situation, while his advisors in Washington were encouraging escalation with no guarantees of success. Political factors, however, were overriding. If the United States quit Vietnam and "let Ho Chi Minh run through the streets of Saigon," Johnson later told Doris Kearns, it would be rewarding aggression just as the West had done with Hitler in the 1930s. Communist victory in Vietnam would also cause an "endless national debate – a mean and destructive debate – that would shatter my Presidency, kill my administration, and damage our democracy," just as Mao's victory in China had undermined the Truman administration and brought on McCarthyism. In fact, Truman's problems with the PRC "were chickenshit compared with what might happen if we lost Vietnam."[36] Johnson's advisors, civilian and military, likely had similar world views of domestic politics, so, at the Honolulu meeting, they focused on improving conditions in the RVN. Despite understanding the political and military troubles facing the United States in Vietnam, Johnson's foreign policy team did not even consider disengagement.

An "atmosphere of considerable gloom," as Westmoreland put it, permeated the Honolulu meetings. The military situation, the new MACV commander reported, was "tenuous but not hopeless," while the political situation, still the key to success, resembled "the most absurd *opera bouffe*" with Buddhist–Catholic tensions and infighting among junta members making it impossible to achieve stability.[37] While everyone could recognize such problems within Vietnam, there was no consensus on how to reverse the deterioration. The president wanted to integrate American officials extensively into the RVN administrative structure but Westmore-

35. Westmoreland, *A Soldier Reports*, 67–71.
36. Kearns, *Lyndon Johnson and the American Dream*, 252–3, 258.
37. Westmoreland, *A Soldier Reports*, 71.

land, Lodge, and Taylor – who was about to become ambassador
upon Lodge's departure – doubted that there were enough qualified
Americans to fill such positions or that a U.S. takeover was the
politically correct way to bolster the RVN.[38]

The JCS itself was also split over future policy. Over Taylor's
objections, the chiefs – still trying to pin down the White House –
again expressed concern over "a lack of definition" of U.S. objectives, without which they could not "advocate a desirable military
course of action" to achieve American goals. Nevertheless, LeMay,
Greene, incoming JCS chair Earle Wheeler, and Lodge all favored
beginning an air campaign against the north to stop infiltration and
show American resolve. Taylor, however, feared that such strikes
might provoke DRVN or even PRC aggression in the RVN. He also
understood that "political considerations" – it was an election year
and Johnson was running as a peace candidate against the hawkish
Senator Barry Goldwater – would guide U.S. policy, so the JCS
chair-cum-ambassador urged "demonstrative attacks" against limited military targets as a way to show American willingness to
engage the enemy. He, and Westmoreland, also believed that any
decision to widen the war "should be delayed for some time yet."
Thus the conferees adjourned on 3 June committed only to expanding the advisory effort, refining plans for pressuring the DRVN,
and beginning a publicity campaign to prepare Americans for escalation in Vietnam and to secure allied assistance for the RVN.[39]

The failure to develop a strategic concept at Honolulu offered
more evidence that American policy was stagnant in mid-1964.
Earle Wheeler had to admit that "we have never been able to recover the same degree of military success that we were having a year
earlier [before the Diem coup]. The political situation . . . has

---

38. Taylor, *Swords and Plowshares*, 312–13. General Krulak, the commander of the Marines Pacific Fleet, also opposed the "encadrement" of U.S. personnel into the RVN
government or the ARVN. To Krulak, such a move would amount to a "proconsul
arrangement." With such a reorganization, the United States would assume responsibility for the war, "the indigenous group learns nothing, [and] blames you for all misadven-
tures and gradually turns against you." Krulak to CINCPAC, 29 May 1964, "Meeting
on Southeast Asia," Victor H. Krulak Papers, box 2, folder: Correspondence, 1964–
June 1965, MCHC. On Taylor's move from JCS chair to ambassador, which Mark Perry
describes as a coup d'etat staged by the other chiefs, see *Four Stars*, chapter 4.
39. *Pentagon Papers: Gravel*, 3:171–9, 2:323–5.

steadily gotten worse; the government has gotten weaker."[40] The commandant of the Marine Corps seemed to place much of the blame for that predicament on Maxwell Taylor. As General Greene saw it, Taylor assumed "an increasingly more dominant and powerful role" as JCS chair. The commandant also believed that many civilian officials in the Pentagon had supported Taylor's power grab and created a situation where the "position of the chairman is enlarged only at the expense of the corporate body of which he is a member."[41]

Taylor's successor, General Wheeler, and Westmoreland also came under fire at this time. The new JCS leader, his critics emphasized, was a lifetime bureaucrat who had "never heard a shot fired in anger." Wheeler was, maverick Marine Colonel William Corson charged, "the Army's highest-ranking sycophant" who had gained promotion via consistent agreement with his superiors. McNamara, however, developed a strong relationship with Wheeler at the beginning of his tenure as chair. Since the new JCS leader was willing to broker between military and civilian viewpoints, the defense secretary was assured harmony with the chiefs. But to many officers, Wheeler was simply a "political general" who might not defend their interests strongly enough. Apparently the other chiefs also questioned whether Westmoreland, a favorite of John Kennedy and dubbed "the inevitable general," should be commanding the MACV given his limited background in CI warfare and his image-conscious and aloof manner. Westmoreland had not been the JCS's first choice to assume the MACV command, but he was well respected among civilian leaders. The chiefs, however, were confident that he would not overstep his bounds or try to dominate the policy-making process for Vietnam so they, especially Wheeler and Harold K. Johnson, "swallowed hard" and accepted his appointment. Clearly, both the new chair and commander shared a strong sense of the political ramifications of military pol-

---

40. Earle Wheeler Oral History, 64–6, JFKL.
41. Wallace M. Greene, Jr., Opening Remarks, General Officers' Symposium, 7 July 1964, Wallace M. Greene Papers, box 14, folder 167, MCHC. On JCS criticism of Taylor as chair, see Perry, *Four Stars*, chapter 4.

icy, an understanding that would increasingly bear on their handling of the war in Vietnam over the next four years.[42]

By autumn 1964, however, neither political nor military conditions were in America's favor. The MACV again noted a "rise in tempo and intensity" of both small-scale and battalion-size or larger VC actions all across the RVN. American advisors seemed more worried, however, about the foundering pacification campaign. While the VC was impeding CI progress throughout I Corps, the RVNAF's own pacification squads "have displayed much more concern for their own personal safety than for the accomplishment of their mission." In Quang Ngai, in I Corps, the provincial chief had to recall several hundred combat cadre to attend a reorientation course in pacification due to their "lack of ability, supervision, and motivation." In the northern Phuoc Tan district, in what could have been an analysis of the program in general, the MACV reported that Vietnamese personnel "have no clear concept of their mission and role in pacification."[43] Nor were the Americans adequately supporting civic affairs policies, Army advisor Captain Dave Richard Palmer charged; "Lip service – yes, honest effort – no," was his description of the U.S. pacification program.[44]

Despite such problems, Lyndon Johnson thought he would have to wait until November, after the presidential election, to take effective action on Vietnam. But in early August, in the DRVN's territorial waters in the Gulf of Tonkin, the president would find a justification to expand the war. At that time the RVN's navy had been bombarding the northern Vietnamese coast as part of OPLAN 34-A operations. Two U.S. destroyers, the *Maddox* and the *C. Turner Joy*, were also in the area of the Gulf of Tonkin and on 2 and 4 August American naval officials alleged that DRVN torpedo boats had attacked the ships. The strikes, never substantiated, and an attendant congressional resolution authorizing the president to

42. Quotes in Perry, *Four Stars*, 135–7; see also Shapley, *Promise and Power*, 325–6; for more criticism of Westmoreland, see Forrestal to McGeorge Bundy, 30 March 1964, "South Vietnam," Reference File, box 1, folder: Miscellaneous Vietnam Documents, LBJL.
43. U.S. MACV Weekly Military Reports, July 1964, MACV Records, part 1, reels 2–3, UPA.
44. Captain Dave Richard Palmer, Random Notes on the Vietnam War, 1 August 1964, Westmoreland Papers, folder 504: #7 History Backup, 27 July–31 August 1964, WNRC.

"take all necessary steps" to defend the RVN, gave Johnson a virtual carte blanche to wage war in Vietnam, which he soon did with "retaliatory" air strikes against the north. The Gulf of Tonkin Resolution passed the House 416–0, while Fulbright had pushed it through the Senate with just two votes cast against it. One of the dissenters, Wayne Morse of Oregon, had considered calling Generals Ridgway, Gavin, Shoup, and Collins to testify against it, but Fulbright had not allocated adequate time for debate. The resolution, the president later explained in his inimitable Texas style, "was like Grandma's nightshirt, it covered everything."[45] It also gave Johnson political cover for his 1964 campaign, allowing him to claim that he was both standing firm in Vietnam and exercising restraint, unlike Goldwater.

The Tonkin Gulf affair set into motion the American takeover of the war in Vietnam. The U.S. air strikes and the overwhelming vote in Congress convinced the southern leadership of America's resolve to remain in the RVN; as CIA operatives observed at the time, "many [RVNAF] officers feel that the U.S. is now fully committed, and that more of the burden of carrying on the war will now pass to the U.S."[46] As the Johnson administration moved closer to full-scale intervention, however, ranking officials, especially Taylor and even Westmoreland, still hoped to limit American involvement in Indochina yet were also willing to expand the war at the same time. Westmoreland, at the outset of his command, was already taking the dual approach to policy making that would characterize his time in Vietnam. On one hand, his assessments candidly reflected the serious problems existing in the south. On the other, he would optimistically conclude that success would be forthcoming once American resources, weapons, or soldiers reached the battlefield in sufficient numbers. In this way the commander was telling his superiors in Washington what they wanted to hear, but also covering his flanks by offering honest evaluations of the situation on the ground. Such were the politics of the war in Vietnam in mid-1964.

Westmoreland's response to the Gulf of Tonkin incident reflected his concern about escalating the war. U.S. attacks against the north,

45. Kahin, *Intervention,* 219–25; Halberstam, *Best and Brightest,* 507; Johnson in Stanley Karnow, *Vietnam: A History* (New York, 1983), 374.
46. CIA Report, 13 August 1964, in Kahin, *Intervention,* 229.

the MACV commander assumed, would prompt the PRC to increase aid to Ho or even intervene, infiltration into the RVN would
rise to counter American personnel, and the VC would take further
offensive actions, especially by attacking vulnerable American air
bases at Da Nang, Bien Hoa, and Tan Son Nhut. To protect those
bases, he thus recommended that a Marine expeditionary force,
Army elements, and logistics units prepare to deploy to Vietnam.
Already in August 1964 Westmoreland was aware of the barriers to
victory, but preparing for a longer-term commitment in Vietnam,
which, he hoped, would not include combat forces.[47] The MACV
commander was taking a relatively temperate approach compared
with the JCS in Washington. On 26 August, the chiefs pointed out
that the United States was "already deeply involved" in the war in
Vietnam and thus asked McNamara to authorize air strikes against
ninety-four previously selected targets in the north in order to
destroy the DRVN's capabilities to support the insurgency in the
south. Credibility, however, seemed an overriding concern, for,
while the chiefs admitted that such an air campaign "will not necessarily provide decisive end results," they believed that the enemy
would interpret anything less as a "lack of resolve."[48]

McGeorge Bundy wanted to do even more than the JCS. In May
he and his brother had first proposed sending combat troops to
Vietnam. Now, believing that limited air or naval operations would
do little more than show resolve, the national security advisor
thought that Johnson ought to begin thinking about committing a
substantial number of U.S. forces to action against the VC. "Before
we let this country go," Bundy warned, "we should take a hard
look at the grim alternative."[49] In June the JCS also raised the
ground force issue, directing the USARPAC to study the feasibility

---

47. Westmoreland to Sharp and Wheeler, 15 August 1964, "Improvement [of] US Posture
    [in] SVN," Westmoreland Papers, folder 504: #7 History Backup, 27 July–31 August
    1964, WNRC.
48. JCS to Secretary of Defense, 26 August 1964, "Recommended Courses of Action –
    Southeast Asia," *Pentagon Papers: Gravel*, 3:550–2.
49. Bundy also tried to reassure the president that a war in Vietnam would neither require a
    commitment nor have an outcome similar to the Korean War: "It seems to me at least
    possible that a couple of brigade-size units put in to do specific jobs about six weeks
    from now might be good medicine everywhere." Bundy to LBJ, 31 August 1964, in CRS,
    Government and Vietnam War, 349–50. On Bundy's May views, see ibid., 256–7, and
    Demma, "Suggestions for the Use of Ground Forces."

of deploying forces across the RVN and Laotian panhandle to the Mekong River as a way to interdict infiltration. In August the Army estimated that four divisions could accomplish the task and, Chief of Staff Harold K. Johnson contended, moreover could avoid provocative air attacks and put the burden for breaking the defensive cordon onto the DRVN.[50] Critics of both the panhandle and air war plans emerged at once. Admiral Felt attacked the Army plan, citing enormous logistics problems and terrain difficulties to question whether it would stem infiltration. The outgoing Pacific commander also feared that U.S. troops would get tied down in static positions "in an environment worse than that of ARVN pacification forces" in the south. Such an effort would, moreover, indicate that the United States had "shot a big wad at a point of no decision."[51]

The military was also split over the advisability of an air campaign against the north. Both LeMay and Greene found it "now necessary to execute extensive U.S. air strikes" over the DRVN. The Air Force chief, as Mark Perry explained, hoped that an air campaign would stem Communist success before ground troops would have to intervene in a "full-blown conventional ground conflict." So did the commandant. Wheeler, Harold K. Johnson, Admiral McDonald, and Westmoreland, however, agreed with Maxwell Taylor that such measures would "overstrain" the RVN. As the JCS chair saw it, the RVN government, then under Khanh's control in between coups, would be too weak in the foreseeable future to handle the risks of an escalated air war, which could include increased VC or PAVN actions in the south.[52] The MACV commander also questioned the utility of air strikes against the north because the insurgency and continued infiltration in the RVN was

---

50. Demma, "Suggestions for the Use of Ground Forces"; Interview with Harold K. Johnson, conducted by Charles B. MacDonald and Charles von Luttichau, 20 November 1970, 6–8, CMH.
51. Demma, "Suggestions for the Use of Ground Forces."
52. William Bundy Memorandum, 8 September 1964, "Courses of Action for South Vietnam," Wheeler to McNamara, 9 September 1964, "Courses of Action for South Vietnam," Memorandum for the Record, 14 September 1964, "Meeting on South Vietnam, 9 September 1964," all in NSF, Meeting Notes File, box 1, folder: September 9, 1964, LBJL; Perry, *Four Stars,* 141. First Taylor quotation in Kahin, *Intervention,* 230; see also Futrell, *U.S. Air Force in Southeast Asia,* 253–4; Johnson, *Vantage Point,* 120; Mark Clodfelter, *The Limits of Air Power: The American Bombing of North Vietnam* (New York, 1989), 51–2.

his first priority, and air power would not affect that appreciably. Overreliance on air power, Bruce Palmer explained later, led U.S. policy makers to neglect what should have been their principal goal: developing the ARVN to pacify and defend its own country. Harold K. Johnson agreed on the limits of air war and, as Army historian Vincent Demma explained, consistently tried to moderate the JCS's calls for bombing the north. "If anything came out of Vietnam," the Army chief later said, "it was that airpower couldn't do the job."[53]

Given such views, the president wondered whether Vietnam was "worth all the effort," but his advisors, as expected, reassured him that preserving the RVN was essential to preventing a Communist takeover of all of Southeast Asia.[54] Still, no consensus existed on the means to achieve American goals. In NSAM 314 Johnson authorized resumption of naval patrols and OPLAN 34-A operations in the Gulf of Tonkin, limited operations in Laos, retaliatory actions in the event of DRVN or VC attacks against American units, and continued political-economic development programs.[55] The administration would do little more in September 1964 because the presidential election was just two months away and, as John McNaughton, the assistant secretary of defense for international security affairs, put it, "we must act with special care" both to send signals about U.S. intentions to the DRVN and RVN, and to show the U.S. public "that we are behaving with good purpose and restraint."[56] Westmoreland's concerns were more forthright. The MACV commander "did not contemplate" using U.S. troops in a combat role, Taylor reported. Such a course, Westmoreland thought, "would be a mistake [because it] is the Vietnamese's war."[57]

53. Taylor to Department of State, 4 September 1964, *DDRS*, 84, 737; Westmoreland to Taylor, 14 September 1964, Westmoreland Papers, folder 505: #8 History Backup, 1 September–8 October 1964, WNRC; Demma, "Suggestions for the Use of Ground Forces"; Palmer, *25-Year War*, 178–9; Harold K. Johnson Oral History, U.S. Army, Military History Institute, Senior Officer Oral History Program, 10, used at CMH.
54. Johnson, *Vantage Point*, 120.
55. NSAM 314, 10 September 1964, *Pentagon Papers: Gravel*, 3:565–6.
56. McNaughton draft, 3 September 1964, "Plan of Action for South Vietnam," ibid, 3:556–9.
57. Westmoreland added that, in the interests of morale, he would not assign any U.S. military personnel unaccompanied by family to Vietnam for more than a year. To expect longer tours would be "self-defeating and unfair." Taylor to Department of State, 4 September 1964, *DDRS*, 84, 737.

Even more, U.S. officers continued to admit, they still lacked a coherent approach to the war. Vice Admiral Thomas Moorer, the Navy's Pacific Fleet commander, argued that the United States had to give more than "lip service" to the need for an integrated politicomilitary strategy in Vietnam, a concept that "has really never been meaningfully applied." [58] In a radio interview in early October Westmoreland also stressed that Vietnam was "decidedly different from conventional wars" like World War II or Korea. As well as fighting against an elusive enemy in a battle without fronts, American leaders had to take account of "political considerations" in developing strategy. Anti-Communist success, he noted, "requires a combination of military force, psychological activities, and means of improving the physical welfare of the people." [59]

In October 1964 the United States was markedly deficient in meeting such criteria. Less than half of the southern provinces had made any progress in pacification, while the residents in only about 20 percent of the villages were willing to provide the RVN officials there with any information about the VC. [60] Urban residents, Taylor added, simply expected the political turmoil to drag on, while rural dwellers were more concerned with their own security than government intrigue in Saigon. As a result, reports from the field cited political instability and continued high levels of VC activity to explain the lack of progress in southern Vietnam. Although hoping for reform, Taylor assumed that a coming showdown between Generals Khanh and Minh would only magnify the government's shortcomings. [61]

Despite the risks of deeper involvement amid the endless political clashes in the RVN, John McNaughton believed that it was "essential" for America to maintain its status as a world power, "however badly [Southeast Asia] may go over the next 2–4 years." The

58. Moorer message, 29 September 1964, in Marolda and Fitzgerald, *U.S. Navy and Vietnam*, 456–7.
59. Remarks Made for Mutual Broadcasting Network, 4 October 1964, Westmoreland Papers, folder 3, WNRC.
60. Pacification Reports, October 1964, Westmoreland Papers, folder 505: #8 History Backup, 1 September–8 October 1964, and folder 506: #9 History Backup, 9 October–13 November 1964, WNRC.
61. Taylor to Department of State, 7 October 1964, *DDRS*, 85, 1750; Taylor to Department of State, 14 October and 20 October 1964, VN C.F., NSF, box 195, folder: President/Taylor NODIS CLORES, LBJL.

United States would have to emerge from Vietnam as a "good doctor," he asserted; "we must have kept promises, been tough, taken risks, gotten bloodied, and hurt the enemy very badly" in order to prevent other adversaries from questioning U.S. power and resolve. Credibility, not victory, was McNaughton's goal in Vietnam.[62] The MACV was not achieving either in late 1964. While various critics reported continued stasis throughout all four Corps Tactical Zones,[63] Westmoreland was more worried that the political maneuvering in the capital had further damaged the RVNAF. Fearing a purge after the Khanh–Minh feud was resolved, southern officers might lose their will to fight or else make a "desperate move to regain power."[64]

Back in Washington, the Joint War Games Agency was pointing out even more problems. In Sigma II-64, sponsored by Wheeler, the JWGA again offered a comprehensive and desolate outlook regarding U.S. prospects. American officers fully expected their military role in Vietnam to expand, but recognized the risks of such action. Whether they sent American ground forces into the RVN or intensified the air war over the DRVN, they could expect Communist powers to respond to such offensive measures with either Soviet countermoves in Europe, especially Berlin, or PRC intervention into northern Laos. Even more, JWGA officials warned, "the US would be branded the aggressor for using regular units to fight the people of Vietnam." Representatives of both the Red [Communist] and Blue [U.S.] teams, moreover, recognized that an increased American commitment would face serious military and political problems. A majority of participants believed that, despite heavy bombing of industrial and military targets in the north, the insurgency in the south was not weakening.[65]

62. McNaughton draft, 13 October 1964, "Aims and Options in Southeast Asia," *Pentagon Papers: Gravel,* 3:580–3.
63. U.S. MACV weekly military reports, August-October 1964, Records of the MACV, part 1, reel 3, UPA; General Richard Stilwell, 12 October 1964, "Monthly Report or Pacification Progress and Population and Area Control," VN C.F., NSF, box 165, folder: Vietnam, Monthly Reports of Pacification Progress . . . [I], LBJL.
64. Westmoreland to Taylor, 6 September 1964, "Assessment of the Military Situation," Westmoreland Papers, box 4, folder: #10 History Backup, I, LBJL (I did research in the Westmoreland Papers at both the Washington National Records Center and the LBJ Library. Since the filing designations are slightly different, I will indicate the archives from which the particular document cited came).
65. JWGA, Final Report, Sigma II-64, September 1964, NSF, Agency File, JCS, box 30, folder: JCS War Games, volume II [I], LBJL.

Because of the "stoic attitude of a regimented oriental population," and the "racial undertones of [a] war in which US pilots kill
women and children," the Sigma II participants questioned the
reliance on an air campaign over the DRVN. Citing stiffened
civilian morale during the Battle of Britain, "Red" officers boasted
that, in the DRVN, "the people's rage had been turned against the
American murderers" and also pointed out that the air war had
shown diminishing returns. "The more you attack us," they told
their American counterparts, "the less we have to lose" because
American pilots had hit most of the valuable targets in the north. As
Sigma II and previous games indicated, the DRVN economy, already strained for over a year, was now much worse, but that had
little impact on the war. The VC, Communist team members observed, could simply continue operations in the south utilizing existing stockpiles, captured arms, and levies on the population.
"Red" representatives also reminded the others that U.S. military
escalation would be sure to spark political quarrels at home. The
American public might say that "we're not doing so well, so why
not just let it die on the vine and pull out of there" rather than
taking over the war. The Sigma II participants knew that the
Johnson White House would not withdraw and had developed
their approaches to Vietnam accordingly, but they had nonetheless
confirmed that the military and political odds were not in America's
favor at that time.[66]

General Donald Bennett, a war game participant, thought that
U.S. officials just did not understand Vietnam in 1964. If anything,
however, the Sigma II conclusions revealed a sharp understanding
of the risks of involvement in the war in Indochina. George Ball, the
undersecretary of state and primary war critic within the administration, later cited the results of Sigma II to argue that air war
against Hanoi would accomplish little.[67] Notwithstanding the
JWGA's bleak assessments, many of Johnson's advisors urged him
to subject the DRVN to an extended bombing campaign. Those

66. See source cited in previous note.
67. Bennett participated in Sigma II along with Robert McNamara, Dean Rusk, and Walt
Rostow, among others. Rostow, he later observed, was "startled" that no political
leaders could identify the U.S. objectives in Vietnam. As a result, Bennett concluded that
it was a "no win war." Donald Bennett Oral History, section 7, 26–3, MHI; Ball to
Rusk, 5 October 1964, "How Valid Are the Assumptions Underlying Our Viet-Nam
Policies?" NSC History – Troop Deployment, UPA.

advocates of air strikes became more vocal after the VC successfully mortared a U.S. air base at Bien Hoa on 1 November, causing several casualties, damaging planes and helicopters, and destroying five B-57 bombers. The JCS again urged a progressive air campaign against the north while Admiral Ulysses S. Grant Sharp, the CINCPAC, thought that American pilots should make an "inexorable and increasingly destructive march toward Hanoi."[68] As the director of an NSC Working Group on Vietnam, William Bundy, explained, the president was also moving toward reprisal bombing of the north.[69]

The military remained divided, however, on the extent and efficacy of the projected air war. Although he observed that "all of Southeast Asia . . . was sort of going to hell in a hand basket" after the Bien Hoa attack, Harold K. Johnson remained the military's most vocal critic of the American air strategy.[70] The chiefs, however, urged a controlled and swiftly applied program of military pressure against the DRVN – to include strikes in Laos, on airfields and industrial and petroleum installations in Hanoi and Haiphong, against infiltration routes, and against the ninety-four targets compiled previously – but they also reiterated that the administration should establish a "clear set of military objectives" before deepening its involvement in Indochina.[71] Dean Rusk, while urging a "clearly tougher" approach to the DRVN, nonetheless wanted to conduct "less drastic" air operations than the "full and relentless" attacks against the ninety-four targets, while William Bundy expected Ho to accept extensive damage to his transport and industrial systems in a test of wills against the United States.[72]

68. Clodfelter, *Limits of Air Power*, 52–4; Marolda and Fitzgerald, *U.S. Navy and Vietnam*, 473–7, Sharp quotation on 477; *Pentagon Papers: Gravel*, 3:210–15; Johnson, *Vantage Point*, 121; Westmoreland, *A Soldier Reports*, 88.
69. *Pentagon Papers: Gravel*, 3:211.
70. Johnson in Krepinevich, *Army and Vietnam*, 132–3.
71. "JCS Policy Statements concerning Operations in Southeast Asia," n.d., Warnke-McNaughton, box 7, folder: VNS 2 [Vietnam 1966–8] (1), Wheeler to McNamara, 18 November 1964, "Courses of Action in Southeast Asia," Warnke-McNaughton, box 8, folder: book III – DOS Material, 1964, LBJL.
72. "JCS Policy Statements concerning Operations in Southeast Asia," n.d., Warnke-McNaughton, box 7, folder: VNS 2 [Vietnam 1966–8] (1); Wheeler to McNamara, 18 November 1964, "Courses of Action in Southeast Asia," Warnke-McNaughton, box 8, folder: book III – DOS Material, 1964, LBJL; Rusk to Taylor, 8 November 1964, VN C.F., NSF, box 195, folder: President/Taylor NODIS CLORES, LBJL; see also Dean Rusk with Richard Rusk, *As I Saw It*, ed. Daniel S. Papp (New York, 1990), 446–7.

Maxwell Taylor, who would play both sides of the air war issue in 1964–5, was the most vocal critic of the air campaign in November, because of both military and political factors in the RVN. After the attack at Bien Hoa, Taylor counseled patience amid the various calls for retaliation. The southern government was not stable enough to handle the type of wider war that such measures were likely to produce, and, despite the JCS's views to the contrary, the ambassador observed that too much coercion would likely alienate Hanoi, just as too little would embolden DRVN leaders to take further offensive action. Above all, he warned, "what we don't want is an expanded war in [Southeast Asia] and an unresolved guerrilla problem in [the RVN]."[73]

Taylor was especially anxious because the political situation in the RVN had deteriorated further, with Tran Van Huong of the civilian-led High National Council replacing Khanh in September, only to be ousted due to Buddhist pressure three months later. In January 1965 both Huong and Khanh would return to power only to be removed again. All told, the RVN experienced about a half-dozen changes of government between September 1964 and February 1965. It was thus easy to understand why Taylor told Rusk that the RVN lacked the "minimum level of government required to justify military pressures against the North."[74] Because of the pervasive "war weariness and hopelessness" already evident in 1964, the ambassador found it "impossible to foresee a stable and effective government under any name in anything like the near future."[75]

73. Taylor to Department of State, 2 November 1964, *DDRS,* 83, 542; Taylor to Department of State, 3 November 1964, *Pentagon Papers: Gravel,* 3:590–1. The ambassador also suggested that the VC strike at Bien Hoa demonstrated the futility of expanding U.S. operations. Taylor saw "nothing but disadvantage" in pursuing rebels outside the RVN's borders. "We don't often catch the fleeing VC in the heart of SVN," he conceded, so "I see little likelihood of doing better in Cambodia." Taylor to Department of State, 4 November 1964, *DDRS,* 85, 1777; on the JCS's criticism of Taylor's recommendations – which it derisively termed "tit-for-tat" bombing – see Earle Wheeler JCSM 955-64, 14 November 1964, *Pentagon Papers: Gravel,* 3:628–30; the Army's vice chief of staff, General Creighton W. Abrams, also regarded the Bien Hoa attack as a "very serious step" and added that recent intelligence reports had detected shifts in PRC air and land forces in southern China, which could possibly signal a buildup for use in Vietnam. Memorandum for the Record, 2 November 1964, Creighton W. Abrams Papers, box: Messages Creighton Abrams, 1964–9, MHI.
74. Taylor to Rusk, 10 November 1964, VN C.F., NSF, box 195, folder: President/Taylor NODIS CLORES, LBJL.
75. Taylor also observed that an American accommodation with Ho might be possible. If

He was merely stating the obvious. By early December, although the president had affirmed his support of the RVN, Taylor noted that the chaos in Saigon had "completely dismayed the staunchest friends of South Vietnam" in the United States.[76] By late December, conditions had worsened to the point that Taylor, reporting on "another first-class governmental crisis in Saigon," described a "three fronts" war: the government against the military, the RVNAF against the U.S. embassy, and the Buddhists against the government. No one, apparently, was fighting the VC.[77] Indeed, the situation in Vietnam had become so dire that the embassy was looking into "various degrees of controlling US aid" and, although unlikely, admitted that "one possibility would be to go home."[78]

Others were also wary of expanding American involvement. Like the ambassador, Westmoreland warned that the U.S. had to limit its response to the Bien Hoa attack to avoid expanding the war "to a level inconsistent with our objectives in this area." The MACV commander thus opposed JCS proposals for a massive air campaign and instead called for increased efforts in the south and continued covert, 34-A operations at sea.[79] General Krulak, the Marines's CI expert, also questioned America's preoccupation with the DRVN, believing that the conflict between U.S. and PAVN-VC

the DRVN would "remain aloof" from the PRC in a "Tito-like state," he envisioned that the United States could support such a government, providing it allowed the RVN to survive. Taylor, 27 November 1964, "The Current Situation in South Viet-Nam, November, 1964," *DDRS*, 83, 557.

76. Taylor, 7 December 1964, "Report on Washington Attitudes," Westmoreland Papers, folder 509: #11 History Backup, 7–31 December 1964, WNRC; see also Taylor Oral History (2), 22–4, LBJL.

77. Taylor 1826 to Rusk, 23 December 1964, VN C.F. NSF, box 195, folder: President/ Taylor NODIS CLORES, LBJL; see also Taylor to Rusk, 21 December 1964, *DDRS*, 79, 206D.

78. M. Bundy to Johnson, 24 December 1964, "Report of Taylor Backgrounder to Media," *DDRS*, 79, 222C. Though not as gloomy as Taylor, Harold K. Johnson returned from a visit to Vietnam in December with his judgment reinforced about the problems facing the United States there, especially pointing out the "insensitive conduct" of the ARVN, which was alienating the population and thus undermining the struggle. Krepinevich, *Army and Vietnam,* 132–3.

79. Untitled document, 14 November 1964, Westmoreland Papers, folder 508: #10 History Backup, 14 November–7 December 1964, WNRC. Although it is untitled, I am reasonably certain that Westmoreland authored this document because it expressed sentiments consistent with those in the documents cited in the subsequent notes and it reflected the concern he expressed to Taylor in early 1965 about committing combat troops. See also Marolda and Fitzgerald, *U.S. Navy and Vietnam,* 477–9.

forces "could move to another planet today and we would still not have won the war." The insurgency could only be thwarted, he maintained, when U.S. and Vietnamese forces began to stop the subversion and guerrilla war in the south.[80]

But the RVN was in no condition to fight an expanded war, as Westmoreland saw it. With deficient leadership, more desertions, and tactical weaknesses which "run the entire gamut," the southern military was unable to fight effectively, and pacification efforts were still foundering.[81] Even worse, the ARVN's senior officers were "absorbed in political activity," while there was "undoubtedly a preoccupation" with government intrigue at lower levels as well.[82] Given such assessments, Westmoreland, although "generally more optimistic" than Maxwell Taylor, was hoping to wait six months or so "to have a firmer base for stronger actions."[83]

Such a delay, however, was neither militarily nor politically practical. American policy makers had clearly recognized the U.S. dilemma in Vietnam in late 1964. Without a stable government in the south, an expanded U.S. role would likely be counterproductive, if not fatal, to the RVN. The American presence could alienate the local population and provoke the Communists, yet the various Saigon governments were not likely to survive without increased American support and perhaps a U.S. combat role. Even then, there was great division within American circles over the means to develop a stable situation in the RVN. While almost all U.S. officials agreed on the need for some type of bombing campaign, Taylor, Westmoreland, Harold K. Johnson, the JWGA, and others had pointed out the limited impact, but great risks, such actions might carry. Nonetheless, American policy makers, although aware of the shortcomings of their attempts to develop a viable southern state so

80. Victor H. Krulak Oral History, interview of June 1970, 200, MCHC.
81. Westmoreland to Taylor, 24 November 1964, *DDRS*, 77, 288E; see also Westmoreland to Taylor, 14 November 1964, "Assumption by U.S. of Operational Control of the Pacification Program in SVN," and Colonel Daniel Richards to Westmoreland, 30 November 1964, "Major Hop Tac Problems," Westmoreland Papers, box 4, folder: #10 History Backup, LBJL; on military developments, see U.S. MACV Weekly Military Reports, October–December 1964, Records of the MACV, part 1, reel 3, UPA.
82. U.S. MACV Weekly Military Report, 19–26 December 1964, Records of the MACV, part 1, reel 3, UPA.
83. William Bundy, 27 November 1964, Memorandum of Meeting on Southeast Asia, *Pentagon Papers: Gravel*, 3:674–6.

far, continued to do more of the same, thus leading to the Americanization of the war in short order.[84]

Indeed, the NSC Working Group on Vietnam, administration officials, and the president himself all understood the hazards of expanding the war in 1964 but, having cast their lot with the RVN to that point, had to prove their credibility by deepening the American involvement in Vietnam. When the JCS continued to press for heavy air assaults to force the DRVN to stop supporting the NLF and VC in the south, most officials rejected the chiefs' position because it risked "major military conflict" with the DRVN or PRC and might lead to a massive commitment in Vietnam that could be "extremely adverse" to America's international position.[85] While McNamara and Rusk led the fight against the JCS plans, Taylor urged reprisal bombings and intensified covert operations, both to dissuade the DRVN from supporting the insurgency and to stabilize the government in the south. The United States could then gradually escalate the air war, preventing northern success unless it "paid a disproportionate price."[86] Taylor's views must have made an impact on the Working Group, which forwarded his recommendations to the president for a 1 December approval.[87]

The president approved the Working Group's suggestions, fully aware that the United States would have to do much more in Vietnam. Indeed Johnson and his advisors, though committed to the RVN, were also trying to buffer themselves from the political consequences of defeat at some future date. In a strikingly honest memorandum to the president, his close advisor Jack Valenti advised Johnson to "sign on" the JCS before making any "final decisions" about Vietnam. Fearing the "future aftermath" of such decisions, and invoking Omar Bradley's support of Harry Truman at the MacArthur hearings during the Korean War, Valenti wanted the JCS's support of the president's policy to be made public so as to

---

84. *Pentagon Papers: Gravel,* 3:215–18; W. Bundy draft, 26 November 1964, "Proposed Courses of Action in Southeast Asia," ibid., 3:656–66; Clodfelter, *Limits of Air Power,* 53–6.

85. See sources cited in previous note.

86. Taylor briefing, 27 November 1964, "The Current Situation in South Vietnam – November 1964," *DDRS,* 83, 557.

87. Clodfelter, *Limits of Air Power,* 55–6; Marolda and Fitzgerald, *U.S. Navy and Vietnam,* 477–9.

avoid future recriminations. In that way the chiefs "will have been heard, they will have been part of the consensus, and our flank will have been covered in the event of some kind of flap or investigation later."[88]

Valenti's memorandum was indeed instructive, for, as the president himself indicated at a 1 December meeting, those "final decisions" would involve a greater American commitment in Vietnam. Though alarmed by the situation in the RVN, Johnson warned his advisors to "keep [the] problem from looking worse here than it is." The president, however, did see a "day of reckoning coming" and thus wanted "to be sure we've done everything we can" to preserve the RVN. Again Johnson stressed that political stability was a prerequisite to U.S. escalation, and a purpose of the meeting was "*to pull a stable gov[ernmen]t together.*" In fact, the president told his advisors, "if need be, create a new Diem, so when [we] tell Wheeler to slap, we can take [a] slap back." Johnson also pressed for third-country assistance to the RVN so that it did not seem as though the United States alone was supporting the south, or to provide cover for an American takeover of the war. If Vietnam was "as serious as [we] believe," then the administration needed to approach other nations to help the RVN and would have to "get big numbers from them." Such assistance was especially important because the RVN's leaders were aware of America's strategic role in the Far East and knew that Johnson's credibility would require staying the course in Vietnam. The president too understood this, and wondered whether "we oversold them on our necessity of being [a] power in the Pacific."[89]

Lyndon Johnson's outlook in December was indeed sobering. His suggestions to establish a new government in the south and obtain third-country assistance clearly signaled his desire to do much more in Vietnam. The president, in fact, more explicitly indicated his intentions. He understood that the conflict would require a long-term commitment, noting that it was "easy to get in or out,"

---

88. Valenti to Johnson, 14 November 1964, CF, CO 312, VN, box 12, folder: CO 312, Vietnam, 1964–5, LBJL. A handwritten note at the bottom of the document indicates that the president discussed this memorandum with Valenti.

89. "Are they drunk on [prowar journalist Joseph] Alsop," Johnson added. Notes of 1 December Meeting, Cabinet Room, NSF, Meeting Notes File, box 1, folder: 1 December 1964, LBJL; emphasis in original.

but "hard to be patient." Johnson would, however, do whatever was needed. When Maxwell Taylor told him that effective CI action would be costly – approximately 20 billion piasters, or $175 million – the president urged full support, joking that he did "not want to send [a] widow woman to slap Jack Dempsey." The United States, he stressed, "must do [its] damndest" in the RVN.[90]

So, for the time being, he would pursue Taylor's program of reprisal bombing against the north, but the president also made it clear that intensified action would be forthcoming. Aware that Wheeler and McNamara believed that "it's downhill in SVN no matter what we do *in* country," Johnson was ready to expand the air war over the north, as well as the ground war in the south. The president was aware that U.S. air power was not going to bring victory in Vietnam and so was "now ready to look with great favor" on an increased ground effort, "although I know that it may involve the acceptance of larger American sacrifices." The United States had "been building our strength to fight this kind of war ever since 1961," the president emphasized, "and I myself am ready to substantially increase the numbers of Americans in Vietnam if it is necessary to provide this kind of fighting force against the Viet Cong."[91]

The president was not the only American official thinking about sending ground troops to Vietnam, although his position was more certain than many others. In October Admiral Sharp and Vice Admiral Moorer, for instance, had opposed a JCS plan to commit units to Quang Ngai because they believed that RVN forces, not U.S. Marines, should fight the war. Moorer in fact termed the conflict in Vietnam a "dirty little war," only to be reprimanded by the White House, not for using the word "dirty" but for calling it a "war." In mid-November, Maxwell Taylor, reversing his October 1961 policy, advised against sending logistics and combat units to flood-ravaged areas in the central provinces because such moves would

90. Ibid.
91. Ibid.; also Vice Admiral Mustin to Sharp and Westmoreland, 2 December 1964, Westmoreland Papers, box 4, folder: #10 History Backup, LBJL; Westmoreland, *A Soldier Reports,* 113; quotation in Johnson cable to Taylor, cited in Larry Berman, "Coming to Grips with Lyndon Johnson's War," *Diplomatic History* 17 (Fall 1993): 521.

lead to increased casualties and the RVN would assume that America was prepared to take over more of its responsibility.[92] Westmoreland added that "a purely military solution is not possible" and, while he might ask for more advisors if that could hasten the pace of the war, he did not mention any need for ground troops at all.[93]

Marine Commandant Wallace Greene, a great advocate of military pressure against the north, was just as hesitant to send his soldiers into combat in the south. Invoking public opinion, he anticipated that "any major commitment of U.S. troops (casualties), money (tax $), [and] rationing will arouse a storm of protest" at home and be "extremely unpopular throughout the world." Although the Johnson administration was "sinking in a quagmire of indecision" in Vietnam and had to take positive action, the commandant also understood the requirements and perils of expanding the war, which would include indoctrinating the U.S. public, introducing large numbers of troops, widening the war and making America vulnerable in other areas, gaining third-country assistance, and trying to accomplish all this without U.S. forces in combat. Despite this litany of tasks, Greene did not urge withdrawal from the RVN, although he did emphasize that Johnson should "avoid [the] commitment of [a] large ground force." The commandant had thus analyzed the war in a manner that would typify the military's response to Vietnam policy making. Although candidly recognizing the serious disadvantages to overcome, Greene and other senior officers continued to encourage escalation and to force the White House to make and be accountable for major decisions on the war.[94]

92. Marolda and Fitzgerald, *U.S. Navy and Vietnam*, 522–3; Taylor to Department of State, 14 November 1964, DDRS, 83, 553; Perry, *Four Stars*, 146.
93. Consolidation of Military Questions and Answers, November 1964, Westmoreland Papers, box 4, folder: #10 History Backup, I, LBJL.
94. Remarks of General Wallace Greene, CMC, Naval War College, Newport, R.I., 5 November 1964, Greene Papers, box 16, folder 188; CMC Address, Foreign Service Institute, Washington D.C., 9 November 1964, Greene Papers, box 16, folder 189; CMC Remarks before Joint Assembly of National War College and Industrial College of Armed Forces, Fort McNair, Washington D.C., 1 December 1964, Greene Papers, box 17, folder 194, MCHC. Greene's rhetoric could become quite hawkish as well; see Halberstam, *Best and Brightest*, 594. General Raymond Davis, the assistant commander

Such decisions, it was clear in late 1964, could not be long delayed, even if political and military officials seemed reluctant to press for an expanded war. The military itself was still divided over the best approach to Vietnam, with the Air Force and Marine leaders urging air war over the north, while Taylor, Harold K. Johnson, and Westmoreland knew that bombing was no panacea for the problems of Vietnam. Civilian officials, too, avoided making hard choices on Vietnam. In fact, when Westmoreland, in the United States for his father's funeral, passed through Washington to meet with the Joint Chiefs in mid-December, neither Lyndon Johnson nor Robert McNamara met with the MACV commander. "When I learned later that at the time of my visit major new steps for escalating the war were under consideration," Westmoreland observed, "I deemed it odd that neither the President nor the Secretary had sought my views."[95]

Apparently wanting to maintain a low profile on Vietnam issues at the time, Johnson, with Dean Rusk's encouragement, also refused to respond to a Christmas Eve attack on a U.S. officers' billet in Saigon – in which more than a hundred Vietnamese and Americans were wounded – despite pressure from the chiefs and Taylor for strikes against the north. Such an attack, the president feared, would provoke "a major reaction from Hanoi and its friends" while the political base in the south was "too shaky to withstand a major assault by the Communists."[96] As even the MACV staff pointed out, the government of the RVN was "unstable and ineffective," military, civic, and religious leaders had shown "no letup in political maneuvering" since Diem's ouster, and the ARVN was passive and outgunned.[97] But American leaders would not be able to wait for conditions in the south to stabilize before taking military action.

of the 3d Marine Division, had visited Vietnam with Navy Secretary Paul Nitze in the fall of 1964, and sensed that "there was no . . . really clear indication that we would be committed" prior to the March 1965 Marine landings at Da Nang. Raymond Davis Oral History, 5, MCHC.

95. Halberstam, *Best and Brightest*, 594–5; Westmoreland, *A Soldier Reports*, 89.
96. Johnson, *Vantage Point*, 121; Rusk, *As I Saw It*, 446–8; Westmoreland, *A Soldier Reports*, 89–90.
97. MACV Command History, 1965, 2–3, used at MCHC.

American troops would thus begin to pour into Vietnam, although U.S. officials would continue to recognize that the vexing problems there would not be resolved for the remainder of the war. In deciding to intervene despite political turmoil, military stasis, and gloomy prospects, Lyndon Johnson was carrying Kennedy's policies to their natural outcome. Despite the artificial optimism of earlier months, the new president had inherited a situation in November 1963 that was heading steadily downhill. Committed to fulfilling his predecessor's pledges and maintaining his own credibility, Johnson was quickly making the protection and preservation of the RVN the centerpiece of his foreign policy, and he was willing to take whatever measures deemed necessary, including using U.S. combat forces, to achieve his objectives. Many of his advisors supported the president's commitment, with McNamara, the Bundys, and McNaughton especially urging intensified efforts in southern Vietnam. In large part these advocates of intervention believed that American credibility was in question and that the United States had to assume the role of "good doctor," as McNaughton had termed it, even if the patient was terminally ill. Throughout 1964, then, the Johnson White House demonstrated its resolve by authorizing more sorties, deploying more military personnel, and sending more resources into the RVN.

At the same time, military leaders continued to react ambiguously to the war. American officers were divided over the requirement for and advisability of an air war over the DRVN, with Army leaders especially challenging sanguine projections of bombing success. The war, they asserted frequently, would be won or lost in the south, not over the skies of the north. Most military leaders also did not seem enthused about combat involvement in the war. Maxwell Taylor, Westmoreland, Felt, Greene, and Moorer, among others, all were on record opposing U.S. ground force entry into Vietnam, with the JCS chair-turned-ambassador most stridently rejecting U.S. combat in Vietnam. As Taylor saw it, without a stable government and effective military in the south, there was little America could do to contain VC expansion. Once American troops started landing, Vietnamese politicians and generals would simply allow the United States to assume an increasing burden against the VC. Westmoreland shared many of Taylor's doubts and his reports from

Saigon candidly described the problems and risks facing American military personnel in Vietnam. While hoping to limit U.S. participation in the war, however, the MACV commander was at the same time preparing for a large-scale, long-term commitment.

As such, political considerations, as much or more than military factors, were prompting Westmoreland's and many other policy makers' approaches to Vietnam. With the White House committed to the RVN, eager to do more, and concerned about U.S. credibility, military leaders made the political calculation to follow the administration line on Vietnam despite any misgivings they might have had. By doing so, the armed forces, in the pursuit of their own institutional interests, were making the White House determine the objectives and levels of commitment involved in an American war in Southeast Asia and take responsibility for intervention.

American officers both honestly assessed the chances of success in Vietnam and told U.S. politicians what they wanted to hear. In the process, military critics and politicos eclipsed the dissenters and doubters of just a few years earlier. The brass, it seemed, wanted to accept credit for any success in Vietnam, but avoid blame for future misfortune. The White House too was concerned with the issue of political accountability, as demonstrated by Valenti's advice to Johnson to "sign on" the military to cover his political flanks if Vietnam turned sour. For the next several months the White House and military would continue such maneuvering while more soldiers landed in Vietnam and the United States took over the war.

7

Hope for the Best, Expect the Worst: U.S. Ground Troops Enter the Vietnam War, January–July 1965

In order for the [U.S. government] to evaluate [Westmoreland's] requests properly when submitted, a policy determination must be made in the near future that will assure the question: What should the Vietnamese be expected to do for themselves and how much more must the U.S. contribute directly to the security of South Vietnam?

Harold K. Johnson[1]

As political and military conditions in the RVN deteriorated throughout 1964, it became manifestly clear to the White House that the United States would have to increase significantly its presence in Vietnam to stave off defeat. With U.S. credibility at stake and his own political fortunes attached to the outcome of the war, the president never wavered from his commitment to Vietnam, notwithstanding the ample evidence of decay there. Thus Johnson, McNamara, and McGeorge Bundy, among others, took crucial steps in early 1965, such as intensifying the air war, deploying ground troops, and authorizing offensive operations against the VC. By midyear the United States was well on its way toward taking over the war.

At the same time, military critics and politicos were divided over U.S. policy and prospects in Indochina. Maxwell Taylor and Westmoreland initially pointed out the risks of greater intervention and urged that the United States maintain its support role, but not engage in combat. Within two months, however, Westmoreland, sensing that defeat was imminent and recognizing the political real-

---

1. Johnson in *Pentagon Papers: Gravel*, 3:429.

187

ities of escalation, would request combat forces and assign them an offensive mission. It would then become immediately clear that the U.S. presence in Vietnam would have to expand exponentially to make any impact amid the political chaos and military disintegration in the RVN. The air war, counted on by some military and political officials as the keystone to U.S. strategy in Vietnam, would not decisively affect the DRVN's support of the insurgency and would make a negligible impact in the RVN, as Army representatives had argued. Neither the Rolling Thunder air operations nor the initial deployment of ground troops would do much to stabilize the political situation in Saigon, which was a prerequisite for U.S. success. Many American officers understood this but went to war in Vietnam nevertheless.

In part, U.S. service leaders suffered from the hubris endemic to hegemonic powers and were seduced by the prospects of waging technological warfare against Asian guerrillas.[2] They also understood, however, the Johnson administration's determination to show its resolve in the RVN to whatever degree necessary. Thus, U.S. officers consistently produced gloomy reports on the war, yet developed sanguine assessments of U.S. prospects in Vietnam. In that way, they would continue to fulfill their obligation to evaluate honestly conditions in the RVN, thereby covering their flanks if things turned sour, while at the same time telling the president, the secretary of defense, and other war advocates what they wanted to hear. There was, it seemed, little military compulsion to fight in Vietnam. Political considerations overrode such factors, however, so American leaders optimistically went to war in Vietnam while fully aware of the risks and problems there.

To be sure, there were many true believers inside the armed forces, although even they were well aware of conditions in the RVN. General William DePuy, who would help develop the MACV strategy of firepower and attrition, was as critical of the ARVN as he was confident of the ability of U.S. forces to alter events in Vietnam,

2. See David Marr, "The Technological Imperative in US War Strategy in Vietnam," in Mary Kaldor and Asbjorn Eide, eds., *The World Military Order: The Impact of Military Technology on the Third World* (New York, 1979), 17–48.

and he saw serious political obstacles in the RVN.[3] "Because we are white – strong and rich," he understood, "we are peculiarly vulnerable to VC propaganda." Any Vietnamese officials supported by Americans would be seen as "collaborators" or "petit bourgeoisie," while, DePuy admitted, "the VC on the other hand prefer to mold their leaders from the common clay." Political reforms, though essential, were "highly unlikely," he added. As a result, DePuy had to conclude that "neither time nor human nature would seem to be on our side."[4]

Despite such predicaments in Vietnam, American political leaders were not softening their commitment. To John McNaughton, "our reputation" was the nation's most important stake in Vietnam and so U.S. leaders had to be "sensitive to how, as well as whether, the area is lost."[5] William Bundy stressed the need to act promptly and decisively, calling for the deployment of U.S. troops into the northern RVN to stiffen morale in Saigon and send a signal to Hanoi.[6] The president, who hoped to "minimize [the] risk of rapid escalation," also remained convinced that it was "of high importance" to preserve the RVN.[7]

Even as the political situation deteriorated, with General Khanh deposing Huong for another return to power, Johnson wanted "all the world" to know "that the US will spare no effort and no sacrifice in doing its full part to turn back the Communists in Vietnam."[8] At the same time, McGeorge Bundy and McNamara met with the president to tell him "that both of us are now pretty well convinced that *our current policy can lead only to disastrous*

---

3. Halberstam, *Best and Brightest,* 657.
4. DePuy, J-3, MACV to Westmoreland, December 1964 or January 1965, "The Revolutionary Spirit," *DDRS,* 78, 236C; Maxwell Taylor added that, in briefings covering the Vietnamese military, DePuy "described very clearly the misbehavior of several ARVN units, complete failure of units which had been, we thought, among the most promising." Taylor Oral History (2), 27–9, LBJL.
5. McNaughton draft, 4 January 1965, "Observations re. South Vietnam," *Pentagon Papers: Gravel,* 3:683–4.
6. William Bundy to Rusk, 6 January 1965, "Notes on the South Vietnamese Situation and Alternatives," ibid., 3:684–6.
7. Johnson to Taylor, 7 January 1965, in The War in Vietnam: Classified Histories by the National Security Council, "Deployment of Major U.S. Forces to Vietnam, July 1965," University Publications of America, microfilm edition, reels 2–3 (hereafter cited as NSC History, "Deployment," UPA).
8. Johnson 1549 to Taylor, 27 January 1965, ibid.

defeat." The United States could no longer "wait and hope for a stable government" while the VC expanded its control over the RVN, they believed, and so urged Johnson to "use our military power . . . to force a change of Communist policy."[9]

Taylor, however, was "caught by surprise" when the administration began to press for combat troop deployments to the RVN. "The President was thinking much bigger in this field," the ambassador recalled, "than the tenor in Washington" had indicated.[10] Clearly, then, America's civilian leadership favored introducing combat troops into Vietnam in early 1965. At the same time, as McGeorge Bundy admitted, "we had no recommendations from the military for major ground deployments."[11] There was in fact no military imperative to intervene. After the VC had bombed an officers' billet in Saigon on Christmas Eve, the White House had encouraged Taylor to ask for ground troops, but the ambassador, Westmoreland, and Taylor's deputy, U. Alexis Johnson, quickly moved to reject such measures.[12]

In a prescient analysis of U.S. policy, Westmoreland and his staff explained their resistance to employing combat forces and recommended that the United States continue on its flawed path of providing operational support and improving the advisory system. As the MACV staff saw it, the United States had already spent a great deal of time trying to develop the ARVN, and "if that effort has not succeeded, there is even less reason to think that U.S. combat forces would have the desired effect." The Vietnamese, Westmoreland assumed, would either let Americans carry the burden of war or actively turn against the U.S. presence in their country. Given such circumstances, MACV officers concluded that the involvement of American ground forces in the RVN "would at best buy time and would lead to ever increasing commitments until, like the French, we would be occupying an essentially hostile foreign country."[13]

9. McGeorge Bundy to Johnson, 27 January 1965, ibid., emphasis in original; see also M. Bundy 1557 to Taylor, 28 January 1965, ibid.; Johnson, *Vantage Point,* 122–3.
10. Maxwell Taylor Oral History (3), 2–5, LBJL.
11. McGeorge Bundy to Johnson, 24 July 1965, "The History of Recommendations for Increased US Forces in Vietnam," VN C.F., NSF, boxes 74–5, folder: 2 E, 5/65–7/65, 1965 Troop Decision, LBJL.
12. Taylor, *Swords and Plowshares,* 333–4.
13. Westmoreland analysis in Taylor 2058 to Johnson, 5 January 1965, NSC History, "Deployment," UPA; and *DDRS,* 83, 2793.

Army Chief of Staff Harold K. Johnson was not unduly optimistic either, telling an audience in Los Angeles that he expected U.S. military involvement in Indochina to last a minimum of five years, and possibly as long as two decades.[14] Johnson, as well as Westmoreland and DePuy, would overcome their reservations about sending ground troops to Vietnam only two months later. Maxwell Taylor, however, continued to oppose such steps vehemently. In a series of memoranda to the president and others throughout the winter months of 1965, the ambassador detailed the risks of U.S. intervention and the bleak prospects facing American soldiers in southern Vietnam. Above all, he still insisted that political turmoil in the RVN was the major obstacle to success, and one that American troops could not remove. In early January, as Khanh maneuvered to return to power, Taylor called for "hard soul searching" to decide whether U.S. officials ought to tolerate another coup, or instead reject Khanh altogether and accept the consequences, "which might entail ultimate withdrawal."[15]

To Taylor, the choices were so stark because the United States could ill afford to fight a ground war in Vietnam. The RVN simply lacked the resources and resolve to engage an impressive enemy and it was not "reasonable or feasible" to expect U.S. or third-country forces to assume the burdens of guerrilla war. As another MACV study found, the United States would need to commit about thirty-four battalions of infantry with additional logistics support, a total of about 75,000 troops, just to provide security to American personnel and facilities already in Vietnam. To the ambassador, this "startling requirement" would inevitably "bring us into greater conflict with the Vietnamese people and the government."[16] After

14. Harold K. Johnson, MHI Oral History Program, 8, CMH.
15. Taylor to Johnson, 6 January 1965, NSC History – Troop Deployment, UPA; see also Taylor to Johnson, 27 January 1965, ibid.; Taylor to Johnson, 2 February 1965, *DDRS*, 77, 34D; on U.S. policy in Vietnam in 1965, the best treatment is Berman's *Planning a Tragedy*; on Taylor, see Kinnard, *Certain Trumpet*, especially chapter 5; on Taylor's resistance to combat intervention in general, see Taylor, *The Sword and the Pen*, 308–14.
16. Among the missions for the thirty-four battalions would be protection of 23,000 U.S. military personnel, 16 airfields, 9 communications centers, 1 large petroleum-oil-lubricants (POL) storage area, and 289 separate installations where Americans lived or worked. Taylor 2056 to Johnson, 6 January 1965, NSC History, "Deployment," UPA. The decision to send U.S. troops to protect troops already in country, Marilyn Young reminded me, also served as a justification for the American deployments to Somalia, apparently another "lesson" of Vietnam learned by national leaders.

192 Masters of War

Khanh had staged another coup on 27 January, Taylor advised against recognizing the new government, telling Bundy that the United States should prepare to "reduce [its] advisory effort to policy guidance [or] disengage and let the [RVN] stand alone."[17]

The ambassador thus had "one basic conclusion" about Vietnam: the United States "is on a losing track and must change course or suffer defeat, early or late as one chooses to interpret the known facts."[18] Dean Rusk also interjected a note of caution into the proceedings, but offered different advice on future policy. As McGeorge Bundy told the president in his memorandum of 27 January, the secretary of state, like Westmoreland weeks earlier, believed "that the consequences of both escalation and withdrawal are so bad that we simply must find a way of making our present policy work."[19]

Unlike Rusk, Taylor continued to see air power as a virtual panacea to America's problems. Graduated air strikes against the DRVN, he believed, would signal to Ho the cost of supporting the insurgency, provide leverage in any negotiations, and improve RVN morale. While Taylor, and most other military and political officials, did not expect an air campaign to alter decisively the situation in Vietnam, they did see it as a way of "producing maximum stresses in Hanoi minds."[20] With the war going so badly, the president had little choice but to finally accept Taylor's strategy. Thus, by mid-February, the United States was beginning a full-scale air campaign in Vietnam.

The immediate cause of the air war came on 7 February, when the VC mortared an Army barracks in Pleiku, killing 9 and wounding 109 Americans, and destroying or damaging twenty-two aircraft. U.S. officials then cited the attack at Pleiku to justify Ameri-

17. Taylor to M. Bundy, 1 February 1965, NSC History, "Deployment," UPA; Westmoreland also pointed out that, amid the political turmoil of late January, ARVN soldiers in Da Nang were participating in anti-U.S. demonstrations. Westmoreland Memorandum for the Record, 28 January 1965, "Discussion with General Khanh," Westmoreland Papers, box 5, folder: #13 History Backup (I), LBJL.
18. Taylor to Johnson, 2 February 1965, DDRS, 77, 34D.
19. McGeorge Bundy to Johnson, 27 January 1965, "Re: Basic Policy in Vietnam," NSC History, "Deployment," UPA; see also Dean Rusk with Richard Rusk, As I Saw It, ed. Daniel S. Papp (New York, 1990), 447; Johnson, Vantage Point, 122–3.
20. Taylor 2052 to Johnson, 6 January 1965, NSC History, "Deployment," UPA; Taylor, Swords and Plowshares, 329–38.

can retaliation, but any provocation would have satisfied the administration's desire to expand the war. Indeed, McGeorge Bundy was in Vietnam with McNaughton and others at the time and, looking to justify stronger military measures, saw the incident as the vehicle by which the president could authorize an air campaign against the north, even sarcastically observing that "Pleikus are like streetcars."[21] Thus, Johnson authorized Operation Rolling Thunder, which in three years would unleash more tonnage of bombs than all previous air wars combined. A new bombing campaign, as Bundy saw it, would demonstrate American credibility, for in the RVN he had found a "widespread belief" that the United States lacked the will and patience to stay in Vietnam. Without a significantly increased American effort, the national security advisor warned, "defeat appears inevitable."[22] Accordingly Bundy, in a memorandum that McNaughton drafted, urged the president to execute a program of "sustained reprisal" against the DRVN, with U.S. air and naval attacks to be justified by and calibrated according to the VC's activities in the south. As enemy "outrages" continued in the RVN, the American air strikes against the north would take their toll.[23]

The president thus authorized reprisal strikes, Operation Flaming Dart, against the DRVN on 8 and 9 February, and Rolling Thunder on 13 February. As Mark Clodfelter has shown, Johnson's decisions did not satisfy everyone. While Taylor, McNamara, McGeorge Bundy, and McNaughton thought that the president had demonstrated American resolve, William Bundy and Rusk doubted that air strikes would deter Ho.[24] The JCS, although satisfied that Johnson had finally acted, continued to press for intensified air operations against the north.[25] Harold K. Johnson con-

21. Bundy in Halberstam, *Best and Brightest*, 646.
22. McGeorge Bundy to Johnson, 7 February 1965, "The Situation in Vietnam," NSF, NSC Meetings File, box 1, folder: volume 3, tab 29, LBJL; see also Johnson, *Vantage Point*, 125–8; Clodfelter, *Limits of Air Power*, 56–62.
23. McGeorge Bundy, 7 February 1965, "A Policy of Sustained Reprisal," *Pentagon Papers: Gravel*, 3:687–9; see also sources cited in previous note.
24. Clodfelter, *Limits of Air Power*, 156–62.
25. Colonel H.M. Darmstandler, 15 December 1967, "Chronology of Significant Requests and Decisions Affecting the Air War against North Vietnam," Warnke-McNaughton, box 7, folder: VNS 2 [Vietnam, 1966–8] (1), LBJL; JCS to CINCPAC, 12 February 1965, "Courses of Action Southeast Asia – First 8 Weeks," NSC History, "Deploy-

tinued to decry the emphasis on the air war over the DRVN since the United States, he believed, still had to focus on defeating the insurgency in the south and did not have to destroy the north to force a settlement in the RVN.[26] Westmoreland, also taking the Army line, "doubted that the bombing would have any effect on the North Vietnamese," although he did hope that it might boost southern morale.[27]

Wheeler hoped to prevent such disagreements from reaching civilian ears. Lyndon Johnson, like his predecessor, preferred to discuss policy only with the JCS chair, not the group as a whole, and expected subservience. In fact, after one White House meeting at which Generals Johnson and Greene argued about U.S. strategy in Vietnam, McNamara had told the chair that he never wanted to see such a session again. The general, also realizing that only a united professional military opinion would be considered by civilian leaders, thus enforced conformity within the JCS. Wheeler, Palmer charged, pressured the Army and Navy into supporting the air war in order to send unified proposals to McNamara. If the JCS chair, who was always aware of the political implications of decision making, forwarded a split recommendation, then the defense secretary and president would have made the final decision on strategy, thus infringing on what Wheeler considered the military's prerogative. As far as Palmer was concerned, Wheeler had done Lyndon Johnson, and the nation, a disservice. "Where there are fundamental differences of opinion among the chiefs," he observed, "the political leaders should know so that they do not embark on a murky path with unclear consequences."[28] Although it was unlikely that the president and McNamara were not aware of military differences over strategy, it was evident to most American officials that air power would not win the war. That would require ground

---

ment," UPA; for the JCS's air plans, see Annex to JCS to McNamara, 7 March 1965, "Air Strike Program against North Vietnam," VN C.F., NSF, box 193, folder: Vietnam, JCS Memos, volume 1 [2 of 2], LBJL.

26. Demma, "Suggestions for Ground Forces."
27. Westmoreland, *A Soldier Reports*, 115.
28. Kinnard, *The Secretary of Defense*, 80–2; Korb, *Joint Chiefs of Staff*, 115–16; Palmer in William Conrad Gibbons, *The U.S. Government and the Vietnam War: Executive and Legislative Roles and Relationships, Part III: January–July 1965* (Princeton, N.J., 1989), 84. "There are times," Palmer added, "when doing nothing is better than doing the wrong thing." Palmer, *25-Year War*, 33–5.

troops, and the momentum toward such deployments had become inexorable in February 1965.

Indeed the air war showed no returns at the outset – with Rolling Thunder delayed until March due to poor weather and continued political chaos in Saigon – and Westmoreland expected conditions in the RVN to worsen. Within six months the government in Saigon might only control a limited number of provincial and district capitals, refugees would clog the roads, "end the war" groups would proliferate and demand a settlement, and the VC might take power within the year. To buy time he, and the JCS, thus asked for the deployment of a Marine Battalion Landing Team (BLT) to Da Nang, which the president authorized on 26 February along with more helicopters, increased air support, and additional advisors at the fighting unit level.[29] While the chiefs had urged the Marine deployments and were, in effect, recycling the request, Westmoreland's support for combat troops marked a distinct reversal of his outlook of just weeks earlier.[30]

In part, the continued deterioration conditioned the call for ground troops to protect the American base at Da Nang. As Westmoreland pointed out, the VC's "strength, armament, professionalism and activity" have increased "to the point where we can ill afford any longer to withhold available military means" from the RVN. But even he was not anticipating the large-scale use of ground troops. The MACV commander believed that there were two areas in which U.S. combat support could have a significant impact, citing air and surface sea power, but not combat personnel. Whatever steps the United States took, Westmoreland found it "most important . . . to avoid the impression by friends and enemies that [the] U.S. has taken over responsibility for war from the Vietnamese."[31]

29. Wheeler to Sharp and Westmoreland, 20 February 1965, Westmoreland to Sharp and Wheeler, 23 February 1965, and Wheeler JCS 0736–65 to Sharp and Westmoreland, 27 February 1965, all in Westmoreland Papers, box 5, folder: #13 History Backup, LBJL; Westmoreland analysis of 25 February in *Pentagon Papers: Gravel*, 3:337–8; Westmoreland, *A Soldier Reports*, 122–4; Johnson, *Vantage Point*, 138.
30. On JCS proposals for ground forces, see abstract of JCSM 100–65, 11 February 1965, in JCS Policy Statements concerning Operations in Southeast Asia, Warnke-McNaughton, box 7, folder VNS 2 [Vietnam, 1966–8] (1), LBJL.
31. Westmoreland to Sharp, 27 February 1965, "Use of U.S. Air Power," Westmoreland Papers, box 5, folder: #13 History Backup, LBJL; see also Westmoreland, *A Soldier Reports*, 123.

The CINCPAC, Admiral Sharp, was also ambivalent over the latest moves. While he, too, recognized the corroded situation in the RVN and accepted Westmoreland's rationale for the BLT in Da Nang, Sharp believed that long-term success would require "a positive statement of national policy and specifically a command decision as to whether or not we are or will participate actively in the fighting in [the] RVN, or whether we will continue to adhere to our long standing policy that this is a Vietnamese war and that we are only advisors."[32] As U.S. officers had done since 1961, Sharp was once more pressing the civilian establishment in Washington to take responsibility for Vietnam. The administration, however, was concerned more with taking action in Vietnam than formulating grand strategy. Thus Wheeler, after a meeting on Vietnam with the president and others, told Sharp and Westmoreland that the White House was determined to "press forward despite difficulties to achieve the limited objectives set by the U.S." in Vietnam. "At the same time," the JCS chair saw "evident concern" that America was "not doing enough to achieve these objectives."[33]

It appeared that American officials were taking a temperate view of their role in Vietnam prior to the Marine deployments of 8 March. In fact, however, the United States was taking its infant steps into a major land war in Indochina. While continued disintegration in the south accounted for the first combat troop movements to the RVN, there was also a strong political component in the decision to send soldiers to Da Nang. The military had abandoned its reluctance to commit ground troops to Vietnam not only because of the declining prospects of the southern half to survive the Communist insurgency, but even more because America's civilian leaders had made it clear that such intervention was their policy choice. As the president, McNamara, Bundy, McNaughton, and others began to advocate ground force deployments to retard or reverse the situation in the RVN, the military followed along.

American officers had not recommended the use of combat troops before February 1965 and, in Westmoreland's case, had

---

32. Sharp to Wheeler and Westmoreland, 26 February 1965, "Security Situation in Southeast Asia," Westmoreland Papers, box 5, folder: #13 History Backup, LBJL.
33. Wheeler JCS 0736–65 to Sharp and Westmoreland, 27 February 1965, Westmoreland Papers, box 5, folder: #13 History Backup, LBJL.

firmly rejected such proposals earlier. But with civilian authorities in Washington rushing in that direction, Wheeler, the MACV commander, and others fell in line, as concerned with the political impact of decision making as with the war in Vietnam itself. The deployment to Da Nang resulted from civilian pressure, not military factors, and was in the cards even prior to the events of early 1965. As General DePuy later observed, the commitment of combat forces was not the "product of a Westmoreland concept for fighting the war." The MACV staff, he explained, still expected U.S. troops to advise and assist the ARVN, not fight the war themselves.[34]

So did Maxwell Taylor. Although he had to acquiesce in the troop commitment, the ambassador persisted in warning about a wider war. Expressing his "grave reservations" about commiting ground forces to Vietnam, the soldier-cum-diplomat warned that "once this policy is breached, it will be very difficult to hold [the] line" on future troop moves. As soon as RVN leaders saw that the United States was willing to assume new responsibilities, they would certainly "seek to unload other ground force tasks upon us," which would inevitably lead to increased political tension with the local population and friction with the RVNAF over command arrangements. Taylor recognized the need to defend U.S. airfields at sites such as Da Nang or Bien Hoa, but thought that accepting a combat role against the VC was just not feasible. The "white-faced soldier armed, equipped, and trained as he is" was "not [a] suitable guerrilla fighter for Asian forests and jungles," he explained. Pointing to the French failure in the First Indochina War, Taylor had to "doubt that US forces could do much better."[35]

He also continued to lament that internal political factors would seriously retard America's ability to improve the situation. In "the most tipsy-turvy week since I came to this post," as Taylor wrote to the president in late February, Khanh had again been ousted, this time replaced by a reformist cabinet minister, Dr. Phan Huy Quat. Without a legitimate and stable government in Saigon, effective

---

34. Demma, "Suggestions for Ground Forces"; DePuy in Gibbons, *Government and Vietnam War, 1965,* 125.
35. Taylor 2699 to Rusk, 22 February 1965, NSC History, "Deployment," UPA.

military action was virtually impossible.[36] The Vietnamese, Taylor observed, were not clamoring for U.S. troops either. RVN leaders, after a 1 March meeting with the ambassador, did not reject using American troops for base protection, but told Taylor to bring them into Da Nang "in the most inconspicuous way feasible."[37]

As Taylor saw it, America's best hope remained reprisal air strikes against the DRVN to force Ho to withdraw support from the VC in the south. Contrary to the Army's emphasis on the insurgency in the RVN, the ambassador believed that "if we tarry too long in the south, we will give Hanoi a weak and misleading signal which will work against our ultimate purpose."[38] In thus arguing against active combat by U.S. troops and in favor of a principally air war, he lost out on two counts. Though he was arguably the most reputable military man in America in the mid-1960s, the administration ignored Taylor's urgent dissent. Civilian officials had already decided to fight in the RVN and so political imperatives overrode Taylor's provocative analysis of America's problems and prospects. At the same time, the ambassador, in urging the use of air power in the north to defeat the VC in the south, had revealed that he did not understand Vietnam much better than anyone else in Washington.

Division and ignorance, however, would be no obstacle to an expanded war. As soon as the Marines arrived at Da Nang, it was clear that their presence would make little impact and within a short while, as many generals had anticipated, those initial deployments led to an American takeover of the war. General Fredrick Karch, the commander of the 9th Marine Expeditionary Brigade (9th MEB), later renamed the 3d Marine Amphibious Force (III MAF), arrived in Vietnam only to have MACV intelligence give him a "rather dismal" briefing about American prospects. The VC controlled vast territory in both the cities and the countryside, making it dangerous for U.S. personnel to travel only two miles outside Da Nang or Saigon. Political intrigue continued to dominate RVNAF affairs, Karch added, and various "warlords" were

36. Taylor to Johnson, 23 February 1965, ibid.
37. MACV Command History, 1965, 31, MCHC.
38. Taylor 2888 to Secretary of State, 8 March 1965, VN C.F., NSF, boxes 45–6, folder: Vietnam, volume 1 (A), NODIS-LOR, LBJL.

engaging in widespread corruption and graft, which made it impossible to channel aid to the village level where it was most needed. "Vietnam was just one big cancer," the Marine commander lamented.[39]

And it was metastasizing. In I Corps, where the Marines were deployed, "the communist guerrillas enjoyed essentially uncontested dominance over most of the rural population," they admitted. The enemy, organized at various levels from main-force units down to hamlet guerrillas, could utilize "a spectrum of military capabilities ranging all the way from coordinated operations of battalion size down to sabotage, terrorism, intelligence, and propaganda activities in the heart of GVN-dominated sectors."[40] Westmoreland further explained that the enemy held the initiative throughout the RVN, was consolidating its political gains in rural areas, continued to infiltrate and recruit military personnel, and was "implanting a sense of the inevitability of VC success" among southerners. Because of such developments, the MACV commander hedged his bets on the troop issue, requesting forces but stressing that "overall responsibility for the defense of the Danang area remains a RVNAF . . . responsibility."[41]

Such gloomy appraisals stiffened the president's will. Johnson reaffirmed his determination to protect the RVN to whatever extent needed, including more combat troops. Toward that end, he directed the military man most supportive of sending combat forces into Vietnam, Harold K. Johnson, to survey the situation and to "get things bubbling." The president "very clearly was not going to lose Vietnam," General Johnson understood, and so he developed policy accordingly.[42] After a week in Vietnam it was clear to the

39. Fredrick Karch Oral History, 58–62, MCHC; see also Jack Shulimson and Charles Johnson, *U.S. Marines in Vietnam: The Landing and the Buildup, 1965* (Washington, D.C., 1978), 19–20.
40. FMFPac, "U.S. Marine Corps Forces in Vietnam, March 1965–September 1967, Historical Summary," 5–1, 9–1, MCHC; see also Shulimson and Johnson, *Marines in Vietnam, 1965,* 19–20.
41. Westmoreland in FMFPac, "Operations of the III MAF, Vietnam, March–September 1965," MCHC [hereafter cited as III MAF Operations, March–Sept. 1965]. Like Westmoreland, the JCS was cautious on the troop deployments, giving directions that the Marines "will not, repeat will not, engage in day-to-day actions against the Viet Cong." JCS to CINCPAC, 6 March 1965, HCAS, *USVN Relations,* book 4, IV.C.4, 1.
42. Harold K. Johnson interview with MacDonald and von Luttichau, CMH; Marolda and Fitzgerald, *U.S. Navy and Vietnam,* 531–3.

Army chief that the situation "has deteriorated rapidly and extensively." Time was "running out swiftly," so "expedient measures will not suffice." Toward that end, the Army chief devised a twenty-one-point program of logistic, financial, intelligence, and training support to strengthen the RVNAF, improve village security, and stem VC expansion in the south. The keystone of his report, however, was a recommendation for substantial ground troops in the RVN, either a division to free the ARVN by assuming base protection or taking defensive responsibility in II Corps, or a four-division force to be deployed across the RVN and Laos to the Mekong (the so-called Panhandle plan).[43]

Although the president had sent the general to Vietnam because of the likelihood of the Army chief recommending ground troop deployments,[44] it was somewhat ironic that Harold K. Johnson had become the military's point man on the combat force issue in early March. Just a month earlier he had met with *New York Times* writers who reported that the general expected "Korea all over again," with the enemy exploiting sanctuaries outside the RVN and the United States unable or unwilling to use its full power. Johnson thus "had no great desire to go to war in Vietnam." He then told Tom Wicker that any troop commitment would have to be vast, requiring 15,000 troops to protect Pleiku alone. The Army chief was equally blunt with Westmoreland during his tour in Saigon, warning of the enemy's determination and capabilities. "We're ready, sir," Westmoreland replied. "No, you're not," Johnson told him.[45] McNamara, however, had no such reservations. On 1

43. Harold K. Johnson, "Report on Survey of the Military Situation in Vietnam," VN C.F., NSF, boxes 190–1, folder: Vietnam, General Johnson Report, LBJL; McGeorge Bundy to Johnson, 24 July 1965, "History of Recommendations," VN C.F., NSF, boxes 74–5, folder: 2E, 5/65–7/65, 1965 Troop Decision, LBJL; Johnson, *Vantage Point,* 139–40; Westmoreland, *A Soldier Reports,* 125–8; Gibbons, *Government and Vietnam War, 1965,* 161–73.

44. Army historian Vincent Demma, in his written work and in a conversation with me, persuasively argues that Harold K. Johnson was the biggest military advocate of deploying combat forces – to be utilized in the four-division Panhandle plan – and that the president sent him to Saigon for precisely that reason. Lyndon Johnson, as the Army chief himself noted, was committed to getting more deeply involved in the war, and expected recommendations to do so. Demma, "Suggestions for Ground Forces"; see also Harold K. Johnson, MHI Oral History Program, and Johnson interview with MacDonald and von Luttichau, CMH.

45. Halberstam, *Best and Brightest,* 595, 630; Johnson in Perry, *Four Stars,* 149.

March he informed the service secretaries that there was an "unlimited appropriation" available for Vietnam and just weeks later told Harold K. Johnson that "Policy is: anything that will strengthen the position of the GVN will be sent."[46]

After the Johnson trip to Vietnam, the United States was well on its way to a large-scale commitment of combat troops. Just days after the general's return McGeorge Bundy advised the president to deploy ground troops to improve America's bargaining position in Vietnam.[47] McNaughton similarly advocated "a massive US ground effort" in the south. The U.S. stake in Vietnam, he reiterated, was psychological and political more than military, and troop deployments would demonstrate resolve and maintain credibility. As McNaughton saw it, 70 percent of the reason for intervention was "to avoid a humiliating US defeat (to our reputation as guarantor)"; 20 percent was to keep the RVN out of "Chinese hands"; while only the remaining 10 percent was to "permit the people of SVN to enjoy a better, freer way of life."[48]

McNaughton's views, George McT. Kahin explains, were typical of the Johnson administration's approach to Vietnam. The White House had made a "political calculation" that a humiliating defeat in Vietnam would open the Democrats to a new version of the "loss of China" charges of the early 1950s and the president would then be vulnerable to a "serious domestic political attack" from his critics.[49] Speaking at Johns Hopkins University on 7 April, the president thus invoked the U.S. commitments to southern Vietnam under Presidents Truman, Eisenhower, and Kennedy to justify continued action. Clearly, America's credibility was on the line; since the 1950s U.S. leaders had pledged to defend the RVN and Johnson intended to "keep that promise." "We will not be defeated. We will

46. *Pentagon Papers: Gravel*, 3:428–9; Leonard B. Taylor, *Financial Management of the Vietnam Conflict, 1962–1972* (Washington, D.C., 1974), 17–25; Kolko, *Anatomy of a War*, 166.
47. McGeorge Bundy to Johnson, 16 March 1965, "Memo for Discussion . . . Policy on Vietnam," NSC History, "Deployment," UPA; Berman, *Planning A Tragedy*, 54–61.
48. McNaughton Draft, 10 March 1965, "Action for South Vietnam," NSC History, "Deployment," UPA; McNaughton to McNamara, 24 March 1965, "Proposed Course of Action Re Vietnam," *Pentagon Papers: Gravel*, 3:694–702.
49. "Domestic political considerations," Kahin pointed out, were "so ingrained in the minds of the president and his advisers as to be taken for granted and require no explicit articulation in [McNaughton's] strictly internal memorandum." Kahin, *Intervention*, 313.

not grow tired. We will not withdraw. . . . [So] we must be prepared for a long continued conflict," he declared. From Berlin to
Bangkok, as well as in Saigon, Communists were attacking America's friends and the United States had to take a stand. "To withdraw from one battlefield means only to prepare for the next," the
president believed. "We must stay in Southeast Asia."[50]

Even though the president's intent was clear, Taylor continued to
warn against further ground troop moves. Perhaps he just did not
understand the depth of the U.S. commitment to the RVN, for the
ambassador found it "curious" that Johnson was reluctant to approve an air campaign against the DRVN, while it was "relatively
easy to get the Marines ashore."[51] And more would be landing if
Westmoreland got his way. On 16 March the MACV commander
requested another Marine deployment, this time to Phu Bai – about
eight miles south of Hue and fifty miles below the DMZ in Thua
Thien province in I Corps – to protect the 8th Radio Research Unit
(RRU) there. "Intrinsic in my proposal," Westmoreland later observed, "was that American troops would be used in offensive
operations."[52] Taylor immediately balked. The request for protection for the 8th RRU, he complained to the president, reinforced his
fear that such proposals would continue unabated and might induce the ARVN to perform even "worse in a mood of relaxation at
passing the Viet Cong burden to the US."[53]

Marine leaders too questioned the move to Phu Bai, an area that
General Krulak thought was "as tactically indefensible as anyone
could imagine" due to its distance from Da Nang, about fifty miles,
and the difficulty of providing logistical support. Westmoreland,
however, had already invested about $5 million in the communica-
tions center there and "was determined not to see it move," Krulak
charged. The troop movements to Phu Bai, as the Marine general

50. Johnson in Berman, *Planning a Tragedy*, 8–9; in Gibbons, *Government and Vietnam
    War, 1965*, 217. Maybe not surprisingly, Johnson's account of the Johns Hopkins speech
    in his memoirs does not include the cited passages. It only quotes those portions of the
    address in which the president discusses his dreams of developing Vietnam along Great
    Society lines and arriving at a peaceful, negotiated solution to the conflict there.
    Johnson, *Vantage Point*, 133–4.
51. Taylor, *Swords and Plowshares*, 338.
52. Westmoreland, *A Soldier Reports*, 129–30.
53. Taylor 3003 to Secretary of State, 16 March 1965, NSC History, "Deployment," UPA.

interpreted it, constituted a case "where dollar economics wagged the tail of military deployment."[54]

Military critics also shared reservations over the conventional, offensive mission Westmoreland was developing for U.S. troops in Vietnam. They preferred, as General Johnson had, that American troops deploy to coastal enclaves, rather than assuming "search and destroy" or other types of missions that would actively engage the Viet Cong. To the ambassador, Sharp, Generals Krulak and Greene, or retired General James Gavin, it was imperative to build up the ARVN and protect U.S. installations rather than conducting a war of attrition against guerrillas.[55] Westmoreland, however, had other ideas. As General DePuy observed, in early 1965 the MACV was in transition "from a staff that originally was very much concerned with counterinsurgency . . . to a staff concerned with [large-scale] operations."[56] At the outset of the U.S. ground war, American generals were thus divided once more over the appropriate strategy for Vietnam. Although such differences may not have seemed critical at the time, overlooked or dismissed in the rush to send forces to the RVN, they would continue and intensify after the major U.S. commitments of mid-1965 and affect the war for the remainder of the Johnson years.

In March 1965, however, military, and civilian, officials were concerned with getting more ground forces into Vietnam amid the continued deterioration there. The initial deployments had not alleviated the situation in the south and Wheeler, as MACV historians explained, "feared that the VC gains might have reached the point where, regardless of US action against [the DRVN], the RVN would fall apart."[57] Other officials had equally forthright reservations. The commitment to Da Nang had alienated various Marine generals who pointed out to Greene that the corps "was overcommitted . . . and unable to meet any kind of challenge in the Atlantic

---

54. Victor H. Krulak, Comments on Shulimson Draft, 11 August 1969, Vietnam Comment File, MCHC; Shulimson and Johnson, *Marines in Vietnam, 1965*, 22.
55. *Pentagon Papers: Gravel*, 3:6, 453; Shulimson and Johnson, *Marines in Vietnam, 1965*; Marolda and Fitzgerald, *U.S. Navy and Vietnam*, 531–3; Palmer, *25-Year War*, 40–2; on Gavin, see Buzzanco, "Division, Dilemma, Dissent," and "The American Military's Rationale against the Vietnam War."
56. DePuy in Krepinevich, *Army and Vietnam*, 139.
57. MACV Command History, 1965, 31.

area."[58] Army General Arthur Collins, a planning officer who believed that the United States was going to "nibble away at this Vietnamese problem" and that the southern Vietnamese had no will to fight, urged Bruce Palmer to oppose the moves to the RVN in early 1965.[59] Collins and the Marines both got nowhere with their complaints. The United States had already passed the point of no return in Vietnam, and in March and April 1965 American policy makers seemed solely concerned with sending more troops to the RVN, not in debating whether they should be there.

Although military authorities had just deployed the 9th MEB to Da Nang, they forbade it from taking offensive action, and it became immediately clear that the Marines would have a negligible impact on the conflict in general. The United States would have to do much more to make a difference. Upon his return from Vietnam, Harold K. Johnson "sent quite a shock wave through the administration," as Wheeler's aide General Andrew Goodpaster put it, by estimating that the United States would have to commit at least 500,000 troops, for a minimum of five years, to achieve success in the RVN. The Army chief, a skeptic on the benefits of air power, assumed that such a vast number of soldiers was required to develop an effective strategy of counterinsurgency. Although the president probably had not previously anticipated such figures, he nonetheless reaffirmed his determination to maintain the RVN with whatever resources were needed.[60] Emboldened by the president's largesse in sending forces to Vietnam, the JCS upped the ante in late March, going beyond General Johnson's recommendations for one division by requesting that two U.S. divisions be deployed for active combat, to Da Nang and the central highlands, and one Korean division be positioned to operate in the RVN.[61]

---

58. General Norman Anderson, Oral History, 170–2, MCHC.
59. Gibbons, *Government and Vietnam War, 1965*, 170.
60. Ibid., 165–6; Harold K. Johnson, MHI Oral History, 8, Marolda and Fitzgerald, *U.S. Navy and Vietnam*, 531–3. There are apparently no written records of this 15 March meeting.
61. JCSM 204–65, 20 March 1965, in "JCS Policy Statements," Warnke-McNaughton, box 7, folder: VNS 2 [Vietnam, 1966–8] (1), LBJL; see also Gibbons, *Government and Vietnam War, 1965*, 169; Palmer, *25-Year War*, 40–1; the JCS also reported that it was making satisfactory progress toward meeting the twenty-one-point program that Johnson had developed in early March. "As a general observation," the chiefs told the president, "all projects appear to be moving swiftly and smoothly." Wheeler CM-522–

Westmoreland had developed the new troop requirements based on a comprehensive analysis of America's alternatives, which he forwarded to his superiors on 26 March. As the MACV commander saw it, the new three-division deployment offered the best hope of success in Vietnam. He again dismissed an expanded air war and buildup of the RVNAF because such measures did nothing to stabilize the political situation in the south or attack the principal problem, the VC insurgency below the DMZ. Citing the impossibility of providing logistics support to forces along the seventeenth parallel in a timely manner, the general also rejected a version of Harold K. Johnson's Panhandle proposal.[62]

Westmoreland, with Wheeler, pitched the new proposal to the president and defense secretary at a 29 March meeting, after which Johnson was publicly noncommittal about future American moves in Vietnam. Although the president was committed to expanding U.S. efforts in Vietnam, he also understood that rising military appropriations could divert resources and attention away from his domestic agenda. On the other hand, a tentative approach to the war would endanger Johnson's domestic program also as congressional allies of the military, and conservatives, would attack the Great Society in retribution for not doing enough in Indochina. The president, predisposed toward increasing the U.S. role in the RVN and more worried about the hawks than the liberals in any event, thus decided to approve what Admiral Sharp pointed out was a "far reaching strategy change – namely, the concept of U.S. forces engaged in ground operations against Asian insurgents in South Vietnam."[63]

Sensing the nature of Johnson's coming moves, Maxwell Taylor continued to challenge White House policy on Vietnam. With an NSC meeting scheduled for 1–2 April, the ambassador returned to Washington to make the case against the military's plans. Prime

65 to Johnson, 27 March 1965, "Status Report on the Recommendations of the Chief of Staff, U.S. Army," VN C.F., NSF, box 191, folder: General Johnson Report, LBJL.

62. U.S. MACV, 26 March 1965, "Commander's Estimate of the Military Situation in South Vietnam," Westmoreland Papers, folder 509a [2 of 2]: #14 History Backup, 1–26 March 1965, WNRC; Westmoreland, *A Soldier Reports*, 124–9; Shulimson and Johnson, *Marines in Vietnam, 1965*, 21–2.

63. Sharp, *Strategy for Defeat*, 70; Brian VanDeMark, *Into the Quagmire: Lyndon Johnson and the Escalation of the War* (New York, 1991), 112, 125.

Minister Quat reported that the RVN leadership was not excited about the new deployments, and anti-American sentiment was sure to rise as more U.S. soldiers arrived in Vietnam.[64] Once more Taylor called for intensified air attacks against the DRVN, and, in apparent agreement with McNamara, urged the Marines in I Corps to establish coastal enclaves. But Taylor, as McGeorge Bundy saw it, had become too antagonistic and obstructionist and should be replaced as ambassador. "In the long pull," he wrote to the president, "we need a McNaughton-type in Saigon."[65] For the time being, however, Rusk and McNamara backed Taylor's position. As a result, rather than three divisions, the president authorized two additional Marine battalions and about 18,000 to 20,000 other support forces for Vietnam, while at the same time approving a change in mission to allow the 9th MEB to actively fight the VC.[66]

Taylor left Washington satisfied that the president was not rushing into a ground war in Vietnam. But the ambassador had gained only a Pyrrhic victory in delaying the three-division commitment. Johnson had in fact significantly extended the U.S. role in Vietnam as American soldiers would now be waging war on the ground in the south.[67] NSAM 328, the formal declaration of the president's directives, significantly expanded the U.S. role in Vietnam. Johnson, as so many had urged, was prepared to engage the enemy directly, but his actions were not wholly accepted. John McCone, the outgoing director of the CIA, questioned the move to active combat operations without a corresponding escalation of the air war. Unless "our airstrikes against the North are sufficiently heavy and damaging" to deter Ho from supporting the insurgency, he believed, American ground forces would have little impact. The United States should "tighten the tourniquet" around the DRVN,

64. McGeorge Bundy to Johnson, 24 July 1965, "History of Troop Recommendations," VN C.F., NSF, boxes 74–5, folder: 2 E, 5/65–7/65, 1965 Troop Decision, LBJL; Krepinevich, *Army and Vietnam*, 145.
65. Bundy added that, although he favored the new troop proposals, the deployment of a Korean division to Vietnam might be unlikely, as Seoul was "very wary" of the plan. McGeorge Bundy to Johnson, 31 March 1965, "Your Meeting with Max Taylor at 5:15 this Afternoon," NSC History, "Deployment," UPA; *Pentagon Papers: Gravel*, 3:6.
66. See sources cited in previous note; also *Pentagon Papers: Gravel*, 2:357–8, 3:454; Shulimson and Johnson, *Marines in Vietnam, 1965*, 22–6; Krepinevich, *Army and Vietnam*, 145–6; Westmoreland, *A Soldier Reports*, 131.
67. Berman, *Planning a Tragedy*, 60–1.

not kill civilians in the south. "If anything," McCone admitted, "the strikes to date have hardened [Ho's] attitude."[68]

Earle Wheeler's evaluation of the air war was more desolate. Since 7 February the United States and RVN had conducted forty-four air strikes, he reported, but DRVN anti-aircraft forces had shot down twenty-five American and six Vietnamese planes. One Vietnamese pilot had died and two were missing, while one U.S. airman was killed, two were captured, and nine more were missing. "The air strikes have not reduced in any major way the over-all military capabilities of the DRV," the JCS chair admitted. Although some bombs had damaged supply depots and ammunition dumps, which did reduce the supply of some matériel, "these losses should not be critical to North Vietnamese military operations." Attacks against barracks, airfields, and radar sites, he added, did not seriously hamper DRVN capabilities, while the economic impact of the air operations was "minimal." At any rate, the JCS chair concluded that Ho had been "uninfluenced" by American air power and was willing to "pay a price for South Vietnam" by withstanding the U.S. assaults from the sky. In fact, Wheeler, apparently desperate to put the best spin possible on Rolling Thunder, resorted to arguing that the DRVN would have to focus more resources on air defense at the expense of other economic and social sectors and that the northern population would be apprehensive about continued bombings. While such observations may have been true, they constituted a rather weak rationale for emphasizing a costly and destructive air war.[69]

Although many of Lyndon Johnson's critics would argue that he undermined the air war by limiting the number of sorties flown and targets struck, it was clear at the outset that air power would not win the war and that, as Mark Clodfelter has shown, American

---

68. NSAM 328, 6 April 1965, *Pentagon Papers: Gravel*, 3:702–4, 3447; McCone to Rusk, McNamara, Bundy, Taylor, 2 April 1965, VN C.F., NSF, boxes 74–5, folder: 2 E, 5/65–7/65, 1965 Troop Decision, LBJL; McCone to Johnson, April 1965, NSC History, "Deployment," UPA.

69. Wheeler CM-534–65 to McNamara, 6 April 1965, "Over-all Appraisal of Air Strikes against North Vietnam, 7 February 1965 to 4 April 1965," VN C.F., NSF, box 193, folder: JCS Memos, volume 1 [1 of 2], LBJL; for JCS bombing requests, see Colonel H. M. Darmstandler, 15 December 1967, "Chronology of Requests," Warnke-McNaughton, box 7, folder: VNS 2 [Vietnam, 1966–8] (1), LBJL.

service leaders remained divided over its priority and prospects.[70] "Even had Washington adopted a strong bombing policy" without target restrictions and pauses, Westmoreland "still doubt[ed] that the North Vietnamese would have relented." To force DRVN leaders to stop supporting the VC in 1965 the United States "had to do more than hurt their homeland; we had to demonstrate that they could not win in the South, and [the RVN] had to make real progress in pacification." U.S. aircraft could not accomplish that, and in fact could provoke a DRVN reaction "that might overwhelm the existing unstable government."[71] Indeed, the Air Force's principal problem was not politically imposed constraints so much as inadequate air base defense. As the earlier VC mortar attacks at Bien Hoa and Pleiku had indicated, America's formidable array of aircraft would have little value if destroyed on the tarmac. Yet the Air Force, despite the military emphasis on CI training, "did not actively consider the impact of insurgency warfare on air base defense," as its own history admits.[72]

With the efficacy of air power seriously in doubt, American leaders recognized that they would have to send more combat troops to Vietnam to have any impact on the VC's progress.[73] As the two Marine BLTs authorized in NSAM 328 were arriving in the Hue-Phu Bai and Da Nang areas in mid-April, bringing the U.S. total to four maneuver battalions, American officials were laying the groundwork for a much larger commitment. Between 8 and 10 April Admiral Sharp sponsored a planning conference at which U.S. military leaders decided to expand markedly American troop levels in Vietnam. Toward that end, Westmoreland requested the deployment of an airborne brigade to Bien Hoa and an Army brigade to the Qui Nhon-Nha Trang areas on the coast of II Corps, each to consist of about five thousand troops plus support person-

---

70. Clodfelter, *Limits of Air Power,* 80–4; for criticism of Johnson's approach to the air war, see, among others, Sharp, *Strategy for Defeat;* Lewy, *America in Vietnam;* Nixon, *No More Vietnams;* Harry Summers, *On Strategy: A Critical Analysis of the Vietnam War* (Novato, Calif., 1982).

71. Harold K. Johnson, MHI Oral History program; Johnson interview with MacDonald and von Luttichau; Westmoreland, *A Soldier Reports,* 113.

72. Roger P. Fox, *Air Base Defense in the Republic of Vietnam, 1961–1973* (Washington, D.C., 1979), 19–25.

73. *Pentagon Papers: Gravel,* 3:443–50; see also CIA Memorandum TS HI185834, "Communist Intentions in South Vietnam," NSC History, "Deployment," UPA.

nel. On 14 April the president met with his advisors and the JCS and then, without consulting Taylor in Saigon, approved the deployment of the 173d Airborne Brigade, which at the time constituted the CINCPAC's airmobile reserve, to the Bien Hoa area.[74]

The White House, the *Pentagon Papers* authors noted, "was well ahead of Saigon in its planning and its anxiety" over coming moves in Vietnam.[75] The president and his advisors were assuming that the worst possible outcome, continued breakdown in the RVN and rapid VC progress to victory, was forthcoming and took action to forestall it. Washington was so eager to engage the enemy that, when Westmoreland anticipated that the Marines might not begin offensive actions for several weeks, Sharp pointed out that, "if I read the messages properly, this is not what our superiors intend. [I] recommend you revise your concept accordingly."[76] The new deployments and mission, as McGeorge Bundy recognized, were sure to be a "very explosive" issue with Taylor as well.[77] Bundy of course was right. The ambassador, left out of the loop at the key mid-April meetings, had heard about the 173d Airborne deployment and reacted with rancor, accusing Washington of reversing its earlier position that it would allow the Marines to experiment with a counterinsurgency role before bringing in other contingents.[78]

Taylor found it "difficult to understand" the administration's enthusiasm for offensive forces. For both military and political reasons, he cabled Rusk, "we should all be most reluctant to tie down Army/Marine units in this country and would do so only after the presentation of the most convincing evidence of the necessity." America's first objective in sending in ground troops – assuring the RVN and DRVN of the U.S. determination to stay the course in Vietnam – had been met with the initial deployments, and Taylor saw no need to make additional moves to reinforce that point. The ambassador also warned that other arguments for U.S. reinforcement, including freeing the ARVN to fight the VC or hav-

74. *Pentagon Papers: Gravel,* 3:450–1; Gibbons, *Government and the Vietnam War, 1965,* 226–9; Krepinevich, *Army and Vietnam,* 146–9.
75. *Pentagon Papers: Gravel,* 3:451.
76. CINCPAC to Westmoreland, 14 April 1965, "Employment of MEB in Counterinsurgency," NSC History, "Deployment," UPA.
77. McGeorge Bundy to Johnson, 14 April 1965, ibid.
78. Taylor 3373 to Secretary of State, 14 April 1965, ibid.

ing a presence in Vietnam as a contingency for future crises, "could be adduced to justify almost unlimited additional deployments of US forces." In time, "the mounting number of foreign troops may sap the GVN initiative and turn a defense of the homeland into what appears a foreign war." Tension between the Vietnamese and their "white allies" would worsen, Taylor added, and the growing American role would likely prompt the PRC to increase its support of Ho.[79] Taylor's apostasy notwithstanding, Johnson, after brief deliberations with McNamara, Rusk, and McGeorge Bundy, decided to proceed with the new commitments and he directed that the ambassador be cabled that the president "believes the situation in South Vietnam has been deteriorating and that, in addition to actions against the North, something new must be added in the South to achieve victory."[80]

Ironically, Taylor, who had consistently opposed an American ground war because of the RVN's fragile political situation, now claimed that the conditions in the south had improved measurably and new U.S. forces were not needed.[81] Complaining that the young Quat government already was being forced to accept "a 21-point military program, a 41-point non-military program, a 16-point Rowan USIS program, and a 12-point CIA program," he sarcastically wondered whether "we can win here somehow on a point score." The White House's best approach, the ambassador told McGeorge Bundy, would be to leave Quat alone for the time being. The RVN could win, he suggested, "unless helped to death."[82] Taylor, however, also understood that his position was untenable in the face of Johnson's desire to send more combat forces into the RVN. So, while still "badly [in] need of a clarification of our purposes and objectives" to justify the new troop moves to the Saigon government, he otherwise obeyed directions and even drafted the instructions needed for approaching Quat about the coming deployments.[83]

By mid-April 1965 Taylor's influence had waned and the White

79. Taylor 3384 to Secretary of State, 14 April 1965, ibid.
80. Joint State-Defense Message to Taylor, 15 April 1965, ibid.
81. Taylor 3424 to Secretary of State, 17 April 1965, ibid.
82. Taylor 3421 to M. Bundy, 17 April 1965, ibid.
83. Taylor 3423 to Secretary of State, 17 April 1965, ibid.

House could essentially dismiss his dissenting views. The embittered ambassador finally realized at that point, as Andrew Krepinevich observes, that the president "had been egging on the JCS all along for a major introduction of U.S. ground forces" despite his objections. Taylor himself later complained that Johnson "was the fellow with the black snake whip behind [the chiefs] saying, 'Let's get going – now!' He did all this behind my back. . . . Once he made his decision he couldn't get going fast enough."[84] At the same time, Taylor remained a strident advocate of air attacks over the north to shut down the insurgency in the RVN. He thus came to embody the U.S. experience in Vietnam as much as anyone. His admonitions about the political turmoil and perils of ground war may have seemed prophetic, but his claims that the war was going well and that air power would prove decisive not only diverged from the military consensus but were examples of Taylor's naiveté, if not ignorance, about Vietnam, and of his awareness of the politics of the war. Taylor was a transitional figure in the evolution of the U.S. military leader from warrior to bureaucratic manager. Although he had sufficient credibility to press his misgivings more forcefully or publicly, Taylor's political education had taught him to defer to the political will and not challenge Washington on policy, as, for instance, Ridgway, Gavin, and others had done in 1954. Having gone into battle against Eisenhower as Army chief and then been given another chance by Kennedy, Taylor was a veteran of civil–military maneuvering and so, in April 1965, he knew he had lost. Lyndon Johnson would get his war.[85]

With Taylor's concerns overridden and Johnson anxious to develop plans for the new commitment to Vietnam, the president directed his principal advisors – including McNamara, McNaughton, William Bundy, Sharp, Wheeler, Westmoreland, and the ambassador – to meet at Honolulu on 20 April. At that point the United States had approximately 33,000 troops in-country and another 20,000 were on their way. Those numbers were about to jump rapidly, and the administration was aware of the political and military implications of the coming American escalation. Jack Val-

---

84. Taylor in Krepinevich, *Army and Vietnam,* 147–9.
85. Kinnard, *Certain Trumpet,* 134–62.

enti, once more stressing the domestic political impact of the war, advised the president to meet with White House correspondents and their editors to sell them on Vietnam. "During the next few weeks," Valenti warned, "the Viet Nam embroilment will come under heavy attack. Some editors are . . . queasy about where it is all leading us."[86]

American officials may have been a bit anxious as well. At Honolulu the conferees, according to McNamara, determined that the enemy would not capitulate anytime in the near future and that "a settlement will come as much or more from VC failure in the South as from DRV pain in the North," which could take "perhaps a year or two" to accomplish. Ignoring Sharp's objections, the defense secretary reported that the officials at Honolulu had agreed that the air war's "present tempo is about right." From that point on, McNamara and Johnson would subordinate the air war to ground operations. Toward that end, U.S. policy makers recommended the prompt deployment of 82,000 American and 7,000 third-country forces, and envisioned the additional transfer of about 56,000 troops to Vietnam later in the year, all of whom could be used in ground operations in the south.[87] Taylor, the good soldier as well as policy critic, had come on board at Honolulu too. In fact he believed that "if we keep up our bombing and introduce substantial US and third-country forces," a favorable settlement in Vietnam might occur in a matter of months rather than the year or two that McNamara was expecting.[88] Although now a team player, Taylor, as his most recent biographer observed, was only a "background figure in Vietnam" after April 1965. "In that fateful spring," as Douglas Kinnard put it, "Mars was on the loose" and neither Taylor nor anyone else would contain him.[89]

Among U.S. military men, however, there were clear signs that

86. Valenti to Johnson, 19 April 1965, Reference File, box 1, folder: Aides' Memos on Vietnam, LBJL.
87. McNamara to Johnson, 21 April 1965, VN C.F., NSF, boxes 74–5, folder: 2 EE, 1965–7, Primarily McNamara Recommendations re. Strategic Actions [1965–6], LBJL; Sharp, *Strategy for Defeat,* 77–9; Taylor, *Swords and Plowshares,* 341–7; Westmoreland, *A Soldier Reports,* 132; Davidson, *Vietnam at War,* 345–6.
88. McGeorge Bundy to Johnson, 26 April 1965, "Cable from Max Taylor," NSC History, "Deployment," UPA.
89. Kinnard, *Certain Trumpet,* 154.

America's problems were only beginning. Taylor reported that Quat was still reluctant to accept U.S. troops. Victor Krulak added that the ARVN commander in I Corps, General Nguyen Chan Thi, opposed any American patrols or offensive action beyond the air-field at Da Nang. "This is enemy country," Thi told the Marine general, "you are not ready to operate there." The Marine Commandant dismissed the ARVN general's counsel, however. "You don't defend a place by sitting on your ditty box," Wallace Greene observed during a visit to Da Nang.[90] The commandant believed that the White House would have to expand the 9th MEB if it was to be able to clear VC from I Corps, but he continued to press for expanded air operations in the north, possibly even strikes against dikes to ruin rice fields and starve the DRVN into submission, as a key to overall success in Vietnam. At the same time, however, Greene recognized the limits of air war. The DRVN's anti-aircraft capabilities were already well developed and U.S. planes flying north, he admitted, "get the living hell beaten out of them by 37, 57, 85, 100 millimeter guns [and] radar control."[91]

Like many American officers, the commandant seemed bellicose on Vietnam but in fact offered ambivalent, if not contradictory, views on the war. Greene, who already understood that much of the public opposed "this unwanted, undesired, miserable war," nonetheless thought that the United States had a "national security stake" in Southeast Asia. If America withdrew, the commandant warned, it would lose two centuries of prestige and credibility, and merely postpone the day "when we're gonna have to meet these bastards somewhere in India, in the Near East, Latin America – It's coming." He thus believed it necessary to conduct a "radical" public relations blitz to impress upon Americans the need to pay "whatever it takes" in Vietnam and to prepare for national mobilization. Given Greene's awareness of problems in Vietnam and the public's already evident antipathy toward the war, however, he

90. Taylor 3496 to Johnson, 23 April 1965, NSC History, "Deployment," UPA; Victor H. Krulak, Comments on Shulimson Draft, 2 August 1977, Vietnam Comment File, MCHC; Greene in Shulimson and Johnson, *Marines in Vietnam, 1965*, 29, see also 20.

91. Meanwhile the Marines were hiring Vietnamese workers to build a base at Chu Lai, about fifty miles south of Da Nang, which meant that it was likely "that our permanent airfield will be built by VC labor." Conference between CMC-FMFPac, at FMFPac Headquarters, 23–29 April 1965, tape #6298, MCHC, my transcription.

must have anticipated that such preconditions would not be met, and that the United States would not succeed in Vietnam.[92]

Taylor and Westmoreland were also pointing out difficulties in southern Vietnam. The ambassador reported that the VC was increasing its infiltration into and action inside the RVN, while the influx of American troops was disrupting life in the coastal areas and straining logistics facilities. The Vietnamese had to absorb the 80,000 troops already in-country, so more soldiers should be sent "only in case of clear and indisputable necessity," Taylor advised.[93] The MACV commander also recognized serious problems in the RVN, but wanted more forces anyway. By May 1965, Westmoreland found that Rolling Thunder "had no measurable effect" on pacification in southern Vietnam. Even during a three-month lull in VC activity, the counterinsurgency program "has continued to regress in I and II Corps to an alarmist degree."[94]

General Krulak, after visiting Da Nang in May, was satisfied with Marine activity to that point, but he too recognized shortcomings. The VC, as a Marine briefer told his Pacific commander, "continue to harass and wear out our forces, forcing us to move out of their operational area out of despair." In addition, native resentment over government and U.S. interference with the people's lives was apparent, while the 9th MEB was experiencing serious logistics, supply, and communications flaws. The "powdered sugar" beaches at Chu Lai made vehicle transportation nearly impossible, Phu Bai was still "relative[ly] indefensibl[e]," and Krulak had "never seen a worse situation" in communications than at Da Nang, where some messages might not get out for thirty hours, while others never arrived. While at Da Nang Krulak also met with Maxwell Taylor and he reported that the ambassador believed that "however successful we are, it is still going to take a long time to win, and he is fearful that the nation at large may not have the requisite patience."[95]

92. Greene in tape #6298, MCHC.
93. Taylor 3632 to Secretary of State, 4 May 1965, NSC History, "Deployment," UPA; Taylor 3808 to Secretary of State, 19 May 1965, VN C.F., NSF, boxes 45–6, folder: Vietnam, volume 2 (A), NODIS-LOR, LBJL.
94. Westmoreland MACJ332 to Taylor, 30 May 1965, "Comparison of the Rural Reconstruction Situation, 25 January and 25 April 1965," Westmoreland Papers, folder 511: #16 History Backup, 10 May–30 June 1965, WNRC.
95. Victor H. Krulak, 22 May 1965, General Summary, FMFPac Trip Reports, CG's Trip Summary, WestPac Visit, 14–21 May 1965, MCHC.

Americans would need a great deal of patience, however, because the U.S. commitment to Vietnam was sure to grow. With political chaos worsening – in June Quat resigned, eventually to be succeeded by a junta headed by Air Marshal Nguyen Cao Ky and General Nguyen Van Thieu – and the DRVN sure to commit whatever forces needed to win in the south, more American soldiers would be headed to Vietnam. The JCS thus called for "a substantial further build-up of US and allied forces in the RVN, at the most rapid rate feasible on an orderly basis." Accordingly, Westmoreland requested an immediate increase of over 40,000 troops, but added that 52,000 more might be needed in a short while. In addition to the forty-four battalions – thirty-four American (twenty-two Army and twelve Marine) and ten from third countries (Korea, New Zealand, Australia) – he also sought authority to conduct operations in the RVN more actively. The MACV commander had asked for even more troops than envisioned by the chiefs, who had up to that point been more eager than Saigon to get reinforcements sent to Vietnam, and when word of his plans reached Washington, the JCS even pressed Admiral Sharp to explain just "where Westmoreland intended to put this force in Vietnam."[96]

Although not articulated as such, Westmoreland's battalion proposal essentially involved taking over responsibility for offensive warfare from the ARVN. Clearly the decay in the RVN, and VC success, had forced U.S. leaders into the stark choice of either vast escalation or defeat. The MACV commander and other brass, however, also understood that their own credibility, as well as Lyndon Johnson's and the nation's, were at stake, and that the president and his principal civilian advisors on Vietnam, McNamara and McGeorge Bundy, had most vigorously pressed for U.S. combat involvement and expected prompt success. Only a substantial U.S. combat role could even offer any such hopes, so American officers, despite their constant recognition of the risks of intervention, not

96. Westmoreland to JCS, 7 June 1965, "US Troop Deployments to SVN," in NSC History, "Deployment," UPA; Wheeler to McNamara, 11 June 1965, "US/Allied Troop Deployments to South Vietnam," VN C.F., NSF, box 193, folder: JCS Memos, volume 1 [1 of 2], LBJL, and in *DDRS*, 79, 270A; *The Pentagon Papers, New York Times* edition, ed. Neil Sheehan et al. (New York, 1971), 423; see also J-2, MACV, Intelligence Estimate, 1 May 1965, III MAF Command Chronology, July 1965, MCHC (hereafter cited as III MAF Chronology); MACV Command History, 1965, 6–7; Embassy, Saigon, to Department of Defense, 5 June 1965, *DDRS*, 79, 325A; Taylor 4035 to Secretary of State, 3 June 1965, NSC History, "Deployment," UPA.

only accepted the White House's determination for a ground war in the south, but indeed upped the ante by requesting deployments in excess of what the civilians had envisioned. If the president wanted a war in Vietnam, the U.S. military apparently reasoned, he would have to be responsible for its outcome.

By mid-1965, service leaders were obviously suspicious of their civilian counterparts and worried about their conduct of the war. Earle Wheeler bemoaned what he saw as "overcontrol and over-management" by Pentagon civilians and wanted his field commanders to be free of having "their hands tied by . . . theorists at higher headquarters." Admiral David McDonald, the CNO, like-wise was concerned that Johnson's graduated bombing campaign would fail, but that the president would eventually leave office and "the only group left answerable for the war would be the mili-tary."[97] Admiral Sharp explicitly addressed such political consider-ations in his instructions to Westmoreland. Although the ambas-sador had already told MACV commanders that they could commit their forces to battle against the VC, and Sharp had reiterated that authorization, the CINCPAC also urged that Westmoreland "real-ize that there would be grave political implications involved if siz-able U.S. forces are committed for the first time and suffer a defeat." The commander should thus "notify CINCPAC and JCS prior to [the] commitment of any U.S. ground combat force."[98]

Indeed, such political maneuvering would be an implicit yet crit-ical element in Vietnam policy making from that point on because military men were aware that civil–military relations as well as battlefield conditions would determine the nature of U.S. involve-ment in the war. American officers – although not usually as candid as Sharp in discussing the "grave political implications" of their decisions – did recognize that the president and defense secretary would never authorize unlimited resources or operations in Viet-nam. Military policy was not made in a vacuum; public opposition to the war, Johnson's domestic agenda, and international political

97. Wheeler and McDonald in Betts, *Soldiers, Statesmen, and Cold War Crises,* 11.
98. U. S. G. Sharp to Westmoreland in NMCC to White House, 13 June 1965, NSC History, "Deployment," UPA; for background see Westmoreland to Taylor, 3 June 1965, "Au-thority for the Commitment of US Ground Combat Forces," Westmoreland Papers, folder 511: #16 History Backup, 10 May–30 June 1965, WNRC; Taylor 4036 to Secretary of State, 3 June 1965, NSC History, "Deployment," UPA.

considerations, as well as the situation on the ground in the RVN, would always be significant elements in the formulation of strategy. The president himself made this clear at a mid-June NSC meeting on Vietnam. To Johnson, dissent at home, trouble in the field, and the threat of PRC intervention meant that the United States had to limit both its means and ends in Vietnam. It thus had to contain the enemy "as much as we can, and as simply as we can, without going all out." By approving Westmoreland's forty-four-battalion request, he explained, "we get in deeper and it is harder to get out. . . . We must determine which course gives us the maximum protection at the least cost."[99]

The president's concern about a deeper commitment was revealing, indicating that he would not authorize unlimited resources to or wholly unrestrained operations in Vietnam. Johnson would, however, escalate the war to levels not imagined just years earlier. Military leaders, despite recognizing the risks of intervention in Vietnam and having arrived at no consensus on how to conduct the war, nonetheless continually pressed the White House to expand the U.S. commitment. Unable to develop any new ideas to alter conditions in the RVN, or to admit that they were not likely to reverse the situation there, American officers asked for more of the same. The president in turn would "get in deeper" yet not fully satisfy the military's requests. Either way, Lyndon Johnson would be responsible for what happened in Vietnam.

This process was already evident during the deliberations over Westmoreland's proposals in June and July 1965. Military leaders continued to take an equivocal, if not contradictory, approach to the war. The JCS urged the president to meet Westmoreland's request but opposed MACV plans to use American forces in the highlands of the RVN, instead preferring to employ them as a mobile reserve near the coast. Westmoreland, however, believed that only RVNAF soldiers could conduct the pacification program, so he planned to commit U.S. forces against "hardcore" PAVN and VC units, both "in reaction and [in] search and destroy operations." By assuming such security tasks, Westmoreland hoped to

99. Bromley Smith, summary Notes of 552d NSC Meeting, June 11, 1965, NSF, NSC Meetings File, box 1, folder: volume 3, tab 34, LBJL; see also Kahin, *Intervention,* 348–52.

free the Vietnamese to attack VC strongholds in populated regions along the coast, in the delta, and around Saigon.[100] The MACV commander, of course, would get his way on the employment of U.S. forces, giving them principally a conventional mission in an otherwise guerrilla war. His decision, however, would remain a divisive issue within military circles for the duration of the war.

In July 1965 American officers subordinated such differences to the need to take action in Vietnam. The RVN leadership, now under General Ky's direction, was pressing Taylor for troops in late June. The ambassador, now on the team regarding Vietnam, relayed the request to Rusk with his support because the air campaign had not produced significant results and he did not expect Hanoi to "show weakness under the pressure generated thus far."[101] McNamara too advised the president to authorize the forty-four-battalion deployment to Vietnam and once more urged him to expand the air war against the north. Underlying his, and Westmoreland's, approach was their determination that the war had entered the "third stage" of people's war as formulated by Mao Zedong: the defense secretary and MACV commander now believed that the struggle in Vietnam was a "conventional war in which it is easier to identify, locate and attack the enemy." McNamara was well aware, however, that the introduction of additional American troops in Vietnam did not ensure success. Although Westmoreland hoped to "re-establish the military balance" by year's end, he admitted that the new commitments "will not per se cause the enemy to back off." Accordingly, MACV leaders could not yet estimate the troop levels that might be needed in coming years "to gain and maintain the military initiative," although Westmoreland "instinctively" expected "substantial US force requirements" in 1966. The number of battalions eventually required, Westmoreland alerted McNamara, "could be double the 44 mentioned above."[102]

100. See sources cited in previous note; also Text of Cable from General Westmoreland, COMUSMACV 20055, 14 June 1965, NSC History, "Deployment," UPA.
101. Taylor 4422 to Secretary of State, 28 June 1965, NSC History, "Deployment," UPA; Taylor to Secretary of State, 11 July 1965, VN C.F., NSF, box 19, folder: Vietnam, volume 37, LBJL; see also Taylor Memorandum, 11 July 1965, VN C.F., NSF, boxes 190–1, folder: Vietnam, NODIS-MAYFLOWER, LBJL.
102. McNamara to Johnson, 26 June 1965 (revised 1 July 1965), VN C.F., NSF, box 20,

The president expected to increase his commitment to Vietnam as well. At a White House meeting on 2 July, Johnson was clearly predisposed toward accepting McNamara's recommendations, which Rusk had also supported. At a press conference a week later the president announced that America's manpower requirements in Vietnam "are increasing and will continue to do so. . . . Whatever is required I am sure will be supplied."[103] McNaughton also backed the new deployments to Vietnam, even though he assumed that perhaps 400,000 troops would eventually be needed to give the United States just a 50 percent chance of success by 1968.[104] Lyndon Johnson was clearly heading toward a wider war, but he remained aware that a significant number of Americans continued to question or oppose U.S. involvement in Vietnam. As a result, the president directed McNamara to visit Saigon again to examine the situation and prepare the public for the coming measures.[105]

McNamara and his party departed for Vietnam on 14 July to determine whether the new deployments would assure ultimate success, or rather cause the ARVN to "let up" while engendering greater resentment against Americans among the Vietnamese.[106] Neither Westmoreland nor Taylor, who was in his last days as ambassador, could guarantee decisive results even with the reinforcements. The VC and PAVN would likely expand their force levels to correspond with American increases or, if needed, could avoid "conclusive military confrontation" against U.S. or ARVN regular units by resorting to guerrilla tactics. Unless the VC abandoned the insurgency due to a variety of highly improbable developments – such as the effectiveness of Rolling Thunder, Soviet or Chinese pressure, continuing signs of American resolve, political stability in Saigon, and an improved performance from the

folder: Vietnam, volume 37, Memos (C), also in NSF, NSC Meetings File, box 1, folder: volume 3, tab 35, LBJL; *Pentagon Papers: Gravel*, 4:296.

103. Gibbons, *Government and Vietnam War, 1965*, 343–4, and Johnson quotation on 367; Rusk, *As I Saw It*, 450.
104. McNaughton to McGeorge Bundy, 13 July 1965, "Analysis and Options for South Vietnam," VN C.F., NSF, box 20, folder: Vietnam, volume 37, Memos (A), LBJL.
105. Adam Yarmolinsky, McNamara's deputy, later explained that the defense secretary "regarded his trips as theater" and even drafted his reports before departing the United States so then he would only have to revise them based on what he had observed in Vietnam. Gibbons, *Government and Vietnam War, 1965*, 369.
106. McNamara to Taylor, 7 July 1965, NSC History, "Deployment," UPA.

ARVN – the troop expansion, according to Westmoreland, was
"not believed to be sufficient to eliminate the widespread VC
capability for control of major segments of the country."[107]

McNamara received more sobering news during a meeting in
Saigon with Westmoreland, Wheeler, and MACV briefers on 16
July. The DRVN continued to infiltrate men into the south at high
levels despite the U.S. air strikes, and was supporting the insurgency with only fourteen tons of supplies per day, according to a
JCS study. To the defense secretary this meant that the United States
had only a "very small" chance of upsetting infiltration via air
attacks. To stop even the "meager supplies" moving into the RVN
would require "tremendous activities on the ground." Such increased operations, however, carried grave risks. Although hoping
that the proposed reinforcements would force the enemy to stand
and fight in conventional battles and suffer greater losses, Westmoreland conceded that "the chances of [the VC] standing up to
fight US forces is questionable; they may be hard to find." In addition to this not insignificant point, the MACV intelligence chief,
General Joseph McChristian, observed that the insurgents could
shift between various phases of warfare easily. "With 100,000 guerrillas," he explained, the VC "can fight now and then return to the
plow." Overall, McChristian added, the enemy had approximately
1 million men within its manpower pool and could increase its
strength at the rate of about 100,000 troops per year.[108]

Because of such enemy capabilities, Westmoreland anticipated
that he would require another vast reinforcement in 1966, including twenty-four maneuver, fourteen artillery, three air defense, eight
engineer, and six helicopter battalions, as well as twelve helicopter
companies and additional support units. With such forces the

---

107. Westmoreland in Gibbons, *Government and Vietnam War, 1965,* 373–4; see also
 Taylor, *Swords and Plowshares,* 348–52.
108. General DePuy, the planning chief, disagreed with McChristian's analysis of the enemy's ability to make the transition between stages of warfare. The VC's main-force
 battalions, not guerrillas, were America's principal opponents, as he saw it. Once U.S.
 troops began to locate and engage those forces, DePuy believed, the war would change
 in their favor. Record Group 407, Records of the Adjutant General's Office, DA/
 WNRC Administrative Files Relating to Westmoreland/Capital Legal Foundation v.
 Columbia Broadcasting System, Litigation Research Collection (LC), box 44, folder:
 Questions and Answers, WNRC (hereafter cited as Westmoreland v. CBS with appropriate filing information).

MACV commander planned to defeat the enemy in a three-phase war, initially halting the losing trend by the end of 1965, then taking the offensive in high-priority areas after that, and finally destroying any remaining VC forces and base areas by 1968. McNamara essentially accepted Westmoreland's assessment, but because of the VC's potential manpower reserve of one million the defense secretary also recognized that American deployments could conceivably expand well beyond current estimates for phase three operations.[109]

McNamara returned to Washington and delivered his report to the president on 20 July, touching off the most intense week of deliberations on Vietnam policy until the 1968 Tet Offensive. To achieve a "favorable outcome" – which would involve an end to the insurgency, the survival of the RVN, and the withdrawal of U.S. combat forces – the secretary of defense advised Johnson to authorize the deployment of thirty-four additional maneuver battalions, and forty-three if the Koreans failed to contribute nine battalions as planned, by October 1965. Those troops, along with support personnel, would raise the U.S. force structure in Vietnam to 175,000 or more. McNamara also urged a national mobilization for Vietnam, recommending that the administration activate 235,000 men in the Reserve and National Guard, increase the size of the armed forces by 375,000 via recruiting, draft calls, and extended tours of duty, and seek a supplemental appropriation to cover the costs of this new buildup. Once in place, this American force could take the offensive against the VC in the south while the air war over the north would expand from 2,500 to 4,000 sorties per month. At the same time, the reserve call-up and other military augmentations would create about sixty-three additional maneuver battalions to use as a contingency force.[110]

The defense secretary's report sparked a series of intense meetings on the war, although the president had already told

---

109. See source cited in previous note; and *Pentagon Papers: Gravel*, 4:296–7.
110. McNamara to Johnson, 20 July 1965, "Recommendations of Additional Deployments to Vietnam," NSF, Memos to the President, McGeorge Bundy, box 4, folder: volume 12, July 1965 [1 of 2], LBJL; "Proposed 63 Battalion Plan," 19 July 1965, ibid.; Johnson, *Vantage Point*, 145. McNamara's memorandum of 20 July contained much of the same language as McNaughton's draft of 13 July. Adam Yarmolinsky was the chief drafting officer for both. Gibbons, *Government and the Vietnam War, 1965*, 382.

McNamara's deputy, Cyrus Vance, that he would approve the reinforcements.[111] In July 1965 U.S. officials consciously had decided
to take responsibility for a war in Southeast Asia with their eyes
wide open to the realities and drawbacks of intervention. George
Ball, the undersecretary of state, Clark Clifford, an informal advisor to the White House, and Maxwell Taylor actually opposed
McNamara's plans, with Ball in particular offering a spirited and,
as it turned out, prophetic assessment of the hazards of war.[112] But
the advocates of intervention were aware of what the future held as
well. McNamara was prepared to request at least $2 billion in
supplemental funding for Vietnam in 1965, while Vance thought
that the costs of national mobilization could reach $8 billion.
McGeorge Bundy, however, warned the president that such a vast
appropriation would be a "belligerent challenge" to the Soviet
Union, become a propaganda tool for the Communists, and hurt
economic confidence at home.[113] Jack Valenti urged Johnson to
take whatever steps necessary to alter the war conclusively in as
short a time as possible, but he also warned that Republicans as
well as liberal Democrats would be sure to find fault with the
president's policy as the war became "long, protracted, [and]
uglier."[114]

American military officials, while supporting the Westmoreland-
McNamara proposals, once more did not offer sanguine views of
the situation in Vietnam. While Wheeler was optimistic that U.S.
forces could, if need be, "handle" both the DRVN and PRC, some

111. Gibbons, *Government and Vietnam War, 1965,* 380.
112. Ibid., 399–419; Clifford to McGeorge Bundy, 21 July 1965, VN C.F., NSF, box 20,
     folder: Vietnam, volume 37, Memos (B), LBJL; Clark Clifford, Memorandum for the
     Record, 22 July 1965, "Meetings on Vietnam, July 21, 1965," VN C.F., NSF, boxes
     74–5, folder: 2 E, 5/65–7/65, 1965 Troop Decision, LBJL.
113. Bundy was also concerned about McNamara's program of reinforcements. While urg-
     ing the president to approve the forty-four-battalion plan, he also advised him to defer
     making any further commitments for a few months. "After all," the national security
     advisor pointed out, "we have not yet had even a company-level engagement with the
     Viet Cong forces which choose to stand their ground and fight." McGeorge Bundy to
     Johnson, 23 July 1965, "Reasons for Avoiding a Big Military Appropriation in Viet-
     nam," NSC History, "Deployment," UPA; McGeorge Bundy to Johnson, 21 July 1965,
     "Timing of Decisions and Actions in Vietnam," and McGeorge Bundy to Johnson, 24
     July 1965, "History of Recommendations," both in VN C.F., NSF, boxes 74–5, folder:
     2 E, 5/65–7/65, 1965 Troop Decision, LBJL.
114. Valenti to Johnson, 22 July 1965, Reference File, box 1, folder: Aides' Memos on
     Vietnam, LBJL.

of his associates were not so bold in predicting success. John Mc-
Connell, the Air Force chief of staff, hoped that the new measures
would "at least turn the tide where we are not losing anymore."
Wallace Greene, still advocating the enclave concept rather than
MACV's conventional strategy, urged both combat reinforcements
and air strikes against the DRVN's industrial base, and a blockade
of Cambodia to choke off infiltration into the south. As the commandant saw it, such measures would require a 500,000-troop
commitment in the RVN for at least five years. "I think the US
people will back you," he optimistically told the president. Harold
K. Johnson, who believed that the Vietnamese Communists were
prepared to fight for twenty more years if needed, was not so hopeful. "We are in a face-down," he explained. "The solution, unfortunately, is long-term. Once the military solution is [found], the problem of political solution will be more difficult."[115]

Despite such blunt assessments and his own fear of provoking
the PRC or Soviet Union to intervene in Vietnam, Lyndon Johnson
believed that he had "very little alternative to what we are doing."
To Johnson it was "more dangerous" to lose the war "than [to]
endanger a greater number of troops." Should he not come to the
RVN's rescue, the president feared that other nations would consider the United States a "paper tiger." "Wouldn't we lose credibility by breaking the word of three presidents" concerning America's
pledge to preserve an independent southern state, Johnson asked
George Ball.[116] But the president also recognized the serious political consequences of a total commitment to Vietnam. If Johnson
accepted the McNamara-MACV program in whole, with possibly
endless deployments, a Reserve call-up, and supplemental appropriations, Hanoi would then use the American escalation as leverage to receive more aid from Chinese and Soviet sources. At home,
"this dramatic course of action" would involve declaring a state of
national emergency and additional funding of several billions of
dollars. The president did not want such drama and tension, especially when civil rights and Great Society legislation dominated his

---

115. Notes of Meeting, 22 July 1965, Meeting Notes File, box 1, folder: 21–27 July 1965,
   LBJL.
116. Notes of Meeting, 21 July 1965, Meetings Notes File, box 1, folder: 21–7 July 1965,
   LBJL.

domestic agenda. "I think we can get our people to support us without having to be provocative," Johnson observed wistfully.[117]

The president's steadfast commitment to see the war in Vietnam to a successful conclusion had come into conflict with his fear of provoking a wider war in Asia and of the domestic political and economic implications of national mobilization. Accordingly on 28 July Johnson announced that he was increasing the total of U.S. forces in the RVN from 75,000 to 125,000 and would send additional troops "as requested." The president would also double the number of monthly draft calls to 35,000, but would not activate the Reserves. Although he gained no pleasure in sending "the flower of our youth" into war, Johnson had to prevent the RVN from being "swept away on the flood of conquest." For such reasons, "we will stand in Vietnam."[118]

With the president's decision that day, the United States took a major step on the path to disaster. Despite the parlous situation facing U.S. forces in Vietnam, which included costs and risks recognizable to virtually all American officials, Johnson essentially decided that the United States would take responsibility for the war. By pledging to meet the military's requests for more troops, the president, as new Ambassador Henry Cabot Lodge lamented, "has just given up the only real power he has over the conduct of the war." At the same time, he alienated U.S. military officials by refusing to mobilize the country for war in Vietnam or to activate large numbers of reservists. Service leaders were already aware of the implications of the newly established policy. When Harold K. Johnson, who had assumed until the last moment that the president would mobilize for war, learned that the commander in chief was not going to utilize the National Guard, he assured McNamara that "the quality of the Army is going to erode to some degree that we can't assess now. I just know that."[119]

117. Bromley Smith, Summary Notes of 553d NSC Meeting, 27 July 1965, NSC Meetings File, box 1, folder: volume 3, tab 35, LBJL; Notes of NSC Meeting, 27 July 1965, Meeting Notes File, box 1, folder: 21–7 July 1965, LBJL. On the connections between the Great Society and Vietnam in Johnson's policy making, see Doris Kearns, *Lyndon Johnson and the American Dream.*
118. Johnson in Gibbons, *Government and Vietnam War, 1965,* 437–8; Johnson, *Vantage Point,* 151–2.
119. Lodge in Trewhitt, *McNamara,* 227; as the Army chief of staff saw it, not using the

Marine General Raymond Davis later made the same point about the failure to activate the Reserves and added that the military had initially requested $11 billion for Vietnam but, because of political pressure from advocates of domestic programs, ended up with just a small percentage of that amount. Such military complaints about Johnson's decisions were somewhat disingenuous, however. While ranking officers understood that Johnson and McNamara would be wary of their requests for troop increases because of the impact such moves would have on the Great Society, the JCS too played politics with the issues of troops and funding. Throughout the Vietnam era, the various services and the unified commanders were supposed to coordinate force levels in Indochina, but the chiefs rarely took the advice of the latter group because, as Lawrence Korb explained, they "were wary of losing any power to these men [the unified commanders] who were theoretically their equals."[120]

Given such political considerations on their own behalf, military critics and politicos should not have been shocked by Johnson's decisions. Their own assessments of the war had always pointed out the barriers to success in Vietnam and they had decried the continued erosion there. Their often sanguine projections for the future were thus born of either bold confidence in the capabilities of the American war machine or, just as likely, recognition that war in Vietnam was politically inevitable and, like it or not, they would have to wage it. "No longer was the United States pursuing the more limited objective of denying the enemy victory in the South and convincing him he could not win," Bruce Palmer observed. The U.S. goal "now was to defeat the enemy in the South, relying primarily on American troops. Unfortunately these actions gave the impression . . . that the United States intended to win the war on its own."[121]

General William Rosson, the MACV chief of staff, further saw the president's July 1965 decision as a "major strategic mistake" that "entailed risks we need not have taken." Many officers were as

Reserves was the "single greatest mistake we made." Harold K. Johnson, MHI Oral History Program, 13.
120. Raymond Davis Oral History, 93–4, MCHC; Korb, *Joint Chiefs of Staff*, 107; Palmer, *25-Year War*, 170; Gregory Palmer, *The McNamara Strategy and the Vietnam War: Program Budgeting in the Pentagon, 1960–1968* (Westport, Conn., 1978), 116.
121. Palmer, *25-Year War*, 41–2.

skeptical as he was, "but the course of action selected by the administration was clear" and the military went along with it, despite the "unrealistic" prospects for success.[122] Rosson and other officers in Saigon and Washington nonetheless accepted the responsibilities of war in mid-1965 although they were well aware of both the difficult situation in the RVN and the political constraints on their war-making potential.

Despite such awareness, those military officials would conduct an expanding war of destruction and attrition in Vietnam while, at the same time, recognizing their limited ability to produce the desired results. Even more, American service leaders would continue to urge the president to authorize the very measures – a fully unrestrained air campaign, geographical expansion of the conflict, national mobilization, and a call-up of Reserves, among others – that could not ensure success and that Lyndon Johnson had rejected already. Either the military thought that it could break the president's will through repeated pressure or, failing that, make him responsible for the stasis that was sure to result from U.S. involvement in the war. Either way, Larry Berman was surely right in contending that, with the July 1965 decisions, American officials had "decided to lose the war slowly."[123]

In just over eighteen months the United States had extended its involvement in southern Vietnam from supporting the ARVN, to protecting bases with U.S. soldiers, to engaging the enemy in combat, and eventually to turning the conflict into an American war. For Lyndon Johnson and other civilian officials such as McNamara, McGeorge Bundy, and McNaughton, the grave conditions in Vietnam and the need to maintain U.S. credibility made it imperative to take such action. Military leaders too understood the stakes involved in Vietnam, but took a somewhat tortured path toward their commitment to the war. The services themselves were initially divided over the proper approach to the conflict, with some generals urging air war over the north as the means to end the rebellion while others, especially Army leaders, rejected it as a diversion from the heart of the struggle, the southern insurgency. At

---

122. William Rosson interview, Senior Officer Oral History Program, used at CMH.
123. Berman, *Planning a Tragedy,* 124.

the same time, the brass, with the exception of Harold K. Johnson, showed little interest in assuming the responsibilities of ground war in the RVN. Indeed, only two months before U.S. Marines hit the beaches at Da Nang, General Westmoreland had advised against such deployments because they were of questionable military value and could lead also to a political situation not unlike that of France in the 1950s. Even more, the respected General Maxwell Taylor stridently opposed American combat in Vietnam for a variety of military and political reasons.

The Johnson White House, however, dismissed such criticism and caution and went to war in the RVN. General Matthew Ridgway, a critic of U.S. policy in Indochina for two decades, later observed that the president was "gung-ho on that thing." Johnson's increasing commitments to Vietnam and imprudent decision to enter combat there "far exceeded what you would hope would be the activities of the Commander-in-Chief," as Ridgway saw it. While the president did push the United States into war, it was also clear that American military leaders did not serve him well either. Rather than contemplate their own misgivings about the situation in Vietnam and the prospects of an effective military response there, U.S. officers generally ignored their own warnings, followed the White House lead on Vietnam, kept asking for measures that they knew would not be forthcoming, and then blamed the president when things, inevitably, turned sour. Neither military nor civilian officials had been adequately introspective in early 1965 and so they optimistically intervened in a foreign war that would cause unimaginable distress, internationally and at home. Some Americans saw it coming, however. When Ridgway met with the secretary of state shortly after the president's decision to engage in combat in Vietnam he lamented, "My God, Dean, don't we learn anything?" Maybe Rusk thought that the general's concerns were valid for, Ridgway added, "there was no answer."[124]

124. Ridgway Interview/Question Period at Command and General Staff College, 1984, 15–16, 22–3, MHI.

8

War on Three Fronts:
U.S. Forces versus the Viet Cong,
Westmoreland versus the Marines, and
Military Leaders versus the White
House, July 1965–December 1966

Those [Pentagon] officials and some White House and State Department advisers appeared to scorn professional military thinkers in a seeming belief that presumably superior Ivy League intellects could devise some political hocus-pocus or legerdemain to bring the enemy to terms without using force to destroy his war-making capability.

William Childs Westmoreland[1]

Dean Rusk may have used silence to express his reservations, but other officials would become increasingly vocal throughout 1965 and 1966 in pointing out the pitfalls facing U.S. forces in Vietnam and in criticizing Westmoreland's approach to the war. During that period the three factors that had principally characterized America's problems in Vietnam – the U.S. military's recognition of its foundering position, interservice feuding, and political maneuvering – became more pronounced and showed just how elusive success had become. By late 1966 it was clear that American forces had not been able to reverse conditions on the ground, while military leaders were aware of the limits to be placed on their operations. The services themselves were brawling over MACV strategy, and influential officials were sounding alarms about the U.S. future in Vietnam. Maybe most important, Lyndon Johnson's political career was on the line as the war in Indochina replaced the War on Poverty as the dominant national issue. Although the conflict would continue for many more years, the blueprint for failure had been drawn at the outset of intervention.

1. Westmoreland, *A Soldier Reports*, 120.

Throughout the year and a half of full-scale military involvement in Vietnam following the president's July 1965 decisions, the administration's problems in the RVN and in Washington mounted. Despite public claims of progress and often rosy outlooks from Westmoreland, Wheeler, and others, U.S. officers still realized that the ARVN was allowing American forces to carry the brunt of the war and that the enemy showed no signs of quitting. Although service leaders often complained, during the war and thereafter, that political constraints undermined their efforts, in reality they recognized that Communist infiltration, morale, and capabilities remained strong. They additionally conceded that the enemy held the military initiative, would simply avoid combat except on favorable terms, and had time on its side. Even more, they understood that the NLF was making further political headway among the Vietnamese people, while RVN leaders were still unable to develop a stable administrative structure or provide security. Under such circumstances, any military expectations of future success were delusive at best.

Just as critically, the U.S. military itself was engaged in an increasingly sharp fight over Westmoreland's strategy in Vietnam. Rather than address what they saw as the fundamental needs of the Vietnamese people – security and political stability – military critics such as Generals Krulak, Greene, Johnson, and others charged that the MACV strategy was needlessly bleeding American forces by engaging the enemy in big-unit encounters while the VC infrastructure remained virtually untouched. Westmoreland, however, would continue his ultimately futile strategy of attrition for the remaining two years of his command. At the same time, civil–military relations continued to deteriorate and political factors were ever present in the policy-making process. To the military, Johnson's failure to mobilize and activate Reserves, his bombing pauses and restrictions on air operations, and his concern over widening the war were fatal missteps with grave long-term implications. But American officers already understood that Johnson would try to limit the war, in terms of troop numbers, sorties flown, and geographical areas of combat. Nonetheless, they consistently pressed Johnson to declare a national emergency throughout 1965 and 1966 without success, yet, as the president's domestic problems mounted, continued to call for such measures even though they would not be authorized as the war dragged on. Rather than devise strategy based on such political realities, however, U.S. officers kept urging the president to approve the stronger measures that he had repeatedly rejected.

Given the president's concerns, such a reevaluation may not have been possible in any case. Johnson assumed that the United States could force Hanoi to abandon its support of the VC via incremental military pressure, but also feared both the international repercussions of escalation and the impact of Vietnam on his Great Society programs, so he hoped to find a way to end the war promptly and successfully. Given such objectives, it was not surprising that the military pursued the course of attrition and air power. Even if the Marines and Harold K. Johnson had convinced Westmoreland to emphasize nation building and turn over responsibility for combat to the ARVN, the war would have continued for years to come, and there was no guarantee that counterinsurgency tactics would have succeeded. To the president, an interminable commitment in Vietnam was simply unacceptable from a political viewpoint. Thus Johnson would wait for Westmoreland to achieve success; the military, when not fighting itself, would try to expand the war; and both sides would try to pin the other with responsibility for the disaster that was surely coming.

Following Johnson's moves of July 1965, the military began to prepare for full-scale combat in Vietnam, but without Reserves or other extraordinary measures. The Army, as Harold K. Johnson explained, thus faced a great dilemma as it had to support the war in Vietnam without mobilization and without reducing its worldwide commitments.[2] Still, Westmoreland and his staff planned on

2. Harold K. Johnson, MHI Oral History Program, 12–13, CMH; Harold K. Johnson, *Challenge: Compendium of Army Accomplishments – 1968*, a Report by the Chief of Staff, Washington, D.C., July 1964–April 1968, iii–x, used at CMH (courtesy of Graham Cosmas). When Creighton Abrams learned of the president's decision against using Reserves, he complained that "the only Americans who have the honor to die for their country in Vietnam are the dumb, the poor and the black"; in Sorley, *Thunderbolt,* 183. See also Douglas Kinnard, *The War Managers* (Hanover, N.H., 1977), 118–21; Palmer, *25-Year War,* 42.

waging a huge, conventional war in Vietnam, much as had Harkins during his time in Saigon. Thus the MACV commander and the JCS forwarded their "Concept for Vietnam" to McNamara in August. The generals assumed that the DRVN and VC would continue to control more territory, that the inchoate political situation in Saigon would persist, and that PRC intervention remained a possibility in Southeast Asia, and they also understood that the VC would avoid risky engagements with American forces and would instead conduct smaller-scale operations "to bleed and humiliate US forces." Notwithstanding that recognition – and Westmoreland's earlier claim that the war had entered Mao's "Third Phase," with set-piece conventional battles – the MACV intended to conduct the very type of war that the enemy would probably avoid. To attack both the "source" of aggression in Hanoi and "vigorously" eliminate the VC in the south, Westmoreland would intensify military pressure in the north via air and naval power, interdict supplies and reinforcements heading southward, and use "aggressive and . . . superior military force" to defeat the enemy in three of his own phases by 1968.[3]

Implementing such plans would obviously require additional forces, so Westmoreland immediately asked for, and McNamara approved, the dispatch of an additional 85,000 troops, thereby raising the number of U.S. military personnel in the RVN to over 200,000.[4] Such requests would continue, the chiefs pointed out, so again they pressed the administration to activate Reserves, extend terms of service for active-duty soldiers, expand the manpower base, and mobilize the industrial and financial sectors. In that way, the United States could both fight the war in Vietnam and maintain American commitments in Europe.[5] The JCS signed off on West-

3. JCS JCSM-652–65 to McNamara, 27 August 1965, "Concept for Vietnam," VN C.F., NSF, box 193, folder: JCS Memos, volume I [2 of 2], LBJL; MACV Concept of Operations in the Republic of Vietnam, 1 September 1965, Westmoreland v. CBS, LC, box 3, folder: Concept of Operations in RVN, WNRC; General Westmoreland's History Notes, Entry of 29 August 1965, Westmoreland Papers, folder 458 [2 of 2]: #1 History Files, 19 August–24 October 1965, WNRC; Palmer, *25-Year War*, 42.
4. McNamara to Johnson, 1 September 1965 and 22 September 1965, both in NSC History, "Deployment," UPA.
5. Admiral David McDonald, Acting CJCS, JCSM-721–65, to McNamara, 24 September 1965, "U.S. Military Posture," VN C.F., NSF, box 193, folder: JCS Memos, volume I [1 of 2], LBJL.

moreland's new requirements, but was concerned about the inflated troop numbers for Vietnam. Westmoreland suspected that Harold K. Johnson and senior staff members thought that "I was being unreasonable in stating my requirements for Army resources," while a conflict of interest between him and the Army chief was "inevitable" given the demands of the war in Vietnam and the limited resources available to Johnson in Washington. Although Westmoreland had no trouble receiving authorization for his requests in 1964 and early 1965, his latest requirements were "cutting into the meat and vitals of the Army and therefore the seeds of resentment are bound to appear."[6]

The seeds of disaster were already sprouting. Despite the new American commitments, conditions in Vietnam remained parlous and the outlook for future improvement was uncertain at best. In another war game, Sigma II-65, the JWGA expected the Communists in Vietnam to wait out the U.S. buildup and focus their attention on longer-term objectives such as destroying the political order and disrupting the economy in the south. Still believing that "time is on our side," the insurgents did not expect the United States to sustain its expansion in Vietnam, the JWGA said. Massive buildup on the ground notwithstanding, the United States could not convince the DRVN and VC that it was willing "to take appropriate action" to prevent their victory.[7] Even General DePuy offered a bleak appraisal of the war. Speaking at Marine headquarters in late October, he described the military situation only as "tolerable" and found pacification "totally unsatisfactory." Although confident that U.S. combat efforts could reverse battlefield conditions, DePuy anticipated a long-term commitment. "The thing that's going to keep U.S. troops in Vietnam for a long, long time," the planning chief told the Marines, "is the fact that the government . . . is really bankrupt." In addition to the VC subversion and Buddhist–Catholic division, the "congenitally conspiratorial" Ky-Thieu junta

6. General Westmoreland's History Notes, Entry of 27 September 1965, Westmoreland Papers, folder 458 [2 of 2]: #1 History Files, 19 August–24 October 1965, WNRC; Westmoreland MAC 4919 to Harold K. Johnson, 3 October 1965, Westmoreland Papers, folder 358c: Message File, WNRC; see also Abrams to General James Polk, 28 September 1965, Abrams Papers, box: Messages, Creighton Abrams, 1964–9, MHI.
7. Sigma II-65, Final Report, August 1965, NSF, Agency File, JCS, boxes 31–3, folder: War Games, Volume III, LBJL.

was exacerbating the political turmoil in the south, he charged, and most southerners expected the Communists to win the war. It was just October 1965 but he recognized that, if the people of Vietnam "lose morale again, I'd hate to try to buy it back one more time. I suppose it could be done . . . but each time it's more difficult."[8]

DePuy was barely more positive in evaluating the ARVN. Though he saw some improvements, the planning chief admitted that the MACV was working hard simply "to put ARVN back into the war." American officers had to teach the RVNAF "simple tasks, and short, step-by-step objectives," while U.S. personnel would work on longer-range goals. The VC, however, did not suffer from such shortcomings. Enemy troops, DePuy admitted, "fight like tigers." During Operation Starlite in I Corps in August, the VC "maneuvered in the jungle, maintained tactical integrity, withdrew their wounded, lost practically no weapons, and did a first-class job." Paying the enemy the ultimate compliment, DePuy confessed that "we'd be proud of American troops of any kind who did as well against such a large force that surprised them in the middle of the jungle."[9]

The VC, in fact, was operating effectively throughout the RVN. The insurgents, MACV officers explained, "have penetrated Vietnamese society in depth. It is a problem US forces have not encountered before."[10] It was also likely to worsen, for, as Westmoreland reported to Sharp, recent enemy infiltration was "greater than suspected." Ironically, Westmoreland predicted that the number of infiltrators would expand as the weather improved "and [as] US forces increase." In large measure American soldiers were having such difficulties containing infiltration because they were often protecting U.S. installations. At each U.S. airfield in the south, Westmoreland observed, there was a "serious risk" of VC mortar,

8. General DePuy, J-3, Briefing on Plans and Force Requirements, 21 October 1965, HQMC, tape #6173, MCHC, my transcription.
9. See source cited in previous note.
10. General James Collins, Jr., Special Assistant to COMUSMACV, Memorandum for the Record, 6 November 1965, "Conference at Nha Trang on 24 October 1965," Westmoreland Papers, folder 458 [1 of 2]: #1 History Files, 19 August–24 October 1965, WNRC; see also MACV Command History, 1965, 7; Lansdale to McGeorge Bundy, 23 October 1965, Lansdale Papers, folder 1485, Hoover Institution; Shulimson and Johnson, *Marines in Vietnam, 1965*, 91–7.

light artillery, or commando attack "even though a significant proportion of ground forces are tied to air base defense roles."[11]

Despite these problems, Westmoreland and other officers still
insisted that the war was going well, especially after the mid-
November battle of Ia Drang valley. While patroling in the central
highlands close to the Cambodian border, near Pleiku, units attached to the 1st Cavalry Division came into contact with and
routed PAVN regulars. Using their superior mobility and firepower
against the northern army, which was fighting without heavy
weapons, American forces killed over 2,000 Communist troops in
the Ia Drang valley, while losing about 240 of their own during the
battle. Ia Drang, as Westmoreland and DePuy interpreted it, validated their strategy of attrition. To General Phillip Davidson, a
MACV intelligence officer, it was a "major victory" for the Americans. Even the normally skeptical Harold K. Johnson initially believed that the worst was behind the United States after November
1965.[12]

In Washington, however, the war's biggest booster was not so
enthused. Robert McNamara, who, as George Ball put it, "more
than almost anyone else had led the country into" the war, was
clearly shaken by the events in the Ia Drang valley. To the defense
secretary the United States, despite inflicting great losses on the
enemy, had incurred an inordinate amount of casualties itself. On
top of such concerns, McNamara, just a week after the battle,
received another troop request from Westmoreland, this time for
additional battalions, instead of his initially projected twenty-eight,
to meet rising Communist infiltration into the RVN. In fact, the
number of PAVN forces in the south had risen from 6,000 to

---

11. Westmoreland MAC 5358 to Sharp, 27 October 1965, and Westmoreland MAC 5663
    to Sharp, 11 November 1965, "Airfield Security," both in Westmoreland Papers, folder
    358c: Message File, WNRC.
12. Westmoreland, *A Soldier Reports,* 157–8; Sheehan, *Bright Shining Lie,* 571–9; Kinnard,
    Certain Trumpet, 165–6; Krepinevich, *The Army and Vietnam,* 168–9; Davidson, *Viet-
    nam at War,* 360–2; U. S. G. Sharp and William C. Westmoreland, *Report on the War in
    Vietnam (as of 30 June 1968)* (Washington, D.C., 1968), 99–100; the most recent and
    comprehensive treatment of Ia Drang is Harold G. Moore and Joseph L. Galloway, *We
    Were Soldiers Once . . . and Young: Ia Drang – The Battle That Changed the War in
    Vietnam* (New York, 1992).

71,000 during the summer of 1965 while the number of guerrillas had increased to 110,000.[13]

McNamara, in Paris for a NATO meeting, took a detour to Saigon to meet with Westmoreland, who revealed that the enemy had been building up its forces at double the initial MACV estimates. The commander, while invoking Ia Drang as proof of the effectiveness of his strategy, nonetheless told the defense secretary that "the war had been characterized by an underestimation of the enemy and overestimation of the [southern] Vietnamese." He also made what he termed a "passing observation" that the war was increasingly taking on "an attritional character with heavy losses on both sides." Westmoreland, like Harkins before him, was committed to waging a conventional war of attrition in Vietnam, but also suggested that U.S. leaders "take a good hard look at our future posture."[14] McNamara did precisely that, concluding that earlier force projections were inadequate. The United States, he believed, could negotiate a compromise solution – an option he dismissed immediately – or "stick with our stated objectives and with the war, and provide what it takes in men and materiel." Staying the course, the secretary explained, would involve an intensified air campaign against the north and an increase from thirty-four to seventy-four combat battalions in 1966, which would expand the U.S. presence in Vietnam to about 400,000 troops within a year, with possible reinforcements of 200,000 in 1967. Even with such deployments, McNamara estimated that about 1,000 American soldiers would die every month "and the odds are even that we will be faced with a 'no-decision' at an even higher level."[15] The

13. George Ball, "The Rationalist in Power," *New York Review of Books* (22 April 1993), 30–6; Sheehan, *Bright Shining Lie*, 579–80; Shapley, *Promise and Power*, 355–8.
14. Westmoreland to Sharp, 23 November 1965, "Add-On to Phase II Deployments," VN C.F., NSF, boxes 24–5, folder: volume 43, Cables, LBJL; *Pentagon Papers: Gravel*, 4:303–9; General Westmoreland's History Notes, Entry of 29 November, Westmoreland Papers, folder 459: #2 History Files, 25 October–20 December 1965, WNRC; Sheehan, *Bright Shining Lie*, 568; Shapley, *Promise and Power*, 357–8.
15. McNamara to Johnson, 30 November 1965, VN C.F., NSF, boxes 74–5, folder: 2EE, 1965–7, Primarily McNamara Recommendations re. Strategic Actions [1965–6], LBJL (the 30 November memorandum was a supplement to a McNamara memo to the president of 3 November 1965 titled "Courses of Action in Vietnam," in ibid.); see also McNamara to Johnson, 6 December 1965, "Military and Political Recommendations for South Vietnam," same source as above. McNamara's commitment to let Westmore-

secretary of defense recognized, as had Westmoreland, just how badly the war was going at the end of 1965, but both urged more of the same. The United States had thus arrived at a pivotal point in the war. Despite increased troop levels and perceived success at Ia Drang, the American military position in Vietnam had not improved to any appreciable degree. In fact, Ia Drang had been instructive to General Giap too, and he would thereafter avoid big-unit engagements unless PAVN forces already held the initiative and maintained access to cross-border sanctuaries.[16]

As such battlefield developments continued to impede U.S. progress, various politicoeconomic factors took on greater importance. Both civilian and military leaders recognized that more than the survival of the RVN was at stake in the conflict in Indochina. To Lyndon Johnson the Great Society, and his own political legacy, would crumble if the war became divisive and boundless. By autumn 1965, however, the costs of Vietnam were already affecting the president's domestic goals and his relationship with the military, and, in time, would prove crucial in causing American defeat. As a result of the U.S. commitment to Indochina, various economic problems surfaced and worsened throughout the mid- and later 1960s, including inflation, budget and balance-of-payments deficits, and, maybe most important, a dollar and gold crisis. Inflation averaged 4.5 percent during the Vietnam years, while budget deficits rose from $3.8 billion in fiscal year 1966 (FY 66) to over $25 billion in FY 68, the largest in postwar history and 3 percent of the gross national product. America's share of world trade, which neared 50 percent after World War II, was down to 25 percent in 1964, and had fallen to just 10 percent by the end of the Johnson years. At the same time, the balance-of-payments deficit almost tripled between 1964 and 1968, when it rose to over $9 billion. Meanwhile, U.S. gold stocks, $23 billion in 1957, had dropped to

---

land establish strategy was obvious to his aides. When Pentagon staffers complained that the Ia Drang valley was not an advantageous place to fight because of its proximity to Laos and distance from Saigon, McNamara rebuked them, explaining that "we can't run this war from Washington; let Westmoreland run it." In Shapley, *Promise and Power*, 356–7.

16. Kinnard, *Certain Trumpet*, 165–6.

$16 billion by 1962 and annually decreased further throughout the war.[17]

Obviously, such economic distress had a tremendous impact on policy making for Vietnam as the spiraling costs of the war became a major factor in civil–military relations. In order to pay for the growing commitment to Indochina while keeping political attention at home focused on the Great Society, McNamara's budgets always underestimated the amount of money needed for Vietnam. The defense secretary always assumed, for budgeting purposes, that the war would end on 30 June of the following year (the end of the fiscal year at that time), which meant that the defense budget included no provisions for additional military funding for Vietnam and that the administration had planned for no alterations in its monetary or fiscal policies.

When, inevitably, the funds appropriated for Vietnam proved too limited, the administration would return to Congress with requests for supplemental expenditures for the war, an essentially political device first used in May 1965, when McNamara asked for another $700 million, and in August, when Congress established an "Emergency Fund, Southeast Asia" capitalized at $1.7 billion. By underfunding the military in Vietnam in his budgets and using supplemental requests to make up for the shortfalls, the defense secretary was providing political cover for the administration, which wanted to avoid debate on the costs of the war, and placing the burden for the economic consequences of escalation on the armed forces, which were always asking for more money, and the Congress, which approved the additional expenditures. Lyndon Johnson then had it both ways, proposing extensive spending for domestic welfare but also making the case to the military that he had met their needs in Vietnam. This budgeting strategy, not surprisingly, had serious implications for the war and the economy. Not only did it make it more difficult to discover the true cost of the war, but it also increased the military's tendency to focus on domestic political battles rather than seek alternatives in Vietnam, while at home it led to exorbitant defense spending – real funding for

17. Kolko, *Anatomy of a War*, 283–90; Campagna, *Economic Consequences of the Vietnam War*, 19–40.

Vietnam outpaced budget estimates by $1.5 billion in FY 66, over $9 billion in FY 67, and $13 billion in FY 68 – and ultimately caused greater inflation, higher interest rates, and tax increases.[18]

By autumn 1965, as McNamara and Westmoreland were debating the meaning of Ia Drang, the dollar–gold crisis added more problems to the policy-making mix. In August, French treasury officials feared that the Vietnam-induced balance-of-payments deficits were damaging European economies, and months later American bankers warned that the dollar's role as the world's currency might be in jeopardy. In fact, by the end of the year foreign banks had redeemed dollars for $1.7 billion in gold. Just a year later, David Rockefeller, Douglas Dillon, and other financial leaders insisted that the war not further upset the balance-of-payments ledger. After that, the situation became grave. In July 1967, Britain devalued the pound, triggering a run on a gold pool established by eight European nations in 1965 as the war in Vietnam had been "Americanized." Within a month, $1.5 billion of gold had been withdrawn from the pool, 60 percent of it from American gold reserves, while for the year U.S. gold stocks dropped another $1.2 billion.[19]

Such economic consequences of the war could not have escaped Wheeler, the consummate "political general," or Westmoreland, a product – like the secretary of defense – of the Harvard Business School.[20] All parties must have understood as early as the 1965 commitments that significant reinforcements of ground troops were the most costly way to escalate the war, and that technological means would have to be used to offset such expensive manpower.[21] In the coming years, the economic situation would progressively worsen to the point where McNamara, to conceal further the true

---

18. See sources cited in previous note; also Leonard Taylor, *Financial Management of the Vietnam Conflict*, 17–25.
19. Kolko, *Anatomy of a War*, 283–90.
20. The MACV commander, while assigned to the Pentagon on Ridgway's staff in the early 1950s, attended the advanced management program at the Harvard Business School, which, as he put it, "afforded insights into the management techniques of civilian business and some indication of the motivation of senior business executives." Though written without a trace of sarcasm, Westmoreland may very well have been thinking about McNamara as he composed those lines. Westmoreland, *A Soldier Reports*, 28.
21. Zeb B. Bradford, Jr., and Frederic J. Brown, *The United States Army in Transition* (Beverly Hills, Calif., 1973), 46.

costs of the war, began to postpone equipment overhauls, stretch out the purchases of new weapons systems, cannibalize matériel stocks in Europe, and extend repair and maintenance cycles by 50 percent. Such measures outraged the military hierarchy and helped make it impossible for service and civilian leaders to coordinate policy on Vietnam.[22]

For its part the military, just marginally optimistic about American prospects in Vietnam in any case, understood that the president would constrain its tactics in Vietnam for political and economic reasons. Nonetheless U.S. officers would continue to seek authorization for more resources and extended operations, although they too recognized the limited value of such measures and the political pitfalls associated with expansion, and failure, in Vietnam. Although such political–military maneuvering was commonplace during the Vietnam era, it entered a new, more intense phase in 1965. For the next two and a half years the White House and the armed forces would continue to play politics with the Vietnam War and, by early 1968, would create one of the gravest crises in civil–military relations in contemporary times.

For Lyndon Johnson, the final days of July 1965 had capped what he called "the most productive and most historic legislative week in Washington during this century." Congress had either passed or was prepared to vote on bills that would establish the Great Society, including Medicare, voting rights, War on Poverty, and education legislation. Johnson, however, had also increased the American stake in an overseas war and "the lowering cloud of Vietnam," as he noticed, was beginning to affect his domestic political agenda. As the costs of the war grew, Charles Schultze, the administration's budget director, informed the president that tax increases would be necessary to subsidize the U.S. presence in Vietnam, while Wilbur Mills, powerful chair of the House Ways and Means Committee, saw the beginnings of a "very serious inflationary crunch." Among others, Gardner Ackley, chair of the Council of Economic Advisers, told Johnson that 1966 "would not be a good year."[23]

22. Korb, *Joint Chiefs of Staff*, 117, and *Fall and Rise of the Pentagon*, 12.
23. Johnson clearly understood the significant interrelationship between Vietnam and the Great Society. In his memoirs he wistfully observed that on 27 July 1965 "two great

American political leaders, including Senators Warren Magnuson, John Pastore, and Bobby Kennedy, were at the same time urging the White House to find a way out of Vietnam before it became even more militarily difficult and politically divisive.[24] Maxwell Taylor, now an advisor to the president on military affairs, likewise warned McNamara to show "more concern about the homefront." Taylor, who thought that the public generally backed the president, also noted "gnawing questions and uneasiness" that could seriously hamper U.S. efforts in the war.[25]

International politics were affecting U.S. policy as well. In late 1965 Ambassador Anatoly Dobrynin and other Soviet officials were pressuring Rusk, William Bundy, Harriman, and others to establish a bombing pause and negotiate with the NLF. Dobrynin pointed out that the United States was a "big power" yet made no peace overtures. Were the Americans "trying to impress the Soviets?" the ambassador from Moscow asked. Bundy reported that another Soviet official told him that, if the United States truly wanted peace in Vietnam, it would have to make a gesture that was "quite major and specific relating to the South (perhaps, for a guess, suspension of reinforcements)."[26]

Active-duty military leaders were well aware of such relationships between politics and war in Vietnam. In August, Westmoreland, recognizing the tactical limits that the White House would place on American forces, rejected an Abrams proposal to cut off infiltration in the Laotian panhandle. Such a plan, he explained, "was not in the cards for the foreseeable future because of complex

streams in our national life converged – the dream of a Great Society at home and the inescapable demands of our obligations halfway around the world. They were to run in confluence until the end of my administration." Johnson, *Vantage Point*, 322–5; Mills and Ackley in Merle Miller, *Lyndon: An Oral Biography* (New York, 1980), 539–40; Campagna, *Economic Consequences of the Vietnam War*, 34.

24. McNamara, Memorandum of Telephone Conversations with Members of Congress Relating to South Vietnam," 9 December 1965, NSF, Memos to the President, McGeorge Bundy, box 5, folder: volume 17, 11/20–12/31/65 [2 of 2], LBJL.
25. Taylor to McNamara, 6 December 1965, "Comments on Reference Documents," VN C.F., NSF, box 25, folder: volume 43, LBJL.
26. Memorandum of Conversation between Rusk, Dobrynin, and Llewellyn Thompson, 8 December 1965, "Viet-Nam," and Memorandum of Conversation between William Bundy and Alexander I. Zinchuk, Minister Counselor, Soviet Embassy, 16 December 1965, "Vietnam," both in NSF, Memos to the President, McGeorge Bundy, box 5, folder: volume 17, LBJL.

political and other considerations." Not surprisingly, he resented such "considerations." When Rusk and Lodge expressed their concern over the CI campaign, Westmoreland lamented what he saw as their "violation of the prerogatives of the military commander." Should civilians continue to pressure the military on strategic matters, the MACV commander expected a return "to the situation of a year ago when Washington attempted to call all the shots, project all plans, and dictate how this war would be fought." Westmoreland thus pledged to "do everything I can to discourage this tendency."[27]

DePuy also recognized that the administration would determine the course of affairs relating to Vietnam. During his October briefing to Marine leaders, the planning chief conceded that the MACV would not receive the full measure of its troop requests. The United States, he explained, would never be able to maneuver the VC into a big-unit war on terms favorable to American forces, so "it's more likely we'll be forced to win the war by attrition and penny packets [a derisive term for incremental reinforcement]."[28] Nor would the RVNAF pick up the slack any time soon. Although the Marines wanted authorization for 40,000 more Vietnamese forces in I Corps, Commandant Wallace Greene admitted that such an increase was a "virtual impossibility" because of manpower shortages in southern Vietnam and because a "considerable number" of local villagers supported the VC.[29]

Harold K. Johnson had also resigned himself to the political realities of the war. In a visit to Vietnam after the battle of Ia Drang, the Army chief feared that the United States would never find a suitable way to end the war. Despite questioning Westmoreland's strategy, he and the other chiefs were also looking for ways to provide the requested reinforcements to the MACV. Johnson, however, was "not optimistic" about reinforcements "because virtually

---

27. General Westmoreland's History Notes, Entries of 29 August and 16 September 1965, Westmoreland Papers, folder 458 [2 of 2]: #1 History Files, 19 August–24 October 1965, WNRC.
28. "This will take more troops, [and] it will take longer," DePuy admitted, but he concluded optimistically that "it will succeed." DePuy Briefing at HQMC, 21 October 1965, tape #6173, MCHC.
29. Greene in Annex C, FMFPac: CG's Visit to Western Pacific, 3–11 December 1965, FMFPac Trip Reports, MCHC.

all the blood is out of the turnip." While the United States "could overcome our deficiency very quickly with an extension of terms of service or a selected Reserve call-up," the Army chief saw "no inclination to declare a national emergency." Westmoreland too raised the issues of Reserve activation and extended tours with Ambassador Lodge, but acknowledged that those steps "might re- quire some drastic action that would be politically difficult for the President." Although he offered a "grim prospect" for the war, Westmoreland "felt in all fairness" that he should inform Lodge of conditions in Vietnam as he saw them.[30]

At the same time, the military continued to pressure the president to intensify the air war. The Rolling Thunder campaign, however, was but a palliative to the problems of Vietnam, as U.S. service leaders recognized.[31] Admiral Sharp, arguably the military's strongest booster of the air war, pointed out that the United States had already caused heavy damage to most of the important military targets in the DRVN by August 1965, yet no American commander was suggesting that such measures had significantly altered the military situation in Vietnam. In fact, the JCS had reported that even an increased program of interdiction would not appreciably reduce the flow of matériel required for current, or even expanded, VC and PAVN activity.[32]

Given that limited impact, McNamara, upon his return from Vietnam in late November, urged the president to halt the air war for the time being. To the defense secretary such a pause would give Hanoi a chance to slow down the war, could convince other nations that the United States was sincerely interested in a negotiated settlement, and would, in the event that Ho did not respond favorably,

30. Johnson WDC 10453 to Westmoreland, 1 December 1965, Westmoreland Papers, folder 358b: Message File, WNRC; General Westmoreland's History Notes, Entry of 9 December 1965, Westmoreland Papers, folder 459: #2 History Files, 25 October–20 December 1965, WNRC; Perry, *Four Stars,* 156–7.
31. McNamara to Johnson, 31 July 1965, "Evaluation of the Program of Bombing North Vietnam," VN C.F., NSF, box 20, folder: volume 37, Memos (B), LBJL.
32. Sharp to JCS, 22 August 1965, "Rolling Thunder Appraisal," VN C.F., NSF, box 21, folder: volume 39, Cables, LBJL; Wheeler JCSM-613–65 to McNamara, 27 August 1965, "Effects of Accelerated Interdiction in North Vietnam," VN C.F., NSF, boxes 74– 5, folder: 2EE, 1965–7, Primarily McNamara Recommendations re. Strategic Actions [1965–6], LBJL; Sharp's criticism of the president's handling of air war is the dominant theme in his book on Vietnam, *Strategy for Defeat.*

justify resuming and intensifying the bombing.[33] On Christmas Eve
Johnson accepted McNamara's proposal and began a thirty-seven-
day bombing pause. To General Taylor, a long-time advocate of air
power in Vietnam, the military costs of such actions were not significant but the political rewards could be, so he urged the president
to continue the pause.[34] Most military representatives, however,
reacted vitriolically, especially Sharp and Westmoreland, with the
CINCPAC calling it a "retreat from reality."[35]

Although a contentious military issue, the bombing pause, as
General Phillip Davidson observed, was even more a divisive political issue. Under the guise of determining how to conduct the air
war, civilian and service officials were in fact vying for control of
military operations. Writing after the war ended, Davidson wondered "where, in 1965–1966, the real war was actually being
fought – in the jungles and skies of Vietnam or in the corridors of
the Pentagon."[36] The "real war" included the services fighting
among themselves as well. Indeed, struggles between military
branches over the management of and strategy to be used in the
war, already an irritant in policy-making considerations, reached
new levels and became an explosive issue by late 1965 and 1966.

On one level, the interservice feuding was a continuation of the
fight for larger roles and more influence that had characterized
military affairs since the 1950s. By 1965, internecine struggles
within the military were as intense as ever, for the JCS could not
seem to unite on major budgetary issues. The Army and Navy did
not support the development of the B-70 bomber for the Air Force;
the Air Force and Army opposed Navy attempts to develop a
nuclear-powered fleet; and the Air Force and Navy argued against
the Army's Antiballistic Missile Program. Such squabbling only
made it easier for McNamara to play the services off against one
another and increase his control over the defense establishment.[37]

33. See McNamara's Memoranda to Johnson of 30 November and 6 December 1965, cited
    in note 15.
34. Taylor in McGeorge Bundy to Johnson, 27 December 1965, NSF, Memos to the Presi-
    dent, McGeorge Bundy, box 5, folder: volume 17, 11/20–12/31/65 [1 of 2], LBJL.
35. Westmoreland 45189 to Sharp and McConnell, 26 December 1965, VN C.F., NSF, box
    25, folder: volume 44, LBJL; Sharp, *Strategy for Defeat*, 105.
36. Davidson, *Vietnam at War*, 389–90.
37. Korb, *Joint Chiefs of Staff*, 115–16, and *Fall and Rise of the Pentagon*, 116–17.

Such interservice rivalries spilled over into the conduct of the war in Vietnam. The Air Force and Marines continued to press the Army-dominated MACV for greater representation on Westmoreland's staff and for more autonomy in conducting their own operations. That situation, however, had worsened so much that Wheeler found himself trying to stave off a "major blow up" between the Army and Air Force in November over the placement of Air officers on the MACV staff.[38] More critically though, the services were engaged in a virulent battle over the type of military strategy to be used in Vietnam. As it had since the Kennedy years, much of the contention revolved around whether the United States should follow conventional military doctrine, with maneuver battalions, firepower, and attrition, or stress counterinsurgency warfare. Westmoreland opted for the former, the Army "Concept" as Andrew Krepinevich called it, deploying heavy weapons to Da Nang in March although Maxwell Taylor considered howitzers and tanks "inappropriate for counterinsurgency operations."[39] As noted earlier, the ambassador, Harold K. Johnson, and Marine officers favored the establishment of coastal enclaves from which the U.S. troops could maneuver against enemy forces, and they also wanted to emphasize the important political tasks of nation building while holding the RVNAF responsible for the brunt of the war.[40]

By June, however, the MACV had abandoned the pretense that it would follow the enclave concept. With Rolling Thunder unable to force the DRVN to capitulate and the situation in the south still deteriorating, U.S. officers could not experiment with the time-consuming tasks of pacification and political reform, nor, the MACV commander pointed out, did the RVN possess the political

---

38. Throckmorton WDC 9824 to Westmoreland, 13 November 1965, Westmoreland Papers, folder 358b: Message Folder, WNRC; see also General Westmoreland's History Notes, Entries of 3 September, 5 September, and 16 October, Westmoreland Papers, folder 458 [2 of 2]: #1 History Files, 19 August–24 October 1965, WNRC; Shulimson and Johnson, *Marines in Vietnam, 1965,* 149–52.
39. Taylor to Rusk, 14 April 1965, *DDRS,* 79, 211C.
40. *Pentagon Papers: Gravel,* 3:452–4; Harold K. Johnson to JCS, 12 April 1965, NSC History, "Deployment," UPA; Conference between CMC/FMFPac, at FMFPac HQ, 23–9 April 1965, tape #6298, MCHC; Krulak to Sharp, 27 April and 14 May 1965, Krulak Papers, box 2, folder: Correspondence, 1964–June 1965, MCHC; Krulak, General Summary, 22 May 1965, FMFPac Trip Reports, CG's Trip Summary, WestPac Visit, 14–21 May, 1965, MCHC.

stability requisite for such measures.[41] Westmoreland thus began to employ search-and-destroy tactics, utilize the MACV's heavy advantages in weaponry and mobility, and conduct a war of attrition. While doing this he also admitted that Vietnam "is no place for either tank or mechanized infantry."[42] General Krulak – who had earlier attacked Vann's strategic heresies but was on his way to becoming Westmoreland's biggest critic within the military – questioned the MACV approach. Military success was impossible, he charged, "without corresponding non-military programs aimed at exploiting the benefits of the security brought by an effective military plan."[43]

In a meeting with McNamara in July, Krulak boasted of Marine pacification efforts in I Corps and expressed concern about Westmoreland's strategy, even believing that he had convinced the defense secretary "of the imprudence of trying to stage decisive battles with the VC on the Tannenberg design."[44] The commandant weighed in on the strategic issue as well, telling fellow officers that he still preferred the "constant enclave concept." Greene and his deputies believed that "we can't afford to go into [Vietnam] – not only from the Marine Corps point of view, but from the over-all point of view – and do what the French did." U.S. forces should not be deployed in land where "thousands upon thousands" of Vietnamese could surround them. The French had placed twelve battalions at Dien Bien Phu, Greene reminded other Navy and Marine officers, but "what the hell happened to them? They lost 10,000 men."[45]

In a similar vein, Marine General Lewis Walt, commander of the reorganized 3d Marine Amphibious Force (III MAF), found that VC-controlled villages "were tidy and well run, [and] the people were adapted to government by the communists. . . . Where Viet

41. Davidson, *Vietnam at War,* 346–8; Westmoreland and Sharp, *Report on the War in Vietnam,* 105.
42. Westmoreland MAC 3407 to Harold K. Johnson, 5 July 1965, Westmoreland Papers, folder 512: #17 History Backup, 1 July–28 August 1965, WNRC.
43. Victor Krulak, June 1965, "A Strategic Concept for the Republic of Vietnam," Krulak Papers, box 2, folder: Point Papers, Briefings, Trip Reports, 1965, MCHC.
44. Krulak to Greene, 18 July 1965, Krulak Papers, box 2, folder: Correspondence, July–November 1965, MCHC.
45. Wallace M. Greene, Address at Flag/General Officer Selectees Briefings at the Pentagon, 10 August 1965, Greene Papers, box 20, folder 234, MCHC.

Cong control was absolute, it was superficially reasonable and often appeared mild." Accordingly, Walt urged that U.S. forces "temper . . . the fight with an understanding of the people, compassion toward them, and the exercise of good works, even in the midst of war."[46] Westmoreland acknowledged such concerns, rhetorically at least. As a MACV directive put it, the conduct of its soldiers and use of military force would have to be "carefully controlled at all times." U.S. goals – crushing the VC but minimizing collateral damage – thus required "the exercise of judgment and restraint not formerly expected of soldiers."[47]

Such restraint, many other officers believed, was unlikely, given Westmoreland's strategy. Maxwell Taylor, for instance, objected to the MACV/JCS "Concept for Vietnam," which entailed using conventional means to extend Saigon's control over the entire RVN. Reiterating themes that he had been stressing over the previous several years, the White House's military consultant "anticipate[d] an endless requirement for American troops if we undertook to pursue the enemy into the remote vastnesses of the Vietnam frontier," as Westmoreland's plan envisioned. In such areas, the VC "would be close to his cross-border sources of supply and . . . the terrain would be favorable to his hit-and-hide tactics."[48] John Paul Vann, in Vietnam as a civilian official connected with the embassy, still complained of the "widespread use of air and artillery as a substitute for getting into the countryside."[49] The emphasis on military operations, he continued, had alienated the southern population, not only because American forces were destroying the countryside but because they had also ignored the need for political reform. The U.S. government simply kept propping up the regime

46. Lewis Walt, *Strange War, Strange Strategy: A General's Report on Vietnam* (New York, 1970), 16, 29. General Edward Lansdale, in Saigon as a special assistant to Lodge, similarly told the ambassador that U.S. forces, using conventional military tactics, "cannot defeat [the Communists] short of genocide unless our side puts the war on a political footing in Vietnam." Lansdale to Lodge, 29 July 1965, "Your Working Paper on the 'Politico' Part of the Vietnam Problem," Lansdale Papers, folder 1532, Hoover Institution.
47. MACV Directive 525–4, 17 September 1965, "Tactics and Techniques for Employment of US Forces in Republic of Vietnam," Westmoreland Papers, folder 458 [2 of 2]: #1 History Files, 19 August–24 October 1965; WNRC; see also MACV Directive 525–3, 7 September 1965, VN C.F., NSF, box 22, folder: volume 40, Memos (B), LBJL.
48. Taylor, *Swords and Plowshares*, 363–4.
49. Vann to Lansdale, August 1965, Lansdale Papers, folder 1392, Hoover Institution.

in Saigon even though it could not "establish stability, even with dictatorial powers, let alone achieve a popular base among the people."[50]

Maxwell Taylor added that the ARVN, as he had warned, was shirking its duty and he feared that American forces were about to take on a "preponderant ground role" in Vietnam. If that happened, Taylor expected 50 to 75 percent of Vietnamese units to end up in static defense roles, American casualties to rise sharply, and, in turn, public criticism of the war to become more vocal.[51] Such concerns were apparently widespread, for various junior officers told Harold K. Johnson during his December visit that Westmoreland would have to "end the big-unit war; we're just not going to win doing this." Others did recommend to the Army chief that the United States take the fight to the DRVN but, as Mark Perry explains, this was "an option [that] Johnson knew was out of the question."[52] Westmoreland, however, believed that he could not divert from a strategy of attrition and firepower because the White House, for ostensibly political reasons, would limit his military options in Vietnam.[53]

More than anyone, the Marines challenged Westmoreland's views. Although they agreed with the MACV commander that politicians would constrain them, Krulak, Greene, and others attacked Westmoreland as harshly as many civilian critics of the war. Where the MACV leader had planned a three-phase effort to halt the slide in Vietnam, then go on a limited offensive, and, finally, destroy the enemy, the III MAF urged an "oil spot" approach. From their coastal deployments the Marines would extend their areas of operations, like spreading oil, as pacification efforts bore fruit and as resources became available.[54] General Karch, the first Marine commander at Da Nang, believed that "there was only one way that that war could be won, and it was going to take a force of 250,000

50. Vann's analysis was presented in a widely circulated memorandum – "Harnessing the Revolution in South Vietnam" – in early September. Although disseminated and commented upon by various U.S. officials in the RVN, Vann's views ultimately got nowhere, again. See Sheehan, *Bright Shining Lie*, 537–58; Kahin, *Intervention*, 408–12.
51. Taylor in Jeffrey J. Clarke, *Advice and Support: The Final Years of the U.S. Army in Vietnam* (Washington, D.C., 1988), 121–4.
52. Perry, *Four Stars*, 156–7.
53. Westmoreland, *A Soldier Reports*, 145–53.
54. Shulimson and Johnson, *Marines in Vietnam, 1965*, 115–16.

troops ten years of pacification to do it." American soldiers, Karch advised, should root out the VC and pacify the south at increments of about a half mile at a time.[55] Westmoreland, however, had countered that U.S. forces had to "forget about the enclaves and take the war to the enemy."[56]

By December 1965, General Krulak – who offered the most comprehensive and trenchant critique of the MACV strategy – had become more frustrated and angry about Westmoreland's approach, considering it "wasteful of American lives [and] promising a protracted, strength-sapping battle with small likelihood of a successful outcome." Continued Communist infiltration and poor ARVN morale, which Westmoreland conceded, and the results of Ia Drang, a great triumph to MACV leaders, had actually confirmed to Krulak the futility of the U.S. approach to the war.[57] The Marine general in turn produced a widely disseminated seventeen-page memorandum on strategy that presented a markedly different view of the war from anything written in Saigon. Krulak began his evaluation by asserting that Westmoreland's strategy of attrition, despite "limited progress, in recent months," was wholly inadequate. While geography, political and religious friction, and economic underdevelopment were all making America's task in southern Vietnam more difficult, it was the MACV reliance on attrition that principally impeded progress. With over 100 million men available for duty in the DRVN and PRC, it was the Communists who were effectively waging attritional warfare. In just three months, he reported, the U.S.-RVN advantage in the ratio of enemy soldiers killed had decreased from 2.8:1 to 1.5:1.[58]

Even if U.S. troops killed ten enemy soldiers for every one of their own lost, Krulak added, it would still require a tremendous sacri-

55. Karch Oral History, 77, MCHC.
56. Westmoreland, *A Soldier Reports,* 140; for further criticism of the Marines by Westmoreland, see General Westmoreland's History Notes, Entries of 20 October and 8 December, folders 458 [2 of 2] and 459, WNRC; and General Underwood, December 1965, "Noteworthy View Points Encountered and Observations Made on Vietnam Trip," Harold K. Johnson Papers, box 135, folder: Trip to Vietnam, December–January 1965–6, MHI.
57. Krulak, *First to Fight,* 221–6; Victor Krulak, December 1965, "Visit with COM-USMACV," FMFPac: CG's Visit to Western Pacific, 3–11 December 1965, FMFPac Trip Reports, MCHC; Sheehan, *Bright Shining Lie,* 630–3.
58. Victor Krulak, December 1965, "A Strategic Appraisal – Vietnam," Krulak Papers, box 2, folder: Point Papers, Briefings, Trips, Reports, 1965, MCHC.

fice in American blood. The DRVN and VC, without Chinese support, could recruit from a manpower base of about 2.5 million men. If the United States just continued its current rates of attrition, the general estimated that "it will cost something like 175,000 U.S./ GVN lives to reduce the enemy pool by only a modest 20 percent." As Krulak saw it, only if American officials "put the full weight of our top level effort into bringing all applicable resources – U.S. and GVN – into the pacification program," as well as providing village security and expanding air strikes, could progress be made. Krulak offered "only two basic points" in his conclusion. No military strategy, he warned once more, could succeed without addressing the political, economic, and sociological factors driving the war. Manpower, Krulak added, was the enemy's "greatest strength" and thus "we have no license and less reason to join battle with him on that ground."[59]

Krulak's assessment had shown just how desolate America's prospects in Vietnam had become. His critique of the Westmoreland strategy was detailed and biting, but his solutions, more air power and pacification, were neither militarily appropriate nor politically feasible. Although they did not concede so, military leaders had consistently forwarded reports showing the limited effectiveness of air operations. Pacification, moreover, would take too long and, more importantly, could not succeed amid the political instability and corruption in the RVN. Nonetheless, the Marine general had offered an alternative to the strategy of attrition and had forced a debate within the military about Westmoreland's planning for the war.

The Marine commandant added to the feud, reinforcing Krulak's views during a January 1966 visit to Vietnam. U.S. and ARVN forces, General Greene noted, "could kill all [the] PAVN & VC [in the south] & still lose the war" unless pacification was given priority. The commandant compared Westmoreland's strategy of attrition to "a grindstone that's being turned by the Communist side,

---

59. See source cited in previous note. The conflict between the U.S. and Communist forces in Vietnam, Krulak later added, "could move to another planet today and we would still not have won the war . . . [but] if the subversion and guerrilla efforts were to disappear, the war would soon collapse as the Viet Cong would be denied food, sanctuary, and intelligence." In Shulimson and Johnson, *Marines in Vietnam, 1965,* 212.

and we're backing into it and having our skin taken off of . . . our entire body without accomplishing a damn thing because they've got enough to keep the old stone going." In the end, "although their casualty rate may be fifty times what ours is," the Communists will "be able to win through their capability to wage a war of attrition." Yet, Greene concluded, "this is a thing that apparently the Army doesn't understand." Krulak added that Wheeler "doesn't understand it" either, whereas American congressmen, who were presumably beginning to sense the rising antiwar sentiment at home, were aware of the perils of Westmoreland's program for Vietnam. Krulak, citing the JCS chair's pleasure with recent operations in which the VC suffered about seven times more casualties than Americans, wondered "just how . . . did that bring us nearer to winning the war? . . . [T]his is not the strategy for victory."[60]

Such brash criticism within the military, on top of McNamara's bleak appraisals of late November, ought to have made it clear that America was headed toward even greater problems in Vietnam in the coming years. Some officials did seem to grasp the importance of the attacks on Westmoreland's strategy. Both Admiral Sharp and General Greene supported Krulak's December 1965 analysis and tried to rally other officers to the strategic implications of attrition – in Greene's case, by commissioning a long study on pacification by the Marine staff – but to little avail. The defense secretary too was "struck by Krulak's mathematics of futility," as Neil Sheehan described it, since it had confirmed his own fears about the future in Vietnam. McNamara thus advised the maverick Marine to explain his views to the president. Before that, however, he met with Averell Harriman, then working out of the State Department, to complain about limits on the air war. The meeting with Harriman did not go well and by the time Krulak met with Lyndon Johnson, in August 1966, U.S. military strategy in Vietnam was inflexibly established.[61]

---

60. Greene's handwritten notes, Greene Papers, box 39, folder 415–1: Notes on Trip to WestPac, 3–15 January 1966, MCHC; Greene and Krulak in FMFPac Briefing for CMC, Headquarters, FMFPac, Camp Smith, Hawaii, January 1966, tape #6278, MCHC, my transcription; see also Greene's and Krulak's comments in Vietnam Comment File, 1966, MCHC.
61. Sheehan, *Bright Shining Lie*, 630–3; Krulak, *First to Fight*, 221–6.

Krulak and other military critics, it is safe to say, were fighting a losing battle from the beginning. Since Paul Harkins had gone to Vietnam in early 1962 the MACV had decided to defeat the enemy with technology and attrition, the warnings of John Vann, Harry Felt, Maxwell Taylor, Krulak, or others notwithstanding. By late 1965, the Army, which dominated the U.S. military establishment in Saigon, was not about to give up its primary mission – conventional warfare using heavy weapons – and the attendant material benefits to adopt a strategy of pacification. Less than a decade earlier, the Army had feared for its existence, but it had gained a preponderant role in Vietnam and was not about to relinquish it. Indeed, Westmoreland and his Army deputies attacked the Marines and their concepts as strongly as Greene and Krulak had challenged the MACV approach. Westmoreland, despite fearing an "interservice imbroglio," wanted to "get the Marines out of their beachheads" and onto the offensive. He was "increasingly concerned," he wrote to a subordinate commander, "that we are not engaging the VC with sufficient frequency . . . to win the war in Vietnam" and thus reiterated his emphasis on the big-unit war.[62]

Others more stridently attacked Marine theories and practices. General Harry Kinnard, commander of the 1st Cavalry Division, was "absolutely disgusted" with the situation in I Corps. The Marines "just would not play," he charged. "They don't know how to fight on land, particularly against guerrillas." DePuy similarly observed that the III MAF "just sat down and didn't do anything." Their attempts at counterinsurgency were "of the deliberate, mild sort."[63] Maxwell Taylor, despite his harsh critique of ground intervention, was not a fan of pacification either. That approach, he believed, would undermine both Vietnamese and U.S. morale by putting their forces in passive positions, would constitute an abandonment of those Vietnamese who lived further away from enclaves, and would raise greater suspicions in the RVN about American resolve. Most important, the only U.S. official whose opinion mattered in the end rejected the Marines' strategic recommendations. Deploying soldiers to enclaves, Lyndon Johnson told re-

---

62. Westmoreland in Shulimson and Johnson, *Marines in Vietnam, 1965,* 116; Westmoreland, *A Soldier Reports,* 165–6.
63. Kinnard and DePuy in Krepinevich, *Army and Vietnam,* 174–5.

porters aboard Air Force One in early 1966, was "like a jackass hunkering up in a hailstorm." Unhindered escalation, his other military option, was also impossible due to political considerations, so the president concluded that the United States would have to continue its policy of "pressure with restraint."[64]

No matter how passionate, or sometimes accurate, Westmoreland's critics and the advocates of pacification might have been, their strategy was essentially impossible to implement. By later 1965, with Vietnam beginning to affect the Great Society at home, public resistance growing, and other military figures pressuring his administration to intensify the war, the president could not afford to accept a military policy that was time-consuming and difficult to measure in terms of progress.[65] Johnson, still unwilling to make difficult strategic decisions for Vietnam, needed results – enemy soldiers killed, northern targets destroyed, reduced infiltration – and U.S. troops could not produce them if "hunkered up."[66] Politics and warfare, converging since the United States had intervened in Vietnam, had collided sharply in 1965 and would shape the course of the war thereafter.

Lyndon Johnson, however, maintained his commitment to Vietnam in spite of the myriad military and political problems associated with the war. "This nation is mighty enough, its society is healthy enough," he observed in his 1966 State of the Union address, "to pursue our goals in the rest of the world while still building a Great Society here at home."[67] Despite such public confidence, the president and other officials would have to confront

64. Taylor, *The Sword and the Pen,* 329; Johnson in Miller, *Lyndon,* 563.
65. The gauge by which pacification progress was measured was the extent of territory in the RVN allegedly made secure – always a difficult evaluation to make with any precision – while the standards by which successful conventional operations were judged included enemy soldiers killed, weapons captured, or targets destroyed. Not surprisingly, the military preferred the latter approach because it could use its overwhelming advantage in firepower to inflict awesome damage on the Communists and then claim to be "winning" the war. Pacification was not so easily or empirically assessed. See Gregory Palmer, *The McNamara Strategy and the Vietnam War,* 117.
66. On the president's failure to tale decisive strategic action, see, for example, George Herring, "'Cold Blood': LBJ's Conduct of Limited War in Vietnam," Paper Presented at the Military History Symposium, U.S. Air Force Academy, Colorado Springs, Colo., October 1990 (special thanks to David Humphrey of the LBJ Library for bringing this article to my attention).
67. Johnson in Miller, *Lyndon,* 551.

greater problems in Vietnam throughout 1966 as military difficulties, division within the U.S. camp over strategy, and political maneuvering worsened. Neither civilian nor military leaders had changed their positions on the war to any appreciable degree since mid-1965, so fundamental questions of troop deployments, mobilization, strategy, and the role of the Vietnamese military were still being debated as the war raged on. Although there were already about 220,000 American soldiers in Vietnam, Westmoreland had just asked McNamara for seventy-five additional battalions, thirty above his initial request, which would bring the total number of American military personnel in the RVN to 400,000 by year's end.[68]

While deliberating over that request, the president, at an NSC meeting in late January, asked the chiefs "what do you want most to win?" Harold K. Johnson answered. "A surge of additional troops into Vietnam," the Army boss replied. "We need to double the number now and then triple the number later. We should call up the reserves and go to mobilization. . . . This involves declaring a national emergency here and in Vietnam."[69] General Johnson, however, had to know that such measures were not going to be authorized. McNamara had already told reporters as much, and various military officials, after meeting in Hawaii in mid-January, reported to Westmoreland that "everyone here is of the opinion that mobilization is not in the cards."[70] Clearly U.S. officers recognized at that early date the manpower limits under which they would fight. Whether American service leaders – who at that time and since have attacked Johnson's decision not to activate Reserves and declare a national emergency – have a credible argument is thus beside the point. The president was not going to mobilize, ever, and everyone associated with the war understood that. Continued calls for him to do so served primarily as political capital to be used

68. Jack Valenti's Notes of Meeting in Cabinet Room, 22 January 1966, NSF, Meeting Notes File, box 1, folder: January 22, 1966, LBJL.
69. Summary Notes of 556th NSC Meeting, 29 January 1966, NSF, NSC Meetings File, box 2, folder: volume 3, tab 38, LBJL.
70. DePuy HWA 0211 to Westmoreland and Rosson, 19 January 1966, Westmoreland v. CBS, LC, box 14, folder: MACV Backchannel Messages to Westmoreland, 1–31 January 1966, WNRC.

when recriminations began to fly around Washington for the disaster in Vietnam.

It was also clear that U.S. leaders would not reassess their military strategy in Vietnam. Prior to the president's meeting with Ky and Thieu in Honolulu in February 1966, the MACV reaffirmed its conventional approach in its campaign plan for 1966.[71] Westmoreland, in fact, asked for more of the same at the conference, proposing that U.S. manpower be more than doubled, to 429,000, in 1966 but also understanding that no Reserve call-up would be included in any force structure package. Westmoreland also devised a set of objectives for U.S. forces in the coming year, including increased security in the south, more opened road and railway use, greater destruction of VC and PAVN base areas, improved pacification, and most important, attrition of enemy forces at a rate greater than their capacity to reinforce in the RVN. This final goal, reaching the "crossover point," was crucial to U.S. strategy, but flew in the face of the earlier McNamara and Krulak infiltration estimates.[72] Nonetheless, American officials, many of whom would later blast Westmoreland's conduct of the war, accepted his evaluation and plans in 1966.

Lyndon Johnson, under pressure in Washington as Fulbright was holding televised hearings on Vietnam featuring war critics James Gavin and George Frost Kennan while he was in Honolulu, nonetheless agreed to Westmoreland's request for more troops. The president, however, also made it known that his patience was not unlimited, telling Westmoreland to "nail the coonskin to the wall" in 1966 with the new reinforcements. Johnson, satisfied that the MACV commander was "sufficiently understanding" of the political constraints driving American policy, further warned Westmoreland, "General, I have a lot riding on you. I hope you don't pull a MacArthur on me."[73] Such admonitions notwithstanding,

---

71. Rosson 03847 to CINCPAC, 3 February 1966, "Ground Operations in SVN," Westmoreland v. CBS, LC, box 28, folder: Message, dated 3 February 1966, WNRC.
72. General Westmoreland's Historical Briefing, 16 February 1966, Westmoreland v. CBS, box 7, folder: Historical Briefing, 16 February 1966, WNRC; "1966 Program to Increase the Effectiveness of Military Operations and Anticipated Results Thereof," 8 February 1966, Westmoreland Papers, folder 461: #4 History Files, 20 January–13 March 1966, WNRC.
73. Johnson in Kinnard, *Certain Trumpet*, 168; Johnson in Herring, "Cold Blood," 8–9.

Honolulu was a clear victory for advocates of the MACV strategy and a repudiation of the Marine views. As Westmoreland later put it, the decisions made in February 1966 "basically set . . . the tactics of the war." The commander, moreover, did "not recall any dissent that was made" by administration officials at the time.[74] Accordingly, American leaders had decided to continue their war of attrition in Vietnam, but with a vastly expanded U.S. force there. Rather than develop a strategic plan, Westmoreland would just continue to establish a program for troop increases.[75]

Increasing U.S. troop numbers, however, seemed to have little impact in Vietnam. Despite MACV statistics indicating an erosion in enemy strength in the south, it was still clear that the United States faced serious problems in the war.[76] Jack Valenti, the president's trusted advisor, urged Johnson "to find some way out of Vietnam. . . . [There] is no reasonable hope. All your military advisors insist you must double your force, and still they give you no prophesy of victory, however shapeless, however mild."[77] While Washington continued to worry about the war, the situation in Vietnam in the spring of 1966 worsened. In March the Buddhist-led "Struggle Movement," which included ARVN officers and units, conducted large-scale antigovernment demonstrations in Da Nang, Hue, and elsewhere in I Corps. The impact of such political turmoil on the U.S. effort was obvious. The MACV deputy commander, General John Heintges, warned that "our people back home are going to get their dander up and want to wash their hands of this mess over here." Krulak was more bleak. "Repressive measures are all that is left" to quash the Buddhists "and you will recall," he reminded Admiral Sharp, "what happened after Diem launched his repressive measures." The uprising in I Corps also

74. Westmoreland Oral History, 7, MCHC.
75. Kinnard, *Certain Trumpet*, 165–6.
76. Westmoreland MACJ00 08328 to Sharp, 17 March 1966, Westmoreland v. CBS, LC, box 28, folder: Message, dated 17 March 1966, WNRC; Westmoreland 16210 to Sharp, 11 May 1966, Westmoreland v. CBS, LC box 28, folder: Message, dated 2 May 1966, WNRC.
77. Valenti to Johnson, 3 April 1966, Reference File, box 1, folder: Aides' Memos on Vietnam, LBJL. On criticism of the government and military of the RVN, see also Walt Rostow, April 1966, "Issues Hard to Learn from the Cables," NSF, Memos to the President, Walt Rostow, box 7, folder: volume 1, 1–30 April 1966 [3 of 3], LBJL; Krulak to McNamara, 9 May 1966, Krulak Papers, box 2, folder: Correspondence, March–July 1966, MCHC.

prompted the Marine general to admit to Navy Undersecretary Robert Baldwin that, "despite all our public assertions to the contrary, the South Vietnamese are not – and never have been – a nation."[78]

Wheeler's outlook from Washington was just as alarming. Several "key congressmen," he informed Westmoreland and Sharp, believed that America was now "overextended in our military commitments . . . and will be unable to support adequately our present forces and surely cannot support additional forces." Many civilians expressed concern over not only the political disarray in the RVN but also the "very low level of Vietnamese military activities" during the Buddhist crisis. American officials were particularly upset about the ARVN's casualty rates, which were lower than those of U.S. forces although the Vietnamese were supposed to be carrying the greatest burden of the war.[79] By late May, the JCS chair worried that the American people, "rightly or wrongly," saw developments in the RVN as "proof positive" of antiwar leaders' charges that U.S. soldiers were fighting and dying while RVN officials "squabble pettily among themselves to achieve political advantage." Wheeler also realized that even a "farfetched" – to use his description – proposal by Senator Jacob Javits to stop the air war and cease offensive ground operations would have "distinct appeal," both to political doves and "even more importantly, to the relatives of our men in South Vietnam whose lives are at risk." And Wheeler himself admitted "much sympathy" for the latter group.[80]

The JCS chair's operating procedure – reporting on events in Washington via back-channel messages to Westmoreland and Sharp – amounted to an even greater politicization of the policymaking process, to the detriment of military realities. By sending his

78. Heintges MACJ01 to Westmoreland, 23 March 1966, "Demonstrations in I Corps," Westmoreland Papers, folder 462: #5 History Files, 13 March–23 April 1966; Krulak to Sharp, 31 March 1966 and Krulak to Navy Undersecretary Robert Baldwin, 20 April 1966, Krulak Papers, box 2, folder: Correspondence, March–July 1966, MCHC.
79. Wheeler CJCS 1974–66 to Sharp and Westmoreland, 13 April 1966, Westmoreland v. CBS, LC, box 15, folder: MACV Backchannel Messages to Westmoreland, 1–30 April 1966, WNRC; Wheeler CJCS 2644-66 to Westmoreland and Sharp, 12 May 1966, Westmoreland v. CBS, LC, box 15, folder: MACV Backchannel Messages to Westmoreland, 1–31 May 1966, WNRC.
80. Wheeler CJCS 2837–66 to Westmoreland and Sharp, 20 May 1966, Westmoreland v. CBS, LC, box 15, folder: MACV Backchannel Messages to Westmoreland, 1–31 May 1966, WNRC.

interpretations of political affairs in the capital to the MACV commander and CINCPAC, Wheeler could preempt, or at least prepare responses to, civilian complaints about the military's conduct of the war. Even more, Westmoreland could then base his own proposals for troops, air operations – *whatever* – on the JCS chair's reading of Washington politics.[81] Again, civil–military affairs, rather than battlefield conditions, were a principal factor driving the war.

Such maneuvering was particularly critical because time was not on Earle Wheeler's side in early 1966, as public opinion at home, the continuing enemy buildup in the south, interservice friction, and civil–military gambits were conspiring to hamper even more seriously the U.S. military campaign.[82] Even if, as Westmoreland was claiming, the media had exaggerated the gravity of U.S. problems in the war, the perception among Americans of stasis in Vietnam could not be ignored.[83] Wheeler, citing Gallup Poll statistics on rising antiwar sentiment, understood the public's unease as well and observed that press reports, albeit "highly colored," would "if true" point to a "far more serious situation, both current and impending, than you and your officers on the scene believe to be the case."[84]

The MACV, however, was well aware of the gravity of its problems in the RVN, as made eminently clear in an early May intelligence estimate for the coming year. Intelligence chief Joseph McChristian again warned of the enemy's strength and determination. As of mid-May 1966 the MACV Order of Battle listed 144 Communist battalions, both confirmed and probable, and that number

81. I would like to thank Richard Immerman for bringing this process more clearly to my attention.
82. For details see, among others, Wheeler to Westmoreland, 18 May 1966, Westmoreland Papers, #6 History Files, 24 April–28 May 1966, WNRC; Westmoreland 16210 to Sharp and Wheeler, 11 May 1966, "Arc Light Forces Reaction Capability," Westmoreland v. CBS, LC, box 28, folder: Message, dated 2 May 1966, WNRC.
83. Westmoreland MAC 4081 to Wheeler and Sharp, 22 May 1966, Westmoreland v. CBS, LC, box 28, folder: Message, MAC 4081, WNRC.
84. Wheeler JCS 2844–66 to Westmoreland and Sharp, 23 May 1966, Westmoreland v. CBS, LC, box 15, folder: MACV Backchannel Messages to Westmoreland, 1–31 May 1966, WNRC; Dwight Eisenhower, more hawkish on Vietnam in the 1960s than when he occupied the White House, also recognized the public's hesitation to support the war and was "much concerned" that Americans would begin to lament that it was "simply dragging on inconclusively." General Andrew Goodpaster Memorandum for the Record, 22 June 1966, "Meeting with General Eisenhower, 22 June 1966," NSF, Memos to the President, Walt Rostow, box 8, folder: volume 7, 21–30 June 1966 [2 of 2], LBJL.

would probably rise to 180 by early 1967. With those forces, the VC "will exert continuous pressure to interdict roads and railroads, to terrorize areas of government control and to wear down our will to resist." American units, however, could do little to counter such measures for, as McChristian conceded, "the VC will avoid combat unless they expect victory."[85]

As for the enemy above the seventeenth parallel, the PAVN's ground forces now included nine divisions, six infantry brigades, ten infantry regiments, and six artillery regiments, as well as twenty-nine anti-aircraft regiments and growing air assets. The DRVN, which had been capable of moving 195 tons of supplies daily into the RVN in mid-1965, had just completed a major truck-building and road construction effort and would be able to transfer over 300 tons a day in the coming months. In addition to such Vietnamese advantages, MACV intelligence pointed out that the PRC – with thirty Army divisions deployed in southern China and forty-five infantry divisions ready to be used as reinforcements, over twenty submarines, about four hundred jet fighters and bombers based just north of the DRVN, and a population psychologically prepared to wage war against the United States – was capable of supporting the Vietnamese Communists with matériel and military personnel if needed.[86]

Despite recognizing such conditions, McChristian incredibly concluded that the MACV strategy of attrition would show decisive results over the next twelve months and, by mid-1967, the United States would reach the crossover point at which it was killing more enemy soldiers than were infiltrating into the south.[87] Again the MACV had ignored its own potentially explosive analysis of the war and decided to remain on its present course in Vietnam, however specious the reasoning behind that policy may have been. There was, in fact, more evidence than the intelligence assessment to testify to America's troubles in Vietnam. An MACV study pointed out that the RVN's primary manpower pool, 20- to 30-year-old men, would be exhausted by 1968, and the secondary

85. MACV J-2, 11 May 1966, "Intelligence Estimate for CY 1967, as of 10 May 1967," Westmoreland v. CBS, LC, box 9, folder: Intelligence Estimate for CY 1967, WNRC.
86. Ibid.
87. Ibid.

groups – those 16 to 19, 31 to 45, and others previously considered unqualified for service – would run out by mid-1969. The RVN, moreover, lacked the material resources to sustain its economy, creating serious inflation and "diluting the focus of the war effort." To Westmoreland it was thus "obvious . . . [that] the RVN has failed to organize itself to meet the heavy demands placed upon its manpower and its economy by the pressures of war."[88] Corruption within the ARVN, which could not be overcome by "changing a man or two or by other half-way measures," remained a serious problem as well. As one of Westmoreland's deputies put it, "the entire administrative system must be overhauled."[89]

As structural problems in southern Vietnam exacerbated the MACV's problems, the interservice feud over strategy continued at a fever pitch. The Marines were still attacking Westmoreland's strategy of attrition and use of search-and-destroy operations. Such tactics, Wallace Greene charged, involved U.S. forces "traversing the same terrain repeatedly against a nebulous foe – while the people were untended." While American troops had assumed responsibility for destroying the VC, they were overlooking the need to provide security. The government and army of the RVN, meanwhile, had "paid scant regard to the needs and interests of the people." Southern villagers, Greene explained, feared the ARVN as much as the VC.[90]

The dissonance between Greene's position and that of the Army was publicly evident as well. In testimony before the Senate Armed Services Committee, Wheeler, defending Westmoreland's conduct of the war, explained that the U.S. mission was "to kill as many Viet Cong" as possible and to "destroy" areas used by the VC. At the same hearings, the Marine commandant countered that "we aren't executing this program by the rifle and the sword. We are helping these people help themselves." Victory in Vietnam, Greene be-

88. Westmoreland to Lodge, 15 June 1966, "Mobilization of the RVN," Westmoreland v. CBS, LC, box 13, folder: Memo, 16 May 1967, WNRC.
89. General John Freund Memorandum for the Record, 25 June 1966, "Discussion with General Tran Van Don, 24 June 1966," Westmoreland Papers, folder 463a: #7 History Files, 29 May–16 July 1966, WNRC.
90. Greene in Vietnam Comments File, 1966, MCHC.

lieved, "will hinge on the success of the pacification program."[91] Krulak added that the VC, despite suffering heavy losses, was tying down American forces in big-unit engagements and was diverting U.S. soldiers away from the village level. The Marine general was thus "deeply concerned that the enemy has played the tune, [and] induced us to dance to it." Westmoreland's "mutation strategy" of conducting conventional operations and paying lip service to pacification, Krulak contended, had "no virtue." If U.S. forces "persisted in such a compromise," he later lamented, "we would bleed ourselves – which we did."[92]

It was also likely that ranking officials would dismiss such complaints – which they did. "Barring unforeseen changes in the enemy strategy," Westmoreland announced in August, "I visualize that our strategy for South Vietnam will remain essentially the same throughout 1967." The president felt the same way. Johnson, after being pressured by McNamara and the commandant to meet with Krulak, finally agreed to talk to the general. After listening to him advocate unrestrained air operations and pacification, the president, as Krulak told it, "put his arm around my shoulder, and propelled me firmly toward the door."[93]

Although they would maintain their dissent throughout the war, the Marines had thus been rebuffed by their Army commander in Vietnam and by the president. Potentially more serious criticism of the MACV's concepts for Vietnam, however, was found in an Army report on strategy that reached Harold K. Johnson's desk in the spring of 1966. Commissioned by the Army chief several months earlier and worked on by the service's brightest young officers, the "Program for the Pacification and Long-Term Development of South Vietnam," or PROVN, study "forthrightly attacked [Westmoreland's] search-and-destroy concept," as General Phillip Davidson put it.[94] After detailing the NLF's popularity and military

91. Wheeler and Greene in U.S. Congress, Senate, Armed Services Committee, *Supplemental Procurement and Construction Authorizations, Fiscal Year 1966*, 89th Cong., 2d. Sess., 1966, 274–8; see also Greene in *U.S. News and World Report*, 28 February 1966, 14.
92. Krulak to Greene, 7 October 1966, Krulak Papers, box 2, folder: Correspondence, August–December 1966, MCHC; Krulak in Vietnam Comment File, 1966, MCHC.
93. Krulak, *First to Fight*, 225–6.
94. Davidson, *Vietnam at War*, 410–11.

prowess and the ARVN's incompetence and corruption, the
PROVN officers could only conclude that "the situation in South
Vietnam has seriously deteriorated" and "1966 may well be the last
chance to achieve eventual success." To gain "victory" it was imperative to gain the support of the Vietnamese people "at the village, district, and provincial levels." After years of American claims
that DRVN aggression had caused the war, the PROVN document
argued that the southern leadership was inefficient and rotten and
thus responsible for the conditions that had led to the rebellion.[95]

Because the grass-roots level was "where the war must be fought
. . . [and] won," the PROVN study argued that "rural construction," its term for civic action or pacification, "must be designated
unequivocally as the major US/GVN effort. It will require the commitment of a preponderance of RVNAF and GVN paramilitary
forces, together with adequate U.S. support and coordination and
assistance." To facilitate this shift in strategy, Army officers recommended that the United States use whatever leverage at its
disposal – spanning a "continuum from subtle interpersonal per-
suasion to withdrawal of U.S. support" – to induce RVN compliance.[96] Although a strong indictment of strategy with influential
advocates – such as Harold K. Johnson, vice chief Creighton
Abrams, and the Army's Pacific commander, General Dwight
Beach – behind it, the PROVN study ultimately suffered the same
fate as other criticism of U.S. strategy.[97]

The MACV either dismissed or ignored the main charges and
recommendations found in the PROVN report – downgrading it
from a "study" to a nonbinding "conceptual document" – and
continued its strategy of attrition, even though Westmoreland
seemed to realize that the prospects were not bright. In a mid-1966
analysis requested by McNamara, the MACV staff concluded that
it would need about 1 million Vietnamese and 500,000 U.S. troops
for another ten years to wrap up the war. Westmoreland refused to

95. PROVN Report, used at CMH (courtesy of Graham Cosmas); *Pentagon Papers: Gravel*,
   2: 501–2, 576–80; Eric M. Bergerud, *The Dynamics of Defeat: The War in Hau Nghia
   Province* (Boulder, Colo., 1991), 81–4, 110–13.
96. See sources cited in previous note.
97. Perry, *Four Stars*, 157–8; Krepinevich, *The Army and Vietnam*, 181; Davidson, *Vietnam
   at War*, 409–11; Beach to Westmoreland, n.d., Westmoreland Papers, folder 551: Personal Correspondence, WNRC.

forward the report, telling his subordinates that its implications were "politically unacceptable."[98] Despite his public advocacy of firepower, Wheeler also warned Westmoreland that continued failure to show progress on counterinsurgency, along with ARVN passivity, would cause increased problems for the MACV staff from U.S. political leaders.[99]

Many of those problems, as the military saw it, were caused by the Whiz Kids in the Pentagon's Systems Analysis (SA) division, headed by Alain Enthoven. McNamara had established SA to coordinate "rationally" budgeting for new weapons system, formerly the military's responsibility. Enthoven, whose assignment was to motivate the JCS to "hunt for deadwood without being prodded," instead joined McNamara as the chief's biggest pariah. The SA, using economic models of cost effectiveness and statistics on American military operations, discovered by the mid-1960s that MACV claims to success were suspect at best. Yet, as Enthoven complained, any attempts to have SA analyze Vietnam strategy and operations "would meet with such strong military resistance as to make it politically impossible." In fact, the JCS went so far as to attempt to restrict circulation of the SA's publication, the *Southeast Asia Analysis Report*, to just senior leaders at the Pentagon.[100]

Despite the political infighting over strategy and continued recognition of the barriers to progress in Vietnam, Westmorland remained sanguine about the war. During a meeting with the president at his ranch in mid-August, the MACV commander accepted Johnson's reasoning behind the decision against mobilization. The United States had "benefitted [from the] fact [that] Reserves haven't been called up," they agreed. The MACV as constituted at that point had professional leadership, and its soldiers were "not overseas against their will." Activating Reserve units, Johnson believed, would force Americans to break their ties with family and business and undermine morale on the home front. Westmoreland, however, chose not to challenge the president on this crucial point

98. *Pentagon Papers: Gravel*, 2:576–80; Westmoreland in Sorley, *Thunderbolt*, 192–3.
99. Wheeler CJCS 7859–66 to Westmoreland and Sharp, 21 December 1966, Westmoreland Papers, folder 362 [2]: Eyes Only Message File, WNRC.
100. Enthoven and Smith, *How Much Is Enough?*, 292; Hewes, *From Root to McNamara*, 307–10; Perry, *Four Stars*, 169–70; Kolko, *Anatomy of a War*, 194; Kinnard, *Secretary of Defense*, 88.

of disagreement. "We're going to win this war for you without mobilization," he assured his commander in chief.[101] Writing to Harold K. Johnson a month later, Westmoreland reiterated such views. Although he hoped for a "maximum buildup" to 542,000 troops by mid-1967 to bring "an earlier successful conclusion" to the war, the MACV commander added that "considerations of quality, including morale, may well justify a smaller force" than originally envisioned. Such considerations, he understood, "include the assumption that there will be no major call up of reserves." Nevertheless, Westmoreland continued to make that very request throughout the war.[102]

The Army chief of staff also understood that Washington was wary of a further buildup of U.S. forces in Vietnam and of expanding either air or ground operations into the north. The more Harold K. Johnson deliberated over the MACV's troop requests, "the more uncertain I am as to my ability to give you a [satisfactory] answer." With voluntary enlistments lower than expected, draft calls inadequate to meet Westmoreland's goals, too little time to train new troops, and congressional criticism that the Army was overextended in Southeast Asia, Johnson saw "no indication here to carry the war outside South Vietnam." In fact, "the tendency to limit the war to South Vietnam is hardening." Westmoreland then claimed to be shocked by Johnson's report of Washington's concern over expanding the war, replying to the general that "your analysis of the [political] impact on forces requested by this command is far greater than my wildest assumptions."[103]

Westmoreland's astonishment reminds one of Claude Rains's shock at discovering gambling at Rick's Place. At a debriefing with Marine leaders, the MACV commander and Admiral Sharp reported that U.S. force levels would "have to be consistent with

101. Notes of a meeting between Lyndon Johnson and William Westmoreland at the president's ranch, 13 August 1966, Tom Johnson's Meeting Notes, box 1, folder: August 13, 1966, President and General Westmoreland, Ranch, WNRC.
102. Westmoreland MAC 7720 to Johnson, 5 September 1966, Westmoreland v. CBS, LC, box 16, folder: MACV Backchannel Messages from Westmoreland, 1–30 September 1966, WNRC.
103. Johnson WDC 10846 and 10849 to Westmoreland, 13 September 1966, in Westmoreland v. CBS, LC, box 16, folder: MACV Backchannel Messages to Westmoreland, 1–30 September 1966, WNRC; Westmoreland MAC 8710 to Johnson, 6 October 1966, Westmoreland Papers, folder 362 (1): Eyes Only Message File, WNRC.

political, psychological and economic factors, as they impact on the GVN," while Krulak pointed out that there was a restraint on their military options, and it was "one that cannot be related to shortages back home," namely the shaky southern economy that had begun to suffer runaway inflation so much so that Ambassador Lodge wanted to hold down expenditures by restricting the number of U.S. forces in country. Westmoreland and Sharp thus realized that there was a "definite limit" to the amount of money, and hence the number of U.S. soldiers, that could be put into the RVN without recklessly destabilizing southern society. The MACV commander, however, had to find some solution to such problems because "we have really crossed the Rubicon. We are involved deeply in what is almost certain to be a long war. Everyone knows this, and what we need now is to settle down with a professional force that our country can support for the long pull, without calling up reserves." The MACV leader then estimated that a force of 400,000 troops would be adequate for Vietnam, which was almost precisely the number that McNamara had earlier put forth. The agreement on force levels between Westmoreland and the defense secretary "seems remarkable," Victor Krulak acerbically observed, "and convenient too."[104]

Krulak's sarcasm was appropriate, for McNamara had clearly soured on the military's spiraling requests for reinforcements, and indeed on the war itself. In a memorandum to the president on 14 October, the secretary offered his most bleak assessment of Vietnam yet. Despite inflicting heavy losses on the enemy, McNamara saw "no sign of an impending break in enemy morale" and in fact it seemed likely "that he can more than replace his losses by infiltration from North Vietnam and recruitment in South Vietnam." Although U.S. forces had prevented a Communist victory in 1966, he added, the VC had adapted by employing "a strategy of keeping us busy and waiting us out (a strategy of attriting our national will)." Because of the enemy's patience and continued high morale – as well as the limited achievements of Rolling Thunder and a pacification program that "has if anything gone backward" – McNamara

---

104. Krulak to Greene, 16 October 1966, "CINCPAC/COMUSMACV Debriefing, HQMC Message File [Eyes Only Messages], 1966–7, MCHC; Kinnard, *Secretary of Defense*, 100.

saw "no reasonable way to bring the war to an end soon." The United States, he lamented, was "no better, and if anything worse off" that it had been just years earlier.[105] It is curious that the defense secretary, in his memoirs published in April 1995, admitted that the war was unwinnable in 1967. His pessimism was actually quite clear after Ia Drang in late 1965, while his October 1966 analysis constitutes a frank admission of failure.

As a result of his analysis, the defense secretary urged the president to stop escalating the war. McNamara recommended another bombing pause as a way to convince Ho to negotiate, and, to break the cycle of military attrition and bloodshed, he further urged that the MACV give priority to a vigorous pacification program. Above all, though, McNamara wanted to end "the spectre of apparently endless escalation of U.S. deployments." He thus advised Johnson to establish a ceiling of 470,000 American troops in Vietnam, an increase of only 70,000 over present levels and about 100,000 less than Sharp and Westmoreland wanted. "Even many more than 470,000," the secretary believed, "would not kill the enemy off in such numbers as to break their morale so long as they think they can wait us out."[106] McNamara, sounding like Krulak a year earlier, had thus renounced Westmoreland's program for Vietnam and urged the White House to develop a new approach to the war.

The JCS emphatically rejected the defense secretary's recommendations, even though it conceded that much of his analysis was on target. The chiefs, in evaluating McNamara's report, "agree[d] there is no reason to expect that the war can be brought soon to a successful conclusion." The enemy was prepared to "wait it out" and expected to "win this war in Washington, just as they won the war with France in Paris." Westmoreland agreed, observing that the VC's tactics "suggest that the enemy intends to continue a protracted war of attrition." Given such conditions, the chiefs and the MACV could only weakly defend the military situation in the RVN, essentially arguing that the U.S. presence had prevented Communist victory and ensured a stalemate on the battlefield. Like

105. McNamara to Johnson, 14 October 1966, "Actions Recommended for Vietnam," in NSC History, "Manila Conference and the President's Asian Trip: 17 October–2 November" 1966, reel 5, UPA.
106. See source cited in previous note; see also Sheehan, *Bright Shining Lie*, 681–3.

McNamara the JCS believed that the war had reached a decisive point and "decisions taken over the next sixty days can determine the outcome of the war and, consequently, can affect the over-all security interests of the United States for years to come."[107]

Despite that nearly apocalyptic warning, the military's recommendations for future strategy offered nothing new. Indeed the JCS merely recycled its standard requests, calling for more troops and expanded air operations. McNamara's call for a limit of 470,000 soldiers was "substantially less" than they deemed necessary to conduct operations in Vietnam, the chiefs complained. They also rejected the defense secretary's appraisal of Rolling Thunder and again protested the political constraints imposed upon the air campaign. In leveling such charges, however, the military seemed to overlook the reality of the war in 1966. Lyndon Johnson had been consistently expanding the war per the chiefs' wishes and to that point had acquiesced to their numerous troop requests. "Westmoreland has received all that he has asked for," the president accurately told congressional leaders. "He'll ask for more . . . [and] we'll send whatever he needs."[108]

Wheeler had also notified Westmoreland and Sharp earlier that the White House had been prepared to authorize expanded air strikes against the DRVN until political turmoil in the south forced a reconsideration. "There was surprisingly little opposition" to approving new targets in the north, the JCS chair explained. In fact, as Walt Rostow informed the president, U.S. pilots had struck targets containing 86 percent of the DRVN's petroleum and lubricant storage capacity and had actually destroyed nearly 60 percent of it.[109] In view of such facts, it is clear that the chiefs' advocacy of

107. Wheeler JCSM-672–66 to McNamara, 14 October 1966, "Actions Recommended for Vietnam," Warnke-McNaughton, box 3, folder: VII, Late Vietnam . . . (2), LBJL, and also in NSC History, "Manila Conference," UPA; summary of Westmoreland MACV 27578 to Sharp and Wheeler, 10 August 1966, Warnke-McNaughton, box 7, folder: VNS 2 [Vietnam, 1966–8] (1), LBJL.

108. See sources cited in previous note; Tom Johnson to Lyndon Johnson, 18 July 1966, "Minutes of the Meeting between the President and Bi-Partisan Leaders of House and Senate," Tom Johnson's Meeting Notes, box 1, folder: July 18, 1966, Meeting with Bipartisan Leaders, LBJL; see also Lyndon Johnson to McNamara, 28 June 1966, NSF, Memos to the President, Walt Rostow, box 8, folder: volume 7, 21–30 June 1966 [1 of 2], LBJL.

109. Wheeler JCS 3086–66 to Sharp and Westmoreland, 2 June 1966, Westmoreland v. CBS, LC, box 15, folder: MACV Backchannel Messages to Westmoreland, 1–30 June

more troops and bombing in reality offered little promise of altering the situation in Vietnam and that U.S. forces were in no way fighting with any hands tied behind their backs. The JCS itself, as well as Westmoreland and others, had consistently recognized that the enemy had maintained its posture and morale at the same time that the government and military of the RVN was showing negligible effectiveness or improvement. Yet they would continue to rely on attrition and air power for the duration of the conflict.

Westmoreland and others nonetheless remained upbeat about the war and continued to press Washington for more resources. Such optimism notwithstanding, Harold K. Johnson confessed his "continuing concern with the level and tempo of combat activity that we can support." Concern over inflation in the RVN had forced McNamara to limit U.S. expenditures to about 44 billion piasters and, the Army chief realized, a ceiling on deployments was forthcoming as well. "We are already overcommitted in maneuver battalions for the level of support that is available for them," Johnson warned Westmoreland, and spending limits would continue to affect U.S. combat capability in Vietnam directly.[110]

McNamara made that precise argument to Wheeler, warning that "runaway inflation can undo what our military operations accomplish."[111] Westmoreland, who "frankly could not see an early ending" to the war, told U.S. congressmen that he needed a force that could be "sustained indefinitely."[112] But Thomas Moorer, the new CNO, realized that the United States would have to "carry on an effective war without mobilization, without escalation, without inflation, and without [a] greatly increased gold flow."[113] Like many American officers, Moorer had recognized the limits under which the war would be fought, yet, like so many others, did not reconsider the nature of the U.S. military commitment to Vietnam.

1966, WNRC; Rostow to Johnson, 5 July 1966, NSF, Memos to the President, Walt Rostow, box 9, folder: volume 8, 1–15 July 1966 [2 of 2], LBJL; see also CIA and DIA assessments of Rolling Thunder in appendix to McNamara's 14 October memorandum to the president, NSC History, "Manila Conference," UPA.

110. Johnson WDC 12415 to Westmoreland, 20 October 1966, Westmoreland Papers, folder 362 (2): COMUSMACV Message File, WNRC.

111. McNamara to Wheeler, 11 November 1966, "Deployments to Southeast Asia," Warnke-McNaughton, box 7, folder: VNS 1 [Vietnam, 1966–8] (2), LBJL.

112. General Westmoreland's Historical Briefing, 25 November 1966, Westmoreland Papers, folder 467: #11 History Files, 30 October–12 December 1966, WNRC.

113. Moorer in Krulak to Greene, 8 November 1966, HQMC Message File, 1966–7, MCHC; Westmoreland and Sharp, *Report on the War in Vietnam,* 119.

Civilian leaders, however, were wavering in their support of the war and, more critically, the continued morass in Indochina was surely affecting Lyndon Johnson's political fortunes. Senator Stuart Symington, especially respected on defense issues, told Walt Rostow he was "thinking of getting off the train soon." "Nixon will murder us" in the 1968 election, Symington warned. "He will become the biggest dove of all times. There never has been a man in American public life that could turn so fast on a dime."[114]

Democratic governors expressed similar concerns to the president at a meeting at his Texas ranch in late December. Harold Hughes of Iowa, Warren Hearnes of Missouri, and John Connally of Texas, among others, told Johnson that his reelection was in doubt because of growing public impatience with Vietnam. "Eat out the Republicans as often and as strongly as you can, at every opportunity," was the president's main advice to the state executives, hardly a reassuring approach to the growing domestic crisis caused by Vietnam.[115] American service officials were just as clearly aware of public anxiety about the war in late 1966. Despite constantly clamoring for mobilization, "each of the chiefs replied in the negative" when McNamara asked whether they favored a call-up of Reserves in December. Undoubtedly the brass knew the president was opposed to such measures and that the political risks of continued war in Vietnam were becoming greater for Johnson. Admiral Sharp was more pointedly unnerved by the politics of the war. "With no end in sight" to the U.S. involvement in Vietnam, the American people "are more apt to become aroused against the war." Sharp's "limited sounding" of public and congressional opinion led him to believe that "we had better do what we can to bring this war to a successful conclusion as rapidly as possible." The CINCPAC had recognized that time was working against the United States in Vietnam, yet his answer to the dilemma was typical – more troops and sorties.[116]

114. Rostow to Johnson, 28 November 1966, CF, ND 19/CO 312, box 72, folder: Situation in Vietnam (July–December 1965), LBJL.
115. Tom Johnson to Lyndon Johnson, 22 December 1966, "Notes of a Meeting, December 21, 1966, at the Ranch with Democratic Governors," Tom Johnson's Meeting Notes, box 1, folder: 21 December 1966, Ranch; Meeting with Governors, LBJL.
116. Rostow, Memorandum for the Record, 7 December 1966, NSF, Memos to the President, Walt Rostow, box 11, folder: volume 16, 1–13 December 1966, LBJL; Sharp to Wheeler and Westmoreland, 24 December 1966, Westmoreland v. CBS, LC, box 16,

Despite McNamara's apparent epiphany on Vietnam, the intense military feuding over strategy, congressional and public division engendered by the war, the damage done to Lyndon Johnson's political prospects, and an uncertain if not doomed situation on the battlefield, American officers, as Sharp had, continued to offer up the same shopworn and ill-considered proposals for future policy. The brass, however, did realize that Washington was increasingly anxious over the lack of progress in Vietnam. Various civilian officials, Wheeler reported to Westmoreland, were beginning to raise questions about the conduct of the war "which may in a fairly short time cause us difficulty." Specifically, Washington remained troubled by the continuing lack of ARVN military activity, the quality of enemy arms, and growing Communist infiltration into the south, which was offsetting the VC's huge losses.[117] But thwarting the enemy's movements into the RVN, Westmoreland conceded, was especially hard because the MACV could not even "differentiate between the North . . . and South Vietnamese."[118]

The MACV commander, despite Lew Walt's confidence that pacification would improve, also expected continued deterioration in counterinsurgency operations in the northern provinces in 1967. In fact, the enemy "can attack at any time" in IV Corps with regimental strength, local forces, and guerrillas or throughout the rest of the RVN with divisional strength. In addition, Chinese and Soviet aid to the insurgents would likely increase, as would infiltration into the south and the training of political cadre already there.[119] American officers continued to cite the ARVN's deficiencies as well and made it clear that future success would require "immediate and substantial qualitative improvements in all aspects

folder: MACV Backchannel Messages to Westmoreland, 1–31 December 1966, WNRC; Sharp, *Strategy for Defeat,* 121–4.
117. Wheeler CJCS 7859–66 to Westmoreland and Sharp, 21 December 1966, Westmoreland Papers, folder 362 (2): Eyes Only Message File, WNRC; Westmoreland and Sharp, *Report on the War in Vietnam,* 114–15.
118. Westmoreland 53846 to Sharp, 19 December 1966, "Enemy Strength in South Vietnam," Westmoreland v. CBS, LC, box 29, folder: Message, dated 19 December 1966, WNRC.
119. General Westmoreland's Historical Briefing, 1 January 1967, Westmoreland Papers, folder 468 [2 of 2]: #12 History Files, 13 December 1966–26 January 1967; Westmoreland 00160 to Sharp, 2 January 1967, "Year End Assessment of Enemy Situation and Enemy Strategy," Westmoreland v. CBS, LC, box 29, folder: Message, dated 4 January 1967, WNRC.

of RVNAF capabilities and operations." The MACV itself had also grown by 200,000 troops in just a year, and the attendant costs and strain on logistics systems only added to Westmoreland's problems.[120]

Despite such forthright evaluations, the military continued to emphasize its accomplishments and to expect progress. In a January 1967 evaluation, the MACV claimed that the American and ARVN forces were routing the enemy, many VC were rallying to the RVN, and pacification was likely to improve in the coming year. While the enemy's determination remained strong, "the conflict has taken a decided turn for the best."[121] The JCS had a more ambivalent view of the war. In a report for McNamara on future courses of action, the chiefs pointed out that they had consistently requested a greater bombing effort over the north, mining of ports, cross-border operations, a call-up of Reserves, and extended terms of service for U.S. soldiers. Although the JCS sought to "break the [White House's] pattern of slow escalation and apparent vacillation," it recognized that "fundamental parts" of the military's planning for expanded war "have never been accepted." The chiefs nonetheless put forth the same recommendations that they had been sending to the civilian leaders in Washington for over two years already.[122]

The military's own pattern of dreary assessments and stale recommendations certainly complemented the Johnson administration's slow and vacillating approach to Vietnam. Indeed, both civilian and service leaders were aware of the political and military problems and risks involved in the U.S. takeover of the war. Various

120. Westmoreland MACJ311, 16 January 1967, "Improvements within RVNAF," Westmoreland Papers, folder 424: Top Secret COMUSMACV Signature File, January 1967, WNRC; Westmoreland and Sharp, *Report on the War in Vietnam*, 114.
121. Measurement of Progress Briefing, given by Lt. Col. A. M. Robert Dean, MACJ34, n.d., Westmoreland Papers, folder 468 [2 of 2]: #12 History Files, 13 December 1966–26 January 1967, WNRC; Westmoreland and Sharp, *Report on the War in Vietnam*, 117.
122. Draft Memorandum for Secretary of Defense, "Future Conduct of the War in Southeast Asia," Enclosure in Third Working Paper, Report by the J-3 to the Joint Chiefs of Staff on Courses of Action for Southeast Asia, 13 January 1967, Westmoreland Papers, folder 579: Joint Chiefs of Staff, 13 January 1967, WNRC.

military critics warned that the MACV reliance on conventional warfare and attrition would bleed American forces but make only a negligible impact on the enemy. Opponents of Westmoreland's strategy, however, advocated the time-consuming and deliberate tactics of counterinsurgency and nation building, measures that the American commander and president were sure to reject for both political and military reasons. Though hyped as the solution to America's strategic shortcomings, pacification, as Maxwell Taylor pointed out, was no panacea for the U.S. ills in Vietnam. U.S. forces had already taken over the main-unit war in 1967 and were sustaining an inordinate number of casualties. Should Americans assume a substantial share of the civic action program, the general warned, the ARVN would be even more tempted to sit back and let them suffer greater losses. In the meantime, political stability, a prerequisite for effective counterinsurgency work, was as distant as ever.[123]

At the same time, many officers continued to see the air war as a cure to their problems in Vietnam, even though they admitted that the bombing campaign over the north would achieve limited results and knew that full authorization for unrestrained strikes was not forthcoming. By 1966, then, victory through the air was an elusive, if not desperate, goal. Nonetheless, even Krulak and Greene, who provided the most striking and exhaustive critique of the American strategy in Vietnam, were seduced by the promise of air power. Perhaps the PROVN report, commissioned by the military's biggest critic of air operations, Harold K. Johnson, in reality offered the best, albeit thin, hope for the United States in Vietnam.

Even more than recognizing the failure of U.S. strategy, if not doctrine, in Vietnam, military leaders also understood the impact of politics on their war-making capabilities. Given the president's fear of widening the war and, more important, the impact of Vietnam on his domestic agenda and future, various officers – both critics and politicos – recognized that politics and public opinion would necessarily force Johnson to try to limit the war. The president would not declare a national emergency or activate the Reserves, and military leaders warned fellow officers to resign themselves to receiving "penny packets" rather than large-scale reinforcements.

---

123. *Pentagon Papers: Gravel*, 2: 493–4.

The same military men who had recognized the impact of inflation and military spending in the RVN surely must have understood the relevance of such economic factors at home. Despite that awareness, Westmoreland, Wheeler, Sharp, and others did not pursue any alternative policy course in Vietnam, but instead kept asking the White House for more of the same. The military's criticism of the administration was thus disingenuous on one hand, because Johnson and McNamara had approved the MACV's troop requests through 1966; on the other hand, their attacks on Johnson were politically motivated, because their recycled requests forced the president to repeatedly reject calls for mobilization and expanded war, and to bear the onus for whatever consequences occurred. As General Dave Richard Palmer observed, "to be sure, political considerations left military commanders no choice other than attritional warfare, but that does not alter the hard truth that the United States was strategically bankrupt in Vietnam in 1966."[124]

Rather than adapt to the political-economic-military realities of the war, Westmoreland, Wheeler, and Sharp were, in essence, forcing the president to choose between a politically difficult, if not impossible, escalation, or continued stasis. Since Johnson was no more likely than the brass to reevaluate the war or his commitment to the RVN, and was, if anything, more aware of the domestic ramifications of both escalation and failure, America's service chiefs had put the ball into the White House's court. With American forces unlikely to attain success in Vietnam, civilian and military leaders were scrambling to avoid blame in Washington.

124. Palmer in Davidson, *Vietnam at War,* 354.

9

"The Platform of False Prophets Is Crowded": Public Hope and Private Despair in Vietnam, 1967

The significant point is that no professional military man, not even the Chairman of the JCS, was present at these [Tuesday policy] luncheons until late in 1967. This omission, whether by the deliberate intent or with the indifferent acquiescence of Secretary McNamara, was in my view a grave and flagrant example of his persistent refusal to accept the civilian–military partnership in the conduct of our military operations.

U. S. G. Sharp[1]

Despite foundering efforts in the field, interservice dissension, and an emerging political crisis in the United States, American officials did not fundamentally reevaluate the war in 1967. The White House continued to hope for the best in Vietnam while trying to rein in the military's repeated requests for more soldiers and a wider war. For their part, Westmoreland, Wheeler, and other officers kept forwarding optimistic projections of the war despite continued bleak reports on conditions in the RVN. The ARVN was passive and seemed to be allowing U.S. troops to carry the burden of the fight, they suggested, while the enemy infiltrated and recruited despite American firepower, still determined the scale and nature of engagements, and could be expected to prolong the war to its advantage. Pacification was not going well, U.S. officers added, and their principal response, the air war, was not making a decisive impact.

Even after recognizing such problems, military leaders continued to pressure the White House for more of the same. By recycling

1. Sharp, *Strategy for Defeat*, 86–7.

such requests for escalation – especially evident in an April proposal for a reinforcement of 200,000 troops – the military was effectively admitting its failure. As McNamara, Krulak, and others had prophesied much earlier, the United States simply could not match the Communists in a war of attrition. Even more, political factors plagued American efforts. On one hand, fear of a general war in Asia or of shortchanging European forces, as well as growing domestic opposition to the war, made it imperative to find a prompt way out of Vietnam. On the other hand, both civilian and military leaders wanted each other to find that solution. Thus the president began to express his concerns about reinforcement and escalation to Westmoreland and Wheeler more explicitly, even summoning Westmoreland to Washington in midyear to emphasize that his conduct of the war stemmed from the commander's advice. But, as McNamara's aide Adam Yarmolinsky contended, Johnson was using military officials as advocates for his positions rather than sincerely requesting their counsel regarding his options for Vietnam policy making.[2] For their part, military leaders understood that Lyndon Johnson wanted good news and the brass decided to provide it, to the point of suppressing evidence that indicated otherwise. But Westmoreland, Wheeler, and others were, at the same time, candid about the serious problems that they faced.

On the surface, such behavior may have seemed inconsistent or erratic. Given the history of civil–military relations and the politics of Vietnam, however, it was understandable. By 1967, American officers were disgusted with the war. Many had not wanted a large-scale intervention in Vietnam but, once committed, expected the White House to authorize a fully unrestrained war. From the beginning, however, it was clear that Johnson did not want the conflict in Vietnam to spill over into China or undermine his dream of building a Great Society at home. The president therefore took what the military saw as a piecemeal approach to the war. As a result, service leaders wanted to make it clear that it was Johnson and McNamara, not U.S. commanders in Vietnam, who should be held

---

2. Adam Yarmolinsky, *The Military Establishment: Its Impact on American Society* (New York, 1971), 32.

accountable for the coming disaster. Thus military officials in Saigon and Washington, instead of rethinking the war, kept making the very proposals that the president had already rejected, and would surely turn down again. By late 1967, the JCS, afraid it would "take the fall" for Vietnam, even decided to resign to protest civilian handling of the war. The chiefs, as it turned out, decided to keep their jobs, but they had given up on the war nonetheless.

As American officers analyzed the war in early 1967 it was clear that they expected events in Vietnam to continue along already established lines. In a January summary of the enemy's position, Westmoreland found VC-PAVN forces able to reinforce, resupply, and prepare for a new offensive. The Communists "can attack at any time" in division strength in the northernmost provinces and in regimental strength in IV Corps, he found, while exacerbating political instability via strikes against government and economic targets. Despite its huge losses, the enemy could still infiltrate about 8,400 men into the RVN from the north and recruit about 3,500 in the south, both on a monthly basis. Still controlling the battlefield, the Communists could withdraw or break down their main force units into smaller groups to wage guerrilla war, stop or alter its political attacks if challenged, or move out of disputed areas and resurface elsewhere.[3]

The commander, while denying that the ARVN was avoiding combat, nonetheless forwarded statistics showing that it had actually made contact with the enemy in only 40 percent of its operations. Thus Westmoreland's "constant objective" in coming operations would be "to increase the effective employment of ARVN assets." His level of trust in the southern military's abilities, however, was still questionable. In the MACV battle plan for 1967, Westmoreland continued to assign to U.S. forces the primary responsibility for offensive action against the Communists' main-force units and base areas, while the RVNAF would protect its own

---

3. Westmoreland 00160 to CINCPAC, 2 June 1967, "Year-End Assessment of the Enemy's Situation," NSF, Memos to the President, Walt Rostow, box 35, folder: volume 58 (initially found in Declassified and Sanitized Documents from Unprotected Files [DSDUF], box 4, folder: Vietnam, box 35, volume 58), LBJL.

bases and focus on pacification operations. Just as the ARVN's problems persisted, the enemy's strengths remained evident. Even though he expected U.S. units to continue to inflict sizable casualties on the enemy, Westmoreland thought it would be a "grave error" to assume that the enemy's military or logistics capabilities had been significantly damaged.[4]

Admiral Sharp likewise expected the VC to try to prolong the war, disrupt civic action programs, and resort to conventional operations "only when the odds favor his success."[5] Despite conceding the initiative to the enemy, Sharp agreed with Westmoreland's goals for 1967, namely the "total destruction, or total denial" of Communist bases, weapons, and lines of communication. Although U.S. public opinion might be questioning the war, the admiral believed that "the military" had to "go all out at all levels in SVN if we are to win." American troops were involved in a "full blown and difficult war" in which they had already committed "a huge amount of combat power," yet, Sharp realized, "we are still a long way away from achieving our objectives." To win in Vietnam, even more strength was needed, he believed. "Our ground forces must take the field in long term sustained" operations, notwithstanding the "reticence" of political figures and the American public.[6]

The JCS also wanted the president to take stronger measures in Vietnam, again recommending stepped-up air strikes against the DRVN, additional troops to attack the enemy in the south, extended tours of duty, and, at home, expanded draft calls, activation of Reserves, and economic mobilization. The president had repeatedly turned down this program and there was no indication that he would authorize it in early 1967. The chiefs, of course, were well aware of Johnson's political calculations in developing Vietnam policy. They understood that allied ambivalence about the war, fear

---

4. Westmoreland MAC 0030 to Wheeler and Sharp, 2 January 1967, Westmoreland v. CBS, LC, box 17, folder: MACV Backchannel Messages from Westmoreland, 1–31 January 1967, WNRC.
5. Sharp to Wheeler, 3 January 1967, NSF, Memos to the President, Walt Rostow, box 35, folder: volume 58 (initially found in DSDUF, box 4, folder: Vietnam, box 35, volume 58), LBJL.
6. See sources cited in previous note; Sharp also believed that the United States should diminish its efforts to stem infiltration and focus on the war in the south; at the same time, he continued to encourage massive bombing above the seventeenth parallel. Sharp to JCS, 14 January 1967, in Sharp, *Strategy for Defeat*, appendix C, 280–4.

of provoking the PRC or the Soviet Union, concern about the 1968 elections, growing public protests, and "domestic anti-military feeling" could coalesce to convince policy makers "to give little consideration to military recommendations." Once more, America's military leadership had recognized the military and political factors limiting the war in Vietnam but responded, typically, by calling for a larger war.[7]

In some measure, Westmoreland and others wanted to expand the war because they perceived that large search-and-destroy operations in late 1966 and early 1967 had been successful. In Operations Attleboro, Cedar Falls, and Junction City, the MACV committed large numbers of U.S. and ARVN troops, with B-52 air support and massive artillery fire, against suspected enemy base areas and strongpoints. In all cases, the enemy suffered sizable losses, prompting MACV declarations of success. But U.S. and RVN forces took major casualties as well and even DePuy, now commanding the 1st Infantry Division, admitted that the Communists had "metered out their casualties" and broken off engagements when their losses began to mount. "They just backed off and waited. . . . They were more elusive. They controlled the battle better. They were the ones who decided whether there should be a fight." General Bernard Rogers, who later wrote the Army's history of the early 1967 campaigns, added that it was a "sheer physical impossibility" to keep the VC from escaping.[8]

Yet Westmoreland and his commanders saw Cedar Falls and Junction City as vindication of their strategy, as they had done after Ia Drang in 1965. Again, Victor H. Krulak offered a markedly different evaluation. While the chiefs contended that American forces had turned the corner in Vietnam and were badly hurting the enemy, Krulak believed that the war was in a state of "equilibrium," with both sides capable of intensifying their efforts and prolonging the conflict. The general, moreover, seemed anxious over the possibility of Soviet or Chinese intervention, Ho's ability

7. Third Working Paper, Report by the J-3 to Joint Chiefs of Staff on Courses of Action for Southeast Asia, 13 January 1967, Westmoreland Papers, folder 579: Joint Chiefs of Staff, 13 January 1967, WNRC.
8. DePuy in Krepinevich, *The Army and Vietnam,* 190–1; Bernard William Rogers, *Cedar Falls–Junction City: A Turning Point* (Washington, D.C., 1974), 157; for Westmoreland's analysis of these battles as U.S. triumphs, see *Report on the War in Vietnam,* 137.

to shift between conventional or guerrilla warfare as it suited him, and, even more, political instability in Saigon and the ARVN's passivity. He continued to attack Westmoreland's conduct of the war as well. Although agreeing with the MACV leadership on the desirability of more troops, the Marine leader stressed to McNamara that the United States should avoid the type of manpower-intensive strategy that Westmoreland had implemented, and instead try to damage the Communists while minimizing American losses, preferably via escalating air strikes. As Krulak saw it, Ho had "made a sagacious . . . and a far reaching" decision to engage in protracted combat and erode the American manpower base. By ignoring pacification and trying to win a war of attrition, Westmoreland had played into the enemy's hands.[9]

Westmoreland, however, charged that the Marines were to blame for their problems in I Corps. After visiting General Walt in Da Nang, the MACV commander complained that the III MAF leaders had committed too many troops to inaccessible areas where they could not take offensive action. Conditions in I Corps, he lamented, were deteriorating as the proximity to the DMZ and easy infiltration from the north enabled Ho to reinforce his units to whatever extent needed.[10] The MACV intelligence chief, General McChristian, offered an even grimmer view of the enemy's capabilities. The Communists, he told Maxwell Taylor during his visit to Saigon in late January, would likely infiltrate about 7,000 soldiers per month and recruit another 7,500, for a total reinforcement of 174,000 for the year, which amounted to a net gain in enemy strength of about 65,000 in 1967.[11]

Other officers found McChristian's figures "unduly pessimistic," however, and continued to accentuate the positive. ARVN and U.S. forces "have defeated the enemy in every recent encounter," according to a MACV briefer; the Communists, Westmoreland added, "no longer have the capability of achieving a military vic-

9. Krulak to McNamara, 4 January 1967, Krulak Papers, box 2, folder: Correspondence, 1967–8, MCHC.
10. General Westmoreland's Historical Briefing, 29 January 1967, Westmoreland Papers, folder 468: #12 History Files, 13 December 1966–26 January 1967, WNRC.
11. Maxwell Taylor Memorandum for the Record, 30 January 1967, "Viet-Nam Visit, 20–25 January 1967," NSF, Files of Robert Komer, box 6, folder: General Maxwell D. Taylor, LBJL.

tory." Wheeler agreed, and he told the president that if the United States "applied pressure relentlessly in the North and the South," the DRVN would withdraw support from the VC and "at that point, the war would be essentially won."[12] The MACV commander himself, however, had a more sobering assessment in mid-February. Although U.S. forces had hurt the enemy in 1966, "he is far from defeated." American forces had just begun antiguerrilla operations and had not even made contact with many PAVN and VC main-force units for months. Westmoreland even had to "say without hesitation" that the ground war – beset by intelligence shortcomings, inadequate helicopter support, and uncertain troop availability – "cannot be significantly accelerated" beyond current levels.[13] Harold K. Johnson likewise informed the commander in Saigon that he would have to increase the lead time on troop and equipment requests due to political pressure and budget constraints. While he would continue to press the administration for all available resources, the Army chief "simply want[ed] to point out that the rules of the game are changing."[14]

The "rules" – the political factors involved in developing military policy – may not have been changing so much as becoming even more critical. By early 1967, civilian and military leaders held well-established assumptions about each other and about the war, and they were unlikely to reconsider them. The president wanted a timely end to the conflict without spiraling escalation and at the least cost to his political concerns. The military and its allies on Capitol Hill – 139 members of Congress held Reserve commissions – more boldly criticized civilian policy, and American officers even began feeding information on McNamara to right-

12. Measurement of Progress Briefing given by Lt. Col. A. M. Robert Dean, MACJ 34, n.d., Westmoreland Papers, folder 468 [2 of 3]: #12 History Files, 13 December 1966–26 January 1967, WNRC; Westmoreland DOD 63890, 24 January 1967, "Command Guidance," attached to Rostow to Johnson, 26 January 1967, NSF, Memos to the President, Walt Rostow, box 12, folder: volume 19, 15–31 January 1967 [1 of 2], LBJL; Wheeler JCS 1284–67 to Sharp and Westmoreland, 17 February 1967, Westmoreland Papers, folder 363: Eyes Only Message File, WNRC.
13. Westmoreland MAC 1658 to Sharp and Wheeler, 17 February 1967, Westmoreland Papers, folder 363: Eyes Only Message File, WNRC; Westmoreland 06497 to JCS and CINCPAC, 23 February 1967, Westmoreland v. CBS, LC, box 30, folder: Message, dated 23 February 1967, WNRC.
14. Johnson to Westmoreland, 21 February 1967, Westmoreland v. CBS, LC, box 17, folder: MACV Backchannel Messages to Westmoreland, 1–28 February 1967, WNRC.

wing groups like the American Security Council and Liberty Lobby in their campaign to discredit him.[15] Even more, service leaders, recognizing stalemate in Vietnam, kept asking the White House to expand the war and, if refused, had an excuse for failure. Over the next year, through the Tet Offensive, such political considerations would erupt as the political war in Washington intensified along with the shooting war in Vietnam. As a result, civil–military relations deteriorated to crisis proportions.

By 1967, Vietnam had become a political albatross around Lyndon Johnson's neck. The president "totally agreed" with Senator Fulbright's view that "the war poisons everything else" and had to be ended promptly.[16] He was, however, also accommodating Wheeler and Sharp. Johnson, stung by rising media criticism of the bombing of northern Vietnam, directed the JCS chair to prepare a public relations campaign to show the importance of Rolling Thunder.[17] Sharp, noting the president's efforts to remove restrictions on the air war in Laos, also admitted that "the influx of men and materials" into the RVN had increased "despite considerable air effort expended to hinder infiltration." Although conceding that interdiction strikes were of questionable utility, Sharp still believed that the White House's reluctance to remove even more restrictions was "based primarily on political considerations." Curiously, Wheeler contended that growing antiwar sentiment might induce the president to grant broader authority to conduct the bombing campaign. Johnson, he believed, valued the military's advice above all others. Accordingly, "the only obstacle which could impede additional authority for military action would be one created by us."[18]

15. Richard J. Barnet, *The Economy of Death* (New York, 1970), 80–1; for an example of the right wing's anti-McNamara propaganda, see the "special report" of the Liberty Lobby, *Robert Strange McNamara: The True Story of Dr. Strangebob* (Washington, D.C., 1967).
16. Minutes of Meeting in Cabinet Room, 9 January 1967, Reference File, box 1, folder: Miscellaneous Vietnam Documents, LBJL.
17. Wheeler CJCS 1594–67 to Westmoreland, 2 March 1967, Westmoreland Papers, folder 363: Chief of Staff Message File, WNRC. The chiefs delivered the requested report, "Results of the Air Campaign against North Vietnam," to McNamara that very day, and he forwarded it to the president, see VN C.F., NSF, boxes 74–5, folder: 2 EE, 1965–7, Primarily McNamara Recommendations re. Strategic Actions [1965–6], WNRC.
18. Sharp to Wheeler and Westmoreland, 16 February 1967, "Restrictions on Operations in Southern Laos," Westmoreland Papers, folder 363: Eyes Only Message File, WNRC;

Although the obstacle to which Wheeler referred was public criticism of the president by military leaders, another appeared just days later. In revising its data on enemy action, the MACV found that the number of VC- and PAVN-initiated major unit attacks between January 1966 and January 1967 was actually about four times higher than initially estimated. Even worse, the enemy was getting stronger as the U.S. presence increased. Where the original figures had listed only five Communist-initiated engagements for the period between September 1966 and January 1967, the revised, accurate count was eighty-seven. The implications of the new numbers, Wheeler recognized immediately, were "major and serious." The MACV's statistics on large-scale enemy initiatives had been a principal element in its evaluations for the president, McNamara, Congress, and even the media. "In cold fact," the JCS chair admitted, "we have no other persuasive yardstick." As such, the new totals had just undermined America's *raison de guerre*. Wheeler could thus "only interpret the new figures to mean that, despite our force buildup, despite our many successful spoiling attacks and base area searches, and despite the heavy interdiction campaign in North Vietnam and Laos," the enemy was more effective than ever.[19]

Upon receiving the new estimates, Wheeler directed Westmoreland to suppress the statistics, cabling the MACV commander that "if these figures should reach the public domain, they would, literally, blow the lid off of Washington." He therefore told the MACV to do "whatever is necessary" to avoid disclosure of the new information. The JCS leader surely understood the political impact of the new appraisals. "I cannot go to the President," he said, "and tell him that contrary to my reports and those of the other chiefs as to the progress of the war . . . the situation is such that we are not sure who has the initiative in South Vietnam." But the president could not have been ignorant of that reality. Johnson, as Larry Berman has shown, "never intended" to escalate the war as the military was

Wheeler JCS 1691–67 to Sharp and Westmoreland, 6 March 1967, folder 363: Chief of Staff Message File, WNRC.

19. The original statistics showed 45 enemy-initiated engagements for the thirteen-month period beginning on January 1966; the revised figure was 179. Wheeler CJCS 1843–67 to Westmoreland and Sharp, 11 March 1967, Westmoreland Papers, folder 363: Eyes Only Message File, WNRC.

urging, and developments in Vietnam in early 1967 had reinforced that position.[20]

Wheeler's alarmist response to the MACV statistics showed that he, and certainly other U.S. officers, knew that conditions in Vietnam, rather than in the Pentagon or White House, had made success virtually impossible. Exacerbating such problems for the military, the SA office around that same time completed an extensive study of operations in Vietnam that found that MACV claims on enemy casualties were inflated by about 30 percent and, more important, discovered that the only engagements in which Communist losses were significantly higher than those of U.S. forces occurred when the PAVN or VC main-force units attacked entrenched American positions. Such attacks, however, had accounted for less than one-fourth of all large battles in 1966, and General Giap, sensing the failure of direct strikes, essentially abandoned such tactics until Tet 1968.[21]

Bad as the news was, the military once more sought to burden the president with responsibility for future failure with another huge request for reinforcements. In earlier force projections for 1967, known as Program IV, MACV officials assumed that the U.S. troop total would rise to about 550,000 by the end of the year. Due to economic and political problems in both the RVN and United States, however, the American force structure stood at 470,000. Such numbers were clearly inadequate for Westmoreland because "the enemy has increased his structure appreciably" in the RVN, Laos, and Cambodia. Pacification was another problem, with thirty-five of forty-seven provincial officials reporting that civic action programs were not developing satisfactorily in their areas. MACV intelligence added that the enemy "will continue to avoid combat unless it is on his terms," or, if badly hurt, would alter its course of action in ways that American operatives could not predict.[22]

20. Wheeler CJCS 1810–67 to Westmoreland, 9 March 1967, Westmoreland v. CBS, DA/ WNRC Files, box 2, folder: Suspense, WNRC; Larry Berman, *Lyndon Johnson's War* (New York, 1990), 31–4, 37, 224; see also source cited in previous note.
21. Enthoven and Smith, *How Much Is Enough?*, 295–7.
22. Westmoreland Message of 18 March 1967, reproduced in Krulak to Greene, 18 March 1967, HQMC Message File [Eyes Only Messages] 1966–7, MCHC; Westmoreland in *Pentagon Papers: Gravel*, 4:427–8; charts on pacification progress, Westmoreland Pa-

Such assessments were nothing new by March 1967. Nor was Westmoreland's response. As he had done repeatedly since 1964 the MACV commander followed a bleak evaluation of the war with another request for more troops, this time asking for four and two-thirds additional divisions, or about 201,000 soldiers, in the coming year. If authorized, the U.S. force in Vietnam would rise to over 670,000 by 1968, thereby allowing the MACV, it hoped, to destroy or neutralize the enemy's main-force units and root out the Communist infrastructure.[23] Westmoreland's strategy, as Krulak had charged almost eighteen months earlier, was amounting to an American bloodletting as the MACV commander consistently asked for more troops despite his awareness of the volatile and eroding situation into which they would be thrown. Whether Westmoreland sincerely believed that an additional 200,000 soldiers would turn the tide in Vietnam and bring victory in a short time was beside the point, then, because it was hardly likely that he could have expected Lyndon Johnson to approve that reinforcement in the spring of 1967.

Immediately after forwarding his proposal for more troops, Westmoreland met with the president and U.S. and Vietnamese officials at Guam, where the MACV commander tried to sell his program. To convince the others that he needed more troops to win a war of attrition, Westmoreland explained that "killing guerrillas is like killing termites with a screw driver, where you have to kill them one by one and they're inclined to multiply as rapidly as you kill them."[24] If the Communists maintained their capabilities, "the war could go on indefinitely." Following his briefing, Westmoreland noted the "looks of shock" on the faces of U.S. officials "who had obviously been hoping for some optimistic assessment."[25] Rostow, in a bit of understatement, found Westmoreland's presentation to be "conservative and non-promissory."[26] The record does

pers, folder 469 [2 of 3]: #13 History Files, 27 January–25 March 1967, WNRC; MACV J2 report, 18 March 1967, "An Assessment of the Enemy Situation," Westmoreland v. CBS, LC, box 1, folder: An Assessment of the Enemy Situation, WNRC.
23. Assessment of 18 March, cited in previous note; Johnson, *Vantage Point*, 369.
24. White House Report of Johnson's Trip to Guam, *DDRS*, 85, 002248.
25. Westmoreland in Miller, *Lyndon*, 572–3.
26. Rostow in Berman, *Lyndon Johnson's War*, 34.

not indicate whether anyone asked if 200,000 more screwdrivers could kill an indeterminate number of termites.

Wheeler's and Westmoreland's actions in March 1967 marked another pivotal point in the war. Up to that time U.S. military leaders, despite their awareness of military problems in the RVN, might have convinced themselves that America would turn the corner in Vietnam and begin to wear down the Communists. But after the new MACV statistics showed just how strong the enemy was, prompting Wheeler's anxiety and Westmoreland's massive troop request, American officers had to know that U.S. strategy in Vietnam had failed. Although they now faced nearly a half-million U.S. soldiers, and American firepower and airplanes, VC and PAVN forces had matched enemy escalation and remained as formidable as ever. Given those bleak conditions, there was no chance of receiving another 200,000 troops. Since the early 1960s, U.S. military officials had openly recognized the perils of intervention in Vietnam. Service leaders never felt compelled to go to war, yet always acquiesced to political imperatives and accepted new commitments in the RVN, including combat. In some sense, Wheeler, Westmoreland, and other officers had inherited war from John Kennedy and Lyndon Johnson, but by early 1967 it was clear that they had made the worst of it.

Following Westmoreland's new troop proposal and the Guam conference, military critics noted that the situation in Vietnam showed few visible signs of improvement. Although Westmoreland's conventional strategy should have served him well in the "decisive" northernmost provinces, where the war increasingly became a conflict between the Marine Corps and the PAVN in 1967, it was a "stalemate situation" at best, and Westmoreland had to declare I Corps a "holding area" since he preferred to deploy reinforcements "in more strategically important parts of Vietnam."[27] Ironically, the III MAF, the strongest military advocate of pacification, now faced "a major change in its orientation" and was

27. Westmoreland MAC 3474 to Sharp and Wheeler, 12 April 1967, "Situation in I Corps," Westmoreland Papers, folder 364: Eyes Only Message File, WNRC; General Westmoreland's Historical Briefing, 25 March 1967, Westmoreland Papers, folder 469 [1 of 3]: #13 History Files, 27 January–25 March 1967, WNRC; Allan Millett, *Semper Fidelis: The History of the United States Marine Corps* (New York, 1982), 583–96.

charged with the most intensive conventional warfare responsibilities, and left shorthanded at that, because nation building, as
Westmoreland saw it, was a "relatively unimportant endeavor,"[28]
despite the bloodletting that was taking place in I Corps. In retrospect, the fact that the Marines – who were most vigorously engaged in conventional operations throughout the conflict and
closest to Communist infiltration routes in the DMZ and Laos – so
consistently and forcefully advocated the alternative strategy of
civic action rather than firepower and interdiction provides perhaps the most damning indictment of American warfare possible
and shows that battlefield conditions, not political constraints,
determined the nature and outcome of the war.

With the enemy's strength growing in I Corps and Marine–Army
sniping over strategy continuing, the president, as Westmoreland
later put it, "wanted bad news like a hole in the head" in April
1967. As the commander prepared to visit Washington to press for
200,000 reinforcements, Wheeler informed him to expect intense
questioning over the ARVN contribution to the war. There was a
"wide impression" within the administration, he noted, that the
southern Vietnamese troops "have now leaned back in their fox-
holes and are content for us to carry the major share of combat
activity." Apparently, the president shared such views, for he told
the JCS chair that Westmoreland ought to discuss the matter with
Ky and "explore whether and how the South Vietnamese propose
to carry their fair share of the combat load." John Paul Vann, back
in Vietnam as a civilian pacification official, further testified to the
ARVN's weaknesses. Despite thirteen years of American assistance
and advice, Vann observed that "the problems of leadership in the
[RVNAF] have probably never been more serious."[29]

28. Summary of Westmoreland visit to CINCPAC, in Krulak to Greene, 21 April 1967,
    HQMC Message File [Eyes Only Messages], 1966–7, MCHC.
29. Wheeler JCS 2861–67 to Westmoreland, 19 April 1967, Westmoreland v. CBS, LC, box
    17, folder: MACV Backchannel Messages to Westmoreland, 1–30 April 1967, WNRC.
    Vann also scored American officers who were making sanguine predictions based on the
    ability of U.S. forces to kill large numbers of enemy soldiers in conventional engage-
    ments. Those claims, he asserted, only led American officials to have expectations that
    "cannot be supported by the hard facts of the actual security situation within most of
    South Vietnam." Such optimism, he added, was prevalent among the MACV's senior
    officers, but not sector, regiment, or battalion advisors, who rarely found the security
    situation adequate for pacification. John Paul Vann, Draft Working Paper, 2 April 1967,
    Vann Papers, folder: 1967, MHI.

Such problems in Vietnam surely troubled Lyndon Johnson, but it was the reinforcement issue that dominated his talks with Westmoreland and Wheeler. With the 1968 elections a year off, the president wanted more than ever to find a solution to the war. In February, he had offered the DRVN a bombing halt as a quid pro quo to end infiltration, but Ho rejected the deal. By springtime, many administration confidantes, including the Bundys, Komer, CIA officials, and members of the SA office, were expressing their reservations about any proposals to expand the war.[30] John McNaughton, an architect of intervention, now believed that "we have enough troops to do the job we should be doing." Besides that, "the enemy can in most cases avoid contact with our forces, thus neutralizing the effect of our deployments."[31] And McNamara remained convinced that the war of attrition, as Larry Berman wrote, would ultimately fail "as a military strategy as well as a presidential policy for political survival." Politically, then, major reinforcement was just not in the cards in early 1967.[32]

The president himself had made such concerns clear to Westmoreland and Wheeler when the MACV commander claimed that U.S. and ARVN forces had eroded enemy strength to the "crossover point" at which Communist losses exceeded input into the south. In response, Johnson wondered, "when we add divisions, can't the enemy add divisions? If so, when does it all end?" The president, typically concerned with possible PRC reactions to American escalation, also asked "at what point does the enemy ask for [presumably Chinese] volunteers?" The two generals did not reassure him. The insurgents had eight divisions already in the RVN, Westmoreland reported, and could add four more. By maintaining current U.S. troop levels of 470,000, "we would be setting up a meat grinder." With 100,000 additional forces the war "could well go on for three years," and even with maximum reinforcement to bring U.S. manpower to 670,000 it could continue for another

30. *Pentagon Papers: Gravel,* 4:438–42.
31. McNaughton notes, 16 May 1967, Warnke-McNaughton, box 2, folder: McNTN III-Drafts, 1967 (1), LBJL; see also Alain Enthoven, Systems Analysis, to McNamara, 4 May 1967, in ibid.
32. Berman, *Lyndon Johnson's War,* 37; for a detailed explanation of McNamara's views, see his memo to the president of 19 May 1967, VN C.F., NSF, boxes 74–5, folder: 2 EE, 1965–7, Primarily McNamara Recommendations re. Strategic Actions [1965–6], LBJL.

two years. Wheeler added that such a buildup would have important international repercussions. The JCS chair expected diversionary pressure from North against South Korea; Soviet moves in Berlin to force America to reinforce its thinning force structure in Europe; Chinese, Soviet, or Korean "volunteers" possibly going into the RVN; or even overt Chinese intervention into Vietnam or elsewhere in Southeast Asia. Like Che Guevara before him, Earle Wheeler was raising the specter of "two, three, many Vietnams." The JCS chair also admitted that the air campaign, the military's redundant answer to the problems of the war, "is reaching the point where we will have struck all worthwhile fixed targets except the ports."[33] As a result of such evaluations, on top of the blunt military reports arriving from Saigon, the president rejected the upper-limit request in April 1967. In fact, as General Douglas Kinnard observed, Westmoreland's request for a force level of 670,000 was "never seriously considered."[34]

The White House, however, did not interpret the events of early 1967 as proof of U.S. failure in Vietnam, so still tried to revitalize the war. The civilian leadership directed Wheeler to find new ways to increase the RVN's manpower contribution, "thereby reducing the need for US troops." In turn, the JCS asked Westmoreland to consider extending ARVN tours of duty, reenlisting previously released veterans, or reducing the draft age. While Westmoreland still wanted to expand the war to match the "increasing tempo and scale of the VC/NVN aggression" in the south, he also recognized that the "present intensity of civilian dissent" would inevitably temper such escalation. By May the commander knew that the American "political climate . . . militates against further substantial troop augmentation," at the very least until the Vietnamese themselves demonstrated their own contribution to the war.[35]

---

33. Notes on Discussion with the President, 27 April 1967, Warnke-McNaughton, box 2, folder: McNTN Drafts 1967 [2], LBJL; see also appendix to Wheeler to McNamara, 29 May 1967, VN C.F., NSF, boxes 81–4, folder: 3 E (1)b, 6/65–12/67, Future Military Operations in Vietnam, LBJL.
34. Johnson, *Vantage Point*, 369–71; Kinnard, *Secretary of Defense*, 98.
35. Wheeler JCS 3332 to Westmoreland and Sharp, 5 May 1967, Westmoreland v. CBS, LC, box 18, folder: MACV Backchannel Messages to Westmoreland, 1–31 May 1967, WNRC; Westmoreland to Ellsworth Bunker, 16 May 1967, "Mobilization of the Republic of Vietnam," Westmoreland Papers, folder 428: Signature File, May 1967, WNRC. Maxwell Taylor also sensed "a new wave of pessimism . . . pervading official

The importance of the early 1967 political maneuvering and decisions regarding the future of the war cannot be underestimated. Well before the decisive Tet Offensive, the White House and the JCS and MACV had clearly drawn the lines over which civil–military battles would be fought. The civilian leadership could see that success was hardly imminent, but it continued to reject unrestrained warfare. The military had recognized the continued peril of war in Vietnam as well, and was aware that it would not receive authority to fight without limits. The JCS and MACV knew that Johnson and McNamara would "avoid the explosive congressional debate and U.S. reserve callup" included in Westmoreland's program. Admiral Sharp, who never quit pressing for an unlimited air campaign, nevertheless admitted that "recent strikes in the Hanoi area have raised the temperature of the war in a manner which could elicit additional Soviet assistance to the North Vietnamese." Wheeler was more bleak, adding that, short of population bombing or closing ports – "neither of which would be politically acceptable" – the air war could not reduce infiltration into the south or coerce the DRVN into negotiations. The JCS chair also lamented the White House's understanding that "the Main-Force war . . . is stalemated . . . and there is no evidence that pacification will ever succeed in view of the widespread rot and corruption of the government, the pervasive economic and social ills, and the tired, passive and accommodation prone attitude of the armed forces of South Vietnam."[36]

Even if Wheeler did not subscribe to that description, there was widespread anxiety within the military, over both Vietnam and defense policy in general. The JCS "view[ed] with increasing concern the loss of the strategic initiative in Southeast Asia and the current restrictive worldwide US military posture." With its present force ceiling, the armed services could not vigorously prosecute the war in Vietnam, prepare for any contingencies in Southeast Asia, or

circles in Washington," but urged the president to intensify the air war as a way to overcome it. Taylor to Johnson, 11 May 1967, NSF, Memos to the President, Walt Rostow, box 16, folder: volume 27, LBJL.
36. Wheeler JCS 3891 to Westmoreland and Sharp, 26 May 1967, Westmoreland v. CBS, LC, box 18, folder: MACV Backchannel Messages to Westmoreland, 1–31 May 1967, WNRC; Wheeler JCS 4200 to Sharp and Westmoreland, 6 June 1967, ibid., folder: MACV Backchannel Messages to Westmoreland, 1–30 June 1967.

meet its commitments or new challenges elsewhere, the chiefs told McNamara. Such conditions were likely to worsen. Enemy forces in Vietnam now included sixty-eight PAVN and eighty-five VC infantry battalions in the south and four divisions in the DMZ, the PRC and Soviet Union had raised their assistance to the DRVN, and the northern air defense system was aggressive and expanding. Outside of Southeast Asia, the United States faced serious problems as well. The Soviet Union could still divert American attention from Indochina by staging actions in North Korea or Berlin; meanwhile North Africa, the Middle East, and Latin America continued to "exhibit a high potential for instability, subversion, and violence." With such international crises on the horizon, the chiefs again recommended that the White House significantly expand U.S. troop numbers and escalate the war in Vietnam in order to bring it to a timely conclusion and then "achieve an appropriate worldwide military posture."[37]

Specifically, they urged the president to approve Westmoreland's request for four and two-thirds additional Army divisions, increased Navy assets, and substantially more Air Force tactical fighters and reconnaissance aircraft. Once more the JCS proposed that Johnson activate Reserves and extend terms of service as well. Above all, the JCS wanted to expand Rolling Thunder to "curtail" the DRVN's efforts to support the war by destroying more human and material resources in the north.[38] Westmoreland, however, conceded that air operations had remained at a high peak over the past two months, yet enemy activity in the highlands had "stepped up significantly." Despite Pentagon claims that Ho was sending fewer men into the south, General Phillip Davidson, who had just replaced McChristian as the MACV intelligence chief, confessed that "if anything infiltration is increasing." Even though American attacks had caused huge losses and disrupted the enemy's time

---

37. JCSM-288–67, "Worldwide US Military Posture," NSF, Agency File, JCS, box 30, folder: Joint Chiefs of Staff [1 of 2], LBJL; Harold K. Johnson also pointed out the impact of Vietnam on America's worldwide commitments. The U.S. contribution to NATO was still the country's principal priority, he asserted, but the Army "certainly 'shorted' Europe of company commanders at this time," due to Vietnam. Harold K. Johnson, MHI Oral History Program, 19, used at CMH.
38. JCSM-312–67, 2 June 1967, VN C.F., NSF, boxes 81–4, folder: 3 E (1)a, 6/65–12/67, Future Military Operations in Vietnam, LBJL.

schedule, Westmoreland still believed that the Communists' overall plan remained in effect. The commander continued to assert, however, that American forces were dealing serious blows to the VC, and he remained optimistic that forthcoming offensive action would decisively hurt the enemy.[39]

Krulak again challenged Westmoreland's review of the situation in Vietnam. The Marine general charged that the commander still did not understand "the enemy's announced purposes and obvious capabilities," that the MACV had established no visible objectives for the future, and that Westmoreland still ignored the importance of pacification. Writing to Commandant Greene, Krulak pointed out the contradiction in Westmoreland's view of the war: while he had boasted of blunting the enemy offensive in I Corps, the MACV leader also admitted that Communist infiltration, strength, and armament had increased, and that the enemy position in the highlands was imposing. The VC and PAVN, Westmoreland claimed, had suffered 11,000 battle deaths in just two months, but Krulak questioned those numbers and pointed out that, even if true, the ratio of Communist to U.S.-RVN soldiers killed, about 4 to 1, was not as favorable as the commander believed.[40]

To Westmoreland, the American ability to meet expected Communist threats signaled the success of his strategy. Krulak countered that the United States could not "win" the war simply by "defending our positions and maintaining a good posture to meet each new enemy threat." To achieve victory, he reiterated, the MACV had to emphasize civic action, now referred to as "revolutionary development." Even if all the enemy main-force units in the RVN were to "vaporize" immediately, Krulak cautioned, U.S. forces "would still have a tremendous war on [their] hands in Vietnam." America's problems would be "much more manageable," he suggested, if U.S. personnel focused on eliminating the guerrilla

---

39. Westmoreland MAC 5310 to Sharp and Wheeler, 4 June 1967, Westmoreland Papers, folder 364: Eyes Only Message File, WNRC; Davidson, J2 MACV, 5287 to Peterson, J2 CINCPAC, 4 June 1967, Westmoreland v. CBS, Administrative Files, box 2, folder: BG [Brigadier General] Davidson's Messages, 1967–8 [2 of 2], WNRC.
40. Krulak to Greene, 10 June 1967, "Recent Operations in Vietnam," HQMC Message File [Eyes Only Messages], 1966–1967, MCHC; see also Krulak to Robert Cushman, 25 May 1967, and Krulak to Walt, 15 March 1967, both in Krulak Papers, box 2, folder: Correspondence, 1967–8, MCHC.

infrastructure rather than the big units. Victor Croizat, a retired Marine colonel conducting a study on Vietnam for the Rand Corporation, added that U.S. leaders may have read Mao, Giap, and Che Guevara, but – fighting the same enemy on the same terrain as the French had in the 1950s – had ignored the lessons of the First Indochina War to their detriment.[41]

Sharp, in another of his candid political evaluations, challenged the most recent JCS and MACV analyses of U.S. policy in Vietnam as well. Both the chiefs and Westmoreland had presented "unacceptable" courses of action to the president, as the admiral saw it. The reinforcements that the JCS requested "are simply not going to be provided," he understood. "The country is not going to call up the Reserves and we had best accept that." On the other hand, Sharp, like Krulak, saw Westmoreland's plans as a "blueprint for defeat." The CINCPAC, as unimaginative as ever, still relied on air power to alter conditions in Vietnam, but also urged Westmoreland to keep the pressure on the White House. "Continue to state your requirement for forces," he told the commander, "even though you are not going to get them."[42] Sharp later alleged in his memoirs that politicians in Washington stabbed the military in the back, but the admiral must have seen the knife headed his way well before the war had ended. Westmoreland too understood the political considerations involved in developing strategy. In a somewhat contradictory reply to his boss's charges, the commander "caution[ed] against too gloomy an appraisal" of his campaign plans, but he also told the admiral that their analyses of the situation in Vietnam were "identical." Accordingly, Westmoreland decided to seek a third course, somewhere between the JCS call for reinforcement and Reserves and his own plans.[43]

In the end, of course, Westmoreland would develop no new approach to the war. Instead he continued to request more troops and resources, despite Sharp's blunt awareness that they would not be

41. See sources cited in previous note; also Croizat in BDM, *Strategic Lessons,* volume 6, book 1, 1–16 to 1–18.
42. Sharp to Westmoreland, 13 June 1967, Westmoreland v. CBS, LC, box 18, folder: MACV Backchannel Messages to Westmoreland, 1–30 June 1967, WNRC.
43. Westmoreland MAC 5601 to Sharp, 13 June 1967, Westmoreland v. CBS, LC, box 18, folder: MACV Backchannel Messages from Westmoreland, 1–30 June 1967, WNRC; Sharp, *Strategy for Defeat.*

forthcoming, and despite similar warnings from Harold K. Johnson. "You are painfully aware of the problems ahead of us," the Army chief cabled Westmoreland, "if we cannot find some way to bring our authorized and operating strengths into line." Calling for "personnel economy" and greater "discipline" in requisitioning resources, Johnson asked for the commander's support to stem the problem before the Defense Department began to investigate the Army's handling of manpower issues.[44] The Pentagon boss, however, had already decided how to handle the request for additional troops and expanded air operations. To McNamara, even a more intense Rolling Thunder "would neither substantially reduce the flow of men and supplies to the South nor pressure Hanoi toward settlement." It would also cost an undue number of American lives and prompt even greater criticism of U.S. policy at home and overseas.[45]

After visiting Saigon in early July, the defense secretary was still steadfastly opposed to committing another 200,000 forces to Vietnam, Westmoreland's and Wheeler's rosy reports there notwithstanding. As a result, the president agreed to send more troops, but urged his advisors to "shave it as best we can." Johnson moreover told McNamara that the MACV should make better use of the U.S. troops already in Vietnam, reiterated that no Reserves would be activated to meet manpower requirements, and insisted that American officials convince the media that "there is no military stalemate." The president, in a compromise between the military and McNamara, also agreed to deploy another 45,000 troops to Vietnam, thereby raising U.S. strength there to 525,000. Surely the White House was not about to cut and run from the RVN, but the authorization was far below the military's request for minimal reinforcement and it presented another unmistakable sign that political conditions in Washington were not conducive to repeated pleas for additional forces.[46]

44. Johnson WDC 8419 to Westmoreland, 27 June 1967, Westmoreland v. CBS, LC, box 18, MACV Backchannel Messages to Westmoreland, 1–30 June 1967, WNRC.
45. McNamara to Johnson, 12 June 1967, "Alternative Military Actions Against North Vietnam," VN C.F., NSF, boxes 74–5, folder: 2 EE, 1965–7, Primarily McNamara Recommendations re. Strategic Actions [1965–6], LBJL.
46. Notes from Meeting of the President with Secretary McNamara to Review the Secretary's Findings during His Vietnam Trip, 12 July 1967, Tom Johnson's Meeting Notes,

Although not receiving the full measure of its troop request, the military forwarded upbeat reports on the war. The JCS, Westmoreland, and Sharp all boasted that the Rolling Thunder campaign, recently expanded by the president, had produced impressive results, destroying about 85 percent of the DRVN's sources of power, one-third of its railway system, and about 7,500 trucks and boats. American bombs, Westmoreland reported, had reduced the north's air defense capability by 50 percent, stopped production at DRVN steel and cement plants, and forced Ho to divert 500,000 people from other tasks to rebuild damaged areas.[47] MACV officials also contended that the land war was going well. American forces were providing security to southerners and maintaining constant pressure on the VC in populated areas, Westmoreland reported in August. In his assessment of the war, General Fred Weyand, an MACV commander in II Corps, saw "an enemy who is on the run, fighting only defensively," a sentiment echoed in Westmoreland's reports to Sharp.[48]

The president, despite his partial authorization, also seemed content with the situation in Vietnam, and pledged to do more. "We are going to send Westmoreland the troops he needs," Johnson told

box 1, folder: 12 July 1967, Meeting on McNamara Trip, LBJL; Notes of Meeting of the President with Rusk, McNamara, etc., 12 July 1967, ibid., folder: 12 July 1967, Tuesday Lunch Group; *Pentagon Papers: Gravel*, 4:511–28; MACV FY 68 Force Structure, July 1968, Westmoreland papers, folder 475: #19 History Files, 6 July–3 August 1967, WNRC.

47. JCS Memorandum, 2 March 1967, "Results of the Air Campaign against North Vietnam," attached to McNamara to President, 2 March 1967, VN C.F., NSF, box 74–5, folder: 2 EE, 1965–7, Primarily McNamara Recommendations re. Strategic Actions [1965–6], LBJL; Westmoreland to Bunker, 21 June 1967, Westmoreland Papers, box 12, folder: #18 History Files, 1 June–1 July 1967, LBJL; Remarks by CINCPAC at Briefing for Secretary of Defense and Others in Saigon, 5 July 1967, in Sharp, *Strategy for Defeat*, appendix D, 285–92.

48. General Westmoreland's Military Assessment for July, 11 August 1967, VN C.F., NSF, boxes 68–9, folder: 2 C (1)a, General Military Activity, LBJL; Weyand HOA 1263 to Westmoreland, 23 August 1967, Westmoreland v. CBS, LC, box 18, folder: Backchannel Messages to Westmoreland, 1–31 August 1967, WNRC; Westmoreland MAC 8073 to Wheeler and Sharp, 25 August 1967, Westmoreland Papers, folder 372: Eyes Only Message File, WNRC; see also Davidson MAC 7928 to Generals Brown, DIA, and Peterson, CINCPAC, 21 August 1967, Westmoreland v. CBS, Administrative Files, box 2, folder: BG Davidson's Messages, 1967–8 [2 of 2], WNRC; Westmoreland MAC 8068 to Wheeler and Sharp, 25 August 1967, Westmoreland Papers, folder 477: #21 History Files, 21 August–9 September 1967, WNRC; Westmoreland MAC 8095 to Wheeler and Sharp, 26 August 1967, Westmoreland Papers, folder 365: COMUSMACV Message File, WNRC.

Wheeler even after the defense secretary returned from Vietnam. In mid-August, as McNamara was trying again to limit air strikes over the north, Johnson observed that "it doesn't look as though we have escalated enough to win." Even so, the president told Democratic congressmen that Westmoreland "has turned defeat into what we believe will be a victory."[49] Johnson, however, was not so sanguine when domestic political affairs intervened in considerations of policy making for Vietnam. Dr. Martin Luther King, Jr., the president's ally on civil rights legislation in 1964 and 1965, had broken with the White House over the war, charging that the United States was the "greatest purveyor of violence in the world today" and that the Great Society had died on the battlefields of Vietnam.[50] The economy was causing equally serious problems. Not only would the president have to refuse appropriations for infrastructure repairs, but, with the deficit nearing $30 billion, Johnson knew that he would have to raise revenues and cut defense spending. Increased taxation, however, would only turn more Americans against the war, while the military was sure to fight any reduction in its budget.[51]

The president also faced a virtual mutiny from senators in his own party. Fulbright, the leading Senate critic of Johnson and the war, told the president that Vietnam was "ruining our domestic and our foreign policy" and that he was considering bottling up the Foreign Assistance bill in committee. Several southern Democrats, usually loyal Johnson supporters, were also unnerved by the political fallout from Vietnam. Richard Russell, John Stennis, Robert Byrd, and Ernest Hollings, among others, had a "general feeling that we are on a treadmill in Viet Nam." The United States was "vastly overcommitted," Stennis had told Hollings, but was none-

---

49. Notes of President's Meeting with McNamara, etc., 14 July 1967, Tom Johnson's Meeting Notes, box 1, folder: 14 July 1967 – 12:50 P.M., LBJL; notes of the President's Meeting with McNamara, etc., 8 August 1967, ibid., folder: 8 August 1967 – 1:25 P.M.; Notes of the President's Meeting with Democratic Congressmen, 8 August 1967, ibid., folder: 8 August 1967 – Democratic Congressmen, LBJL.
50. King in James Cone, *Martin and Malcolm and America: A Dream or A Nightmare* (New York, 1992), 237.
51. Notes of the President's Meeting with Lester Maddox, 2 February 1967, Tom Johnson's Meeting Notes, box 1, folder: 2 February 1967 – Meeting with Lester Maddox, LBJL; Notes of Meeting with Senate Committee Chairmen, 25 July 1967, ibid., folder: 25 July 1967 – 6:10 p.m., LBJL.

theless "fighting at the level the enemy dictates." Clark Clifford, who had just returned from a trip with Maxwell Taylor to press American allies for greater involvement in Vietnam, told foreign heads of state that the president faced great budget problems and public disenchantment with the war and thus would have to limit the U.S. role in Vietnam some time soon. The American people, Clifford observed, were asking, "if we have to put this much money in the war, what are our allies going to do?" Given such conditions, it was clear to Johnson that the "greatest deterrent" to finding a solution to the war was the "anticipation in Hanoi that we won't be able to hold out in America."[52]

Johnson had correctly judged public displeasure with the war, but he could have acknowledged that there were great impediments to progress in Vietnam as well as at home. John Chaisson, a Marine general and director of the MACV Combat Operations Center (COC), lamented that, after several years in the RVN, American troops could still not adequately protect U.S. airfields. The "most significant tactical issue" in Vietnam in August 1967, he told Marine debriefers, was finding some way to prevent Communist rockets from "plastering the airbases." A VC attack on the Marine base at Da Nang alone had caused about $40 million in damage. The Army was at even greater risk, Chaisson charged, because "every one of their air bases is wide open." This problem was particularly disturbing because the airfield strikes were the enemy's "cheapest investment in manpower and energy," yet had brought great returns in damage on American installations.[53]

Although not adequately protecting their bases, Air Force and Marine leaders did find time to have "quite a rhubarb," as Chaisson described it, over control of air assets in I Corps. The Air Force

---

52. See source cited in previous note; Rostow to Johnson, 1 August 1967, VN C.F., NSF, box 56 (initially found in DSDUF, Vietnam, box 2, folder: Country File Vietnam, box 56), LBJL; Notes of the President's Meeting with Clifford and Taylor, 5 August 1967, Tom Johnson's Meeting Notes, box 1, folder: 5 August 1967 – 1:49 P.M., LBJL; Clifford-Taylor Report to the President, 5 August 1967, VN C.F., NSF, boxes 85–91, folder: 5 D (1), 3/67–1/69, LBJL; Notes of President's Meeting with Harry Reasoner, CBS, 14 August 1967, Tom Johnson's Meeting Notes, box 1, folder: July 1967–May 1968 – Meetings with Correspondents, LBJL; see also Notes of President's Meeting with Democratic Congressmen, 9 August 1967, Tom Johnson's Meeting Notes, box 1, folder: 9 August 1967 – 9:02 A.M., LBJL.

53. General John Chaisson Debriefing, 1 August 1967, in Chaisson Oral History Transcript, 61–3, MCHC.

commander in Vietnam, General William Momyer, refused "under any circumstance" to coordinate his operations with the Marine Corps near the DMZ. For their part, III MAF leaders wanted to employ their own aircraft at their discretion, without receiving Air Force approval via the chain of command.[54] Such infighting had earlier prompted Marine aviator General Keith McCutcheon to observe, only half-jokingly, that "in addition to fighting the VC, we are still fighting the Air Force. They are like Notre Dame, they never give up. We are not going to give up either." Eighteen months later, the general's words still rang true, and American efforts suffered accordingly.[55]

While McCutcheon scored the Air Force, Krulak continued to nip at Westmoreland's flanks. Even though 80 percent of the RVN's population and 90 percent of its wealth resided in the coastal lowlands, the MACV commander was still sending American forces into the "infertile and insignificant" mountain areas further to the west to chase after PAVN units. To the Marines, such tactics were a "maldeployment of forces, [and] a misapplication of power." Yet the corps had "carried out their orders loyally" since 1965, but had "never been shaken of their knowledge where victory really lies," namely civic action.[56] Army leaders, in response, scored the Marines's "beach head mentality" and planted stories critical of the III MAF in U.S. newspapers, prompting Krulak to complain to other media representatives of "an artesian flow of anti-Marine sentiment" within the MACV. The Vietnam War, it is safe to say, was a dreadful experience for the Marines. Its soldiers suffered significant casualties in fighting near the DMZ, the corps experienced serious manpower shortages as the war dragged on, and the commitment to Southeast Asia had a "devastating impact" on other Marine forces, especially the Atlantic fleet.[57]

Other officers were also apprehensive about the war. Admiral Sharp, increasingly concerned with public attitudes on the war,

54. Chaisson Debriefing, 63–5, MCHC.
55. McCutcheon to Col. M. R. Yunck, 7 February 1966, Keith McCutcheon Papers, box 20, MCHC.
56. Krulak presentation at 1967 General Officers Symposium, FMFPac, n.d., Krulak Papers, box 2, folder: Trip Reports, Briefings, 1967, MCHC.
57. Krulak to Don Neff, 25 October 1967, Krulak Papers, box 1, MCHC; Millett, *Semper Fidelis,* 579–80.

complained that service leaders had "trapped ourselves" by attempting to quantify the strategy of attrition by using the enemy body count as a gauge of progress, while at the same time ignoring America's broader objectives in Vietnam. Sharp also lamented that the American public considered Rolling Thunder a failure because the air strikes had failed to reduce infiltration, which did not seem like an illogical interpretation.[58] Westmoreland himself offered a rather oblique endorsement of the war. Because of American pressure, he contended, the enemy's strength was declining, although "not spectacularly and not mathematically provable." As a result, the commander believed that U.S. forces "may have" reached the crossover point, a claim he made with more authority during his talks with the president four months earlier. Westmoreland, it would seem, believed that the military situation in the RVN had validated his strategy of attrition. The commander, however, also argued for more troops and matériel because U.S. combat units were originally structured for conventional war, whereas, he had the temerity to observe, "we now are fighting a counterinsurgency war in the tropics."[59]

Conditions inside Vietnam may have been open to different interpretations, but in Washington the chiefs agreed that it was time to confront the president on his handling of the war, in particular the air campaign. Although Johnson had authorized substantially expanded bombing runs against the north in April, American commanders continued to criticize the restraints under which they operated.[60] General McConnell, the Air Force chief of staff, was, along with Sharp, the strongest military advocate of Rolling Thunder. By mid-1967, however, the limited air war had prompted him to lament, "I can't tell you how I feel . . . I have never been so goddamn frustrated by it all . . . I'm so sick of it."[61] Such alienation came out

58. Sharp to Wheeler and Westmoreland, 3 August 1967, Westmoreland Papers, folder 372: Message File, WNRC.
59. Westmoreland Background Session with Media, 17 August 1967, Westmoreland Papers, folder 476 [2 of 2]: #20 History Files, 4–20 August 1967, WNRC; Westmoreland MACJ321 to Deputy CG, USA, VN, 24 August 1967, "Force Requirement Review," Westmoreland Papers, folder 431: COMUSMACV Signature File, August 1967, WNRC.
60. Clodfelter, *Limits of Air Power*, 106–7.
61. McConnell in Thomas Boettcher, *Vietnam: The Valor and the Sorrow* (Boston, 1985), 242.

clearly in August when Senator Stennis, chair of the Preparedness
Investigating Subcommittee of the Senate Armed Services Committee, opened hearings on the air war. Stennis, hoping to offset
Fulbright's antiwar hearings, gave the military an open microphone
with which to blast civilian control of the war over the north.
Wheeler thus charged that the administration's failure to increase
pressure against the DRVN was making it impossible for the United
States to win the war. Unless the president authorized the military's
full target list, including attacks on Haiphong harbor, significant
progress was unlikely.[62]

McNamara, testifying after the JCS chair, challenged Wheeler's
analysis. The White House had approved 302 of 359 suggested
targets, about 85 percent of the chiefs' list, the secretary of defense
maintained. The military may have believed that Rolling Thunder
was a failure because of imposed restraints, but as McNamara saw
it the air war was going well, making infiltration more costly and
difficult. The chiefs could not believe such claims. The defense
secretary had simply dismissed their evaluation of the air campaign
and had rejected the JCS argument that American pilots would
have to shut off the flow of supplies from Communist allies to the
DRVN, rather than focus on the south, to win the war. McNamara,
in essence, told the nation that the U.S. air war had a negligible
impact at best in the RVN.[63]

The JCS–McNamara feud then set off what might have become
the gravest crisis in civil–military relations in modern U.S. history.
The chiefs believed that they had been betrayed by their civilian
superiors and did not expect a successful conclusion to the war.
Harold K. Johnson, expecting the worst, feared that the military
would "take the fall" for the impending disaster, and he noted "a
very substantial closing of the ranks" among the chiefs.[64] The JCS

62. Perry, *Four Stars,* 161–3; Clodfelter, *Limits of Air Power,* 106–7; Kinnard, *Secretary of
    Defense,* 104–5.
63. Perry, *Four Stars,* 163–5; Shapley, *Promise and Power,* 432–3; Sharp, *Strategy for
    Defeat,* 187–98.
64. Harold K. Johnson, MHI Oral History Program, 10, used at CMH; from 1966 onward,
    Lawrence Korb pointed out, the JCS tended to work out its differences prior to meeting
    with McNamara and, by presenting him with a united front on important issues, get
    more of what it wanted. For instance, the Air Force had wanted thirty-five wings of
    tactical aircraft and the Navy sought seventeen attack carriers, both requests that the
    defense secretary was not likely to authorize. But, before meeting with McNamara,

closed ranks so much that, at the chair's suggestion, the respective service leaders apparently agreed to resign en bloc to protest Johnson's and McNamara's conduct of the war. In August 1967 Wheeler wanted the president to "make an unambiguous stance in Vietnam – or get out," but, especially after McNamara's testimony, it was clear that Johnson would choose neither of those stark options. Claiming that it was being blamed for an intervention over which it had no control, the military opted to publicly disavow Lyndon Johnson, and the Vietnam war as well.[65]

The chiefs ultimately did not follow through on their threatened resignation, and Wheeler in fact denied to the president in November that the JCS had even considered quitting.[66] Nonetheless, it was obvious that civil–military relations had fallen to new depths. In retrospect, however, the events of August 1967 may have been the natural outcome of the political battles that political and military officials had been waging since the New Look and Bay of Pigs controversies. Despite its public optimism and constant calls for escalation, the military, in truth, always recognized that it probably would not achieve success in Vietnam, and feared that its institutional integrity and influence would diminish as the war worsened. By mid-1967, victory was more unlikely than ever, so the chiefs, fearing that they would be blamed for the failure, more directly than ever tried to pin the White House with responsibility for the war. After forcing Johnson to refuse authorization for more troops and bigger operations, American officers escalated their own political tactics in August. With Wheeler blasting administration policy at the Stennis hearings and the JCS considering group resignation, the military gave a clear signal that it would engage the president in political warfare in Washington.

For the remainder of the year, then, public relations became an even more critical factor in developing U.S. policy for Vietnam. While being careful to "avoid charges that the military establishment is conducting an organized propaganda campaign, either

---

Wheeler pressed the services to agree on asking for twenty-nine wings and fifteen carriers, which the secretary agreed to fund. Korb, *Joint Chiefs of Staff,* 115–16.
65. See sources cited in previous note; also Korb, *Joint Chiefs of Staff,* 117, 175–6; Korb, *Fall and Rise of the Pentagon,* 115.
66. Notes on NSC Meeting, 29 November 1967, Tom Johnson's Meeting Notes, box 1, folder: 29 November 1967 – 12 Noon NSC Meeting, LBJL.

overt or covert," Westmoreland found it imperative to counter media reports of military inaction or stalemate. Despite challenging a report by the journalist Peter Arnett that the RVNAF was essentially paralyzed, the commander had to admit that leadership problems still plagued the ARVN, "corruption is everywhere," night operations were unproductive, U.S. advisors were having difficulty working with their Vietnamese counterparts, and the desertion rate remained high.[67] In addition, Westmoreland, Sharp, and Harold K. Johnson, the acting JCS chair at the time, were all concerned with the heavy casualties American forces were suffering in the northern provinces, both because of their political impact and because of the limited operational benefits that were "not consistent with the losses incurred."[68]

Nor were they compatible with the political heat the MACV was taking. In a *New York Times* article, an unnamed U.S. general charged that Westmoreland's continued need for reinforcements "is a measure of our failure with the Vietnamese." The president seemed to agree, directing the JCS to "search for imaginative ideas . . . to bring this war to a conclusion." The chiefs, the president told Harold K. Johnson, should not "just recommend more men or that we drop the Atom bomb" since he "could think of those ideas" himself.[69] Creativity was apparently in short supply, however, as the MACV still insisted that the enemy was weakening and that U.S.-ARVN forces had taken the initiative. Although the president claimed to have approved all but 19 of 479 recommended targets, the JCS continued to score the White House for imposing limits on

67. Westmoreland MAC 7180 to Wheeler, Johnson, Sharp, 2 August 1967, Westmoreland v. CBS, LC, box 18, folder: MACV Backchannel Messages from Westmoreland, 1–31 August 1967, WNRC; Westmoreland MAC 8875 to McConnell and Sharp, 20 September 1967, Westmoreland Papers, folder 478: #22 History Files, 10–30 September 1967, WNRC.
68. Johnson JCS 7987 Sep 1967 to Sharp and Westmoreland, 25 September 1967, and Sharp to Westmoreland, 26 September 1967, both in Westmoreland v. CBS, LC, box 25, folder: Backchannel Traffic, July 1966–June 1968 [1 of 2], WNRC; Westmoreland to Johnson and Sharp, 27 September 1967, Westmoreland Papers, folder 365: COM-USMACV Message File, WNRC.
69. NYT quotation in Wheeler JCS 6336 to Westmoreland and Sharp, 8 August 1967, Westmoreland Papers, folder 372: Eyes Only Message File, WNRC; Jim Jones Memorandum to the President, 11 September 1967, "Weekly Luncheon," Meeting Notes File, box 2, folder: September 12, 1967, LBJL.

the air war, and said it did not expect to break the DRVN's will if the present pace of Rolling Thunder was not accelerated. Wheeler even continued to press for full mobilization and activation of Reserves, requests that the president of course refused again.[70]

By late 1967 there was no chance that the president would escalate the war to the levels that the military was proposing. The costs of the air war were soaring – the United States was losing almost $2 billion worth of aircraft over the skies of Vietnam annually and spending another $7.5 billion on flight instruction and training aircraft – and McNamara had again presented Johnson with a long report outlining his belief that "continuation of our present course of action in Southeast Asia would be dangerous, costly in lives, and unsatisfactory to the American people." Though not as pessimistic as the defense secretary, Dean Rusk also advised against expanding American ground operations into northern Vietnam, Laos, and Cambodia, or flying sorties against Hanoi and Haiphong, where U.S. pilots would be vulnerable to anti-aircraft fire. The president himself, while opposing McNamara's call for a bombing halt and a standdown in ground operations, did agree that additional American troops would not be sent to Vietnam and that the ARVN would have to take over the war.[71]

Indeed, Johnson had been complaining to Wheeler for some time that the ARVN was avoiding its share of military action. "Why aren't [the Vietnamese] bearing their share of the burden," the president wondered. "Why does this have to be a white man's war?" Many Americans apparently were asking the same questions, causing the president to bemoan the "deteriorating public

70. Davidson to Peterson, 18 September 1967, Westmoreland v. CBS, Administrative Files, box 2, folder: BG Davidson's Messages, 1967–8 [2 of 2], WNRC; Wheeler JCSM-555-67 to McNamara, 17 October 1967, "Increased Pressure on North Vietnam," VN C.F., NSF, boxes 74–5, folder: 2 EE, 1965–7, Primarily McNamara Recommendations re. Strategic Actions [1965–6], WNRC, and in *Pentagon Papers: Gravel*, 4:210–1; Notes of President's Meeting with Colonel Robin Olds, 2 October 1967, Tom Johnson's Meeting Notes, box 1, folder: 2 October 1967 – 11:50 A.M., LBJL; Perry, *Four Stars*, 173.
71. McNamara to Johnson, 1 November 1967, "A Fifteen Month Program for Military Operations in Southeast Asia," VN C.F., NSF, boxes 74–5, folder: 2 EE, 1965–7, Primarily McNamara Recommendations re. Strategic Actions [1965–6], LBJL; Rusk to Johnson, 20 November 1967, and Lyndon Johnson, Memorandum for the File, 18 December 1967, VN C.F., NSF, box 127, folder: March 19, 1970 . . . I, LBJL; Enthoven and Smith, *How Much Is Enough?*, 276, 281.

support" for the war.[72] Facing such criticism regarding ARVN inactivity, Westmoreland blamed the media and politicians who had
derogated the Vietnamese military's skills. Rather than put pressure
on southern commanders to reform their units, the MACV commander opted for a political solution, namely a public relations
campaign to improve the ARVN's image in the United States.[73]
Such a response was not surprising. By that time, civilian and military officials were engaged in a determined battle to avoid blame
for Vietnam. Johnson, aware that "our people will not hold out for
four more years," was desperately seeking a way out of the war,
even proposing to halt all attacks against the north to bring Ho into
negotiations, the so-called San Antonio Formula, an offer that the
DRVN leader rejected. Despite such problems with the Vietnamese
Communists, the president asserted that "the main front of the war
is here in the United States."[74]

General William Yarborough, now in Washington as the Army's
assistant chief for intelligence, agreed. Upon observing antiwar
demonstrations in the nation's capital in late 1967, he feared that
"the empire was coming apart at the seams."[75] Though not so
alarmist, Westmoreland, preparing to depart for a late November
public relations blitz in Washington, did realize that the president
expected his commander to bring home good news about the war in
Vietnam.[76] In Saigon, however, bad news seemed to be spreading.
Various reports from the field challenged Westmoreland's rosy estimates about reaching the crossover point, and Marine officials
noted an "enormous buildup" of enemy troops throughout I Corps
and in Laos. More important, a new MACV Order of Battle study

72. Wheeler JCS 9298 to Westmoreland and Sharp, 31 October 1967, Westmoreland v.
    CBS, LC, box 19, folder: MACV Backchannel Messages to Westmoreland, 1–31 Octo-
    ber 1967, WNRC; Notes of Cabinet Meeting, 4 October 1967, Cabinet Papers, box 10,
    folder: Cabinet Meeting, 10/4/67 [1 of 4], LBJL.
73. Westmoreland 36743 to MACV Officers, 9 November 1967, Westmoreland Papers,
    folder 437: COMUSMACV Signature File, 1967, WNRC.
74. Notes of the President's Meeting with Rusk, McNamara, etc., 3 October 1967, Tom
    Johnson's Meeting Notes, box 1, folder: 3 October 1967 – 6:10 P.M., LBJL; Meeting
    with Saigon Advisors, 21 November 1967, ibid., folder: 21 November 1967 – 8:30 a.m.;
    San Antonio Formula in *Pentagon Papers: Gravel*, 4:678–80, and in Johnson, *Vantage
    Point*, 267.
75. Yarborough quoted in Alexander Cockburn's column, *Nation*, 3 May 1993, 583.
76. Transcript of CBS Reports, "The Uncounted Enemy: A Vietnam Deception," broadcast
    on 23 January 1982, Westmoreland v. CBS, DA/WNRC Files, box 1, WNRC.

had found that VC and PAVN numbers were increasing throughout the RVN. Westmoreland, several MACV intelligence officials would later charge, ordered the new figures suppressed because, he apparently told his former intelligence chief, General McChristian, they would create a "political bombshell" in Washington.[77]

Such allegations and Westmoreland's subsequent and litigious denial are not as important as the political realities underlying such developments. "I am in deep trouble," Lyndon Johnson had earlier admitted, so by late 1967, he had to have good news; not only the war but his political future depended on it. But, given his refusal to escalate, the military saw little reason to accept responsibility for the situation in Vietnam or to develop a way out that might benefit the president. Accordingly, Westmoreland, during his visit in late November, offered a rosy view of the war. Citing enemy losses and RVNAF improvements, the MACV leader anticipated that the Vietnamese themselves would increasingly take responsibility for the war and, within two years, some U.S. troops would begin to withdraw. Although he expected tough times ahead, Westmoreland could see "some light at the end of the tunnel."[78]

Although Westmoreland had received favorable reviews for his performance in Washington, American officials remained reluctant to widen the war. Thus Rusk, McNamara, who had decided to resign as defense secretary, and Clark Clifford, his successor at the Pentagon, all opposed Westmoreland's plan to extend operations into Cambodia and north of the DMZ in an effort to damage PAVN forces. That kind of escalation, they warned, would invite international condemnation of American aggression and provoke greater

77. "The Uncounted Enemy," Westmoreland v. CBS, DA/WNRC Files, box 1, WNRC; Norman Anderson Oral History, 178, MCHC; Westmoreland MAC 8068 to Wheeler and Sharp, 25 August 1967, Westmoreland Papers, folder 477: #21 History Files, 21 August–9 September 1967, WNRC; Wheeler JCS 9567 Nov 67 to Sharp and Westmoreland, 9 November 1967, "Effect of Bombing," Westmoreland v. CBS, LC, box 19, folder: MACV Backchannel Messages to Westmoreland, 1–31 November 1967, WNRC.
78. Notes of the President's Meeting with Educators from Cambridge, Mass., 26 September 1967, Tom Johnson's Meeting Notes, box 1, folder: 26 September 1967 – 5:46 P.M., LBJL; Westmoreland, November 1967, "Notes for Talk with the President," Westmoreland Papers, folder 481 [1 of 3]: #25 History Files, 13–28 November 1967, WNRC; Westmoreland HWA 3445 to Abrams, 26 November 1967, Westmoreland v. CBS, box 19, folder: MACV Backchannel Messages from Westmoreland, 1–30 November 1967, WNRC.

division and dissent within the United States. McNamara was
"scared to death" of fighting outside of the RVN because "the war
cannot be won by killing North Vietnamese [but] only . . . by
protecting the South Vietnamese so they can build and develop
economically for a future political contest with North Vietnam."[79]
Although not explicitly agreeing with McNamara, Harold K.
Johnson was alarmed by Westmoreland's recent moves, particularly
his prediction of success. The Army chief, writing to General
Creighton Abrams, now the MACV deputy commander in Saigon,
could only hope that Westmoreland "has not dug a hole for himself
with regard to his prognostications. The platform of false prophets
is crowded!"[80]

Admiral Sharp's views were more ambiguous, but uncomfortable
just the same. While maintaining that the enemy was badly hurt
and at a critical juncture in its war in the south, the CINCPAC also
knew that the VC remained a formidable foe. More important,
Sharp again emphasized that political factors were driving the war,
and, accordingly, he expected the VC to try to stage some type of
offensive action in early 1968 to increase protests in the United
States and therefore force the president to accept a Communist-
dominated coalition government. Even if such plans failed, the
enemy would "revert to his proclaimed strategy of a protracted
war," albeit at a reduced pace.[81] General John Chaisson offered a
more pointed, and more bleak, analysis. During a radio interview
on New Year's Day 1968, the COC director, just six weeks after his
boss saw light at the end of the tunnel, asserted that there was "a
long road ahead of us in winning this war." Nearly 90 percent of the
geographic area of the RVN and over one-third of the population
were under Communist influence, he admitted. The enemy, though
pounded and weakening, had disrupted the pacification program,

79. Notes of the President's Meeting with Rusk, McNamara, Wheeler, etc., 5 December
    1967, Tom Johnson's Meeting Notes, box 1, folder: 5 December 1967 – 6:02 P.M., LBJL.
80. Johnson WDC 15663 to Abrams, 22 November 1967, Abrams Papers, box: Cables,
    June 1967–June 1972, folder: Dep COMUSMACV, 23 June 1967–4 June 1968, MHI.
81. Though Sharp's warning seems prescient in light of the January 1968 Tet Offensive, the
    admiral also believed that "the likelihood of a final effort in the Winter-Spring offensive
    somewhere after Tet cannot be discounted, but remains remote." Sharp to Wheeler and
    Westmoreland, 26 December 1967, Westmoreland v. CBS, LC, box 25, folder: Back-
    channel Traffic, July 1966–June 1968 [1 of 2], WNRC; CINCPAC to JCS, January
    1968, "1967 Progress Report," in Sharp, *Strategy for Defeat,* appendix G, 301–4.

could still put an effective army in the field, and had a "great ability" to absorb American attacks, rebuild, and fight again. Chaisson thus saw no value to escalating the war, a move that could bring on Chinese intervention. Although not "unduly pessimistic," Chaisson believed that the United States faced "a very difficult military [and] . . . political operation" in Vietnam, and so he found it impossible to predict how much longer the war would take.[82]

Like fellow Marine officers, Chaisson also questioned Westmoreland's strategy. The MACV commander was still focused on, if not obsessed with, the enemy threat in the highlands rather than, as Chaisson and others had advised, the situation near the DMZ or pacification, and he was diverting troops to II Corps from more important areas. Even though U.S. operations had caused substantial losses in II Corps, the Marine general questioned their value. "Is it a victory," he asked, "when you lose 347 friendlies in three weeks," as done in fighting near Kontum in October, "and by your own spurious body count you only get 1200?" Because of such operations, Chaisson, unlike Westmoreland, believed that "we're not anywhere near close to a decision in this country." The Communists were "far from dead," as evidenced by the enemy's ability to "crank up the offensive from one end of the country to the other," as it had done in 1967. American forces, Chaisson anticipated, would "have to do an awful lot of hard, dirty fighting" in 1968.[83]

At the outset of 1967 American military officials had expected an intensified war in Vietnam. The enemy, U.S. generals knew, was capable of expanding its human and material commitment in the south and could pose grave challenges to the American-RVN military position. If the accounts of Chaisson, Sharp, and even Westmoreland and Wheeler are any indication, the situation had not changed appreciably during the year, despite their otherwise positive assessments and sanguine predictions. In reality, service critics,

82. Chaisson interview on WBOR, 1 January 1968, in Chaisson Oral History Transcript, 84–101, MCHC.
83. Chaisson presentation at HQMC, 2 January 1968, in Chaisson Oral History Transcript, 118–23, 141–2, MCHC.

as they had done since U.S. forces began fighting in Vietnam, lamented the enemy's capabilities, complained of the ARVN's short-comings, and criticized American strategy throughout the year. During 1967, U.S. forces in Vietnam killed huge numbers of Communist soldiers, but, as Victor Krulak, Wallace Greene, Harold K. Johnson, and others had warned, that slaughter did not alter the outcome of the war.

As conditions in Vietnam failed to improve, the situation in Washington worsened too. Throughout the year, the political battleground at home became as intense and important as the fighting in southern Vietnam. Civil–military relations, never harmonious to begin with, steadily deteriorated as the White House rejected the military's proposals to expand the war and the president tried to distance himself from responsibility for future failure. "This is not Johnson's war," he told journalist Chalmers Roberts. "This is America's war. If I drop dead tomorrow, this war will still be with you."[84] The president was only partly right, however. The conflict might continue no matter who occupied the Oval Office, but was surely Lyndon Johnson's war just the same.

American military leaders too sought ways to avoid responsibility for the ill-fated effort to preserve the RVN. Even if politicos to that point believed that their approach to Vietnam might work, by late 1966 and early 1967 it was clear that conditions in Vietnam and at home were not changing. Yet the armed forces continued to stay the course and intensified the political maneuvering that had characterized the war from its outset, rather than reappraising its policies or even considering disengagement. Thus Earle Wheeler feared that the release of figures on Communist military action would "blow the lid off" of Washington in March, and Westmoreland likewise understood that statistics on increased enemy infiltration would create a "political bombshell" at home in November. Under intense pressure to produce results, the chiefs closed ranks, as Harold K. Johnson observed, and nearly resigned as a way of humiliating the president and the secretary of defense. If the JCS had to close ranks in midyear, however, one can assume that it was

---

84. Notes of the President's Meeting with Chalmers Roberts of the *Washington Post*, 13 October 1967, Tom Johnson's Meeting Notes, box 1, folder: July 1967–May 1968 – Meetings with Correspondents, LBJL.

earlier divided, and therein lay a fundamental problem for the United States throughout the year, indeed throughout the war.

At no time were American military leaders unified on their goals, needs, or strategy in Vietnam. Variously recommending accelerated air power, pacification programs, search-and-destroy operations, or attritional warfare, American officers could not devise the means to achieve success in their war against Vietnamese nationalists-cum-Communists. By 1967, they faced a frightening situation, with the war going badly, under intense political pressure at home, and facing rampant drug use, fraggings, and dissent among American soldiers in the field.[85] Despite such salient and clearly recognized problems, however, there would be no agonizing reappraisal of the war, either at MACV headquarters, JCS offices, or the White House. Instead the president and Westmoreland, among others, knew that military victory was unlikely but put on their best faces and publicly proclaimed that success was at hand. Events in early 1968 would show otherwise. The platform had indeed been crowded with false prophets.

85. The breakdown of morale among U.S. soldiers, and the concomitant increase in drug use, antiwar activity, and racial problems, was a critical factor in the brass's approach to the war by the later 1960s, with many generals wanting to get out of Vietnam simply to preserve the military as an institution. This subject clearly demands further attention. The best sources so far include Harry Haines, ed., *GI Resistance: Soldiers and Veterans against the War*, special issue of *Vietnam Generation* no. 1 (1990); David Cortright, *Soldiers in Revolt: The American Military Today* (Garden City, N.J., 1975); Edward L. King, *The Death of the Army: A Pre-Mortem* (New York, 1972).

10

The Myth of Tet:
Military Failure and the Politics of War

> We suffered a loss, there can be no doubt about it.
> Harold K. Johnson[1]

The light at the end of the tunnel, William Childs Westmoreland's critics would later joke, was a train headed toward the general, and on the night of 29–30 January 1968, it thundered through the RVN. On that date the enemy began its Tet Offensive, a countrywide series of attacks that would in short time effectively signal America's defeat in Vietnam. Coming just months after U.S. officials were so publicly optimistic about the war, the offensive instead validated the previous warnings of so many military officials and precipitated the final stage in the civil–military crisis that had been developing over the years prior to 1968. Militarily, the United States, after three years of intense combat, could not contain the enemy in southern Vietnam. Politically, the American people were no longer willing to support a war without measurable success or without an end in sight. When, on 27 February 1968, Walter Cronkite, broadcasting from Vietnam, urged disengagement from the war "not as victors but as an honorable people who lived up to their pledge to defend democracy, and did the best they could," it was evident that the United States would not soon or successfully conclude its involvement in Indochina. "If I've lost Cronkite," the president lamented, "I've lost middle America."[2] Lyndon Johnson, it went without saying, had lost the war as well.

1. Johnson WDC 3166 to Westmoreland and Abrams, 1 March 1968, Westmoreland Papers, folder 380: Eyes Only Message File, WNRC.
2. Cronkite in Don Oberdorfer, *TET!* (New York, 1984), 250–1, and in Braestrup, *Big*

311

Over the past decades the Tet Offensive has become probably the central event in considerations of Vietnam. Indeed, as many conservative military and political figures see it, Tet serves as a metaphor for the entire war. The United States was actually successful during Tet, they argue, but had its best efforts undermined at home by the media, the peace movement, and craven politicians who had forced American soldiers to fight with "one hand tied behind their backs." So in reality the United States achieved a decisive military victory but suffered an equally conclusive political and psychological defeat.[3] Even scholarly critics of the war have generally accepted that view, essentially agreeing that "Tet was, as the military believed, a great American victory."[4]

The military's own evaluations and analysis of Tet belie such claims. From the outset of the offensive, Westmoreland, Wheeler, MACV officers, and other military critics recognized that Tet had posed new and even more intense, probably intractable, difficulties for the United States. As Clark Clifford, secretary of defense during

broadcast from Vietnam, see, among others, Oberdorfer, Braestrup, Kathleen Turner, *Lyndon Johnson's Dual War: Vietnam and the Press* (Chicago, 1985); and Herbert Schandler, *Lyndon Johnson and Vietnam: The Unmaking of a President* (Princeton, N.J., 1977).

   Military leaders themselves immediately recognized that Tet marked a definite turning point in the war. The chair of the Joint Chiefs of Staff, General Earle Wheeler, told the president that it was "the consensus of responsible commanders" that 1968 would be a pivotal year. The war might continue but would not return to pre-Tet conditions. Wheeler to Johnson, 27 February 1968, "Report of the Chairman, J.C.S., on Situation in Vietnam and MACV Requirements," in *Pentagon Papers: NYT* 615–21. Similarly General Edward Lansdale, special assistant at the U.S. embassy in Saigon, asserted that 1968 would be a "year of intensity," a "change point" in history, as a result of the Tet Offensive. Lansdale to Members, U.S. Mission Council, 21 March 1968, "Viet-Nam 1968," Lansdale Papers, box 58, folder 1511, Hoover Institution. Later, Bruce Palmer forthrightly added that Tet "ended any hope of a U.S. imposed solution to the war." *25-Year War,* 103.

3. For interpretations of Tet as a military victory but psychological/political defeat, see, among others, Westmoreland, *A Soldier Reports;* Johnson, *Vantage Point;* Taylor, *Swords and Plowshares;* Sharp, *Strategy for Defeat;* Dave Richard Palmer, *Summons of the Trumpet: U.S.-Vietnam in Perspective* (San Rafael, Calif., 1978); Oberdorfer, *TET!;* Braestrup, *Big Story;* Sharp and Westmoreland, *Report on the War in Vietnam.*

4. Quotation is in Loren Baritz, *Backfire* (New York, 1985), 180; see also FitzGerald, *Fire in the Lake;* Sandra Taylor, "Vietnam: America's Nightmare, Lyndon's War," *Reviews in American History* 18 (March 1990): 130–6. For different interpretations of Tet, see, among others, Chalmers Johnson, *Autopsy on People's War* (Berkeley, 1973); Asprey, *War in the Shadows;* Krepinevich, *The Army and Vietnam;* Sheehan, *A Bright Shining Lie;* Kolko, *Anatomy of a War;* David Hunt, "Remembering the Tet Offensive," in Marvin Gettleman et al., eds., *Vietnam and America: A Documented History* (New York, 1985): 355–72.

the Tet crisis, observed, "despite their retrospective claims to the contrary, at the time of the initial attacks the reaction of some of our most senior military leaders approached panic."[5] Indeed the U.S. military recognized its dilemma in Vietnam at once. Despite public assertions of success, American officers candidly reported that conditions in the south had deteriorated, that the RVN government and military lacked the means necessary to recover effectively, and that the Communists were replacing their losses and remained a viable and effective threat. In addition to noting such problems, military leaders also understood that civilian officials – who had rejected substantively escalating the war long before Tet – had been shocked and unnerved by the enemy offensive. Yet in late February Westmoreland and Wheeler requested 206,000 additional troops and the activation of 280,000 reservists.

Rather than change course after Tet, the military had thus sent notice that it would continue to rely on its now discredited war of attrition. That approach, however, again reflected the armed forces' political rather than military appraisal of the war. The MACV and JCS had recognized the enemy's capacity to match American reinforcements, thus seriously limiting the value of any additional troop deployments, and were also aware that the president and McNamara were adamantly opposed to escalating the war and calling up Reserves. Under those circumstances it hardly seems likely that Westmoreland and Wheeler could have expected the White House to approve such an immense reinforcement request.

But given the nature of civil–military relations over the decade preceding Tet, the political maneuvering over the reinforcement request had a certain logic. By February 1968, it was clear to U.S. policy makers in both Saigon and Washington that they would not "win" in Vietnam. Military leaders, who had also seen their privileged position in the American political system and culture progressively erode during the war, then requested additional troops in such vast numbers in order to shift the burden for the conduct of the war more forcefully onto the president. Long aware of the

---

5. Clark Clifford with Richard Holbrooke, *Counsel to the President: A Memoir* (New York, 1991), 474; Clark Clifford and Richard Holbrooke, "Annals of Government (The Vietnam Years – Part II)," *New Yorker* (13 May 1991), 52.

parlous nature of the war, and angry and frustrated by their inability to defeat the enemy and by Johnson's vacillating and indecisive approach to Vietnam, Westmoreland and Wheeler forced the president into the dilemma of either deploying 206,000 more troops, activating the Reserves, and causing inestimable public hostility, or of rejecting the request and thereby providing the armed forces with an alibi for future problems. Barely a month later, Lyndon Johnson's political career was ending, and U.S. officers were charging that civilians were tying their hands in Vietnam. The military's political performance in Washington had exceeded its battlefield efforts in the war.

Less than two months after Westmoreland's tour of the White House, the halls of Congress, and the National Press Club, the MACV began to anticipate large-scale enemy action, and in late January the PAVN massed perhaps 40,000 troops for an attack on U.S. outposts at Khe Sanh, in the northwest RVN near the Laotian border, just below the seventeenth parallel.[6] By late spring, it would become clear that Khe Sanh had been a DRVN ruse to draw U.S. troops from urban centers in anticipation of the Tet attacks. Nonetheless, Westmoreland – facing 20,000 PAVN forces with 6,000 U.S. soldiers – decided to make a stand at Khe Sanh, ultimately expending over 100,000 tons of munitions there. At the same time, he warned of the enemy's "threatening posture" in the north, and also anticipated further Communist initiatives, warning of a "country-wide show of strength just prior to Tet." Wheeler similarly warned that the MACV "is about to have the most vicious battle of the Vietnam War." And during a press briefing just days before the Tet attacks began, General Fred Weyand, one of Westmoreland's deputies, admitted that "there is no question about it, the South Vietnamese Army is outgunned by the Vietcong."[7]

6. Westmoreland to Wheeler and Sharp, 15 January 1968, in Vietnam: A Documentary History – Westmoreland v. CBS, Clearwater Publishing Company, Microform, Joint Exhibit (JX) 400, microfiche card 699 (hereafter cited as Westmoreland v. CBS with appropriate document numbers).
7. Westmoreland to Wheeler, 20 January 1968, subject: Tet Ceasefire, Westmoreland v. CBS, JX 402, card 709; see also Westmoreland to Sharp, 21 January 1968, JX 402, card 699 and Westmoreland assessment of situation, 22 January 1968, JX 981, card 816; Notes of

Wheeler and Weyand were right. Taking advantage of a Tet New Year cease-fire, roughly 60,000 PAVN and VC forces attacked virtually every military and political center of importance, even invading the U.S. embassy grounds. Initially Westmoreland, still focusing on the war in the northern provinces, argued that the attacks were a Communist diversion to move military emphasis from I Corps and Khe Sanh in particular, but he also claimed that the U.S. forces had the situation "well in hand" while President Johnson interpreted the attacks as a "complete failure" for the DRVN.[8]

General Weyand, however, pointed out that the enemy had successfully concentrated on "remunerative" political and psychological objectives in its attacks. Wheeler likewise admitted that the Communist presence was expanding because "in a city like Saigon people can infiltrate easily. . . . This is about as tough to stop as it is to protect against an individual mugging in Washington, D.C." General Edward Lansdale, now serving as special assistant to Ambassador Ellsworth Bunker in Saigon, also lamented that Tet had practically "destroyed all faith in the effectiveness" of the government of the RVN, brought Vietnamese morale "dangerously low," and made southern villagers even more "vulnerable to further VC exploitation." Still worse, any possible American countermeasures appeared to Lansdale to be "rather shopworn and inadequate."[9]

General Chaisson elaborated on such problems. "We have been faced with a real battle," he admitted at a 3 February briefing in Saigon, "there is no sense in ducking it; there is no sense in hiding it." Because of its coordination, intensity, and audacity, Chaisson had to give the Communists "credit for having engineered and planned a very successful offensive in its initial phases." Moreover, the DRVN and VC had withheld their main-force and PAVN units

the President's Luncheon Meeting, 25 January 1968, Tom Johnson's Meeting Notes, box 2, folder: January 25, 1968, LBJL; Weyand in *NYT*, 29 January 1968.

8. Westmoreland to Wheeler and Sharp, 30 January 1968, VN C.F., NSF, boxes 68–9, LBJL: Westmoreland phone report to Walt Rostow, *DDRS*, 79, 367C; Notes of the President's Foreign Affairs Luncheon, 30 January 1968, Tom Johnson's Notes, box 2, folder: 30 January 1968 – 1 P.M., LBJL; Wheeler to JCS, 31 January 1968, VN, NSF, boxes 68–9, LBJL; transcript of President Johnson's press conference in *NYT*, 2 February 1968, 8.

9. Weyand in *NYT*, 31 January–1 February 1968; Wheeler to JCS, 31 January 1968, VN C.F., NSF, boxes 68–9, LBJL; Lansdale to Bunker, 2 February 1968, "GVN Actions," Lansdale Papers, box 57, folder 1510, Hoover Institution; for maps of Tet attacks, see Oberdorfer, *TET!*, 123, 135, 199.

in many areas, with Westmoreland pointing out that the enemy "continues to maintain a strong capability to re-initiate attacks country-wide at the time and place of his choosing." Although Chaisson then concluded that the Communists' sizable casualties might eventually constitute a "great loss," his analysis had revealed the depth and nature of the MACV's dilemma as a result of the offensive.[10]

The JCS in Washington also recognized the perilous situation, conceding that "the enemy has shown a major capability for waging war in the South." But on 3 February the brass requested an intensified bombing campaign against Hanoi, even though the scope of the Tet attacks had demonstrated the ineffectiveness of air power in preventing or containing enemy initiatives. Once more, the military's approach to deteriorating conditions in the south seemed like a non sequitur. Despite admitting that grave problems existed, the armed forces asked for bold but unsound responses that placed the burden for a decision firmly on the shoulders of civilian officials in Washington.[11]

As Washington debated the bombing request and the full dimensions of Tet began to emerge, military officials remained worried. "From a realistic point of view," Westmoreland reported to Wheeler, "we must accept the fact that the enemy has dealt the GVN a severe blow. He has brought the war to the towns and cities and has inflicted damage and casualties on the population. . . . Distribution of the necessities has been interrupted . . . and the economy has been disrupted. . . . The people have felt directly the impact of the war." As a result, the RVN faced a "tremendous challenge" to restore stability and aid those who had suffered. But Westmoreland's report ended on an upbeat note. Because enemy losses were sizable and the VC had not gained political control in the south, he contended, the offensive had been a military failure.[12]

10. Chaisson press briefing, 3 February 1968, Westmoreland Papers, folder 9, WNRC; COMUSMACV 29/68 to VMAC, 4 February 1968, Westmoreland Papers, folder 389: COMUSMACV Outgoing Message File, WNRC.
11. *Pentagon Papers: Gravel,* 4:234–6.
12. Westmoreland to Wheeler, 4 February 1968, in NSC History, "The War in Vietnam, March 31st Speech," box 47, volume 2, LBJL (also in University Publications of America microform edition; hereafter cited as NSC History, "March 31st Speech," UPA.

Westmoreland then contradicted himself, making the crucial recognition that the enemy's objectives were finally clear and "they
were primarily psychological and political." The Communists, he
observed, sought to destroy southern faith in the government of the
RVN, intimidate the population, and cause significant desertions
among the ARVN. The DRVN's military objectives, Westmoreland
admitted, may have been secondary to its political goals, and included diverting and dispersing U.S. forces throughout the south.
The enemy, moreover, posed major threats at many areas, including
Saigon, Khe Sanh, the DMZ, and at Hue, and more attacks were
likely. Thus at the same time that Westmoreland claimed military
success, he conceded that the Communists were engaged in psychological and political warfare. Throughout the next two months, his
and other officers' reports would further reveal that the enemy
criteria for success – undermining the southern government and
military, prompting popular discontent, and destabilizing American policy – had indeed been accomplished throughout the RVN.[13]

Such military concern was further evident when Westmoreland
and the JCS, on 9 February, reported that the DRVN had added
between 16,000 and 25,000 troops in the Khe Sanh area and continued to pose a threat of "major proportions." The enemy,
Wheeler predicted, "is going to take his time and move when he has
things under control as he would like them." To that end, PAVN
infiltration had risen from 78 to 105 battalions and the ratio of U.S.
and ARVN forces to Communist troops, which had been 1.7 to 1,
was now at 1.4 to 1. The Communists were also applying heavy
pressure in Hue and Da Nang, had cut off the much-traveled Hai
Van pass, and threatened Highway 1 – the major transportation
route in southern Vietnam. In Quang Tri and Thua Thien, in northernmost I Corps, the controlling factor in America's performance
would be logistics, which Westmoreland admitted were "now marginal at best" even though he had redirected the 101st Airborne
Division and 1st Cavalry Division to the north. But further to the

Citations will be from box 47 of the LBJ Library or reel 6 of the UPA microfilm edition).
    See also Westmoreland to Wheeler, 4 February 1968, DSDUF, Vietnam, box 4, folder:
Vietnam, box 69, folder: 2C (4), LBJL, and NSC History, "March 31st Speech," UPA.
13. Westmoreland cable, 8 February 1968, *DDRS*, 85, 001576.

south, the MACV claimed, the enemy posed no serious threat.[14] The ally, however, did.

Extensive damage to lines of communication and populated areas, heavy casualties – about 9,100 between 29 January and 10 February – and significant desertion rates had riddled the ARVN. Accordingly, Westmoreland urged RVN President Nguyen Van Thieu to lower the draft age to eighteen to increase the armed forces by at least 65,000 troops, the number depleted in the initial Tet attacks. "Realistically," the MACV commander lamented, "we must assume that it will take [the ARVN] at least six months to regain the military posture of several weeks ago." Consequently, Westmoreland, for the first time since Tet, asked for additional forces. Wheeler had encouraged the MACV commander to seek reinforcements, but admitted he could not guarantee them. "Our capabilities are limited," the JCS chair explained, with only the 82d Airborne Division and half of a Marine division available for deployment to Vietnam. Nonetheless, as Wheeler saw it, "the critical phase of the war is upon us" and the MACV should not "refrain in asking for what you believe is required under the circumstances." The JCS chair's timing in raising the reinforcement issue was appropriate, for Westmoreland had thinned out III Corps by transferring forces to the north after a PAVN strike at Lang Vei days earlier. That diversion had troubled the MACV because it needed those forces to fight the enemy's main-force units and support pacification, but the commander did not see it as an unacceptable risk.[15]

It was "needless to say," however, that Westmoreland would welcome reinforcements to offset casualties and ARVN desertions, to react to the DRVN's replacement of southern forces, which was conditioning the MACV's own plans, and to put friendly forces in a better position to contain Communist attacks in the north and take

14. Notes of President's Meeting with the JCS, 9 February 1968, Tom Johnson's Notes, box 3, folder: 9 February 1968 – 11:02 A.M., LBJL, and in Westmoreland v. CBS, JX 1608, card 872. See also Westmoreland to Wheeler and Sharp, 9 February 1968, in NSC History, "March 31st Speech," UPA, and in *DDRS*, 79, 368B; Westmoreland to Wheeler, 12 February 1968, DSDUF, Vietnam, box 70, folder: 2C(5), GMA, LBJL.
15. Westmoreland to Wheeler, in previous note; *Pentagon Papers: NYT*, 593–6; COMUSMACV 30/68 to VMAC, 4 February 1968, Westmoreland Papers, folder 389: COMUSMACV Outgoing Message File, WNRC.

the offensive if given an opportunity. Again Westmoreland finished an otherwise frank evaluation of the military situation in southern Vietnam with a non sequitur: high hopes that additional forces would facilitate greater U.S. success.[16] Washington was not so enthusiastic. Having turned down the JCS's bombing request three days earlier, on 9 February the Pentagon directed the chiefs to furnish plans to provide for the emergency reinforcement of the MACV. The resulting back-channel memoranda between Westmoreland and Wheeler demonstrated that the military understood that its position in Vietnam was untenable.

Although the MACV publicly claimed that only pockets of resistance remained, Wheeler told the president that the JCS "feel that we have taken several hard knocks. The situation can get worse."[17] In fact, at a 12 February meeting, White House officials found that Westmoreland's reports had raised as many questions and concerns as they had answered. The MACV reports from Vietnam had made the president and his advisors anxious and they had interpreted Westmoreland's messages and requests for reinforcements as indications of the ARVN's weaknesses and evidence that the troubled logistics and transport systems in the north had made deployment of additional forces imperative simply to maintain the American position.[18]

Such candid reports continued to unnerve Johnson, who wondered "what has happened to change the situation between then [initial optimism] and now." Maxwell Taylor, the president's military advisor, also "found it hard to believe" that the bleak reports reaching Washington were "written by the same man," Westmoreland, as the earlier optimistic cables. Against that backdrop Wash-

16. See sources cited in previous note.
17. Notes of President's Meeting with Senior Foreign Policy Advisors, 9 February 1968, *DDRS*, 85, 000747; Notes of President's Meeting with JCS, 9 February 1968, Tom Johnson's Notes, box 2, folder: 9 February 1968 – 11:02 A.M., LBJL; Report on RVNAF strength, February 1968, *DDRS*, 79, 369C; briefing on VC/PAVN threat, 11 February 1968, Westmoreland v. CBS, JX 759, card 775; Westmoreland cable for Sharp, 11 February 1968, Papers of Clark Clifford, box 4, folder: 2d set [Memos on Vietnam: February 1968], LBJL; Notes of President's Meeting with Senior Foreign Policy Advisors, 11 February 1968, Clifford Papers, ibid.
18. Wheeler memo to the President, 12 February 1968, Clifford Papers, box 4, folder: 2d set [Memos on Vietnam: February 1968], LBJL; Wheeler to Westmoreland, 12 February 1968, NSC History, "March 31st Speech," UPA, and in Westmoreland v. CBS, JX 664, card 758; *Pentagon Papers: Gravel*, 4:539.

ington began to discuss the reinforcements issue. The president and McNamara reiterated their reservations over additional deployments because of the impact of Tet and the spiraling financial burdens of the war. General Taylor, however, believed that the situation was urgent, interpreting Westmoreland's cables as proof that "the offensive in the north is against him."[19]

Westmoreland told the White House that defeat was not imminent. Nonetheless, he admitted that he could not regain the initiative without additional forces, and he warned that "a setback is fully possible" without reinforcements, while it was "likely that we will lose ground in other areas" if the MACV had to continue diverting forces to I CTZ. But Westmoreland still maintained that the enemy's strong position at Khe Sanh and the DMZ, not the VC infrastructure in the cities, was the most serious threat, and if it was not contained the U.S. position in the northern RVN would be in jeopardy. The MACV commander also expected another Communist offensive in the north, which he pledged to contain either with *"reinforcements, which I desperately need,"* or at the risk of diverting even greater numbers of forces from other areas. Thus far, Westmoreland added, Vietnam had been a limited war with limited objectives and resources, but, as a result of Tet, "we are now in a new ballgame where we face a determined, highly disciplined enemy, fully mobilized to achieve a quick victory."[20]

19. Westmoreland to Sharp, 11 February 1968, Clifford Papers, box 4, folder: 2d set [Memos on Vietnam: February 1968], LBJL; Notes of President's Meeting with Senior Foreign Policy Advisors, 11 February 1968, Clifford Papers, ibid.; Taylor to Johnson, 12 February 1968, VN C.F., NSF, box 108, folder: 8 I, 1/67–12/68 [2 of 2], LBJL; Report on RVNAF Strength, February 1968, *DDRS*, 79, 369C; Briefing on VC/PAVN threat, 11 February 1968, Westmoreland v. CBS, JX 759, card 775.
20. Emphasis in original. Westmoreland added that the United States had yet to open Highway 1 from Danang and Highway 9 to Khe Sanh, two tasks that were "not unreasonable" if reinforcements were provided. But, the MACV commander explained, even the redeployment of the 101st Airborne from III CTZ to the north "will put me in no better than a marginal posture to cope with the situation at hand." Expecting the enemy to "go for broke" in the Quang Tri–Thua Thien area, Westmoreland was confident that he could contain a Communist offensive. He warned Wheeler, however, that he would have to maintain the U.S. position in other CTZ, which was already a difficult task and was being exacerbated by lack of troops. Westmoreland to Wheeler and Sharp, 12 February 1968, Clifford Papers, box 2, folder: the White House [Vietnamese War], Memos on Vietnam: February–August 1968, LBJL; NSC History, "March 31st Speech," UPA; *DDRS*, 79, 369A.
    In relating Westmoreland's report to the president, Wheeler told Johnson that, without reinforcements in I Corps, the MACV would have to take "unacceptably risky"

Based on such communication with Westmoreland, the JCS developed its analysis for McNamara. As of 11 February, the chiefs noted, the PAVN and VC had attacked thirty-four provincial towns, sixty-four district towns, and all of the autonomous cities. Despite heavy losses, the enemy had yet to commit the vast proportion of its northern forces, while the PAVN had already replaced much of its losses and equaled U.S. troop levels in I Corps. Westmoreland and his deputy Creighton Abrams were moreover concerned that the ARVN was relying even more on American firepower to avoid combat and that widespread looting was alienating the population. The ARVN, additionally, had suffered its worst desertion rates to that point. Its average battalion was at 50 percent strength, its average Ranger Battalion was at 43 percent strength, and five of nine airborne battalions were not combat-effective, according to MACV standards.[21]

Even when using questionable criteria such as enemy losses or inability to capture control of government as measures of military success, the MACV and JCS appraisals pointed out increasing problems. As a result, the chiefs had strong reservations about reinforcing the MACV. Admiral Sharp had urged the White House to meet Westmoreland's request, arguing that additional forces could exploit enemy weaknesses. If U.S. officials had underestimated Communist strength, he added, "we will need them even more." Nonetheless the JCS warned that transferring forces to Vietnam would drain the strategic reserve and exacerbate shortages of skilled personnel and essential equipment. Thus for the first time the chiefs rejected a MACV request for additional support. "At long last," the *Pentagon Papers* authors explained, "the resources

courses such as diverting huge numbers of forces from elsewhere in the RVN. The JCS chair moreover noted that it would be mandatory to open and keep open transportation in the north, and "that will cost troops." Wheeler memo for Johnson, 12 February 1968, NSC History, "March 31st Speech," UPA; *Pentagon Papers: Gravel*, 4:539–40.

21. *Pentagon Papers: Gravel*, 4:539–40; Abrams PHB 154 to Westmoreland, 23 February 1968, Westmoreland Papers, folder 377a: COMUSMACV Message File, WNRC; though the enemy may have lost, through kill or capture, over 30,000 forces, it had nonetheless committed only about 20 percent of its northern forces, with those employed mainly as gap fillers where VC forces were not adequate to launch a full-scale offensive. The PAVN, which had added about twenty-five battalions in three months, might thus begin another round of attacks. Report of JCS (12 February 1968), in Westmoreland v. CBS, JX 453, card 715; see also, Clarke, *Advice and Support*, 327–9; Kolko, *Anatomy of a War*, 259–60.

Masters of War

were beginning to be drawn too thin, the assets became unavailable, the support base too small."[22]

The JCS had rejected Westmoreland's plea for more troops principally to pressure the president to activate Reserves in the United States, or face responsibility for continued deterioration. But McNamara on 13 February directed that an emergency force of 10,500 soldiers, including the remainder of the 82d Airborne – the only readily deployable division among continental U.S. forces – be sent to Vietnam to reconstitute the MACV reserve and to "put out the fire." President Johnson hoped that the additions would reinforce stretched lines and guard against another series of enemy attacks, but clearly the defense secretary and president were not about to increase their commitment in Vietnam by that point. Westmoreland, however, remained alert to the VC threat in the cities and continued to expect a major PAVN blow at Khe Sanh and accordingly sought at least another six combat battalions. At the same time MACV officials and General Lansdale continued to warn of future enemy action and point out problems associated with the ARVN. Because of such appraisals and mounting American losses – for the week of 10–17 February 543 U.S. soldiers were killed and over 2,500 wounded – the president remained anxious about the U.S. position in Vietnam and dispatched Wheeler to Saigon on 23 February to review the situation.[23]

Wheeler visited Westmoreland from 23 to 25 February and filed his report with the president on 27 February. The chair's appraisals contrasted sharply with public optimism about the war. As Westmoreland publicly continued to claim success – concluding that he did "not believe Hanoi can hold up under a long war" – Wheeler

22. *Pentagon Papers: Gravel,* 4:539–40; Sharp to Wheeler, 12 February 1968, NSC History, "March 31st Speech," UPA.
23. *Pentagon Papers: Gravel,* 4:238, 542–6; *NYT,* 14 February 1968, 16; Rostow to Johnson, re. General Johnson's report on conversation with Westmoreland, 22 February 1968, Clifford Papers, box 2, folder: Mr. Clark Clifford, LBJL, and *DDRS,* 82, 001264; Lansdale to Bunker and Westmoreland, 23 February 1968, subject: IV Corps, Lansdale Papers, box 57, folder 1510, Hoover Institution.

With regard to Khe Sanh, the president gave what appeared to be a rather backhanded vote of confidence to the MACV strategy when he asserted that "if General Westmoreland wishes to defend Khe Sanh he will be supported; if he wishes to avoid a major engagement in a fixed position which does not utilize the peculiar mobility of U.S. forces, he will also be supported." In Department of Defense Report, 15 February 1968, *DDRS,* 85, 000052.

told reporters that he saw "no early end to this war," and cautioned that Americans "must expect hard fighting to continue." Privately, Wheeler was more pessimistic.[24]

The JCS chair, a skilled veteran of Pentagon politics, was losing confidence in the MACV commander and, as Clark Clifford put it, "presented an even grimmer assessment of the Tet offensive than we had heard from Westmoreland and Bunker."[25] "There is no doubt that the enemy launched a major, powerful nationwide assault," Wheeler observed. "This offensive has by no means run its course. In fact, we must accept the possibility that he has already deployed additional elements of his home army." The JCS chair also admitted that American commanders in Vietnam agreed that the margin of success or survival had been "very small indeed" during the first weeks of Tet attacks. The enemy, with combat-available forces deployed in large numbers throughout the RVN, had "the will and capability to continue" and its "determination appears to be unshaken." Although the enemy's future plans were not clear, he warned, "the scope and severity of his attacks and the extent of his reinforcements are presenting us with serious and immediate problems." Several PAVN divisions remained untouched, and troops and supplies continued to move southward to supplement the 200,000 enemy forces available for hostilities. The MACV, however, still faced major logistics problems due to enemy harassment and interdiction and the massive redeployment of U.S. forces to the north. Westmoreland in fact had deployed half of all maneuver battalions to I Corps while stripping the rest of the RVN of adequate reserves.[26]

Worse, Wheeler, though surprisingly pleased with the ARVN's performance, nonetheless questioned its ability to continue, pointing out that the army was on the defensive and had lost about one-

24. Wheeler and Westmoreland in *NYT*, 26 February 1968; see transcript of Wheeler telephone conversation in Rostow to Johnson, 25 February 1968, *DDRS*, 84, 002989.
25. Clifford with Holbrooke, *Counsel to the President*, 480, and "The Vietnam Years," 58.
26. Wheeler's February reports concerning his trip to Saigon can be found in several sources, including Johnson, *Vantage Point*, 390–3; Clifford Papers, box 2, folder: Memos on Vietnam: February–March 1968, LBJL; *DDRS*, 79, 382B and 383A; NSC History, "March 31st Speech," UPA; *Pentagon Papers: Gravel*, 4:546ff.; *Pentagon Papers: NYT*, 615–21; Notes of President's Meeting to discuss General Wheeler's trip to Vietnam, 28 February 1968, Tom Johnson's Notes, box 2, folder: 28 February 1968 – 8:35 A.M., LBJL.

quarter of its pre-Tet strength. Similarly, the government of the RVN had survived Tet, but with diminished effectiveness. Thieu and Ky faced "enormous" problems, with morale at the breaking point, 15,000 civilian casualties, and a flood of about 1 million additional refugees, one-third in the area of Saigon – all part of the huge task of reconstruction, which would require vast amounts of money and time. The offensive moreover had undermined pacification. Civic action programs, Wheeler admitted, had been "brought to a halt. . . . To a large extent, the VC now control the countryside." He added that the guerrillas, via recruiting and infiltration, were rebuilding their infrastructure and its overall recovery was "likely to be rapid." Clearly, then, the military had developed its analyses and policy recommendations in February 1968 from candid, at times desolate, views of the effects of Tet. Later claims of success aside, in February Wheeler at best found the situation "fraught with opportunities as well as dangers" and conceded that only the timely reaction of U.S. forces had prevented Communist control in a dozen or so places." Whereas Harold K. Johnson plainly admitted that "we suffered a loss," Wheeler, more euphemistically, admitted that "it was a very near thing."[27]

Having been concerned up to Wheeler's visit with the shorter-term results of Tet, the military understood clearly throughout February 1968 that the enemy offensive had created dynamic new problems for its forces in Vietnam. Subsequently, Tet entered its "second phase" and the MACV and JCS began to discuss longer-term policy in the wake of the enemy's attacks. Yet, in doing so, service leaders continued to acknowledge problems in the RVN but still rejected developing new approaches to the war. Instead, they insisted that the MACV simply continue its war of attrition, but

27. See sources cited in previous note; for figures on civilian deaths and refugees, see Clifford with Holbrooke, *Counsel to the President,* 473; for criticism of the ARVN, see Abrams PHB 154 to Westmoreland, 23 February 1968, Westmoreland Papers, folder 377a: COMUSMACV Message File, WNRC; on the impact of the refugee problem, see Sheehan, *Bright Shining Lie,* 712; John Paul Vann and Lansdale also stressed the damage done to the pacification effort during Tet. See Vann to ACS, CORDS, n.d., "DIOCC-Ops-ICEX [Elimination of the VCI]," and Vann to Komer, 5 March 1968, subject: Attack on the Infrastructure, John Paul Vann Papers, folder: 1968, MHI; Lansdale to Bunker, 27 March, 7 May, 12 May 1968, Lansdale Papers, box 58, folders: 1511 and 1513, Hoover Institution; on Harold K. Johnson's appraisal, see quotation at beginning of chapter.

with a huge increase in American soldiers – 206,000 troops and the activation of 280,000 reservists. With such a proposal, which "simply astonished Washington" and "affect[ed] the course of the war and American politics forever," in Clark Clifford's words, the brass had conceded that substantive success would not be forthcoming, but left it to the president to accept responsibility for subsequent military failures in Indochina.[28] Wheeler's reports and request caused a political hurricane in Washington in February 1968 and, since then, have had central places in considerations of Tet. While scholars correctly point to Wheeler's candid assessments as proof of American problems in Vietnam, they tend to see the subsequent reinforcement request as a military response to the crisis: having failed to stem the enemy's advances with 525,000 forces, the military sought a 40 percent increase in troop strength to either stave off defeat or take the offensive, and also to replenish the strategic reserve at home.[29] There was, however, an essentially political character to the proposal for additional troops. Even before the crises of February and March 1968, military and civilian leaders understood that the political environment in Washington had made reinforcement – especially in such vast numbers – impossible.

Wheeler recognized the pervading gloom in the White House, admitting that "Tet had a tremendous effect on the American public . . . on leaders of Congress . . . on President Johnson." General Dave Richard Palmer, remembering the April 1967 request, observed that "the ground had already been fought over, the sides were already chosen." As a result, while Wheeler was in Vietnam, Bruce Palmer, now an MACV commander, informed Westmoreland that General Dwight Beach, the Army's Pacific commander,

---

28. Clifford, "The Vietnam Years," 58.
29. For interpretations of the reinforcement request, see, among others, Herring, *America's Longest War,* 194; Lewy, *America in Vietnam,* 127–9; Andrew Krepinevich, *The Army and Vietnam,* 241; Schandler, *Lyndon Johnson and Vietnam,* 115–16; Kolko, *Anatomy of a War,* 315; Clarke, *Advice and Support,* 291–337.

    Walt Rostow dismisses Wheeler's February reports, virtually out of hand. Wheeler was ill, Johnson's National Security Advisor asserted, and the reports from his visit to Vietnam were the only instance in which such pessimism was raised. Of course Wheeler's reports prior to his visit and into March show that Rostow was wrong; on this issue, like most others dealing with Vietnam, he still refuses to confront reality. Personal Interview, 27 June 1988, Austin, Tex.

had been aware of the new reinforcement request and "had commented that it would shock them [Washington officials]."[30]

Clearly, then, major reinforcement was not forthcoming in February and March 1968. As Westmoreland himself admitted, he and Wheeler "both knew the grave political and economic implications of a major call-up of reserves." But Westmoreland also suspected that even Wheeler was "imbued with the aura of crisis" in Washington and thus had dismissed the MACV's sanguine briefings. "In any event," the MACV commander added, the JCS chair "saw no possibility at the moment of selling reinforcements" unless he adopted an alarmist tone to exploit the sense of crisis. "Having read the newspapers," Westmoreland wondered, "who among them [civilian leaders] would even believe there had been success?" Wheeler's approach to the issue notwithstanding, Westmoreland suspected that "the request may have been doomed from the first in any event" due to long-standing political pressure to deescalate.[31]

Harold K. Johnson suspected as much. In their initial meetings after the Tet attacks began, the chiefs decided to wait for the dust to settle before making recommendations for future strategy. Within days, however, it was clear that the JCS and MACV did not have that luxury, and would have to make a prompt policy statement. Instead of deliberating over the proper course for the future, Johnson observed, the chiefs just endorsed a program for major reinforcements. "I think this was wrong," the Army chief later asserted. "There should have been better assessment" of the situation before forwarding military plans to the White House. The chiefs, despite their misconceptions, approved the reinforcement

30. Wheeler in Miller, *Lyndon,* 611; Palmer, *Summons of the Trumpet,* 261; Record of COMUSMACV Fonecon with General Palmer, 0850, 25 February 1968, Westmoreland Papers, folder 450: Fonecons, February 1968, WNRC.
31. Westmoreland added, disingenuously it would seem, that he and Wheeler "had developed our plans primarily from the military viewpoints, and we anticipated that other, nonmilitary considerations would be brought to bear on our proposals during an intensive period of calm and rational deliberation." Westmoreland paper, "The Origins of the Post-Tet 1968 Plans for Additional Forces in the Republic of Vietnam," April 1970, Westmoreland Papers, folder 493 [1 of 2]: #37 History Files, 1 January–31 June 1970, WNRC; Westmoreland, *A Soldier Reports,* 469. Ironically, both Westmoreland and Gabriel Kolko believe that Wheeler was trying to exploit the circumstances of Tet with his alarmist reports in order to get reinforcements and a Reserve call-up. In Kolko's case, however, he argues that Wheeler was "conniving" for more troops principally to meet U.S. needs elsewhere: see *Anatomy of a War,* 315.

request anyway, essentially because they did not want to reject the chair's suggestion. "If you want it bad," Johnson sardonically remarked, "you get it bad."[32]

And the brass did get it bad. Political leaders had also made it clear that substantive reinforcements would not be forthcoming. Even before Tet, the PAVN strike at Khe Sanh had alarmed Lyndon Johnson. Now, meeting with his advisors, the president charged that "all of you have counseled, advised, consulted and then – as usual – placed the monkey on my back again . . . I do not like what I am smelling from those cables from Vietnam."[33] During his first post-Tet press conference the president asserted that he had already added the men that Westmoreland thought were necessary. "We have something under 500,000," Johnson told reporters. "Our objective is 525,000. Most of the combat battalions already have been supplied. There is not anything in any of the developments that would justify the press in leaving the impression that any great new overall moves are going to be made that would involve substantial movements in that direction." By the following week, with more advisors expressing their concern about Tet and the war in general, it was clear to the president that the military could exploit White House division over Vietnam. "I don't want them [military leaders] to ask for something," Johnson worried aloud, "not get it, and have all the blame placed on me."[34]

Dean Rusk was also arguing that the United States and RVN had adequate numbers of troops to achieve American objectives, and he thus recommended against any increase. Moreover, even congressional hawks began to waver, thereby complicating the political nature of the reinforcement request. As Stanley Karnow observed, hard-line senators such as John Stennis and Henry Jackson who had "consistently underwritten the military establishment now began to see the hopelessness of the struggle." McNamara, though on his way out, was still pointing out the costs of escalation. The

32. Harold K. Johnson interview, MHI Senior Officer Debriefing Project, section 11, 14–15, used at CMH.
33. Notes of the President's Meeting with Senior Foreign Policy Advisors, 9 February 1968, Tom Johnson's Meeting Notes, box 2, folder: 9 February 1968 – 10:15 P.M., LBJL.
34. Johnson in *NYT*, 2 February 1968, 8; Notes of the President's Meeting with Senior Foreign Affairs Advisory Council, 10 February 1968, Tom Johnson's Meeting Notes, box 2, folder: 10 February 1968 – 3:17 P.M., LBJL.

Wheeler–Westmoreland request would require an increase in uniformed strength of 400,000 men, which, the defense secretary estimated, would require additional expenditures of at least $10 billion in FY 69, with an automatic addition of $5 billion for FY 70. McNamara further questioned the military's motives in asking for the additional 206,000 men, which, as he saw it, was "neither enough to do the job, nor an indication that our role must change."[35]

Thus, by mid-February, as Clark Clifford has pointed out, "the President did not wish to receive a formal request from the military for reinforcements, for fear that if it leaked he would be under great pressure to respond immediately." More important, Clifford added that the military was conscious of the situation and so "a delicate minuet took place to create the fiction that no request was being made." Similarly, Philip Habib, a State Department specialist in East Asian affairs, reported that there was "serious disagreement in American circles in Saigon over the 205,000 request." White House aide John P. Roche elaborated that "Johnson hadn't under any circumstances considered 206,000 men. Wheeler figured this Tet offensive was going to be his handle for getting the shopping list okayed." Along those lines, Ambassador Bunker, in late February, had warned Westmoreland about asking for those troops, explaining, as Neil Sheehan reports, that such reinforcement was now "politically impossible" even if the president had wanted it, which was also more unlikely than ever.[36] To say the least, the military's candid, bleak outlooks throughout the first month of Tet followed by the huge reinforcement request had badly unnerved the White House.

Even worse, the dollar–gold crisis was becoming more acutely dangerous in February and March 1968. In January, the president,

---

35. Rusk, *As I Saw It*, 478; the secretary of state did not seem surprised by the reinforcement request. "It is in the very nature of the military to request more troops. General Marshall used to tell me: 'Give the generals one-half of the troops they ask for and then double their mission.'" Schandler, *Johnson and Vietnam*, 183; Stanley Karnow, *Vietnam: A History* (New York, 1983), 557; Clifford, "The Vietnam Years," 70; McNamara in Notes of Meeting, 27 February 1968, VN C.F., NSF, box 127, folder: 19 March 1970 . . . I, LBJL; Clifford with Holbrooke, *Counsel to the President*, 484.
36. Clifford and Habib in Clifford, "The Vietnam Years," 54, 60; Roche in Miller, *Lyndon*, 611; Bunker in Sheehan, *Bright Shining Lie*, 720; see also *Pentagon Papers: Gravel*, 4:239–43, 549–53.

alarmed by a $7 billion balance-of-payments deficit for the fourth quarter of 1967, proposed a tax surcharge to finance the war. Congress, no doubt annoyed by Johnson's repeated attempts to shift the burden for economic sacrifice onto it, stalled, thereby creating even greater anxiety among European bankers. At home, even before Tet, Gardner Ackley was warning of a "possible spiraling world depression" if the dollar and gold issues were not resolved, while Allan Sproul, past head of the New York Federal Reserve Bank, lamented that the Vietnam War was "at the core" of America's "domestic and international political, social, and economic difficulties." By late February, as Senator Jacob Javits called for an end to the gold pool and another $118 million in bullion left the United States in just two days, "the specter of 1929 haunted [the president] daily."[37]

By mid-March European banks had withdrawn another $1 billion in gold, and, on 14 March, the U.S. Treasury lost $372 million in bullion, and, fearing the possible loss of another billion the next day, closed the gold market. Administration officials then called an emergency meeting in Washington of European central bankers, who rejected an American request to give up their right to claim gold for dollars from the U.S. Treasury. The Europeans essentially told the president that they would restrain their gold purchases only if he put the defense of the dollar above all other economic considerations, including Vietnam. Given the confluence of military and economic calamities that had struck Washington in February and March 1968, the administration had to acknowledge that further troop increases in Indochina threatened not only the U.S. economy, but America's position in the world political economy as well. Tet, it is not an exaggeration to suggest, marked the end of America's postwar hegemony.[38]

Accordingly, Johnson, already floored by the dollar–gold crisis and further alarmed by the Wheeler report and similar evaluations from the CIA and SA officials, directed incoming Secretary of

37. Kolko, *Anatomy of a War*, 283–90, 312–15; Schandler, *Johnson and Vietnam*, 227; Kearns, *Lyndon Johnson and the American Dream*, 347; Shapley, *Promise and Power*, 472–3; NSC, "The Gold Crisis: November 1967–March 1968," DDRS, 79, 277A.
38. Kolko, *Anatomy of a War*, 312–15; Campagna, *Economic Consequences of the Vietnam War*, 40–2; Clifford with Holbrooke, *Counsel to the President*, 502.

Defense Clark Clifford to begin an "A to Z Reassessment" of the war. Johnson charged the Clifford group with reviewing current and alternative courses of action, with two questions central to its study: Should the United States stay the course in Vietnam? And could the MACV succeed even with 206,000 additional forces? Both the CIA and SA sent back pessimistic analyses, warning that additional deployments would further Americanize the war and prompt DRVN escalation in kind. General Taylor urged the White House to consider the political effects of future policy. "In the end," the president's military advisor cautioned, "military and political actions should be blended together in an integrated package."[39]

The JCS instead concentrated on military solutions, again urging a wholly unrestrained air war against the north. Westmoreland and Wheeler, moreover, were appalled by the civilian charge that the military sought reinforcements as "another payment on an open-ended commitment." Instead, the MACV argued that it needed the forces to ensure "the security of the GVN in Saigon and in the provincial capitals." In Washington, however, military officials seemed more introspective regarding the impact of Tet. Even the hawkish Joint Staff of the JCS challenged the MACV's assessment and goals. Not only would Westmoreland need another 200,000 forces, but would also have to regain the military initiative, cause heavy enemy losses, train the ARVN, and escalate the air war, all measures that had been recommended, and failed, repeatedly over the previous years. Without such improvements and reinforcement, the DRVN would retain the military initiative and "allied forces can expect increasingly grave threats to their security with high casualty rates." Despite a continued, hopeful reliance on the strategy of attrition and air power, the Joint Staff had provided a desolate view of the war.[40]

By insisting on huge reinforcements and attacking temperate views of the situation, the military rejected opportunities to seek a quicker and less violent solution to Vietnam, but more clearly

39. Clark Clifford, "A Vietnam Reappraisal: The Personal History of One Man's View and How It Evolved," *Foreign Affairs* 47, 4 (1969): 601–22; *Pentagon Papers: Gravel*, 4:240–50, 550–5 (on the importance of Taylor's views, see pages 247, 553; for SA's analysis, see 4:561–7).
40. *Pentagon Papers: Gravel*, 4:553–72; Joint Staff report at pp. 571–2.

thrust onto the White House the burden for an ultimate decision regarding America's future in the war. While the heated debate over reinforcements continued, the situation in Vietnam remained explosive as well. From late February to mid-March, the enemy continued its politicomilitary pressure throughout the RVN, causing significant damage and casualties. In II Corps, John Vann pointed out that native resentment against U.S. and ARVN troops who had damaged homes and villages had risen. "Unless stopped," he warned, "the destruction is going to exceed our capability for recovery and battles we win may add up to losing the war." Similarly, Lansdale warned the embassy that the ARVN command, which included several "notoriously corrupt" officers, was undermining U.S. efforts to recover the pre-Tet military position.[41]

Vann also complained that MACV officers had duped Westmoreland with optimistic briefings. During a visit to II Corps to "kick ass and energize offensive operations," the MACV commander had been preempted by Army briefers who stressed the impressive Tet body counts as measures of success. These officers, however, had ignored government and military inaction in the south and did not mention that the VC was "being given more freedom to intimidate the rural population than ever before in the past two-and-a-half years." Vann, in fact, pitied Westmoreland because "even his best subordinates . . . continually screen him from the realities of the situation in Vietnam. As an honorable man he has no choice but to accept what they say and to report it to all his superiors." Thus the MACV – whether duping its commander, as Vann judged, or openly aware of its problems as the Wheeler reports indicated – no doubt understood the severity and extent of its dilemma in March 1968.[42]

In fact, the MACV itself was in organizational disarray as the Army, Marines, and Air Force, already involved in a long-simmering feud over strategy, heightened their interservice conflict. Under the pressures of Tet many Army officers complained about

---

41. On enemy military success, see *NYT*, 29 February–10 March 1968; John Paul Vann to Weyand, 29 February 1968, Vann Papers, folder: 1968 MHI; Lansdale to Bunker, 2 March 1968, ARVN Generals, Lansdale Papers, box 58, folder 1511, Hoover Institution.
42. Vann to LeRoy Wehrle, 7 March 1968, Vann Papers, folder: 1968, MHI.

the Marines' conduct of the war in I Corps, and thus Westmoreland reorganized the MACV by replacing Marine Commanding General Robert Cushman with Army General William Rosson. General Victor Krulak, the Marines' Pacific Fleet Commander, blasted such developments. After a *Los Angeles Times* article detailed the Army–Marine rift, Krulak, though excoriating the paper in a letter to its publisher and in cables to the MACV commander, privately charged that "the attack – one of several – was launched by the army, of course." If possible, Krulak added, he would publish a rejoinder titled "The Army is at it Again."[43]

Marine Aviation Commander General Norman Anderson similarly complained that the "immense" logistical problems caused by the influx of new units after Tet had become "almost too great to comprehend." Yet, Anderson charged, "in spite of our pleas to slow down the introduction of troops, the four stars in Saigon merely wave their hands and release dispatches directing the units to move. I think much of it is by design, with the ultimate aim of embarrassing" the III MAF. Some of the Marines' "biggest battles," he added, were "with the other Services rather than the VC and NVA [North Vietnamese Army]." Indeed, infighting over operation control of tactical aircraft was so intense that Air Force commanders "would rather see Americans die than give in one iota of the Air Force's party line."[44]

Amid such uncertainty and division the Clifford group forwarded its recommendations to the White House on 4 March. The new defense secretary had been particularly alarmed by the Wheeler

43. Krulak to "Bill," March 1968 (Enclosures include cables to and from Westmoreland, *Los Angeles Times* article, and Krulak's letter to publisher), Krulak Papers, box 2, MCHC.
44. Anderson to McCutcheon, 19 February 1968, McCutcheon Papers, box 20, MCHC. Similarly, Marine General Homer Hutchinson concluded that his complaints concerning aviation control were an "empty exercise" because the Marine leadership offered little support. To Hutchinson's "utter amazement," Marine Commandant Leonard Chapman "folded completely" when discussing with Admiral John McCain, the CINCPAC, the return of fixed-wing assets to the Marines. Chapman's "cave in," Hutchinson suspected, resulted from continued threats from Westmoreland and the Army to "relieve or alter in a major way" Marine control in I Corps. Hutchinson to McCutcheon, July or August 1968, McCutcheon Papers, box 20, MCHC. Other officers seemed to corroborate McCutcheon's charges about the logistics mess in the RVN. The United States had over 700,000 tons of supplies stockpiled in southern Vietnam, "all literally deteriorating in place." General Frank Mildren, January 1968–July 1970 Debriefing, *DDRS*, R, 228A.

report and thus urged Johnson to meet the first increment of West-moreland's request with a 22,000 troop deployment, but he other-wise rejected the MACV proposals. Citing instability in the govern-ment and ARVN, the Clifford group found "no reason to believe" that 206,000 more forces – "or double or triple that quantity" – could oust the Communists from southern Vietnam. Once granted, reinforcement requests might then continue "with no end in sight." The new secretary then called for the MACV to consider new strat-egies. Wheeler balked, principally because he resented Pentagon civilians developing strategic guidance for field commanders, and because the 22,000 reinforcements, though useful, were insuffi-cient. The MACV needed assistance urgently, Wheeler asserted, particularly because Westmoreland had reported "no change in his appraisal of the situation" since the chair's visit two weeks earlier.[45]

In early March 1968 the United States was surely at the crossroads in Vietnam. Following a month of candid, bleak assess-ments, Wheeler and Westmoreland unleashed their bombshell re-quest on Washington. But if, as the MACV boasted, it had decisively eliminated the enemy during Tet, Westmoreland would hardly have needed 206,000 more troops to complete the rout. Even if the MACV sincerely believed that more forces would turn the tide, it certainly understood that they would not be forthcom-ing. Indeed, given the brass's pessimistic evaluations and the presi-dent's attendant anxiety, it is not likely that the military was sur-prised that Tet seemed to be an American defeat. Although the *New York Times* front-page story of 10 March shocked Americans with its stark portrayal of the U.S. position in Vietnam, it in large mea-sure reflected the military's own appraisals of the war from the previous six weeks.[46]

Obviously the continuing public outcry over Tet did little to assuage the White House. The president, who on 13 March had

45. *Pentagon Papers: Gravel,* 4:575–85; Draft Memos of Clifford Group, Clifford Papers, box 2, folder: Draft Memo for the President – Alternative Strategies in Vietnam, 1 and 4 March 1968, LBJL; Notes of President's Meeting with Senior Foreign Policy Advisors, 4 March 1968, Tom Johnson's Notes, box 2, folder: March 4, 1968 – 5:33 P.M., LBJL.
46. For the president's views on the reinforcement debate, see *Vantage Point,* especially 365–438; *NYT,* 10 March 1968, 1; on public perception of Tet as an American failure, see Clarke, *Advice and Support,* 291; on impact of *New York Times* story, see West-moreland, *A Soldier Reports,* 471, and Clifford, "The Vietnam Years," 70.

agreed to send 30,000 more forces to Vietnam with two Reserve call-ups to sustain the deployments, then called on the "Wise Men" – former government and military officials – to help decide the reinforcement issue. General Ridgway, an increasingly outspoken critic of the Vietnam War, was one of the Wise Men, and he urged that the United States equip and train the ARVN for two additional years and then hand over responsibility for the war and begin troop withdrawals. With a few exceptions, including, ironically, Maxwell Taylor, Ridgway and the other Wise Men urged the president to deescalate. At the same time, General Shoup, a hero among doves for his attacks on the war, gave the White House another political setback as he told the Senate Committee on Foreign Relations that "it would take a rather great stretch of the imagination" to believe that Tet was an American victory. The general also scored the reinforcement request, pointing out that the United States might need 800,000 troops just to protect the cities attacked during the offensive. When asked how many forces might be required to actually repel the enemy, Shoup lamented, "I think you can just pull any figure you wanted out of the hat and that would not be enough."[47]

Simultaneously, Johnson met with Wheeler and Creighton Abrams, who had just been designated the new MACV commander, replacing Westmoreland, who had been "fired upstairs" to become Army chief. Days earlier Abrams had sought to "divorce myself from somewhat more optimistic reports coming out of Saigon" and he recognized "a tough fight ahead against a skilful and determined enemy." Wheeler reported that the MACV did not

---

47. For accounts of the Wise Men meetings, see Johnson, *Vantage Point*, 409–22; *Pentagon Papers: Gravel*, 4:592–3; Oberdorfer, *TET!*, 308–15; Schandler, *Lyndon Johnson and Vietnam*, 256–65. Ridgway's suggestions during the Wise Men meetings formed the genesis of a 1971 article in which he lamented that America was continuing along the same paths in Vietnam after the shock of Tet, and he renewed calls for U.S. withdrawal. "Indochina: Disengaging," *Foreign Affairs* 49, 4 (1971): 583–92. Shoup in U.S. Congress, Senate, Committee on Foreign Relations, *Present Situation in Vietnam*, 90th cong., 2d. sess., 1968, 7–27; Shoup's associate, Marine Colonel James Donovan – past editor of the *Armed Forces Journal* – likewise complained to the commandant that the "current news reports of the administration's lame attempts to white-wash the successes of the recent V.C. offensives is sickening." Donovan to Shoup, 19 February 1968, David Monroe Shoup Papers, box 26, Donovan Envelope, Hoover Institution; on Shoup's importance in the national debate over Vietnam, see Buzzanco, "The American Military's Rationale against the Vietnam War."

fear general defeat, but pointed out that continued DRVN infiltration – possibly 60,000 Communist forces had moved southward – and lack of adequate reserves "could give the enemy a tactical victory." The ARVN remained "frozen" in a defensive posture while the enemy had established a "stranglehold" around numerous cities, especially near Saigon and Hue. Khe Sanh, Wheeler also conceded, had suited the DRVN's purposes by diverting U.S. forces to the north as Communist troops moved south- and eastward. Worst of all, U.S. losses continued to mount, with nearly four thousand American soldiers killed in eight weeks. Meanwhile the ARVN, confirming American suspicions about its distaste for battle, had suffered the smallest losses proportionally among the major combatants, with five thousand troops killed.[48]

Upon receiving such appraisals Johnson interpreted the reinforcement request as a defensive reaction to continued Communist success rather than as a means to defeat the enemy, and he lamented that *"everybody is recommending surrender."* Clearly the president was feeling the political heat from Tet. In a sometimes rambling soliloquy to Wheeler, Abrams, and Rusk, he expressed greater alarm at the economic and political repercussions of the war. "Our fiscal situation is abominable," Johnson pointed out, and the military's request for more troops and reserves, at a cost of $15 billion, "would hurt the dollar and gold." Such economic considerations, the president admitted, were "complicated by the fact it is an election year [and] we have no support for the war." Johnson then complained that the media and "Senator Kennedy and the left wing" were undermining his efforts to find a solution to Vietnam. As a result, "I will have overwhelming disapproval in the polls and

---

48. Abrams MAC 03966 to Wheeler, Westmoreland, Sharp, 22 March 1968, Westmoreland Papers, folder 380: Eyes Only Message File, WNRC; Notes of the President's Meeting with Generals Wheeler and Abrams, 26 March 1968, Tom Johnson's Meeting Notes, box 2, folder: 26 March 1968 – 10:30 A.M., Meeting with Wheeler and Abrams, LBJL and in Westmoreland v. CBS, JX 1611A, card 873; see memo of NSC meeting, 27 March 1968, *DDRS,* 82, 001267; Notes of President's Meeting with Foreign Policy Advisors, 26 March 1968, Tom Johnson's Meeting Notes, box 2, folder: 26 March 1968 – 1:15 p.m., Foreign Policy Advisors Luncheon, LBJL; Clifford with Holbrooke, *Counsel to the President,* 473; on enemy capabilities in late March 1968, see Peers NHT 0305 to Westmoreland, 6 March 1968, Westmoreland Papers, folder 380: Eyes Only Message File, WNRC.

elections. I will go down the drain. I don't want the whole alliance and the military pulled in with it."[49]

Westmoreland's 28 March report was equally depressing. The enemy, in its post-Tet strategy, was targeting the people of the RVN; its "main objective is to destroy, or greatly weaken, the GVN." Accordingly, the VC was continuing to isolate the cities, put the ARVN on the defensive, agitate against the government, and proselytize among villagers. The Communists also maintained the politicomilitary initiative. The enemy "has no predesignated point for his main effort, no timetable, only a constant opportunism which will take advantage of vacuums [*sic*] in rural and border areas, weakness in city defenses, or any other favorable circumstances that provides [*sic*] an opening in the tactical situation." And, Westmoreland conceded, the VC retained the capability to exploit circumstances. It had between 100 and 110 combat-effective battalions in the south and was replacing its losses with infiltration and by taking advantage of the absence of U.S. and ARVN forces to recruit in the countryside. "In view of past performances and capabilities, the enemy could bring two division equivalents into the RVN over the next two or three months."[50]

Given such considerations, it was an obviously dismayed president who addressed the nation on 31 March. Johnson again claimed that Tet had been a U.S. success and he announced a token increase of 13,500 troops to be deployed to Vietnam. But he also ordered a partial bombing halt as an incentive for peace talks, and he stunned the country by withdrawing from the 1968 presidential campaign. So, precisely two months after the initial enemy attacks, Lyndon Johnson had become the latest and best-known casualty of the Tet Offensive.[51] Westmoreland, however, continued to smile through the storm, optimistically claiming in early April that the

49. Emphasis in original. Briefing by DePuy and Carver, 27 March 1968, Tom Johnson's Meeting Notes, box 2, folder: 27 March 1968 – CIA-DOD Briefing, LBJL; Notes of President's Meeting with Wheeler and Abrams, 26 March 1968, Tom Johnson's Meeting Notes, box 2, folder: 26 March 1968 – 10:30 A.M., Meeting with Wheeler and Abrams, LBJL.
50. Westmoreland to Wheeler and Sharp, 28 March 1968, Clifford Papers, box 3, folder: Southeast Asia: Cables, LBJL, and in *DDRS*, 85, 000054; on enemy infiltration capabilities see Msg., Westmoreland MAC 04324 to Sharp, 30 March 1968, Westmoreland Papers, folder 382: COMUSMACV Message File, WNRC.
51. On Johnson's 31 March decision, see *Vantage Point,* 425–38.

enemy had suffered a "colossal military defeat" and that the United States had "never been in a better position in South Vietnam." Yet he also informed Wheeler that the enemy had infiltrated between 35,000 and 40,000 troops into the south, and feared that such figures were "increasing almost daily. . . . The final total may be significantly higher." Such admissions, in fact, continued for the next two months as Communist replacement of its Tet losses, human and material infiltration, and recruiting persisted.[52]

Even into late summer, military leaders continued to lament the impact of Tet. Westmoreland and Sharp reported that pacification had suffered a "substantial setback" as Vietnamese forces withdrew from the countryside to defend urban centers. General Abrams added that counterinsurgency had ground to a "virtual halt," and that Tet attacks had devastated local Vietnamese units charged with village protection (so-called Rural Forces/Provincial Forces units). Due to continued VC infiltration, only provincial capitals and district towns were "marginally safe" but the "situation was subject to further deterioration." Abrams also scored the inchoate political atmosphere in the RVN, conceding that perhaps the "most serious – and telling – flaw in the GVN/Allied effort has been the conspicuous shortage of good Vietnamese leadership (both civilian and military) at all levels of command."[53]

52. Westmoreland in *NYT,* 7 April 1968; Notes of President's Meeting with Westmoreland, 6 April 1968, Tom Johnson's Notes, box 3, folder: 6 April 1968 – 1:30 P.M., LBJL. For the next two months Westmoreland, Wheeler, and others would report that Communist infiltration into the south was continuing, and that the enemy retained the capacity to wage war effectively. The military's public claims of decisive success simply do not stand up to the close scrutiny of such documents. See, for instance, Westmoreland to Wheeler, 16 April 1968, *DDRS,* 85, 001578; Honolulu Meeting with Foreign Policy Advisors, 16 April 1968, Tom Johnson's Notes, box 3, folder: 16 April 1968 – 10:25 A.M., LBJL; MACV estimate, 11 May, in *DDRS,* 86, 000669; Notes of Tuesday Luncheon Meeting with Foreign Policy Advisors, 21 and 28 May 1968, Tom Johnson's Notes, box 3, LBJL; Department of Defense report, 11 June 1968, *DDRS,* 85, 000923.
53. Sharp and Westmoreland, *Report on the War in Vietnam,* 170; COMUSMACV [Abrams] to CINCPAC, 6 August 1968, subject: Pacification in South Vietnam During January–June 1968, Vann Papers, folder: 1968, MHI; on the impact of Tet on pacification efforts, see also COMUSMACV 08814 to CINCPAC, 29 March 1968, Westmoreland Papers, folder 390: COMUSMACV Outgoing Message File, WNRC.
   General Lansdale had also long warned that the byzantine politics of the RVN might doom the U.S. effort. See Lansdale to Bunker, 7 May 1967, "Thieu and Ky," Lansdale Papers, box 58, folder: 1527, and Lansdale to Bunker, 14 June 1968, folder: 1514, Hoover Institution.

Only months after Westmoreland had forecast America's bright prospects in Vietnam, the Communist Tet offensive had torpedoed U.S. efforts and shocked a hopeful nation. Yet in early 1968 and thereafter supporters of the war claimed that Tet was in fact a decisive American victory undermined at home by antiwar forces. Such claims, however, are disingenuous at best, for American military leaders themselves had consistently recognized that the enemy offensive was laying bare the contradictions inherent in the U.S. war in Indochina. Despite committing billions of dollars and 500,000 men, and inflicting huge casualties and massive hardship, the United States could neither contain the enemy nor protect its allies. Communist attacks had continued throughout 1968, and the DRVN retained the capacity to match American escalation of the war. American forces also suffered sizable losses of their own in early 1968. If, as Westmoreland and others contend, such conditions constituted a decisive military victory, then America had been waging war through the looking glass.

On a more salient level, the military also recognized that Tet had been a devastating political failure for the United States. Accusations of being "stabbed in the back" notwithstanding, the military realized that political factors in Vietnam, far more than in Washington, had doomed the American effort. Westmoreland and others had recognized the DRVN's conception of political warfare, understood the enemy's psychological goals, and lamented the RVN's instability. The military also understood that the already volatile domestic situation seemed ready to boil over. Media and public perceptions of Tet, as military leaders charged at the outset of the offensive and repeatedly since, had made any attempt to escalate the war politically risky. Most important, America's position in the world economy verged on collapse, in principal measure because of its vast commitment to Indochina. When considered in light of such factors and the president's, defense secretary's, and key political leaders' misgivings about, and opposition to, an increased commitment, reinforcement became politically impossible. Yet after the shock of Tet, Westmoreland and Wheeler chose to continue their war of attrition and asked for 206,000 more troops and 280,000 reservists. Why was American military thought so apparently barren in early 1968?

The military implicitly expected and understood the impact of its proposals. Operating from the recognition that the war had descended to its nadir and that reinforcements would not be forthcoming, U.S. officers made their immense request for troops in order to defer their share of responsibility for the American failure in Vietnam onto the White House.[54] Although recognizing the American dilemma in Vietnam, Westmoreland and Wheeler discounted advice to change strategy and instead proposed a massive escalation of the war, which necessarily would have made the president accountable for the failed conduct of Vietnam policy. Bewildered by the enemy's initiative and under increasing fire at home, the military asked for more of the same and forced Johnson to choose between the Scylla of reinforcement and its attendant consequences or the Charybdis of staying the course and bearing responsibility for the continued stasis. More than simply conniving for troops, military leaders sought to immunize themselves from greater culpability for the U.S. failure in Indochina and in the process forced the president into an intractable political dilemma. By rejecting the military's request to escalate, Johnson provided the services with an alibi for future failures, as the emergence of postwar revisionism on the war attests.

U.S. forces continued to fight for nearly five years after the Tet Offensive, but America's fate was effectively sealed by mid-1968. Intervention in Vietnam, as so many officers had predicted for over a decade, had become a catastrophe. American soldiers kept pouring into Southeast Asia, pilots dropped millions of tons of bombs on Vietnam, north and south, and U.S. weapons killed untold numbers of enemy soldiers and civilians and ravaged a country. Yet William Westmoreland was no closer to being a victorious commander in the spring of 1968 than when he had arrived in Saigon in 1964. Tet, as it were, had become the U.S. obituary in Vietnam.

The MACV commander, Wheeler, Sharp, and others, however, conducted their political warfare more skillfully. The president,

54. For other interpretations of the failure of U.S. military policy and the meaning of the reinforcement request, see George Herring, "The War in Vietnam," in Robert Divine, ed., *Exploring the Johnson Years* (Austin, Tex., 1981), 27–62; Schandler, *Lyndon Johnson and Vietnam;* and Townsend Hoopes, *The Limits of Intervention* (New York, 1969).

who never seemed to determine clearly his own objectives and strategies for Vietnam, had simultaneously escalated the war to unexpected levels while trying to limit it because of the political implications of total war. Lyndon Johnson, his critics would later allege, had tied his commanders' hands throughout the war, especially in early 1968. By that time, civilian, and military, leaders had already established patterns of behavior that had more to do with avoiding blame for failure than finding a solution to the war. Under such circumstances, victory, no matter how defined, was not possible. Escalation and attrition, it was just as obvious, did not constitute a viable strategy. American forces, no matter the number deployed or tactics used, could not stop the enemy. Lyndon Johnson and Robert McNamara, for all their shortcomings, did not cause America's defeat. The Vietnamese Communists did.

11

Conclusion: Bringing It All Back Home

I believe that if we had and would keep our dirty, bloody, dollar-crooked fingers out of the business of these nations so full of depressed, exploited people, they will arrive at a solution of their own. That they design and want. That they fight and work for. [Not one] crammed down their throats by Americans.

David Monroe Shoup[1]

Tet – with its images of firefights at the U.S. embassy compound, besieged soldiers at Khe Sanh, and the public execution of a VC guerrilla by an ARVN officer – had brought the already unpopular war home to Americans more starkly than ever. As a result, and as virtually every high-level policy maker recognized, Lyndon Johnson had to reject new attempts to expand the war. Escalation, never terribly effective as a military strategy, had finally become politically impossible as well. Even though Johnson and his successor, Richard Nixon, would continue fighting for five more years – leading to 20,000 additional American combat deaths and causing untold destruction throughout Indochina – the events of early 1968 had effectively dashed U.S. hopes for success in Vietnam. The Communist offensive, the dollar–gold crisis, and the massive reinforcement request had converged to create a sense of doom only surpassed by the Cuban Missile Crisis in postwar America.

Tet also brought home the various warnings and dire predictions

1. Shoup speech at Junior College World Affairs Day, Los Angeles, 14 May 1966, reprinted in U.S. Congress, Senate, Committee on Foreign Relations (SCFR), *Present Situation in Vietnam,* 90th Cong., 2d sess., 1968, 47.

about the war of so many military leaders who had analyzed American involvement in Vietnam. Although the enemy attacks shocked almost everyone from the White House down, such a denouement was in fact consistent with military thinking on Vietnam for an entire generation. During the Vietnam era U.S. officers candidly recognized their problems and uncertain future in the war, understood the likely consequences of intervention and escalation, and often urged American political leaders either to avoid or temper any commitment to Indochina. Indeed, in the early months of 1968 the messages of the most forceful military dissenters of the Vietnam generation were brought home as Matthew Ridgway counseled the president as one of the "Wise Men"; James Gavin published *Crisis Now,* his analysis of the twin crises of the war and growing poverty at home; and David Shoup testified before the Senate Foreign Relations Committee about the futility of continued war in Indochina.

Ridgway, Gavin, and Shoup had been outspoken opponents of the war long before the Tet Offensive, and the events of February and March 1968 had publicly vindicated their warnings about involvement in Vietnam.[2] These three respected and decorated generals, who had resisted intervention from within the defense establishment in the 1950s and early 1960s, began to speak out against the war publicly while the domestic consensus in support of U.S. involvement was still strong. Gavin first detailed his criticism openly during the nationally televised Vietnam hearings held before Fulbright's committee in February 1966. Just months later, a Ridgway essay in *Look* questioned the morality and conduct of the war. And Shoup, in a May speech, blasted intervention in much stronger terms than almost anyone associated with the antiwar movement.[3]

These and other dissident officers insisted that the war in Vietnam damaged the national interest. Gavin, in 1966, contended that the U.S. role in Indochina had already grown "alarmingly out of balance" while Shoup doubted whether all of Southeast Asia was

2. For a more thorough analysis of these three generals, see Buzzanco, "The American Military's Rationale against the Vietnam War."
3. Gavin testimony in U.S. Congress, Senate, Committee on Foreign Relations, *Supplemental Foreign Assistance, Fiscal Year 1966 – Vietnam,* 89th Cong., 2d sess., 1966 (later published by Vintage Books as *The Vietnam Hearings*); Matthew B. Ridgway, "Pull-Out, All-Out, or Stand Fast in Vietnam?" *Look,* 5 April 1966, 81–4; Shoup speech at Junior College World Affairs Day, Los Angeles, 14 May 1966, in SCFR, *Present Situation.*

"worth the life or limb of a single American." The past commandant further excoriated the U.S. decision to support the RVN's
corrupt leadership. To Shoup, the insurgents in Vietnam were "99
percent South Vietnamese" and he accordingly described the war as
a conflict between "those crooks in Saigon" and Vietnamese nationals fighting against class oppression.[4] Rear Admiral Arnold
True likewise attacked President Ky, who was "naturally willing to
fight to the last American soldier and the last American dollar"
and, after spending seventeen days in Vietnam and then meeting
with National Security Advisor Henry Kissinger, he attacked the
Nixon administration for still "shoring up the dictatorial regime"
of Nguyen Van Thieu.[5] Ridgway added that the United States did
not have to support such oppressive leaders for reasons of national
security; such claims, he scoffed, "strained the credulity of the most
naive believer."[6]

Military dissenters also criticized Westmoreland's conduct of the
war, in terms even more strident than active-duty military critics,
and they denounced the lavish use of American air power with
particular vehemence. Shoup ridiculed the idea of halting infiltration via air strikes and referred to Communist supply routes as the
"Ho Chi Minh autobahn." Decrying the destruction of Vietnam,
he demanded an end to the air war "unless we want to commit
ourselves to genocidal actions." Ridgway likewise found "nothing
in the present situation . . . that requires us to bomb a small Asian
nation 'back to the stone age.'" As Gavin saw it, American bombs
had already turned Vietnam into a "parking lot" and he even went
so far as to observe, after William Laws Calley's trial for war
crimes, that it was "tragic when a lieutenant in the infantry gets
convicted and officers flying bombers don't."[7]

4. Gavin, *Supplemental Foreign Assistance, 1966,* 235, 258, 260, 302–3; Shoup interview
   with Rep. William Ryan, 19 December 1967, in David Shoup biographical file, MCHC;
   Shoup in SCFR, *Present Situation* (1968), 8, 47.
5. True in *Palo Alto Times,* 3 March 1966, also in antiwar advertisement in *NYT,* 22 May
   1967; True in *NYT,* 18 July 1969.
6. Ridgway, "Indochina: Disengaging," 586.
7. Transcript of Shoup interview with John Scali on "ABC Scope," 6 August 1967, and
   transcript of Shoup interview with Ryan, 19 December 1967, both in Shoup file, MCHC;
   Ridgway, "Pull-Out," 84; Gavin in U.S. Congress, Senate, Committee on Foreign Relations, *Moral and Military Aspects of the War in Southeast Asia,* 91st Cong., 2d sess.,
   1970.

Unlike military critics and politicos in Vietnam and Washington, who kept their bleak views of Vietnam inside the beltway for the most part, dissenters like Ridgway, Gavin, and Shoup reached a national audience and provided significant evidence of the disaster in Vietnam not only to the antiwar movement but to many of the "silent majority" who could not quarrel with their unimpeachable loyal opposition. As Doctor Benjamin Spock saw it, the dissent of one general "was easily worth the objections of ten professors or ministers."[8] Government officials apparently feared that Spock's equation was accurate. During the Johnson and Nixon years, the FBI maintained surveillance on the activities of Shoup and other antiwar military leaders; Admiral True alleged that the Navy spied on him for two years and warned of "serious consequences" should he continue his outspoken opposition; a military judge refused to allow Shoup and True to testify at the court-martial of a Navy seaman who had distributed antiwar literature; and the Marine Corps tried to withhold William Corson's retirement pay in retaliation against the publication of *The Betrayal,* his book highly critical of the war.[9]

Notwithstanding the government's efforts to silence them, dissident officers had no trouble reaching the public with their antiwar message and they arguably played an important part in the national debate over Vietnam. In the end, though, those officials charged with conducting the war – both civilian and military – essentially dismissed such critics even though events in Indochina had consistently confirmed their outspoken warnings. In principal measure, the war continued as a result of political maneuvering throughout the 1950s and 1960s. Although most service leaders recognized the inherent peril of war in Vietnam, they paradoxically proposed totally unfettered escalation, seemingly unlimited troop reinforcements, the geographic expansion of the war, activation of reservists, and national mobilization, even though it was always

8. Spock in Charles DeBennedetti, *The Peace Reform in American History* (Bloomington, Ind., 1980), 176.
9. FBI reports on Shoup and others in FBI file on Vietnam Veterans against the War, 100–448092–80, Federal Bureau of Investigation, Washington, D.C.; True in *Washington Post,* 13 January 1971, 10; trial details in *Washington Post,* 21 April 1970, 8, and in *NYT,* 21 April 1970, 17; Corson, *The Betrayal* (New York, 1968).

apparent that such measures would never be authorized to the extent requested.

Alain Enthoven, whose irritation with ranking officers was mutually shared, complained after the war that military planning for Vietnam was "absolutely predictable: do what General Westmoreland and Admiral Sharp ask."[10] In truth, service leaders had asked for the same measures time and again, but Enthoven's observation does not take account of the context in which the military engaged in such conduct. Over the course of a generation, military officials, even true believers, did question the American way of war in Vietnam and they realized that conditions in the RVN were troubled at the start and had deteriorated progressively thereafter. At the same time, the civilian response was predictable as well: limit the war, end it quickly, and minimize the damage to the president's credibility and domestic agenda. In such circumstances, neither civilian nor military officials sincerely pursued alternatives in Vietnam, and the armed forces, accordingly, substituted proposals for escalation in place of strategic planning and thus left the greater burden for the war at the White House doorstep.

Although constitutionally structured to defer to civilian authority, the military was institutionally trying to pin down the administrations of John Kennedy and Lyndon Johnson and make them determine Indochina policy. By constantly proposing to expand the war, rather than offering their objective counsel, American officers could make the civilian establishment deny their requests and thus be accountable for a coming failure in Vietnam. Although political and uniformed officials were supposed to be fighting a common enemy in the jungles of Indochina, there was always insufficient cooperation between the civilian sector and the armed services. Kennedy, Johnson, McNamara, Taylor, Wheeler, Westmoreland, and many others simply continued to muddle along the same paths they had recognized as so seriously flawed years earlier.

Indeed, the American policy-making community was always anguished and divided regarding Vietnam. In the early 1950s, despite the military's bold stand against intervention, Eisenhower and Dulles continued to seek ways to get American troops involved in

10. Enthoven and Smith, *How Much Is Enough?*, 300.

Masters of War

Indochina; for nearly a decade after that, military leaders tried to
pin down their political superiors about U.S. policy in Vietnam
while trying to limit the war there; and, once committed to combat
in 1965, American officers fought among themselves and against
the White House and Pentagon to the serious detriment of their
efforts in Vietnam. As Marine General Edwin Simmons pointed out
in an understated fashion, there was "more diversity of thinking
about Vietnam amongst the senior officers" than one would
expect.[11]

By 1968 military leaders had in fact developed a comprehensive
critique of the war in Vietnam, recognizing the enemy's strengths
and their own shortcomings. Westmoreland himself admitted that
Ho Chi Minh was the most respected figure in Vietnam on both
sides of the seventeenth parallel, and he "was not necessarily a
communist hero; he had gained Vietnam's freedom from the
French." Meanwhile, the various southern leaders could develop
no effective government, while the Americans in Indochina were
tainted with the image of a colonial power. As a result, the Vietnamese people never welcomed the United States into their land.
Many of them, Marine General Raymond Murray feared, "were
ready to slit our throats the first chance they would get."[12] Military
officials, just as importantly, recognized the skill and dedication of
the VC and PAVN, admitting that they fought "like tigers" and
conceding their stamina and growth, although MACV representatives could not even agree on the number of enemy soldiers in the
south.

Perhaps no issue sparked more virulent dissent than the U.S.
strategy in Vietnam. Krulak, Greene, Vann, the PROVN officers,
and many others repeatedly warned that firepower and attrition
could not work. In a text used at West Point, General Dave Richard
Palmer charged that a commander who resorted to attrition "admits his failure to conceive of an alternative. . . . He uses blood in
lieu of brains." Harold K. Johnson likewise complained that Westmoreland and his staff "were indiscriminate in our use of firepower

11. Simmons interview in *NYT*, 24 March 1982, in Simmons Oral History Transcript, 25–7,
   MCHC.
12. Westmoreland Oral History (2), 4, LBJL; Raymond Murray Oral History, 22–3,
   MCHC.

... I think we sort of devastated the countryside." To prove his point, the Army chief, in 1968, computed that U.S. pilots had dropped enough bombs in the DRVN alone to cover it with one-eighth inch of flat steel; by 1970, he estimated that another one-fourth inch could be added to that total. Despite such massive air power, Rolling Thunder did not appreciably damage Communist capabilities or will. In fact, when General Douglas Kinnard surveyed American commanders after the war, about one-third of them believed that close air and artillery support was excessive, "considering the nature of the war," while over half said that B-52 strikes were neither vital nor worth the costs involved.[13]

Despite such candid observations, military leaders never advised the president or defense secretary that they would be unable to achieve their objectives in Vietnam. The "only explanation" for this that General Bruce Palmer could offer was that those officers were imbued with the "can do" spirit and did not want to appear disloyal to their commander in chief. Harold K. Johnson, who had discussed the chiefs' failure with Palmer, "could offer no logical rationale for this lapse" either.[14] More than a "lapse" or omission, the military's failure to admit its inability to succeed in Vietnam was the result of long-term political maneuvering over its role in policy making. For over a decade American officers had wanted a greater role in establishing national defense policy, and Vietnam became the vehicle for attaining that objective.

An entire generation of military leaders had accepted commitments in the RVN despite their own knowledge of conditions there and pessimism about America's ability to make a difference. Because their evaluations were so often bleak and they feared the political fallout from "losing" Vietnam, American officers let politics guide their approach to the war, as did the White House. The politics of the cold war had guided America's initial commitments

13. Palmer in Currey, *Self-Destruction,* 73; Harold K. Johnson interview, Senior Officer Debriefing Project, section 10, 31–2, used at CMH; Harold K. Johnson interview with MacDonald and von Luttichau, 64, CMH; Kinnard, *The War Managers* (Hanover, N.H., 1977), 45–8; Air Force General Otto Weyland anticipated Kinnard's findings by two decades, observing in 1957 that he did not expect to see "B-52s finding and dropping weapons on a small guerrilla troop concentration in the jungles of Indo-China." Weyland in Mrozek, *Air Power and Ground War,* 123.
14. Palmer, *25-Year War,* 46, 213 n. 26.

to Indochina in the 1950s, as U.S. advisors and resources poured into Vietnam even though it was an admittedly peripheral interest. American military leaders recognized this; thus the chiefs acquiesced to a training mission in the RVN because "political considerations are overriding." By the latter part of the decade, the brass and the White House were in open conflict as Generals Ridgway, Taylor, Gavin, and others attacked Eisenhower's decision to cut military budgets per his New Look national security strategy. Although these political battles did not directly pertain to Vietnam, they indeed had a great impact on events there. Military leaders, Army officers in particular, developed the idea of flexible response as a way to boost their institutional power and, with that, provided John Kennedy with a military strategy for Vietnam. More important, civilian and military officials became increasingly mistrustful of each other, thereby setting the stage for the politics of war in Vietnam.

During the Kennedy years, political maneuvering became more commonplace and critical in policy making. Kennedy needed foreign policy success after accepting a coalition government in Laos and especially following his ill-fated attempt to overthrow Fidel Castro. Vietnam then became the place where the United States would stop the Communists. Despite the recent hagiography of Kennedy as a dove who was prepared to quit Vietnam and end the cold war, the evidence indicates that the young president and his civilian advisors were the driving force behind the growing U.S. role in Indochina. Had Kennedy, or his successor for that matter, wanted to disengage from Vietnam, either could have cited the military's own doubts and reservations to deescalate or withdraw from the war with the least amount of political fallout at home. Neither Kennedy nor Johnson chose to do so.

For their part, military leaders did not clamor for intervention. But in the aftermath of the Bay of Pigs disaster, the military had come under attack for its failure to prevent Kennedy from invading Cuba. From that point on, civil–military relations worsened and had a growing impact on Vietnam policy. As a result, American officers, especially Maxwell Taylor and Paul Harkins, accepted Kennedy's commitments to Vietnam and increased the U.S. military stake there, even though Taylor, the president's most trusted military advisor, urged him to avoid combat in Indochina. At the same time, to prevent a repeat of the Cuban episode, the brass kept pressing the White House to identify its objectives, the level of American involvement, and the strategy to be used in Vietnam. Civilian leaders, not soldiers, would thus have to be responsible for the war. The military's primary concern, as General McGarr frankly observed, was to avoid blame for failure in Vietnam.

During the Johnson years, as combat troops entered the battlefield and took over the war despite the reservations of many military leaders, politics increasingly determined the U.S. approach to Vietnam. The administration pursued the contradictory objectives of "winning" the war – that is, preserving an independent southern state – while limiting it in order to avoid Soviet or Chinese countermeasures and to keep its political focus on building a Great Society at home. As the chiefs saw it, this vacillating and piecemeal approach, along with McNamara's arrogance, showed that wars could not be run like corporations or managed by "defense intellectuals."[15] Rather, the military should make and conduct policy. But, in truth, the armed forces itself had recognized that even totally unrestrained warfare would not have brought victory, and, in any case, correctly understood that the president's efforts would be far from decisive. Thus Wheeler, Westmoreland, Sharp, and others played politics, and held their own against the master politician from Texas. Even though Jack Valenti wanted to "sign on" the JCS in the event of a "flap or investigation later," the chiefs always kept the pressure on Johnson to make the crucial decisions regarding the war. Certainly that was his job as commander in chief, but ranking officers did not make it any easier with their repeated calls to escalate a futile war. Indeed, as Sharp put it, there were "grave political implications" involved in military failure. Evidence of stalemate or deterioration, Earle Wheeler likewise understood, would "blow the lid off of Washington." By mid-1967, Harold K. Johnson saw the military taking the fall for the coming disaster. Preserving their own and the armed forces' reputation, not maintaining the RVN, had become the principal goal of American generals by that time.

15. Perry, *Four Stars*, 172.

The president, too, played politics with the war. Caught between his anti-Communist convictions in Southeast Asia and his commitment to civil rights and a war on poverty at home, Johnson spent the better part of four years waiting for "Westy" to achieve success at the least cost to his political agenda. The military, of course, instead kept pressing the White House to do more in Vietnam. Thus, by early 1968 Johnson complained that American officers had placed the monkey on his back for decisions on Vietnam, albeit that was where it belonged, and, after Tet, worried that he would have to turn down the military's proposals and then "have all the blame placed on me" for the subsequent failure.

In large measure, America's leading civilian and military figures spent the better part of a generation trying to avoid blame for Vietnam and, since the end of the war, have accelerated their efforts. Vietnam is now a memory and a valuable political symbol, a "noble cause" or, on the other side of the street, a "dirty little war." To defenders of U.S. intervention, Lyndon Johnson forced American boys to fight with their hands tied behind their backs, while critics still attack the strategy of "General Waste-more-men." The evolution of "Vietnam" as a resonant issue in the American political and cultural arena has indeed been curious. Military dissent and criticism led to political intrigue, which, in turn, brought the United States into an unpopular war in Indochina. Since then, the war has been rehabilitated to an appreciable degree. In the process, truth and lies have been confused.

Both the president and military leaders of the Vietnam era were fighting the war with an eye toward history. As they confronted the abyss in Indochina, political and uniformed officials seemed to be as concerned with maintaining power at home and with the way they would be judged after the war as with finding a way out of the conflict. American leaders had legitimate choices other than their massive commitment to Vietnam. With so many officers questioning various facets of U.S. involvement, the war was avoidable on military grounds alone. American generals, rather than being naive or unduly optimistic, had forthrightly evaluated the risks and likely outcome of a campaign in Indochina. They nonetheless ignored their own bleak analyses with the full complicity of the civilian policy-making establishment.

Rather than reappraise the commitment to and conduct of the war in Vietnam, American officials deluded themselves that success was possible, or at least that they might avoid responsibility for the coming disaster. A black wall in Washington with over 58,000 names on it and a small Asian nation devastated almost beyond recognition suggest otherwise.[16]

16. By the time the United States withdrew from Indochina in 1973, it had dropped 4.6 million tons of bombs on Vietnam and another 2 million tons on Cambodia and Laos (compared with a total of 3 million tons dropped by Allied forces in World War II). American forces additionally sprayed 11.2 million gallons of the dioxin-carrying herbicide Agent Orange, and dropped over 400,000 tons of napalm. The impact of such massive warfare was catastrophic. The United States destroyed over 9,000, out of 15,000, southern Vietnamese hamlets, 25 million acres of farmland, and 12 million acres of forest, while creating over 25 million bomb craters. The human toll was worse: about 2 million Vietnamese, and another 300,000 Cambodians and Laotians, died in the war, while over 3 million Indochinese were wounded. By 1975 there were also nearly 15 million refugees in the area. Figures cited in the *Nation*, 18 February 1991, 184.

Epilogue
"This Is a Real War":
Military Dissent and Politics after Vietnam

I did some checking. I found that it had been traditional that the
JCS spied on the White House. They wanted to know what was
going on.

Richard Milhous Nixon[1]

The U.S. military may have checked out of Vietnam in the 1970s,
but it still had not left. Just as that war continues to shape American
foreign and military policy and the nation's cultural politics, it has
also conditioned the armed forces' approach to policy making and
civil–military relations for the past two decades. Even before the
war ended, service leaders feared that they were bearing the burden
for the U.S. failure in Vietnam as the military's previously respected
standing in American public life dropped markedly. Thus Harold
K. Johnson complained that "the whole onus for Vietnam . . . has
fallen upon 'the military,'" while Matthew Ridgway lamented that
"not before in my lifetime – and I was born into the Army in the
nineteenth century – has the Army's public image suffered so many
grievous blows and fallen to such low esteem in such wide areas of
our society."[2]

The decline in military prestige and influence did not last long,
however. In the aftermath of Tet, American service leaders intensified their efforts to score political points and regain traditional
levels of credibility and power, while civilian leaders in turn continued their own political struggles against the brass. Although

---

1. Nixon in Walter Isaacson, *Kissinger: A Biography* (New York, 1992), 384–5.
2. Harold K. Johnson, Senior Officer Debriefing Project, section 11, 8, CMH; Ridgway in
   NYT, 2 April 1971, 39; Korb, *Fall and Rise of the Pentagon.*

happy to see Lyndon Johnson finally leave the White House and thankful that his successor Richard Nixon was authorizing air strikes against new targets in the DRVN and against Cambodia, military leaders also understood that political feuding against the civilian establishment would likely persist. Thus when the Nixon administration told the military to develop a "one-and-a-half war concept" to fight a major and a limited war at the same time, none of the chiefs thought it was possible but, as the CNO, Elmo Zumwalt, put it, "all of us were under heavy political pressure not to let on." Simultaneously, the JCS requested increased funding in the FY 72 budget but, as Zumwalt explained, "we knew – who could know better? – how unpopular the war in southeast Asia, and by extension the entire Defense establishment, was and how much political pressure the President was under to shift his emphasis to domestic programs."[3]

Such political concerns eventually led to bizarre forms of civil–military maneuvering. During the early Nixon years, Defense Secretary Melvin Laird and National Security Advisor Henry Kissinger were vying for control of foreign policy making and both attempted to use the military to their advantage. Laird thus arranged for Vice Admiral Noel Gayler of the National Security Agency (NSA) to provide him with copies of every back-channel message that the national security advisor sent; for his part, Kissinger directed the chiefs to report directly to him rather than to the secretary of defense.[4] Caught between Laird and Kissinger, and frustrated by the White House's "secret diplomacy" on Vietnam while escalating the war, the chiefs struck back by establishing a "spy ring" to keep abreast of the activities of Kissinger and the president. Admiral Robert Welander, the NSA's liaison to the JCS, enlisted Navy Yeoman Charles Radford to steal and copy documents from Kissinger and send them along to JCS Chair Thomas Moorer.[5]

3. Elmo R. Zumwalt, *On Watch: A Memoir* (New York, 1976), 279–81.
4. Isaacson, *Kissinger,* 201–6; Len Colodny and Robert Gettlin, *Silent Coup: The Removal of a President* (New York, 1991), 3–12.
5. Seymour M. Hersh, *The Price of Power: Kissinger in the Nixon White House* (New York, 1983), 465–79; Colodny and Gettlin, *Silent Coup,* 3–12; Zumwalt, *On Watch,* 369–75; Isaacson, *Kissinger,* 380–6.

The White House soon learned of the spy ring due to a leak that appeared in a column by journalist Jack Anderson. Nixon, however, did not strike back publicly, instead telling Kissinger that he was reluctant to discipline Welander and Moorer because of "the impact on the military services and the country of washing such dirty linen in public" and the "pitiless attack on the military establishment" that was sure to follow. The president accordingly told Chief of Staff H. R. Haldeman to "sweep it under the rug."[6] Though Nixon professed his concern for the military's reputation, his motives for letting the spy ring controversy drop were indeed more complicated. Even before the scandal broke in 1970 and 1971, Moorer had been willing to take orders from Kissinger and the White House behind Laird's back; with the spy ring exposed, the JCS chair would be even more compliant. As a result, Kissinger essentially kept the military in the dark about negotiations over the Strategic Arms Limitation Treaty in May 1971 and Moorer, who did not like the deal, had to accept it because he had been "preshrunk" by the spy scandal.[7]

The JCS's involvement in the politics of the Nixon White House, along with reductions in defense spending in the post-Vietnam era, heightened military insecurities in the mid-1970s. By the latter part of the decade, as Jimmy Carter became president pledging further cuts in spending and weapons systems, the military was as suspicious of civilian leaders as ever, as evidenced by the public challenge to Carter's plan to withdraw some American troops from Korea put forth by the two ranking U.S. officers on the peninsula, Generals John Vessey, Jr., and John Singlaub.[8] Relief for the military, however, was on the way. Ronald Reagan's successful campaign for the presidency included a pledge to "make America strong again" and his first budget included a $32 billion defense increase, as well as funding for both the B-1 bomber, previously

---

6. Henry Kissinger, *Years of Upheaval* (Boston, 1982), 805–9; Nixon in Isaacson, *Kissinger*, 385–6.
7. Kissinger in fact told Admiral Moorer that he would withdraw support for the Trident submarine, a Navy favorite, unless the JCS chair supported limits on submarine-launched ballistic missiles in the SALT pact. Hersh, *The Price of Power*, 540.
8. Korb, *Fall and Rise of the Pentagon*, 140–66; Perry, *Four Stars*, 264–7, 304.

scrapped by Carter, and the MX missile, stalled in the previous administration due to controversies over its mode of basing.[9]

In terms of appropriations, and public respect, the armed forces enjoyed something of a renaissance during the Reagan years. Behind the scenes, however, dissent and politics were still commonplace. Despite the Reagan administration's obsession with indigenous leftist movements in Nicaragua and El Salvador, the military rejected attempts to intervene directly in Central America. At the same time, however, the services exchanged their strict loyalty, if not subservience, for Reagan's budgetary and rhetorical largesse. As Richard Perle, the assistant secretary of defense at the time, saw it, the Joint Chiefs were "pushovers and patsies for whoever leans on them the last, the longest, and the hardest."[10]

No one was pushing the military longer or harder in the 1980s than Congress. In the Goldwater-Nichols Defense Reorganization Act, signed into law on 1 October 1986, the Senate, by a unanimous vote, and the House overhauled the military establishment. The JCS chair, rather than the individual chiefs, was given responsibility for developing strategic plans and budget proposals, and he gained complete control over the JCS staff and obtained a seat on the NSC. Unified commanders also received new powers at the expense of the respective services, who no longer controlled their own budgets and staff assignments. Goldwater-Nichols, depending upon one's perspective, either ended forty years of armed forces' ascendancy in the political arena by eliminating the pursuit for money and glory that had led to internal power struggles and interservice division, or it gave the JCS chair "all inclusive authority" to determine military policy without adequate civilian input.[11]

Notwithstanding the JCS reorganization, the reality of civil–military relations for the duration of the Reagan administration did not change markedly. During the greatest scandal of the 1980s, the Iran–Contra affair, the president, not unlike his predecessors in the cold war era, made policy over the military's reservations. Reagan

9. Perry, *Four Stars,* 267–75, 288–90.
10. Perle in Perry, *Four Stars,* 334–5.
11. On the benefits of Goldwater-Nichols, see Perry, *Four Stars,* 337–40; on its potential dangers, see Robert Previdi, *Civilian Control versus Military Rule* (New York, 1988), 10–38.

and his advisors simply kept JCS Chair Admiral William Crowe, and the other chiefs, out of the loop regarding the arming of Nicaraguan terrorists and illegal weapons transfers to Iran. Crowe himself only learned of the scandal from an assistant who had attended a briefing with Oliver North, and he believed that military leaders were kept in the dark intentionally "to keep dissent out of the decisionmaking calculus." Theodore Draper, who has given the closest scholarly attention to the affair, accurately observed that "the humiliation of the chairman of the Joint Chiefs of Staff was part of the price of the Iran initiative."[12] For his part, Crowe exacted a bit of revenge after his retirement in 1989 as he publicly rebuked the Bush administration for its aggressive posturing toward Panama and testified before Congress – along with another past chair of the JCS, General David Jones – against war in the Persian Gulf.[13]

Crowe's disputes, though serious, seemed like family bickering when compared with the armed services battles with the White House at the outset of the Clinton era. Taking advantage of the significant disdain shown for the commander in chief whom many perceived as a Vietnam draft dodger, the military has gained its greatest stake in defense policy making in the modern era. In addition to publicly foreclosing the use of American force in Somalia and Bosnia while limiting intervention in Haiti, and rejecting the president's plan to allow admitted homosexuals to enlist and serve without qualification, the military has played a principal role in the ouster of the Pentagon's civilian leader and it has staved off the type of significant budget cuts that many, including candidate Bill Clinton, had advocated as the cold war ended.[14]

The military challenged Clinton's plans on virtually every front as soon as he assumed the presidency in 1993. Although Defense Secretary Les Aspin and his staff talked of "reasserting civilian authority," the JCS forced Pentagon officials to abandon their "win-hold-win" strategy – fighting one major enemy while simulta-

12. Theodore Draper, *A Very Thin Line: The Iran-Contra Affairs* (New York, 1991), 391–3.
13. Crowe letter to the editor, *NYT,* 16 October 1989, 23; Woodward, *The Commanders,* 331–2.
14. On the military's rejection of intervention, see *Washington Post,* 20 June 1993, A1 and A12, 14 November 1993, A16; *NYT,* 15 March 1994, A6, 6 April 1994, A1.

neously holding off another with air power – and publicly rejected the president's call for $88 billion in defense cuts. Not surprisingly, the defense secretary, his top aides, and the military establishment all recognized an "open rift" over strategy, force structures, and money less than six months into the Clinton administration.[15] Echoing military complaints from three decades earlier, top officers charged that Aspin did not trust or respect them, and they scored the arrogance of the "faculty club" – civilian Pentagon officials from RAND and Harvard dubbed the new "whiz kids." The secretary of defense conversely lamented that the services were divided between "new thinkers" and the "old guard," and that there were too few of the former.[16]

The old guard indeed had plenty of life left in it, and continued to deride civilian leadership openly. Military officials made little effort to veil their contempt for Bill Clinton. During a Memorial Day ceremony at the Vietnam Wall in 1993, veterans jeered and booed him, while an Army colonel, after a Pentagon visit by Hillary Rodham Clinton, sarcastically told reporters that "the president's here, and Bill stayed home."[17] The armed forces, which had lost about 400,000 troops and $10 billion in appropriations after the Gulf War, feared further decline and warned Clinton that "something will have to give" if he attempted to cut spending any further. Simultaneously, Director of the Office of Management and Budget (OMB) Leon Panetta told the president that he would have to reduce defense spending by another $30 billion to meet spending ceilings established in the deficit reduction package of August 1993. Clinton looked for middle ground, hoping to keep spending in check while avoiding the wrath of the military, but the armed forces kept the heat on. "This is a real war," a ranking general

---

15. *Washington Post*, 20 June 1993, A1 and A12, 25 June 1993, A6. As they were challenging Aspin's strategic vision, service officials were also attacking the conclusions of a bipartisan commission to decide which military bases should be closed. Ex-Republican representative Jim Courter, who chaired the group, recognized the military's strength and Aspin's weakness as he complained that "there's nobody there to restrain the military leadership from doing what they think is best for their own service. There was no cross service analysis. They'll never get together until they're forced to. . . . They'll start a war first." *Washington Post*, 3 July 1993, A5.
16. Ibid., 20 June 1993, A1 and A12.
17. Ibid., 20 November 1993, B1 and B8.

bluntly told reporters. "It is a war with O.M.B. and a war among ourselves."[18]

The chiefs, as they had done throughout the Vietnam era, showed Clinton that they were prepared to wage political warfare at home. As Aspin and Panetta looked for ways to keep the military appeased while decreasing appropriations, the new JCS chair, General John Shalikashvili, offered a "graceful Washington threat" during his first press conference. "If we see that there isn't a solution" to a five-year funding shortfall of $50 billion, he explained, "then I think we can talk about what the fallout would be. So I think it's a little premature for me to say what the dire consequences might be if we can't get together and solve the problem."[19] Just a day later – in what was neither a surprise nor a coincidence – Aspin resigned as defense secretary. According to one four-star commander, Aspin "was not well-suited for the job." Senior officers publicly complained that he was disorganized and tardy for meetings at the Pentagon, and that he often shut them out of key decisions. Because of his ruminative style and academic cohorts, officers mocked the Pentagon as "Aspin U."[20]

The ouster of the defense secretary marked a significant victory for the military. "The guys in the Pentagon like the smell of one of their own," a Clinton official conceded, and Aspin was simply not accepted by uniformed officials.[21] Clinton realized as much, and Aspin's removal and the president's choices to replace him – first Bobby Ray Inman and then William J. Perry – were designed "to stop senior uniformed leaders from rebelling against" civilian leadership.[22] As the military continued to flex its political muscle, Clinton backed away further from his original goals to reduce the budget by $88, or $50, billion over five years. In late 1993 the president gave the Pentagon $10 billion to cover previously mandated salary increases and he agreed to fund the military at $240 billion, later raised to $260 billion, annually.[23] In his 1994 State of the Union Address, Clinton publicly acquiesced to the military's will. "The

18. *NYT*, 10 December 1993, A1 and A28; *Washington Post*, 11 December 1993, A12.
19. *Washington Post*, 15 December 1993, A14.
20. Ibid., 16 December 1993, A1, A8, and A9.
21. Ibid., 17 December 1993, A1; *NYT*, 26 January 1994, A10.
22. *Washington Post*, 17 December 1993, A1; 7 April 1994, A1.
23. *NYT*, 27 December 1993, A14; *Nation*, 4 April 1994, 437.

budget I send to Congress draws the line against further defense cuts," he asserted. "We must not cut defense further. I hope the Congress without regard to party will support that position."[24]

Clinton, obviously seeking a modus vivendi with the military, apparently had sacrificed his earlier goal to reduce defense spending because he wanted a political truce with the armed forces. His FY 95 military budget, his acquiescence to military decisions on intervention in various trouble spots, and his impressive performance in Normandy on the fiftieth anniversary of D-Day seemed to signal a new Clinton, more respected and at ease with the armed services.[25] Any armistice with the brass was short-lived, however. Within weeks of his well-received appearance in France, Army generals forced the administration to retreat from its plans to open most combat positions to women, and Navy officials embarrassed the White House staff with charges that it stole over $500 worth of towels and robes from the ship that was ferrying the president and others across the English Channel during the D-Day festivities.[26]

By the time the 1994 elections – in which the Democrats took a drubbing – came around, Clinton was in full retreat. Just days before the vote, Pentagon officials complained that the president's defense cuts had jeopardized their plans to win two regional conflicts simultaneously and would force the services to make "painful choices" to the detriment of the national security. Shortly thereafter Defense Secretary William Perry publicly agreed with military charges that Army deployments to Haiti and Rwanda – comprising only about 30,000 troops – had seriously endangered U.S. combat readiness. In perhaps the biggest blow of all, the incoming Republican chair of the Senate Foreign Relations Committee, Jesse Helms, warned that the president might be assassinated if he visited Fort Bragg in the senator's home state of North Carolina.[27]

24. Clinton in *Washington Post*, 26 January 1994, A12 and A13.
25. Ibid., 7 June 1994, A1 and A14.
26. Simultaneously, Republican Congress members and conservative media figures began to attack Clinton for the costs involved (about $6 million) in transporting White House and defense officials to Europe for the D-Day observance, and Republican representatives even tried, unsuccessfully, to reduce the White House budget by a similar amount in retribution for the expenses. Such charges and legislative retaliation, it almost goes without saying, would never have been levied against the Reagan or Bush administrations. *NYT*, 17 June 1994, A1 and A18; *Washington Post*, 17 June 1994, A3.
27. *Washington Post*, 6 November 1994, A19; 16 November 1994, A1; 2 December 1994,

Given such readiness to confront the Clinton administration openly, and the civilian leadership's willingness to see the world through military eyes, it is safe to say that ranking officers in the past decade – especially since Goldwater-Nichols and Colin Powell's tenure as JCS chair – have emerged as virtual partners in a ruling coalition government, or in fact may have the upper hand whenever questions of American defense policy are being debated.[28] Such consequences, however, come with a price attached. As the military accrues more political influence, fewer people – be they civilian officials, Congress members, or just concerned and informed citizens – play a role in the development of policy. As the noted military historian Richard Kohn has observed, "the Republic is not in immediate danger. But a consciously separate military participating in policy and national debate can only erode democracy."[29]

Certainly, trends have been running in that direction for some time now, and the current shape of civil–military relations forms a direct continuum with the military criticism and political maneuvering of the Vietnam era. In the future, it is likely that we will continue to see more battles between civilian and uniformed officials at home than between American and foreign forces on the battlefield.

A1; and 9 January 1995, A7. At the same time, interservice squabbling intensified as outgoing Air Force Chief of Staff Merrill McPeak blasted the Army, Navy, and Marines for their "excessive overhead" and for duplicating aspects of the Air Force's mission. *Washington Post,* 24 October 1994, A1.
28. For a background explanation of the militarization of foreign policy, see Barnet, *Economy of Death,* 82.
29. *NYT,* 10 April 1994, 19.

Bibliography

I: Manuscript Sources

Center of Military History, Washington, D.C.
    Oral Histories: Harold K. Johnson, William Rosson
    PROVN Report
Dwight D. Eisenhower Presidential Library, Abilene, Kans.
    Draper Committee Records
    Dwight D. Eisenhower Papers
        White House Central Files, Confidential File
    Oral Histories: Dillon Anderson, Arleigh Burke, Lyman Lemnitzer, Nathan Twining
    Palm Desert-Indio File
    Ann Whitman File
        Dulles-Herter Series
        International Series
        NSC Series
Federal Bureau of Investigation, Washington, D.C.
    Vietnam Veterans against the War File
Hoover Institution on War, Revolution, and Peace, Palo Alto, Calif.
    Edward Geary Lansdale Papers
    David Monroe Shoup Papers
Lyndon B. Johnson Presidential Library, Austin, Tex.
    Cabinet Meetings File
    George Christian File
    Clark L. Clifford Papers
    Declassified and Sanitized Documents from Unprocessed Files
    Tom Johnson's Meeting Notes
    Meeting Notes File
    National Security Files
        Agency File, Joint Chiefs of Staff
        Country File, Vietnam
        International Meetings and Travel File

Robert W. Komer File
Komer-Leonhart File
Memos to the President, McGeorge Bundy
Memos to the President, Walt Whitman Rostow
Name File
National Security Action Memoranda
National Security Council Histories
National Security Council Meetings File
Oral Histories: Maxwell Taylor, William Westmoreland, Earle Wheeler
Reference File
Paul Warnke-John McNaughton Files
William Childs Westmoreland Papers
White House Central Files, ND 19/CO 312
White House Central Files – Confidential File
John F. Kennedy Presidential Library, Boston, Mass.
Roger Hilsman Papers
National Security File
Countries File, Vietnam
National Security Action Memoranda
Meetings with the President, Special Group – Counterinsurgency
Meetings and Memoranda
Regional Security, Southeast Asia
John Newman Papers
Oral Histories: David Shoup, Earle Wheeler
President's Office File, Countries File, Vietnam
Theodore Sorensen Papers
James Thomson Papers
White House Name File
Marine Corps Historical Center, Washington, D.C.
Norman Anderson Papers
Commanding General, Fleet Marine Force, Pacific, Trip Reports
James Donovan Papers
Fleet Marine Force, Pacific: Operations of III MAF in Vietnam, 1965–8
Fleet Marine Force, Pacific: U.S. Marine Corps Forces in Vietnam, March
1965–September 1967, Narrative Summary, 2 vols.
Wallace M. Greene, Jr., Papers
Headquarters, Marine Corps Message File
Victor H. Krulak Papers
Keith McCutcheon Papers
Oral Histories: Norman Anderson, Henry Buse, John Chaisson, Robert Cush-
man, Raymond Davis, Lowell English, Lewis Fields, Fredrick Karch, Victor
Krulak, Keith McCutcheon, Raymond Murray, Herman Nickerson, Jonas
Platt, David M. Shoup, Edwin Simmons, William Westmoreland
Charles Quilter Papers
David Shoup Biographical File
Taped Interviews: Numbers 6173, 6276, 6278, 6298
Task Element 79.3.3.6 Command Diary

III MAF Command Chronologies
Vietnam Comments File
Microform Collections
   Declassified Documents Reference System. Carrollton Press.
   Records of the Military Assistance Command, Vietnam, part 1. The War in
   Vietnam, 1954–73. MACV Historical Office Documentary Collection. Univer-
   sity Publications of America.
   The War in Vietnam: Classified Histories by the National Security Council.
   University Publications of America.
   "Deployment of Major U.S. Forces to Vietnam: July 1965."
   "Honolulu Conference: February 6–8, 1966."
   "March 31st Speech."
   Vietnam: A Documentary History – Westmoreland v. CBS. Clearwater Publish-
   ing Company.
Military History Institute, Carlisle Barracks, Pa.
   Creighton W. Abrams Papers
   Harold K. Johnson Papers
   Matthew Ridgway Papers
   John Paul Vann Papers
   Samuel T. Williams Papers
   Wilbur Wilson Papers
   Oral Histories: Donald Bennett, J. Lawton Collins, Matthew Ridgway, Max-
   well Taylor.
Seeley Mudd Manuscript Library, Princeton, N.J.
   Oral History: Dwight Eisenhower
   H. Alexander Smith Papers
National Archives, Washington, D.C.
   Record Group 59: General Records of the Department of State.
   Record Group 218: Records of the Joint Chiefs of Staff.
   Record Group 218: Chairman's File, Admiral William Leahy, 1942–8.
   Record Group 319: Records of the Army Staff.
   Record Group 330: Records of the Office of Assistant Secretary of Defense for
   International Security Affairs.
Washington National Records Center, Suitland, Md.
   RG 319, Records of the Army Staff, Personal Papers of William Childs West-
   moreland, 1962–72.
   RG 407, Records of the Adjutant General's Office, DA/WNRC Administrative
   Files Relating to Westmoreland/Capital Legal Foundation v. Columbia Broad-
   casting System, Litigation Research Collection.

II: Government Documents and Documentary Collections

Executive Sessions of the Senate Committee on Foreign Relations. (Historical
    Series) Volume 6. 83d Cong., 2d sess., 1954.
Gaddis, John, and Thomas Etzold, eds. *Containment: Documents on American
    Policy and Strategy: 1945–1950.* New York, 1978.

The Pentagon Papers: The Defense Department History of United States Decisionmaking on Vietnam, Senator Gravel Edition. 5 vols. Boston: Beacon Press, 1971.

Porter, Gareth, ed. *Vietnam: The Definitive Documentation of Human Decisions.* 2 vols. Stanfordville, N.Y.: Earl M. Coleman Enterprises, 1979.

U.S. Congress, House Committee on Armed Services. *United States-Vietnam Relations, 1945–1967: Study Prepared by the Department of Defense.* 12 vols. Washington, D.C.: Government Printing Office, 1971.

 House Subcommittee of Committee on Appropriations. *Defense Appropriations for 1967.* 89th Cong., 2d sess., 1966.

 House Subcommittee of Committee on Appropriations. *Department of Defense Appropriations for 1966.* 89th Cong., 1st sess., 1965.

 Senate Armed Services Committee. *Supplemental Procurement and Construction Authorizations, Fiscal Year 1966.* 89th Cong., 2d sess., 1966.

 Senate Committee on Foreign Relations. *Conflicts between U.S. Capabilities and Foreign Commitments.* 90th Cong., 1st sess., 1967.

 Senate Committee on Foreign Relations. *Legislative Proposals Relating to the War in Southeast Asia.* 92d Cong., 1st sess., 1971.

 Senate Committee on Foreign Relations. *Moral and Military Aspects of the War in Southeast Asia.* 91st Cong., 2d sess., 1970.

 Senate Committee on Foreign Relations. *Mutual Security Act of 1959.* 86th Cong., 1st sess., 1959.

 Senate Committee on Foreign Relations. *Present Situation in Vietnam.* 90th Cong., 2d sess., 1968.

 Senate Committee on Foreign Relations. *Supplemental Foreign Assistance, Fiscal Year 1966–Vietnam.* 89th Cong., 2d sess., 1966.

 Senate Committee on Labor and Public Welfare. *Postwar Economic Conversion.* 91st Cong., 2d sess., 1970.

U.S. Department of State. *Papers Relating to the Foreign Relations of the United States, 1950.* Volume 3. *Asia and the Pacific.* Washington, D.C.: Government Printing Office, 1976.

Papers Relating to the Foreign Relations of the United States, 1951. Volume 6. *Asia and the Pacific.* Washington, D.C.: Government Printing Office, 1977.

Papers Relating to the Foreign Relations of the United States, 1952–1954. Volume 13. *Indochina.* Washington, D.C.: Government Printing Office, 1982.

Papers Relating to the Foreign Relations of the United States, 1955–1957. Volume 1. *Vietnam.* Washington, D.C.: Government Printing Office, 1985.

Papers Relating to the Foreign Relations of the United States, 1958–1960. Volume 1. *Vietnam.* Washington, D.C.: Government Printing Office, 1986.

Papers Relating to the Foreign Relations of the United States, 1961–1963. Volume 1. *Vietnam.* Washington, D.C.: Government Printing Office, 1988.

Papers Relating to the Foreign Relations of the United States, 1962. Volume 2. *Vietnam.* Washington, D.C.: Government Printing Office, 1990.

Papers Relating to the Foreign Relations of the United States, January-July

1963. Volume 3. *Vietnam*. Washington, D.C.: Government Printing Office, 1991.

Papers Relating to the Foreign Relations of the United States, August-December 1963. Volume 4. *Vietnam*. Washington, D.C.: Government Printing Office, 1991.

Williams, William Appleman, et al., eds. *America in Vietnam: A Documentary History*. Garden City, N.Y.: Anchor Books, 1985.

III: Memoirs, Books, and Other Published Documents

Acheson, Dean. *Present at the Creation: My Years at the State Department*. New York: W. W. Norton, 1969.

Aliano, Richard. *American Defense Policy from Eisenhower to Kennedy: The Politics of Changing Military Requirements, 1957–1961*. Athens: Ohio University Press, 1975.

Allison, Graham. *Essence of Decision*. Boston: Little, Brown, 1971.

Ambrose, Stephen. *Eisenhower: The President*. New York: Simon & Schuster, 1984.

Ambrose, Stephen, and James Alden Barber, eds. *The Military and American Society*. New York: Free Press, 1972.

Anderson, David. *Trapped by Success: The Eisenhower Administration and Vietnam, 1953–1961*. New York: Columbia University Press, 1991.

Asprey, Robert. *War in the Shadows: The Guerrilla in History*. 2 vols. Garden City, N.Y.: Doubleday, 1975.

Bacevich, A. J. *The Pentomic Era: The U.S. Army between Korea and Vietnam*. Washington, D.C.: National Defense University, 1986.

Ball, George. *The Past Has Another Pattern*. New York: W. W. Norton, 1982.

Baritz, Loren. *Backfire*. New York: Morrow, 1985.

Barnet, Richard. *The Economy of Death*. New York: Atheneum, 1970.

Roots of War: The Men and Institutions behind U.S. Foreign Policy. New York: Atheneum, 1972.

BDM Corporation. *A Study of Strategic Lessons Learned in Vietnam*. McLean, Va.: BDM Corporation, 1980.

Bergerud, Eric. *The Dynamics of Defeat: The Vietnam War in Hau Nghia Province*. Boulder, Colo: Westview Press, 1991.

Berman, Larry. *Lyndon Johnson's War*. New York: W. W. Norton, 1989.

Planning a Tragedy: The Americanization of the War in Vietnam. New York: W. W. Norton, 1982.

Betts, Richard K. *Soldiers, Statesmen, and Cold War Crises*. Cambridge, Mass.: Harvard University Press, 1971.

Biggs, Bradley. *Gavin*. Hamden, Conn.: Archon Books, 1980.

Blaufarb, Douglas. *The Counterinsurgency Era: U.S. Doctrine and Performance*. New York: Free Press, 1977.

Blum, Robert. *Drawing the Line: The Origin of the American Containment Policy in East Asia.* New York: W. W. Norton, 1982.

Boettcher, Thomas. *Vietnam: The Valor and the Sorrow.* Boston: Little, Brown, 1985.

Borden, William. *The Pacific Alliance: United States Foreign Economic Policy and Japanese Trade Recovery, 1947–1954.* Madison: University of Wisconsin Press, 1984.

Bradford, Zeb B., and Frederic J. Brown. *The United States Army in Transition.* Beverly Hills, Calif.: Sage Publications, 1973.

Braestrup, Peter. *Big Story: How the American Press and Television Reported and Interpreted the Crisis of Tet 1968 in Vietnam and Washington.* 2 vols. Boulder, Colo.: Westview Press, 1977.

Campagna, Anthony S. *The Economic Consequences of the Vietnam War.* Westport, CT.: Praeger, 1991.

Caraley, Demetrios. *The Politics of Military Unification.* New York: Columbia University Press, 1966.

Chang, Laurence, and Peter Kornbluh, eds. *The Cuban Missile Crisis, 1962: A National Security Archives Documents Reader.* New York: New Press, 1992.

Chomsky, Noam. *American Power and the New Mandarins: Historical and Political Essays.* New York: Vintage, 1969.

   Rethinking Camelot: JFK, the Vietnam War, and US Political Culture. Boston: South End Press, 1993.

   Year 501: The Conquest Continues. Boston: South End Press, 1992.

Chomsky, Noam, and Edward Herman. *The Washington Connection and Third World Fascism: The Political Economy of Human Rights.* Boston: South End Press, 1979.

Clarke, Jeffrey. *Advice and Support: The Final Years of the U.S. Army in Vietnam.* Washington, D.C.: United States Army Center of Military History, 1988.

Clifford, Clark, with Richard Holbrooke. *Counsel to the President: A Memoir.* New York: Random House, 1991.

Clodfelter, Mark. *The Limits of Air Power: The American Bombing of North Vietnam.* New York: Free Press, 1989.

Collins, J. Lawton. *Lightning Joe: An Autobiography.* Baton Rouge: Louisiana State University Press, 1979.

Collins, James Lawton, Jr. *The Development and Training of the South Vietnamese Army, 1950–1972.* Washington, D.C.: Department of the Army, 1975.

Colodny, Len, and Robert Gettlin. *Silent Coup: The Removal of a President.* New York: St. Martin's Press, 1991.

Cone, James. *Martin and Malcolm and America: A Dream or a Nightmare.* New York: Orbis, 1992.

Congressional Research Service. *The U.S. Government and the Vietnam War: Executive and Legislative Roles and Relationships, Part I: 1945–1961.* Prepared for the Committee on Foreign Relations, United States Senate. Washington, D.C.: Government Printing Office, 1984.

The U.S. Government and the Vietnam War: Executive and Legislative Roles and Relationships, Part II: 1961–1964. Prepared for the Committee on Foreign Relations, United States Senate. Washington, D.C.: Government Printing Office, 1984.

Cooper, Chester. *The Lost Crusade: America in Vietnam.* New York: Dodd, Mead, 1970.

Corson, William. *The Betrayal.* New York: Ace Books, 1968.

Cortright, David. *Soldiers in Revolt: The American Military Today.* Garden City, N.Y.: Doubleday, 1975.

Cumings, Bruce. *The Origins of the Korean War: Liberation and the Emergence of Separate Regimes, 1945–1947.* Princeton, N.J.: Princeton University Press, 1989.

    The Origins of the Korean War, Vol. 2: *The Roaring of the Cataract, 1947–1950.* Princeton, N.J.: Princeton University Press, 1990.

Currey, Cecil. *Edward Lansdale: The Unquiet American.* Boston: Houghton Mifflin, 1988.

    Self-Destruction: The Disintegration and Decay of the United States Army during the Vietnam Era. New York: W. W. Norton, 1981.

Davidson, Phillip R. *Vietnam at War: The History, 1946–1975.* New York: Oxford University Press, 1991.

Davis, Vincent. *The Admirals Lobby.* Chapel Hill: University of North Carolina Press, 1967.

DeBennedetti, Charles. *The Peace Reform in American History.* Bloomington: Indiana University Press, 1980.

DeBennedetti, Charles, and Charles Chatfield. *An American Ordeal: The Antiwar Movement of the Vietnam Era.* Syracuse, N.Y.: Syracuse University Press, 1990.

Donovan, James. *Militarism U.S.A.* New York: Scribner's, 1970.

Donovan, Robert. *Tumultuous Years: The Presidency of Harry S Truman, 1949–1953.* New York: W. W. Norton, 1982.

Draper, Theodore. *A Very Thin Line: The Iran-Contra Affair.* New York: Hill and Wang, 1991.

Eckhardt, George. *Command and Control, 1950–1969.* Washington, D.C.: Department of the Army, 1974.

Edsall, Thomas Byrne, and Mary D. Edsall. *Chain Reaction: The Impact of Race, Rights, and Taxes on American Politics.* New York: W. W. Norton, 1991.

Eisenhower, Dwight. *The White House Years: Mandate for Change, 1953–1956.* Garden City, N.Y.: Doubleday, 1963.

    The White House Years: Waging Peace, 1956–1961. Garden City, N.Y.: Doubleday, 1965.

Ellsberg, Daniel. *Papers on the War.* New York: Simon and Schuster, 1972.

Enthoven, Alain and K. Wayne Smith. *How Much Is Enough? Shaping the Defense Program, 1961–1969.* New York: Harper and Row, 1971.

FitzGerald, Frances. *Fire in the Lake: The Vietnamese and the Americans in Vietnam.* New York: Random House, 1972.

Fox, Roger. *Air Base Defense in the Republic of Vietnam, 1961–1973.* Washington, D.C.: Office of Air Force History, 1979.

Franklin, Bruce. *M.I.A., or Mythmaking in America.* New Brunswick, N.J.: Rutgers University Press, 1993.

Fulbright, J. William. *The Arrogance of Power.* New York: Random House, 1966.

Futrell, Robert. *The United States Air Force in Southeast Asia: The Advisory Years to 1965.* Washington, D.C.: Office of Air Force History, 1981.

Gaddis, John. *Strategies of Containment: A Critical Appraisal of Postwar National Security Policy.* New York: Oxford University Press, 1982.

Galbraith, John Kenneth. *How to Control the Military.* New York: Signet, 1969.

Gardner, Lloyd. *Approaching Vietnam: From World War II through Dienbienphu, 1941–1954.* New York: W. W. Norton, 1988.

Gavin, James. *Crisis Now.* New York: Random House, 1968.

War and Peace in the Space Age. New York: Harper and Row, 1958.

Gelb, Leslie, and Richard Betts. *The Irony of Vietnam: The System Worked.* Washington, D.C.: Brookings Institution, 1979.

Gibbons, William Conrad. *The U.S. Government and the Vietnam War: Executive and Legislative Roles and Relationships, Part III: January–July 1965.* Princeton, N.J.: Princeton University Press, 1989.

Haines, Harry, ed. *GI Resistance: Soldiers and Veterans against the War.* Special issue of *Viet Nam Generation* 2, no. 1 (1990).

Halberstam, David. *The Best and the Brightest.* New York: Fawcett Crest, 1972.

The Making of a Quagmire. New York: Random House, 1965.

Hallin, Daniel C. *The "Uncensored" War: The Media and Vietnam.* New York: Oxford University Press, 1986.

Halperin, Morton. *Bureaucratic Politics and Foreign Policy.* Washington, D.C.: Brookings Institution, 1974.

Hammond, William. *Public Affairs: The Military and the Media, 1962–1968.* Washington, D.C.: United States Army Center of Military History, 1988.

Healy, David. *US Expansionism: The Imperialist Urge in the 1890s.* Madison: University of Wisconsin Press, 1970.

Herman, Edward, and Noam Chomsky. *Manufacturing Consent: The Political Economy of the Mass Media.* New York: Pantheon, 1988.

Hersh, Seymour M. *The Price of Power: Kissinger in the Nixon White House.* New York: Summit Books, 1983.

Hewes, James E., Jr. *From Root to McNamara: Army Organization and Administration, 1900–1963.* Washington, D.C.: Department of the Army, 1975.

Hilsman, Roger. *To Move a Nation: The Politics of Foreign Policy in the Administration of John F. Kennedy.* Garden City, N.Y.: Doubleday, 1967.

Hogan, Michael J., and Thomas G. Paterson, eds. *Explaining the History of American Foreign Relations.* Cambridge: Cambridge University Press, 1991.

Hoopes, Townsend. *The Limits of Intervention.* New York: David McKay, 1973.

Inaugural Addresses of the Presidents of the United States from George Washington 1789 to John F. Kennedy 1961. Washington, D.C.: Government Printing Office, 1961.

Isaacson, Walter. *Kissinger: A Biography.* New York: Simon and Schuster, 1992.

James, D. Clayton, with Anne Sharp Wells. *Refighting the Last War: Command and Crisis in Korea, 1950–1953*. New York: Free Press, 1993.

Johnson, Chalmers. *Autopsy on People's War*. Berkeley: University of California Press, 1973.

Johnson, Harold K. *Challenge: Compendium of Army Accomplishments: A Report by the Chief of Staff, July 1964–April 1968*. Washington, D.C.: Department of the Army, 1968.

Johnson, Lyndon. *The Vantage Point: Perspectives of the Presidency, 1963–1969*. New York: Holt, Rinehart and Winston, 1971.

Kahin, George McT. *Intervention: How America Became Involved in Vietnam*. Garden City, N.Y.: Doubleday, 1987.

Kahin, George McT., and John Lewis. *The United States in Vietnam*. New York: Delta, 1969.

Karnow, Stanley. *Vietnam: A History*. New York: Viking, 1983.

Kaufman, Burton. *The Korean War: Challenges in Crisis, Credibility, and Command*. Philadelphia: Temple University Press, 1986.

Kearns, Doris. *Lyndon Johnson and the American Dream*. New York: Harper and Row, 1976.

Keiser, Gordon. *The US Marine Corps and Defense Unification, 1944–1947: The Politics of Survival*. Washington, D.C.: National Defense University, 1982.

King, Edward. *The Death of the Army: A Pre-Mortem*. New York: Saturday Review Press, 1972.

Kinnard, Douglas. *The Certain Trumpet: Maxwell Taylor and the American Experience in Vietnam*. New York: Brassey's, 1991.

President Eisenhower and Strategy Management: A Study in Defense Politics. Lexington: University Press of Kentucky, 1977.

The Secretary of Defense. Lexington: University Press of Kentucky, 1980.

The War Managers. Hanover, N.H.: University Press of New England, 1977.

Kissinger, Henry. *Years of Upheaval*. Boston: Little, Brown, 1982.

Klare, Michael, and Peter Kornbluh, eds. *Low-Intensity Warfare: Counterinsurgency, Proinsurgency, and Antiterrorism in the Eighties*. New York: Pantheon, 1988.

Knoll, Erwin, and Judith Nies McFadden, eds. *American Militarism 1970*. New York: Viking, 1969.

Kolko, Gabriel. *Anatomy of a War: Vietnam, The United States, and the Modern Historical Experience*. New York: Pantheon, 1985.

Confronting the Third World: United States Foreign Policy, 1945–1980. New York: Pantheon, 1988.

The Roots of American Foreign Policy. Boston: Beacon Press, 1969.

Kolko, Gabriel, and Joyce Kolko. *The Limits of Power: The World and United States Foreign Policy, 1945–1954*. New York: Harper and Row, 1972.

Korb, Lawrence. *The Fall and Rise of the Pentagon: American Defense Policies in the 1970s*. Westport, Conn.: Greenwood Press, 1979.

The Joint Chiefs of Staff: The First Twenty-Five Years. Bloomington: Indiana University Press, 1976.

Krepinevich, Andrew. *The Army and Vietnam*. Baltimore: Johns Hopkins University Press, 1986.

Krock, Arthur. *Memoirs: Sixty Years on the Firing Line*. New York: Funk and Wagnalls, 1968.

Krulak, Victor. *First to Fight: An Inside View of the U.S. Marine Corps*. Annapolis, Md.: Naval Institute Press, 1984.

Leffler, Melvyn P. *A Preponderance of Power: National Security, the Truman Administration, and the Cold War*. Stanford, Calif.: Stanford University Press, 1992.

Lewy, Guenter. *America in Vietnam*. New York: Oxford University Press, 1978.

Liberty Lobby. *Robert Strange McNamara: The True Story of Dr. Strangebob*. Washington, D.C.: Liberty Lobby, 1967.

Littauer, Ralph, and Norman Uphoff, eds. *The Air War in Indochina*. Boston: Beacon Press, 1972.

Louvre, Alf, and Jeffrey Walsh, eds. *Tell Me Lies about Vietnam: Cultural Battles for the Meaning of the War*. Philadelphia: Open University Press, 1988.

MacDonald, Callum. *Korea: The War before Vietnam*. New York: Free Press, 1986.

Marolda, Edward, and Oscar Fitzgerald. *The United States Navy and the Vietnam Conflict*, vol. 2: *From Military Assistance to Combat, 1959–1965*. Washington, D.C.: Naval Historical Center, 1986.

McNamara, Robert S., with Brian VanDeMark. *In Retrospect: The Tragedy and Lessons of Vietnam*. New York: Times Books, 1995.

Military Assistance Command, Vietnam. *MACV Command History, 1965*.

Miller, Merle. *Lyndon: An Oral Biography*. New York: Ballantine Books, 1980.

Millett, Allan. *Semper Fidelis: The History of the United States Marine Corps*. New York: Free Press, 1982.

Moore, Harold G., and Joseph L. Galloway. *We Were Soldiers Once . . . and Young: Ia Drang – The Battle That Changed the War in Vietnam*. New York: Random House, 1992.

Mrozek, Donald. *Air Power and the Ground War in Vietnam: Ideas and Action*. Maxwell Air Force Base, Ala.: Air University Press, 1988.

Newman, John. *JFK and Vietnam*. New York: Warner Books, 1992.

Nixon, Richard. *No More Vietnams*. New York: Arbor House, 1985.

Oberdorfer, Don. *TET!* Garden City, N.Y.: Doubleday, 1984.

Palmer, Bruce. *The 25-Year War: America's Military Role in Vietnam*. New York: Simon and Schuster, 1985.

Palmer, Dave Richard. *Summons of the Trumpet: U.S.-Vietnam in Perspective*. San Rafael, Calif.: Presidio Press, 1978.

Palmer, Gregory. *The McNamara Strategy and the Vietnam War: Program Budgeting in the Pentagon, 1960–1968*. Westport, Conn.: Greenwood Press, 1978.

Parmet, Herbert. *JFK: The Presidency of John F. Kennedy*. New York: Penguin Books, 1984.

Perry, Mark. *Four Stars*. Boston: Houghton Mifflin, 1989.

Podhoretz, Norman. *Why We Were in Vietnam.* New York: Simon and Schuster, 1982.

Previdi, Robert. *Civilian Control versus Military Rule.* New York: Hippocrene Books, 1988.

Prouty, Fletcher. *JFK: The CIA, Vietnam and the Plot to Assassinate John F. Kennedy.* New York: Birch Lane, 1992.

Raymond, Jack. *Power at the Pentagon.* New York: Harper and Row, 1964.

Ridgway, Matthew B. *The Korean War.* Garden City, N.Y.: Doubleday, 1967.
    Soldier: The Memoirs of Matthew B. Ridgway. New York: Harper and Row, 1956.

Rogers, Bernard William. *Cedar Falls–Junction City: A Turning Point.* Washington, D.C.: Department of the Army, 1974.

Rotter, Andrew. *The Path to Vietnam: Origins of the American Commitment to Southeast Asia.* Ithaca, N.Y.: Cornell University Press, 1987.

Rusk, Dean, with Richard Rusk. *As I Saw It.* Edited by Daniel S. Papp. New York: W. W. Norton, 1990.

Salisbury, Harrison, ed. *Vietnam Reconsidered: Lessons from a War.* New York: Harper and Row, 1984.

Schandler, Herbert. *Lyndon Johnson and Vietnam: The Unmaking of a President.* Princeton, N.J.: Princeton University Press, 1977.

Schlesinger, Arthur, Jr. *Robert Kennedy and His Times.* Boston: Houghton Mifflin, 1978.
    A Thousand Days: John F. Kennedy in the White House. Boston: Houghton Mifflin, 1965.

Scott, Peter Dale. *The War Conspiracy.* Indianapolis, Ind.: Bobbs Merrill, 1972.

Shapley, Deborah. *Promise and Power: The Life and Times of Robert McNamara.* Boston: Little, Brown, 1993.

Sharp, U. S. G. *Strategy for Defeat: Vietnam in Retrospect.* San Rafael, Calif.: Presidio, 1978.

Sharp, U. S. G., and William C. Westmoreland. *Report on the War in Vietnam (as of 30 June 1968).* Washington, D.C.: Government Printing Office, 1968.

Sheehan, Neil. *A Bright Shining Lie: John Paul Vann and America in Vietnam.* New York: Random House, 1988.

Shulimson, Jack. *U.S. Marines in Vietnam: An Expanding War, 1966.* Washington, D.C.: History and Museums Division, U.S. Marine Corps, 1982.

Shulimson, Jack, and Charles Johnson. *U.S. Marines in Vietnam: The Landing and the Buildup, 1965.* Washington, D.C.: History and Museums Division, U.S. Marine Corps, 1978.

Sick, Gary. *October Surprise: America's Hostages in Iran and the Election of Ronald Reagan.* New York: Times Books, 1991.

Smith, Gaddis. *Morality, Reason, and Power: American Diplomacy in the Carter Years.* New York: Hill and Wang, 1986.

Sorensen, Theodore. *Kennedy.* New York: Harper and Row, 1965.

Sorley, Lewis. *Thunderbolt: General Creighton Abrams and the Army of His Times.* New York: Simon and Schuster, 1992.

Spector, Ronald. *Advice and Support: The Early Years of the U.S. Army in Vietnam, 1941–1960*. New York: Free Press, 1985.
   After Tet: The Bloodiest Year in Vietnam. New York: Free Press, 1993.
Summers, Harry. *On Strategy: A Critical Analysis of the Vietnam War*. Novato, Calif.: Presidio Press, 1982.
Taylor, John. *General Maxwell Taylor: The Sword and the Pen*. New York: Doubleday, 1989.
Taylor, Leonard B. *Financial Management of the Vietnam Conflict*. Washington, D.C.: Department of the Army, 1974.
Taylor, Maxwell D. *Swords and Plowshares*. New York: W. W. Norton, 1972.
   The Uncertain Trumpet. New York: Harper and Row, 1959.
Thompson, W. Scott, and Donaldson Frizzell, eds. *The Lessons of Vietnam*. New York: Crane, Russak, 1977.
Trewhitt, Henry L. *McNamara: His Ordeal in the Pentagon*. New York: Harper and Row, 1971.
Truman, Harry S. *Memoirs,* Volume 2: *Years of Trial and Hope*. Garden City, N.Y.: Doubleday, 1956.
Turner, Kathleen. *Lyndon Johnson's Dual War: Vietnam and the Press*. Chicago: University of Chicago Press, 1985.
VanDeMark, Brian. *Into the Quagmire: Lyndon Johnson's Escalation of the Vietnam War*. New York: Oxford University Press, 1991.
Walt, Lewis. *Strange War, Strange Strategy: A General's Report on Vietnam*. New York: Funk and Wagnalls, 1970.
Westmoreland, William C. *A Soldier Reports*. Garden City, N.Y.: Doubleday, 1976.
White, Leonard D. *The Republican Era: A Study in Administrative History, 1869–1901*. New York: Macmillan, 1958.
Whitlow, Robert. *U.S. Marines in Vietnam: The Advisory and Combat Assistance Era, 1954–1964*. Washington, D.C.: History and Museums Division, U.S. Marine Corps, 1977.
Wicker, Tom. *JFK and LBJ: The Influence of Personality upon Politics*. Baltimore: Penguin Books, 1973.
Wirtz, James. *The Tet Offensive: Intelligence Failure in War*. Ithaca, N.Y.: Cornell University Press, 1991.
Woodward, Bob. *The Commanders*. New York: Simon and Schuster, 1991.
Yanarella, Ernest. *The Missile Defense Controversy: Strategy, Technology, and Politics, 1955–1972*. Lexington: University Press of Kentucky, 1977.
Yarmolinsky, Adam. *The Military Establishment: Its Impact on American Society*. New York: Harper and Row, 1971.
Yergin, Daniel. *Shattered Peace: The Origins of the Cold War and the National Security State*. Boston: Houghton Mifflin, 1977.
Young, Marilyn. *The Vietnam Wars: 1945–1990*. New York: Harper Collins, 1991.
Zumwalt, Elmo R. *On Watch: A Memoir*. New York: Quadrangle, 1976.

IV: Articles

Anderson, David. "J. Lawton Collins, John Foster Dulles, and the Eisenhower Administration's 'Point of No Return' in Vietnam." *Diplomatic History* 12 (Spring 1988): 127–47.

Ball, George. "The Rationalist in Power." *New York Review of Books* (22 April 1993): 30–6.

Bassett, Lawrence, and Stephen Pelz. "The Failed Search for Victory: Vietnam and the Politics of War." In *Kennedy's Quest for Victory: American Foreign Policy, 1961–1963*, edited by Thomas Paterson, pp. 223–52. New York: Oxford University Press, 1989.

Berman, Larry. "Coming to Grips with Lyndon Johnson's War." *Diplomatic History* 17 (Fall 1993): 519–37.

Buzzanco, Robert. "The American Military's Rationale against the Vietnam War." *Political Science Quarterly* 101 (Winter 1986): 559–76.

"Division, Dilemma and Dissent: Military Recognition of the Peril of War in Viet Nam." In *Informed Dissent: Three Generals and the Vietnam War, Essays by Robert Buzzanco and Asad Ismi,* edited by Dan Duffy, pp. 9–37. Chevy Chase, Md.: Vietnam Generation/Burning Cities Press, 1992.

"Prologue to Tragedy: U.S. Military Opposition to Intervention in Vietnam, 1950–1954." *Diplomatic History* 17 (Spring 1993): 201–22.

Chomsky, Noam. "The United States and Indochina: Far From an Aberration." In *Coming to Terms: Indochina, the United States, and the War,* edited by Douglas Allen and Ngô Vinh Long, pp. 161–88. Boulder, Colo.: Westview Press, 1991.

"Vain Hopes, False Dreams." *Z Magazine* 5 (October 1992): 9–23.

Clifford, Clark. "A Vietnam Reappraisal: The Personal History of One Man's View and How It Evolved." *Foreign Affairs* 47 (Winter 1969): 601–22.

Clifford, Clark, and Richard Holbrooke. "Annals of Government (The Vietnam Years – Part II)." *New Yorker* (13 May 1991): 45–83.

Costigliola, Frank. "The Pursuit of Atlantic Community: Nuclear Arms, Dollars, and Berlin." In *Kennedy's Quest for Victory: American Foreign Policy, 1961–1963,* edited by Thomas Paterson, pp. 24–56. New York: Oxford University Press, 1989.

Cumings, Bruce. "'Revising Postrevisionism,' or, The Poverty of Theory in Diplomatic History." *Diplomatic History* 17 (Fall 1993): 539–69.

Demma, Vincent. "Suggestions for the Use of Ground Forces, June 1964–March 1965." Unpublished manuscript.

Divine, Robert. "Vietnam Reconsidered." *Diplomatic History* 12 (Winter 1988): 79–94.

Gavin, James. "A Communication on Vietnam." *Harper's* (February 1966): 16–20.

Greenstein, Fred, and Richard Immerman. "What Did Eisenhower Tell Kennedy about Indochina? The Politics of Misperception." *Journal of American History* 79 (September 1992): 568–87.

Herring, George. "America and Vietnam: The Debate Continues." *American Historical Review* 92 (April 1987): 350–62.

———. " 'Cold Blood': LBJ's Conduct of Limited War in Vietnam." Paper presented at the Military History Symposium, U.S. Air Force Academy, Colorado Springs, Colo., 1990.

———. "The Truman Administration and the Restoration of French Sovereignty in Indochina." *Diplomatic History* 1 (Winter 1977): 97–117.

———. "The War in Vietnam." In *Exploring the Johnson Years,* edited by Robert Divine, pp. 27–62. Austin: University of Texas Press, 1981.

Herring, George, and Richard Immerman. "Eisenhower, Dulles, and Dienbienphu: 'The Day We Didn't Go to War' Revisited." *Journal of American History* 71 (September 1984): 343–63.

Hess, Gary. "The First American Commitment in Indochina: The Acceptance of the Bao Dai Solution, 1950." *Diplomatic History* 2 (Fall 1978): 331–50.

Hixson, Walter. " 'Red Storm Rising': Tom Clancy Novels and the Cult of National Security." *Diplomatic History* 17 (Fall 1993): 599–613.

Hogan, Michael J. "Foreign Policy, Partisan Politics, and the End of the Cold War." In *The End of the Cold War: Its Meaning and Implications,* edited by Michael J. Hogan, pp. 229–43. Cambridge: Cambridge University Press, 1992.

Hunt, David. "Remembering the Tet Offensive." In *Vietnam and America: A Documented History,* edited by Marvin Gettleman et al., pp. 355–72. New York: Grove Press, 1985.

Immerman, Richard. "Confessions of an Eisenhower Revisionist: An Agonizing Reappraisal." *Diplomatic History* 14 (Summer 1990): 319–42.

———. "The United States and the Geneva Conference of 1954: A New Look." *Diplomatic History* 14 (Winter 1990): 43–66.

Kahin, George McT. "The United States and the Anticolonial Revolutions in Southeast Asia." In *The Origins of the Cold War in Asia,* edited by Yonosuke Nagai and Akira Iriye, pp. 338–61. New York: Columbia University Press, 1977.

Kinnard, Douglas. "Civil–Military Relations: The President and the General." In *The National Security: Its Theory and Practice,* edited by Norman B. Graebner, pp. 199–225. New York: Oxford University Press, 1986.

LaFeber, Walter. "The Last War, the Next War, and the New Revisionists." *democracy* 1 (1981): 93–103.

———. "Roosevelt, Churchill and Indochina, 1942–1945." *American Historical Review* 80 (December 1975): 1277–95.

Leffler, Melvyn. "The American Conception of National Security and the Beginnings of the Cold War, 1945–1948." *American Historical Review* 89 (April 1984): 356–78.

Long, Ngô Vinh. "Vietnam." In *Coming to Terms: Indochina, the United States, and the War,* edited by Douglas Allen and Ngô Vinh Long, pp. 9–64. Boulder, Colo.: Westview Press, 1991.

Marr, David. "The Technological Imperative in US War Strategy in Vietnam." In *The World Military Order: The Impact of Military Technology on the Third*

World, edited by Mary Kaldor and Asbjorn Eide, pp. 17–48. New York: Praeger, 1979.

Melby, John. "Vietnam – 1950." *Diplomatic History* 6 (Winter 1982): 97–109.

Paterson, Thomas. "Historical Memory and Illusive Victories: Vietnam and Central America." *Diplomatic History* 12 (Winter 1988): 1–18.

Pelz, Stephen. "Documents: 'When Do I Have Time to Think?' John F. Kennedy, Roger Hilsman, and the Laotian Crisis of 1962." *Diplomatic History* 3 (Spring 1979): 215–29.

Pruessen, Ronald W. "John Foster Dulles and the Predicaments of Power." In *John Foster Dulles and the Diplomacy of the Cold War,* edited by Richard H. Immerman, pp. 21–45. Princeton, N.J.: Princeton University Press, 1990.

Ridgway, Matthew. "Indochina: Disengaging." *Foreign Affairs* 49 (Winter 1971): 583–92.

Schaller, Michael. "Securing the Great Crescent: Occupied Japan and the Origins of Containment in Southeast Asia." *Journal of American History* 69 (September 1982):392–414.

Shoup, David. "The New American Militarism." *Atlantic Monthly* (April 1969): 51–6.

Steininger, Rolf. "John Foster Dulles, the European Defense Community, and the German Question." In *John Foster Dulles and the Diplomacy of the Cold War,* edited by Richard H. Immerman, pp. 79–108. Princeton, N.J.: Princeton University Press, 1990.

Thorne, Christopher. "Indochina and Anglo-American Relations." *Pacific Historical Review* 45 (February 1976): 73–96.

Weigley, Russell F. "The American Military and the Principle of Civilian Control from McClellan to Powell." *Journal of Military History* 57 (October 1993): 27–58.

Young, Marilyn. "This Is Not a Pipe." *Middle East Report* (July–August 1991): 21–4.

V: Newspapers and Periodicals

Christian Science Monitor
Harper's
The Nation
National Review
New York Times
Newsweek
Time
US News & World Report
Washington Post

Index